ICAZ

Dogs and People in Social, Working, Economic or Symbolic Interaction

Proceedings of the 9th Conference of the International Council of Archaeozoology, Durham, August 2002

Series Editors: Umberto Albarella, Keith Dobney and Peter Rowley-Conwy

Dogs and People in Social, Working, Economic or Symbolic Interaction

Edited by
Lynn M. Snyder and Elizabeth A. Moore

Oxbow Books

First published in the United Kingdom in 2006. Reprinted in paperback in 2016 by
OXBOW BOOKS
10 Hythe Bridge Street, Oxford OX1 2EW

and in the United States by
OXBOW BOOKS
1950 Lawrence Road, Havertown, PA 19083

Paperback Edition: ISBN 978-1-78570-399-7
Digital Edition: ISBN 978-1-78570-426-0 (ePub)

A CIP record for this book is available from the British Library

For a complete list of Oxbow titles, please contact:

UNITED KINGDOM
Oxbow Books
Telephone (01865) 241249, Fax (01865) 794449
Email: oxbow@oxbowbooks.com
www.oxbowbooks.com

UNITED STATES OF AMERICA
Oxbow Books
Telephone (800) 791-9354, Fax (610) 853-9146
Email: queries@casemateacademic.com
www.casemateacademic.com/oxbow

Oxbow Books is part of the Casemate Group

Contents

Preface

Umberto Albarella, Keith Dobney and Peter Rowley-Conwy

This book is one of several volumes which form the published proceedings of the 9th meeting of the International Council of Archaeozoology (ICAZ), which was held in Durham (UK) 23rd–28th August 2002. ICAZ was founded in the early '70s and has ever since acted as the main international organisation for the study of animal remains from archaeological sites. The main international conferences are held every four years, and the Durham meeting – the largest ever – follows those in Hungary, the Netherlands, Poland, England (London), France, USA, Germany and Canada. The next meeting will be held in Mexico in 2006. The Durham conference – which was attended by about 500 delegates from 46 countries – was organised in 23 thematic sessions, which attracted, in addition to zooarchaeologists, scholars from related disciplines such as palaeoanthropology, archaeobotany, bone chemistry, genetics, mainstream archaeology etc.

The publication structure reflects that of the conference, each volume dealing with a different topic, be it methodological, ecological, palaeoeconomic, sociological, historical or anthropological (or a combination of these). This organisation by theme rather than by chronology or region, was chosen for two main reasons. The first is that we wanted to take the opportunity presented by such a large gathering of researchers from across the world to encourage international communication, and we thought that this could more easily be achieved through themes with world-wide relevance. The second is that we thought that, by tackling broad questions, zooarchaeologists would be more inclined to take a holistic approach and integrate their information with other sources of evidence. This also had the potential of attracting other specialists who shared an interest in that particular topic. We believe that our choice turned out to be correct for the conference, and helped substantially towards its success. For the publication there is the added benefit of having a series of volumes that will be of interest far beyond the restricted circle of specialists on faunal remains. Readers from many different backgrounds, ranging from history to zoology, will certainly be interested in many of the fourteen volumes that will be published.

Due to the large number of sessions it would have been impractical to publish each as a separate volume, so some that had a common theme have been combined. Far from losing their main thematic focus, these volumes have the potential to attract a particularly wide and diverse readership. Because of these combinations (and because two other sessions will be published outside this series) it was therefore possible to reduce the original 24 sessions to 14 volumes. Publication of such a series is a remarkable undertaking, and we are very grateful to David Brown and Oxbow Books for agreeing to produce the volumes.

We would also like to take this opportunity to thank the University of Durham and the ICAZ Executive Committee for their support during the preparation of the conference, and all session organisers – now book editors – for all their hard work. Some of the conference administrative costs were covered by a generous grant provided by the British Academy. Further financial help came from the following sources: English Heritage, Rijksdienst voor het Oudheidkundig Bodemonderzoek (ROB), County Durham Development Office, University College Durham, Palaeoecology Research Services, Northern Archaeological Associates, Archaeological Services University of Durham (ASUD), and NYS Corporate Travel. Finally we are extremely grateful for the continued support of the Wellcome Trust and Arts and Humanities Research Board (AHRB) who, through their provision of Research Fellowships for Keith Dobney and Umberto Albarella, enabled us to undertake such a challenge.

Introduction

Lynn M. Snyder and Elizabeth A. Moore

At the eighth Congress of the International Council for Archaeozoology, held in Victoria, British Columbia August 23–29, 1998, Susan J. Crockford chaired a symposium entitled "The History of the Domestic Dog" which focused primarily on the evolution of the domestic dog, early forms and breed development, skeletal variation in Roman and non-Roman contexts, contemporary examples of modern "primitive dogs" and archaeological methods of analysis including morphometrics and non-metric traits, hair and DNA analysis. In a single session in this large symposium, entitled "Interpreting roles: early practical and ritual uses of dogs", six papers were presented, including ones which considered the sacred and secular uses of dogs in Kazakstan (Olsen 2000), the burial of dogs within an Early Archaic human cemetery in the western United States (Yohe and Pavesic 2000), and the use of dogs for food (as evidenced by cut and butchery marks) in Gallic France (Horard-Herbin 2000) and Roman Period Belgium and Romania (Tarcan et al 2000). As a follow-up to this most impressive collection of papers, and with the intention of focusing more specifically on the multiple and complex roles that dogs may play in human lives, we organized a session for the ninth International Council of Archaeozoology Conference, held in Durham, England, 23–28 August 2002, which was entitled "Dogs and People in Social, Economic or Symbolic Interaction". The papers in this book are the result of that session, which included both presented papers and posters, plus one paper (Barsh, Jones and Suttles) which was submitted after the Conference.

These papers cover a wide range of subjects, considering dogs as animals of sacrifice and animal components of ancient and modern religious ritual and practice; as human companions subject to loving care, visual/symbolic representation, and deliberate or accidental breed manipulation; as working dogs; and finally as co-inhabitors of human dwelling places and co-consumers of human food resources. Other papers which consider the special roles which dogs may play in human lives have also appeared in earlier volumes in the present series, including Kansa and Campbell 2004, Lentacker, Ervynck and Van Meer 2004, and Emery 2004.

Although there has been a degree of debate over the initial separation of ancestral dogs from wolves and the timing and mechanisms of differential separation of early domestic forms, using both metrical (cf. Benecke 1987; Clutton-Brock 1995; Morey 1992, 1994; Olsen 1985) and DNA analyses (cf. Wayne and O'Brien 1987; Wayne et al 1987a,b, 1997), it is now generally agreed, based on genetic evidence alone, that dogs derived from a form of wolf, and that this process may have started as much as 15,000 years ago (Savolainen et al 2002; Vila et al 1997, 1999). Whenever and however these early domestication events occurred, for most archaeologists the true evidence of the developing mutualistic and personal relationships between humans and canids is evidenced by physical association of their remains in archaeological contexts. One of the earliest, and most evocative examples of this growing special relationship comes from the Natufian of Israel, where a number of canids were found buried with humans, including one young animal found beneath the upraised hand of a buried woman (Davis and Valla 1978; Tchernov and Valla 1997).

In the 14,000 plus years since the initial mutual or domestic relationship between humans and dogs developed, this relationship has persisted and taken many interrelated and often complex emotional as well as practical forms. In recent years, a goodly number of volumes have been written on the many forms these relationships have taken. In a very accessible popular account entitled "The Lost History of the Canine Race", M. E. Thurston (1997) considers the many forms that human/dog interaction has taken in the past, ranging from the hunting hounds of ancient Egypt, Greece and Rome, through the development of herding and other working breeds, to the very interesting and sometimes sad history of the exploitation of dogs specially bred for exploitation as spit dogs, cart dogs, and even ordinance pullers in Europe in the 19th through early 20th centuries.

Throughout history, dogs were also considered to have attributes making them suitable for ritual use and sacrifice. And, perhaps because of their close relationships with humans as companions and helpers, the eating of dogs was widespread through time, common in some parts of the world, and deliberately avoided elsewhere (cf Simoons 1994:200–252; Schwartz 1997:60–92).

In the Americas, where nearly all other domestic animals were absent until their introduction by European explorers and settlers, the dog was a near universal domestic helper and resource. Apparently accompanying humans in their initial migrations into these new worlds (cf. Leonard et al 2002; Morey and Wiant 1992; Morey and Aaris-Sorensen 2002; Olsen 1985;), dogs served as human hunt and personal companions, beasts of burden and sacrifice, and a ceremonial and sometimes more staple food resource for First Peoples and Native Americans (cf. Morey 1986, Morey and Wiant 1992; Schwartz 1997; Snyder and Leonard 2006). It is likely that no more personal yet practical account of this mutual relationship exists than that which Buffalo Bird Woman, an Hidatsa, gave to Gilbert Wilson in the early 20th century (Wilson 1924). Born in the last traditional Hidatsa village on the upper Missouri River of the northern plains, Buffalo Bird Woman could still remember the "old dogs" which accompanied the Hidatsa and many other plains groups on their semi-annual bison hunts, and also willingly hauled loads of wood and tipi poles for the village women. It is interesting to note that she reports that dogs, at least in her lifetime (some 100 years after the introduction of the horse into the upper Missouri River through trade with other Native American groups to the southwest) were bred, owned, raised, trained and sold by women only. One can only speculate whether this very valuable animal, particularly before the ready availability of horses as a form of transportation and transport, had always been a part of a womans' capital, to be raised and traded, but never sold – as Buffalo Bird Woman notes – except by and to other women.

The papers in this volume reflect a good deal of the range of relationships, both ancient and modern which have existed between humans and dogs. Not all of them are based solely, or even primarily on archaeological materials, but all can provide us with food for thought in the archaeological analyses of our long standing mutual associations with domestic dogs. Four papers consider the role of dogs in ritual and sacrifice. Barbara Wilkens discusses the use of dogs for sacrifice in Italy from the Neolithic through Roman periods in funerary, ritual, cultic and sanctuary contexts. De Grossi Mazzorin and Minitti also consider dog sacrifice in Italy from the Iron Age through Roman periods, as well as information from ancient texts on the timing and occasions of such sacrifices, and the goddesses who required them. Isabelle Chenal-Velarde discusses evidence of dog sacrifice at a single site, Eretria on the Greek island of Euboea, from primarily Hellenistic contexts, and Salvatore Chilardi reports on burned and cut dog bone recovered from temple contexts of the 7th through 4th century BC from the town of Siracusa, on the island of Ortigia.

A fifth paper also deals with dogs in ritual and symbolic contexts, with a concentration on recent historical and contemporary Afro-Cuban religions. Mason and Snyder consider the role of dogs in the religions of the African diaspora, drawing upon recent archaeological studies of African American and Afro-Cuban sites, contemporary *nganga* installations recovered in cities in the eastern United States, and ethnographic and ethnohistoric accounts of the place of dogs in the rituals and iconography of Afro-Cuban religions.

Two papers offer analyses of historical and modern practical uses of dogs as working or "stock" animals. Barsh, Jones and Suttles provide an analysis of one or more types of "wooly dogs", specially bred and raised by the Coast Salish of the Puget Sound area of northwestern North America, which were regularly sheared for wool used in weaving. Although there are very few documented archeologically recovered specimens and even fewer historically collected "known individual" wooly dogs, they report on recently identified modern zoological specimens which are currently undergoing genetic analysis to determine their origins and potentially unique genetic status. Atsushi Nobayashi presents an account of his ethnoarchaeological studies of boar hunting using dogs on Taiwan. His observations on the differing goals of boar hunting between gundog and snare hunters, the resultant variation in age profiles of the hunted populations, and the contrasting status conferred by boar hunting within the two hunting groups offer possible modern analogies for interpretation of archaeologically recovered hunted animal populations.

Three of the papers in this volume discuss dogs as companions. This is not necessarily the only role of dogs that the author's address but it is an important theme in these papers, where the role of dogs as pets is used as a framework to examine physical, visual, and textual evidence of deliberate human care. MacKinnon and Belanger examine an arthritic Maltese dog from the Roman cemetery of Yasmina in Carthage, Tunisia. This example of a toy breed is unlike other canids recovered around the Mediterranean in both its size and age and the evidence of illness and pathologies that the dog displayed. The authors conclude that the only way this dog would have survived so long was with deliberate human care and treatment.

Prummel presents evidence associated with two Bronze Age sites where cremated dog skeletons were found in association with human burials. These sites provide examples of a treatment usually found later, at the end of the Middle Bronze Age in Northwest and Central Europe. Previous interpretations of other cremated dogs as hunting dogs are expanded to include possible ritualistic, economic, and social roles.

Trantalidou also examines dogs in a variety of

representations and roles from economic to symbolic, social to ideological. Companion dogs are but one of the many types that she describes from artistic representations, texts and osteological remains from ancient Greece. She also examines how dogs were associated with various rites and rituals including birth, healing, rites of passage in youth, and purification in death.

Several of the authors address the physical variability of dogs. Tassi's osteometric work with Medieval dogs from Hungary corresponds to the variability in dogs seen in Medieval art in Central and Western Europe. Baxter's examination of a single Roman period dwarf hound skeleton is used to more thoroughly describe a single morphotype. This dog, like the one described by MacKinnon and Belanger, may have also been a companion dog; remains of dwarf dog types are frequent in Roman period sites.

Valadez, Rodriguez, Manzanilla, and Tejeda present the reconstruction of a dog-wolf biotype from Teotihuacan, and examine the symbolic role of this type in religious life in prehispanic Mexico. Valued characteristics of dogs and wolves combine to provide a symbolically rich type that could be controlled by humans.

Yates and Koler-Matznick describe their work with dog remains in forensic cases. Changing attitudes and national and international laws governing exploitation of dogs as commodities, food, entertainment, ritualistic objects, in science, and as controlled agents are explored in the setting of the United States Fish and Wildlife Service's National Wildlife Forensic Laboratory. Although established to solve crimes against, or involving wildlife, this laboratory provides a setting in which data gathered in forensic work can also provide a more thorough understanding of the various uses of dogs.

The close association of ancient populations with their dogs is illustrated by a paper by Liina Maldre, in which she reports the analysis of animal bones and plant remains contained in domestic dog coprolites recovered from the Late Bronze Age site of Asva. She compares the types of animal resources which apparently made up the dogs diet with the range of animals which composed human diet at the site, as represented by the bone assemblage from the site.

While many of the papers in this volume have a predominant focus, they also demonstrate that the relationships between humans and dogs are rarely, if ever, singular or simple. Instead, these relationships are complex, often combining the practical, the ideological and the symbolic. These papers provide a sample of some of that complexity.

Bibliography

Benecke, N. 1987. Studies on early dog remains from Northern Europe. *Journal of Archaeological Science* **14**, 31–49.

Clutton-Brock, J. 1995. Origins of the dog: domestication and early history, pp. 7–20 in Sherpell, J. (ed.), *The Domestic Dog: Its evolution, Behavior and Interactions with People*. Cambridge, Cambridge University Press.

Davis, S. J. M. and Valla, F. R. 1978. Evidence for the domestication of the dog 12,000 years ago in the Natufian of Israel. *Nature* **276(7)**, 608–610.

Emery, K. F. 2004. Animals from the Maya underworld: reconstructing elite Maya ritual at the Cueva de los Quetzales, Guatemala, pp. 101–113 in O'Day, S J *et al.* (eds), *Behavior Behind Bones*, Proceedings of the 9th ICAZ Conference, Durham, 2002. Oxford, Oxbow Books.

Horard-Herbin, M.-P. 2000. Dog management and use in the Late Iron Age: the Evidence from the Gallic site of Levroux (France), pp. 115–121 in Crockford, S. J. (ed.), *Dogs Through Time: An Archaeological Perspective*. BAR International Series No. 889. Oxford, Archaeopress.

Kansa, S. W. and Campbell, S. 2004. Feasting with the dead? – A ritual bone deposit at Domuztepe, south eastern Turkey (c. 5500 cal BC), pp. 2–13 in O'Day, S. J *et al.* (eds), *Behavior Behind Bones*, Proceedings of the 9th ICAZ Conference, Durham, 2002. Oxford, Oxbow Books.

Lentacker, A., Ervynck, A. and Van Neer, W. 2004. Gastronomy or religion? the animal remains from the mithraeum at Tienen (Belgium), pp. 77–94 in O'Day, S. J. *et al.* (eds), *Behavior Behind Bones*, Proceedings of the 9th ICAZ Conference, Durham, 2002. Oxford, Oxbow Books.

Leonard, J.A., Wayne, R. K., Wheeler, R, Valadez, R., Guillen, S. and Vila, C. 2002. Ancient DNA evidence for Old World origin of New World dogs. *Science* **298**, 1613– 1616.

Morey, D. F. 1986. Studies of Amerindian dogs: taxonomic analysis of canid crania from the northern plains. *Journal of Archaeological Science* **13**, 119–145.

Morey, D. F. 1992. Size, shape, and development in the evolution of the domestic dog. *Journal of Archaeological Science* **19**, 181–204.

Morey, D. F. 1994. The early evolution of the domestic dog. *American Scientist* **83**, 336–347.

Morey, D. F. and Aaris-Sorensen, K. 2002. *Paleoeskimo dogs of the eastern Arctic* **55(1)**, 44–56.

Morey, D. F. and Wiant, M. D. 1992. Early Holocene domestic dog burials from the North American Midwest. *Current Anthropology* **33(2)**, 224–229.

Olsen, S. J. 1985. *Origins of the Domestic Dog*. Tucson, University of Arizona Press.

Olsen, S. L. 2000. The secular and sacred roles of dogs at Botai, North Kazakhstan, pp. 71–92 in Crockford, S. J. (ed.), *Dogs Through Time: An Archaeological Perspective*. BAR International Series No. 889. Oxford, Archaeopress.

Savolainen, P., Zhang, P., Luo, J, Lundeberg, J. and Leitner, T. 2002. Genetic evidence for an East Asian origin of domestic dogs. *Science* **298**, 1610–1613.

Schwartz, M. *A History of Dogs in the Early Americas*. New Haven, Yale University.

Simoon, R. J. 1994. *Eat Not This Flesh: Food Avoidances from Prehistory to the Present*. 2nd Edition. Madison, University of Wisconsin Press.

Snyder, L. M. and Leonard, J. A. 2006. Domestic dogs in North America: An overview, Chapter 3 in Ubelaker, D. (ed.), *Handbook of North American Indians, Vol. 3*. Washington, D. C., Smithsonian Institution Press.

Tarcan, C., Cordy, J.-M., Bejenaru, L. and Udrescu, M. 2000. Butchery evidence on dog faunal remains from Roman Period sites in Belgium (Braives) and Roumania, pp. 123–128 in Crockford, S. J. (ed.), *Dogs Through Time: An Archaeological Perspective*. BAR International Series No. 889. Oxford, Archaeopress.

Tchernov, E. and Valla, F. F. 1997. Two new dogs, and other Natufian dogs from the Southern Levant. *Journal of Archaeological Science* **24**, 65–95.

Thurston, M. K. 1996. *The Lost History of the Canine Race*. Kansas City, Andrews and McMeel; New York: Avon Books.

Vila., C., Savolainen, P., Maldonado, J. E., Amorim, I. R., Rice, J. E., Honeycutt, R. L., Crandall, K. A., Lundeberg, J. and Wayne, R. K. 1997. Multiple and ancient origins of the domestic dog. *Science* **276**, 1687–1689.

Vila, C., Maldonado, J., and Wayne, J. K. 1999. Phylogenetic relationships, evolution and genetic diversity of the domestic dog. *Journal of Heredity* **90**, 71–77.

Wayne, R. K. and O'Brien, S. J. 1987. Allozyme divergence within the Canidae. *Systematic Zoology* **36**, 339–355.

Wayne, R. K., Nash, W. G., and O'Brien, S. J. 1987a. Chromosomal evolution of the Canidae: I. Species with high diploid numbers. *Cytogenetics and Cell Genetics* **44**, 123–133.

Wayne, R. K., Nash, W. G. and O'Brien, S. J. 1987b. Chromosomal evolution of theCanidae: II. Divergence from the primitive carnivore karyotype. *Cytogenetics and Cell Genetics* **44**, 134–141.

Wayne, R. K., Geffen, E., Girman, D. J., Koepfli, K. P., Lau, L. M. and Marshall, C. R. 1997. Molecular systematics of the Canidae. *Systematic Biology* **46**, 62–653.

Wilson, G. L. 1924. The horse and the dog in Hidatsa culture. *Anthropological Papers of the American Museum of Natural History* **15(2)**, 125–311.

Yohee, R. M. and Pavesic, M. G. 2000. Early Archaic domestic dogs from western Idaho,USA., pp. 93–104 in Crockford, S. J. (ed.), *Dogs Through Time: An Archaeological Perspective.* BAR International Series No. 889. Oxford, Archaeopress.

9th ICAZ Conference, Durham 2002
Dogs and People in Social, Working, Economic or Symbolic Interaction
(eds Lynn M. Snyder and Elizabeth A. Moore) pp. 1–11

1. History, Ethnography, and Archaeology of the Coast Salish Woolly-Dog

Russel L. Barsh, Joan Megan Jones, and Wayne Suttles

The indigenous Coast Salish peoples of Puget Sound and Georgia Strait (present day western Washington State and southwestern British Columbia) maintained a distinct phenotype of dog for the production of yarn. Blankets woven of dog hair, often mixed with waterfowl down or with hair from mountain goats, were important trade and gift items, essential to the accumulation of wealth and prestige. Lightweight but very labor-intensive, woven blankets represented wealth that could be transported easily in a coastal hunting and fishing society where seasonal mobility was necessary for survival (Suttles 1987). Dog-hair weaving disappeared quickly after the introduction of machine-made blankets by British and American trading companies in the early 19th century. Although many early explorers referred to woolly-dogs (Gunther 1972: 259–60; Howay 1918), the only depiction of a woolly-dog is of doubtful reliability, and woolly-dogs were reportedly extinct by the third quarter of the 19th century.

Archaeologists have attempted to reconstruct the appearance of the woolly-dog and its relationship to living breeds from osteological evidence (Crockford 1997; Koop et al. *2000), but there is no reliable method for distinguishing the remains of woolly-dogs from those of other Coast Salish dogs (i.e. pure-bred hunting dogs or unmanaged mixed-breed "village dogs") in the absence of a type specimen. The recent re-discovery at the Smithsonian Institution's National Museum of Natural History in Washington, D.C. of two Coast Salish dog specimens collected in 1859, one of them unquestionably a woolly-dog based on a comparison of its coat with dog-hair blankets collected in 1841 from the same geographic area, provides a unique opportunity to describe Coast Salish dogs phenotypically and trace their phylogenetic relationships.*

Ethnohistory

Suttles (1951: 244–46) conducted extensive interviews of Northern Straits Salish people in the late 1940s. Although he obtained only a generic term for "dog", sqéx̌ə , he heard descriptions of two functional dog breeds: one used for hunting, the other used for its woolly hair. Similarly, the Twana-speaking peoples of southwestern Puget Sound reportedly maintained separate breeds for hunting and weaving (Elmendorf 1992: 94). Twana people referred to both kinds of dog as sqʷəbáyʾ but sometimes distinguished the woolly-dog as šiʾášʾalqaʾd or "long-haired" (Elmendorf 1992: 96). The limited linguistic evidence suggests that there was relatively little morphological distinction between the two breeds apart from their coats.

Woolly-dogs frequently shared plank houses with people while hunting dogs were ordinarily kenneled outdoors (Suttles 1990: 460–62; Elmendorf 1992: 97). Hunting dogs and woolly-dogs may have been routinely separated to prevent them from interbreeding. It remains uncertain whether hunting dogs were ordinarily bred and trained by hunters (ordinarily men) and woolly-dogs by weavers (typically women). Julius Charles told Suttles that Charles' older half-sister showed him how to make a dog into a good hunter. Dogs of both types were valued highly, and commanded high prices in trade. Dogs were given personal names, and were often buried ceremonially like humans (Elmendorf 1992: 99). An example of a young woman buried with a dog was recorded at Watmough Bight (45 SJ 280) on Lopez Island in 1968,

Fig. 1. Canadian artist Paul Kane's 1855 painting of a Clallam (S'Klallam) woman weaving a blanket with a woolly-dog sitting beside the loom, loosely based on sketches he made eight years earlier. Photograph of the original with permission of the Royal Ontario Museum © ROM

according to field notebooks of the excavations housed at the Burke Museum on the Seattle campus of the University of Washington.

Captain George Vancouver observed woolly-dogs at Port Orchard in the central Sound in 1792, "shorn as close to the skin as sheep are in England … with very fine long hair," and compared them to large Pomeranians (Gunther 1972: 259). Later that year, the Spanish naval vessels *Sutil* and *Mexicana* visited a village located on Gabriola Island, and commented on "the great number of dogs they keep in their villages, most of which were shorn." The dogs were reported to be "of moderate size, resembling those of the English breed, very woolly, and usually white" (Howay 1918: 87). This description also appears in Wagner's (1933) translation of the official published Spanish account of the voyage in much the same form. It does not appear in Kendrick's (1991) translation of a presumed original manuscript from the voyage, however, so its precise source is obscure.

Simon Fraser observed shorn dogs and blankets made from goat and dog hair in 1806 (Lamb 1960). What he saw may have been very much like the soft white blankets brought back from northern Puget Sound by the 1841 U.S. Naval Exploring Expedition, now in the collection of the Smithsonian Institution's National Museum of Natural History (illustrated in Gustafson 1980; Wright 1991: 44–47).

In 1824, the seamen of the *William & Ann* observed that the Makah kept their woolly-dogs isolated "on a little island a few miles from the coast" where they fed them every day (Young 1905: 196). Woolly-dogs were not always isolated, however. Joseph Whidbey and his party observed native people "walking along the shore" of Camano Island "attended by about forty dogs in a drove, shorn close to the skin like sheep" (Lamb 1984: 565). In 1828, James McMillan observed a flotilla of 160 Cowichan canoes on the Fraser River returning from fall salmon fishing upstream, each canoe with "about half a dozen dogs more resembling Cheviot Lambs shorn of their wool" (MacLachlan 1998: 5).

Canadian artist Paul Kane (1859) sketched Coast Salish people and their dogs in 1847, and described woolly-dogs with long black, brown, or white hair that was sheared with a knife (Eaton and Urbanek 1995: 103; see Fig. 1). One of Kane's later paintings, often reproduced as a standard for the morphology of woolly-dogs (Gustafson 1980), shows a small fluffy white dog that is much smaller than the animal in his original sketches or the specimen in the National Museum of Natural History. It is reasonable to accord greater reliability to Kane's earlier work, although the predominance of light colored yarns in surviving early 19th century weavings casts some doubt on his description.

Dog hair was reportedly combined with other animal and plant fibers. Dog hair and mountain goat wool were sometimes combined in one yarn, as well as being spun separately. Plant fibers such as the cotton from fireweed seedpods, thistles, and cattail heads were often reported

Fig. 2. Speculative reconstructions of a "village dog" by Cameron J. Pye for Crockford (1997), based on measurements of archaeological dogs and Paul Kane's sketches and paintings. See Crockford and Pye (1997) for another version

Fig. 3. Two woolly-dogs by Cameron J. Pye for Crockford (1997), based on measurements of archaeological dogs and Paul Kane's sketches and paintings. See Crockford and Pye (1997) for another version

as additions to the blends, along with bird down. The addition of other fibers would have extended the length of yarn that the spinner could produce from a limited supply of dog hair. Other fibers also enhanced the quality of the yarn; for example, we have found that adding bird down produces a particularly light, soft, warm and opulent textile. To display a blanket made of such a yarn would serve to emphasize the high rank and status of the weaver and the owner.

Dog hair yarn eventually succumbed to the influx of commercially manufactured trade blankets. Although the U.S. Indian Agent stationed near Bellingham, Washington, reported that native dress in the middle of the 19th century still included "blankets made of dog hair and feathers, of their own manufacture" (Fitzhugh 1858), field reports of woolly-dogs after 1860 are few. Franz Boas' Kwakiutl assistant, George Hunt, reported seeing a woolly-dog with very fine, long hair when he was a boy in the late 19th century (Boas 1921: 1317–18). Canadian anthropologist Diamond Jenness (1934: 46) reported a dog of that description on the Saanich Reserve of southern Vancouver Island in 1936, still being shorn for yarn to knit mittens. Elmendorf (1992: 97) was told of a woolly-dog seen at LaPush on Washington's Pacific Coast about 1920, and another woolly-dog at the Skokomish Reservation on Hood Canal in 1940. These isolated individuals may have differed considerably from early 19th century woolly-dogs.

Archaeology

Canid remains have been recovered from a large number of archaeological sites in Puget Sound and Georgia Strait, some as old as 4,000 BP. Crockford (1997) attempted to distinguish woolly-dogs from hunting dogs osteometrically using incomplete skeletons of at least 647 individual dogs from 28 archaeological sites in the Coast Salish area, mainly in British Columbia. Her exhaustive measurements suggest a bimodal distribution in the sizes of individuals, somewhat less size variation amongst the smaller dogs, and a larger proportion of males amongst the larger dogs. The difference in mean size was relatively small (<20%), however, and the conclusion that the smaller individuals were woolly-dogs is based on a number of assumptions about prehistoric dog breeding and hunting, e.g. that hunting dogs needed to be larger and more robust. However, the only documented aboriginal Pacific Coast hunting breed, the Tahltan Bear Dog (Koop *et al.* 2000), was much smaller than the woolly-dog specimen we describe here. One of Elmendorf's (1992: 97) Twana informants described Coast Salish hunting dogs as "small and thin, in coat and general build like a wire-haired terrier, with a ruff around the neck," which is to say that is was similar in size to the Tahltan Bear Dog. According to people interviewed by Suttles, the "training" given to Coast Salish hunting dogs was mainly aimed at improving their sense of smell. This suggests that dogs were used to locate game, and not to bring it to ground. They would not need to be large or robust for this purpose.

Crockford and Pye's (1997) reconstruction of the appearance of a woolly-dog and a "village dog" (Figs 2 and 3) is purely conjectural, and suggests a greater difference in size and build between the two types than is evident in the specimens at the National Museum of Natural History. Differences in hair length is a recessive trait in dogs (Ryder 2000), thus it is conceivable that the careful inbreeding of Coast Salish dogs produced lineages that differed little apart from the length and density of their coats.

Koop *et al.* (2000) extracted DNA from two intact dog

Fig. 4. Coast Salish loom with a twill-weave blanket, reportedly woven of goat hair, photographed by Edward S. Curtis in 1913. Note the basket of yarn at the foot of the loom. National Anthropological Archives, Smithsonian Institution (81-13446)

burials and an isolated dog bone recovered from archaeological sites on the lower Fraser River. It is unclear from their report why they classified one burial as a woolly-dog, and the other burial (as well as the isolated bone) as "village dogs"—these attributions appear to have been *post hoc* rationalizations of the disparate mtDNA results. The "village dog" specimens were most closely related to Yukon Wolf and Tahltan Bear Dog specimens, while a divergent group of specimens included the supposed woolly-dog and four living northeast Asian breeds (Ryukyu, Shikoku, Siberian Husky, and Mongolian).

If Coast Salish woolly-dogs have existed as a distinct breed for over 4,000 years as Crockford (1997) speculates, they may represent a relatively old lineage with stronger ties to Siberian dogs than to the New World wolves. A reliably documented woolly-dog specimen is required to test this possibility.

The National Museum specimens

Coast Salish weavings

We have located 13 Coast Salish weavings at the National Museum of Natural History: nine blankets, capes or robes, and four tumpline straps. The U.S. Navy's 1841 expedition to Puget Sound (the Wilkes expedition) collected seven of the weavings, but did not fully identify their geographic origins or composition in the shipping documents (Peale 1846; Pickering 1841). Included are two spectacular blankets with red, dark blue, gray and brown geometric designs, one faded from exposure to sunlight (USNM catalog number E2124), and the other still bright (E1891A, originally cataloged as E2125 but for many years confused with E1891, a Navajo blanket collected in 1866). Peale's (1846) catalog identifies them as "Blankets, made of the wool of the Rock Mountain sheep, by the natives of Puget Sound, Northwest Coast of America." Krieger (1928) asserted that these two blankets contain a mixture of goat hair and dog hair, but did not explain how he arrived at this conclusion.

The Wilkes collection also includes two "robes" incorporating bird down (E1894) and strips of fur and cedar (E1895) into the weave, both identified as "Blankets, made of feathers, by the natives of the N.W. Coast of America" by Peale (1846); and four woven tumpline straps with herringbone designs (E2120, E2121, E2123), described by Peale as "Belt[s] made of the Rocky Mountain Goats wool, by the natives of the Northwest Coast of America." Krieger (1928) described at least one of the straps (E2120) as a mixture of goat hair and dog hair, once again without explanation.

The geographical origins and eras of other Coast Salish weavings at NMNH are even less certain. One blanket fragment was rescued from artist George Catlin's personal collection after his 1852 bankruptcy, and donated to the Smithsonian in 1879 (E177710). Catlin did not visit the Northwest, and it is unclear how or when he acquired this object. Krieger (1928) speculated that Lewis and Clark had originally collected this object when they traveled through Washington and Oregon in 1805–1806. A woven robe or cape with bird down (E221408), donated in 1903 by the widow of ethnologist Frank Cushing, came with no identifying notes and was originally mistakenly cataloged as Nez Perce art from Idaho. Krieger (1928) suspected that it was a weaving collected by George Gibbs in the 1850s, which Gibbs described in his notes as composed of goat hair, dog hair, and down.

Three woven blankets of more recent origin at the NMNH are identified only as "Cowichan": E311257 is from the collection of the Smithsonian Institution's Bureau of American Ethnology, established in 1879; E233950 was donated by Charles Buchanan, Superintendent of the Puget Sound Indian Agency in the first quarter of the 20th century; and E357408 was bequeathed by antiquities collector Victor Justice Evans (1865–1931). James Teit

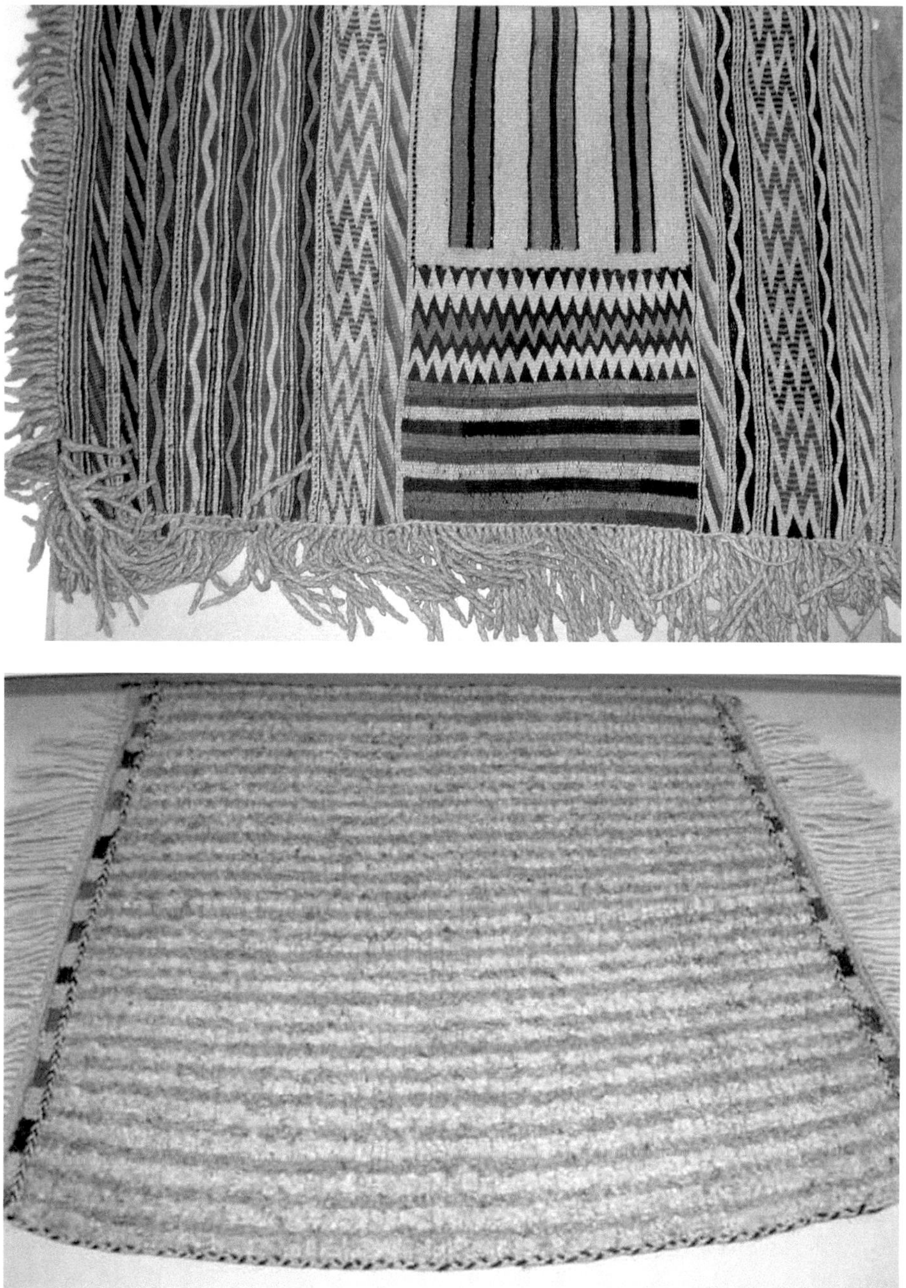

Fig. 5. Coast Salish twined blankets collected in 1841 by Lieutenant Charles Wilkes, commanding officer of the U.S. Exploring Expedition. The brightly colored blanket (NMNH Catalog Number E002124) was originally reported to contain a mixture of dog and goat hair. The ribbed blanket (NMNH Catalog Number E001894) is woven of yarns that incorporate bird down. Photographs courtesy of the Department of Anthropology, Smithsonian Institution; photograph by Repatriation Office staff

was the principal collector of British Columbia antiquities for the Smithsonian Institution as well as the American Museum of Natural History in the early 20th century (Teit 1930). If the Smithsonian acquired E311257 from Teit it could very well have been a product of the Cowichan people who live near Duncan on Vancouver Island. The term "Cowichan" has long been used in the Pacific Northwest as a generic term for all Coast Salish style knitting and weavings, however.

Two "Chilkat" (Tlingit)-style weavings that were probably *not* Coast Salish work also appear in the NMNH catalog: a black and yellow cape (E675) attributed to George Gibbs, secretary of the Indian Treaty Commission and Northwest Boundary Commission in the 1850s, and a blanket (E316360) from the personal collection of early 20th century international legal scholar Charles Hyde.

There have been no systematic microscopic or genetic analyses of the yarn blends in early Coast Salish weavings

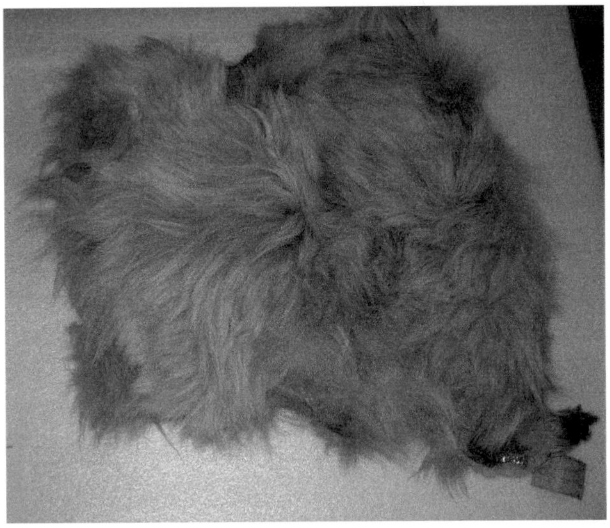

Fig. 6. Pelt of George Gibbs' "famous Indian dog 'Mutton'" collected by naturalist C. B. R. Kennerly in 1859, in the collection of the Mammals Division, National Museum of Natural History, Smithsonian Institution, Catalog Number M4762. Photograph courtesy of the Division of Mammals, National Museum of Natural History, Smithsonian Institution; photograph by Repatriation Office staff

Fig. 7. The Shiba Inu, photographed by J. Megan Jones, 2004

at the NMNH. Upon visual and tactile examination by the weaver in our team (Jones), the white twill woven blankets appeared to be woven from a heavy two-ply yarn of mountain goat wool (Fig. 4), while multi-color twined blankets appeared to contain various blended yarns (Fig. 5). The original Coast Salish weaver probably had a number of materials on hand, collected and traded, from which she could mix, blend, dye and spin different kinds of yarns. She may also have used yarn left over from previous projects. Each multi-colored twined weaving may well contain a unique mixture of different blended yarns, many or all of which include dog hair – very likely shorn from different dogs.

Schulting (1994) used stable carbon isotope ratios (C13:C12) to try to identify the source of the hair in a single Coast Salish blanket from British Columbia. Carbon isotope ratios can distinguish between different photosynthetic pathways, and between terrestrial and marine plants; distinctive ratios persist as plant-derived carbon moves on through the food chain. Schulting's data suggested an animal that gained a considerable amount of its protein from marine sources, and he found similar carbon isotope ratios in the remains of domestic dogs from archaeological sites. These results are consistent with historical and ethnographic accounts of Coast Salish people feeding dogs what they typically dined on themselves: fish. Other candidate sources of hair such as wild goats presumably ate little or no fish. The NMNH weavings have not been subjected to stable isotope ratio analysis to confirm the presence of dog hair. Furthermore, we believe that genetic analysis of the fibers in Coast Salish weavings will tell us more about the size and nature of the woolly dog population.

Woolly dog specimens

The specimens described below were independently rediscovered by one of the authors (Barsh) and by historian Candace Wellman, while each was tracing the fate of notes and specimens collected for the U.S. National Museum in the 1850s by American naturalist C. B. R. Kennerly.

Kennerly shipped two dog pelts and a skull to the U.S. National Museum in 1858–1859. On March 5, 1858, he wrote to museum curator Spencer Baird about the fate of the river otters he had collected at Semiahmoo Bay (near the present-day town of Blaine and the Lummi Indian Reservation):

> … I had two nice skeletons of the otters, & packed them in a box with weights on the top, & intended to clean them in the morning when to my horror & chagrin the abominable Indian Dogs during the night got out the bones & gnawed them to pieces. In pay for this a beautiful skin of a large woolly Dog now hangs outside in a state of preparation for the Smithsonian Museum & as a warning to all others that may come around here without their owners with them [Baird 1833–1887].

This skin was assigned field number 106 and is now cataloged as USNM 3512. It is a medium sized dog with a relatively long, uniformly tawny coat. The undercoat does not match the material in the Smithsonian's 19th century Coast Salish weavings in either color or texture.

Kennerly had been in the Northwest barely a year, and had little direct contact with Coast Salish communities; local ethnography and linguistics had been left to his colleague George Gibbs, who had been Territorial Governor Isaac Stevens' secretary at the Indian treaty negotiations of 1854–1855. Kennerly may have mistaken a "village dog" for a woolly-dog. The original tag on USNM 3512 simply states: "Indian dog."

Kennerly's notebook describes his field number 106 as: "Indian dog Skin & Skull Semiahmoo February 1858" (Kennerly 1858). "Skull" most likely refers to the *Canis* skull assigned catalog number USNM 3437, which we have been unable to locate in the Smithsonian Institution's collections. USNM 3437 has subsequently been confused with a second dog skull sent to the National Museum by Kennerly a year later, in 1859.

A packing list sent to the museum with one of Kennerly's shipments of specimens includes field number 327 "Canis-skull Chiloweyuck Depot July [1859] This is the wooly dog which the Indians shear & use the hair for making blankets, generally mixing it with the wool of the mountain goat" (Kennerly 1859). Farther down the same list is field number 406: "Mr G[ibb]'s dog 'Mutton' Chiloweyuck Indians [September 1859]". We have found no notebook entry or letter describing the circumstances in which Kennerly acquired the "Canis-skull" originally numbered 327, which is now USNM 3820. The original Smithsonian catalog entry is 3671, but refers to field number 327 as "*skin* and skull" [emphasis added], which must be mistaken.

Fortunately, a better record of the provenance of field number 406 has survived. On August 19, 1859, Kennerly wrote to Baird:

> We got another splendid goat skin which was sent to Camp Skagit where Mr. Gibbs happened to be & he took charge of it; but most unfortunately his famous Indian dog "Mutton" got at it and ate the head off. He sent it to me yesterday & when I opened the bag & saw the injury I could almost have cried. Mutton was sheared a short time ago, & as soon as his hair grows out we will make a specimen of him [Baird 1833–1887].

Kennerly's reference to shearing indicates that Mutton was a woolly-dog. Our visual examination of field number 406, now cataloged as USNM 4762, confirms this conclusion (Fig. 6). He is approximately the same size as USNM 3512, the dog that Kennerly mistakenly identified as a woolly-dog. However, Mutton has a pure white, very dense coat, with unusually long guard hairs and an exceptionally fine, dense undercoat of woolly or cotton-like appearance, perfectly matching the fine frizzy fibers found in 19th century Coast Salish dog hair blankets. The original Smithsonian catalog contains a note that this is "The dog whose hair is used by the Indians in manufacturing of blankets".

Fig. 8. The American Eskimo, photographed 2004 by J. Megan Jones, 2004

Mutton's geographical origin remains unclear. The original tag on USNM 4762 reads: "Indian Dog 'Mutton' Cheloweyuck Depot G. Gibbs". The town of Chilliwack on the Fraser River, about 75 km east of Vancouver, British Columbia, derives its name from sc̓əlxʷíqʷ , the name of the Halkomelem-speaking Coast Salish people of the area (Suttles 1990: 455). Kennerly did considerable collecting in southwest British Columbia using "Chiloweyuck Depot" as a forward camp (Kennerly 1858). Gibbs also spent time there with Kennerly, and it is plausible that Mutton was bred nearby. First Nations of the Chilliwack area today regard themselves as part of the Stalo or Sto:lo Nation; see Carlson (2001). Further archival research may reveal Mutton's precise origins.

Robert Fleischer and his students at the Smithsonian Institution's National Zoo have collected tissue from the National Museum of Natural History's woolly-dog specimen at our request, for genetic comparison with other Old World and New World dogs (see Leonard *et al.* 2002), but at the time of this writing they had not yet completed their analysis.

Similar present-day dogs and the reproduction of Coast Salish weaving techniques

Early explorers compared Coast Salish woolly-dogs with European spitz dog breeds, characterized by triangular upright ears on a fox-like head, a brushy tail curled over the back, a compact sturdy build and heavy, double coat (see e.g. "Finnish Spitz," American Kennel Club 2003). The European spitz shares a number of characteristics with "northern" breeds that were not yet familiar to Europeans in Vancouver's time, such as the Malamute, Samoyed, Husky, and Eskimo: upright pointed ears, tail

Fig. 9. Two-ply yarn spun from dog hair (American Eskimo), spun and photographed by J. Megan Jones, 2004

curled forward over the back and a compact sturdy body with shoulders larger and higher than the hips. At least some of these dogs also fit Kane's description of howling rather than barking. A crucial shared characteristic of spitz-like breeds is the double coat, consisting of a very dense undercoat and thick layer of denser guard hairs. This adaptation to cold climates tends to be associated with seasonal molts, resembling the molts of sheep.

Coast Salish methods of blending and spinning yarns on a rolling spindle have been described (e.g. Elmendorf 1992; Gunther 1972; Suttles 1990) and one of us (Jones) has reproduced them using hair from three modern spitz-type breeds Samoyed, American Eskimo, and Shiba Inu. The latter two breeds most closely resemble the size, shape and proportions assumed for the Coast Salish woolly-dog. The specimen Koop *et al.* (2000) regarded as a woolly-dog was more closely related genetically to the Siberian Husky than the Shiba Inu in their sample of living dog breeds, but it may not have been a woolly-dog at all for the reasons discussed above. The Samoyed was not included in Koop *et al.*'s study.

The Shiba Inu (Fig. 7) is the smallest of the living Japanese breeds and is believed to be a direct descendant of ancient Japanese dogs of the Jomon period (up to 8,000 BP), isolated geographically for centuries on small islands and rugged mountain ranges (Ishiguro *et al.* 2000). While Shibas are currently bred for a short coat, longhaired pups are also known. Both long- and short-haired Shibas have dense woolly undercoats that they shed twice each year. The "throwing" of the undercoat takes about a week. It begins with woolly tufts of hair forming at the hips and moves progressively towards the head. The loose hair can be combed out several times each day, but this is laborious and does not recover all of the shed hair. More "wool" can be saved if the dogs are sheared at the beginning of the molt. Complete re-growth of the undercoat takes four to six months. According to historical sources (e.g. Elmendorf 1992; Gunther 1972; Howay 1918; Lamb 1960), Coast Salish woolly-dogs were sheared twice a year. The Shiba Inu occasionally produces longhaired offspring that look very much like Mutton.

The Samoyed also produces a dense woolly undercoat and molts seasonally like the Shiba Inu, but the average Samoyed is much larger in size than the Shiba Inu or Mutton. The American Eskimo dog (Fig. 8) better fits the size, shape, and coat type of Mutton. It is a hardy northern spitz type with a dense undercoat and longer silky outer hairs, all of which spin well. Both the Samoyed and American Eskimo lack the coarse, stiff guard hairs of other breeds, which would compromise the luxurious quality of a yarn spun from their coats.

Several blends and combinations of fibers were tried and all proved to be easy to handle on either the traditional spindle whorl or a modern spinning wheel. The hair was spun and then made into a two-ply yarn that is strong and durable, but also with the soft "hand" characteristic of dog hair. Blends with bird down and plant fibers were also spun and plied (see Figs 9, 10, and 11). An experienced spinner has no difficulty working with these fibers. Gustafson's (1980) statements that "canine hair, no matter from what breed is not a good spinning fiber" and that dog hair yarn exhibits "low tensile strength" are demonstrably in error. Hair from almost any breed of double-coated dog can be spun into acceptable yarn. Breeds vary in the quality of their hair, and individual dogs vary in hair quality depending on diet, overall health, and care. Nevertheless, our research has shown that strong, fine yarns can be spun from dog hair alone, or in combination with a variety of plant and animal fibers.

Discussion and the direction of future research

Our experiments with spinning dog hair raise an important question. Did Coast Salish woolly-dogs comprise a single genetically distinct lineage – that is to say, a true "breed" of dog – or were they simply well maintained, longhaired individuals of mixed and largely indeterminate ancestry? Genetic comparison of a single confirmed specimen (Mutton) with living breeds cannot answer this question; a larger sample of woolly-dogs would be required for reconstruction of the genetic diversity of the population. The best potential source of population level data is hair from Coast Salish weavings preserved in the collections of the Smithsonian Institutions National Museum of Natural History, which should represent a random selection of Coast Salish woolly-dogs living in the early 19th century. We have identified 14 items in the museum's collection that were acquired early enough to be likely to contain at least some dog hairs (E000675, E001891A, E001894, E001895, E002120, E002121, E002122, E002123, E002124, E002125, E177710, E221408,

Fig. 10. Two-ply yarn spun from roughly equal proportions of dog hair (Shiba Inu) and bird down, spun and photographed by J. Megan Jones, 2004

Fig. 11. Two-ply yarn spun from roughly equal proportions of dog hair (Samoyed) and mountain goat wool, spun and photographed by J. Megan Jones, 2004

E233950, E311257). Eight of these weavings were collected by the 1841 U.S. Navy Exploring Expedition, and can be reasonably attributed to Puget Sound provenances.

There is reason to doubt that there was ever any one "breed" of woolly-dog. The sole function of woolly-dogs in Coast Salish society was to produce hair for spinning. Woolly-dogs were separated from other dogs, and not used as hunters, herders, guards, burden haulers, or as food. According to Elmendorf (1992), furthermore, woolly-dogs were not simply thrown scraps of food or left to forage through refuse: they were given a special diet of salmon and elk, which presumably ensured the consistency, quality, and quantity of the spinning fiber. From a weaver's perspective, the value of a particular dog would have been entirely a matter of coat quality: the length, strength, softness, fullness and light color of the hair. Body type, stance, and other traits that preoccupy modern-day breeders would probably have been of little interest to weavers. Assuming that the owner of the dogs was also the spinner and weaver, coat quality would have been the primary criterion applied to breeding decisions as well.

Since the key characteristic of interest to weavers (hair and coat structure) are shared by a number of different living spitz-like breeds, it is reasonable to suppose that Coast Salish weavers both maintained somewhat idiosyncratically local lines of woolly-dogs, and that they traded dogs and recombined lineages. At any moment in time, some local similarities may have been discernible in dogs from different plank houses (perhaps even from different weavers' flocks), but only against the background of even greater variation at the individual level across the entire regional population of woolly-dogs. Individual level variation would have included all the characteristics that are preserved osteologically and have been used by archaeologists to identify Coast Salish dog types: size and build, but not coat structure.

Conclusions

Specimen USNM 4762, the pelt of "Mutton" acquired by George Gibbs some time prior to 1859, likely in British Columbia's lower Fraser River Valley, is the only confirmed specimen of the Coast Salish woolly-dog in the Smithsonian Institution's collections, and probably the only specimen of the skin and coat of this prehistoric Native American breed still in existence. It resembles the infrequently seen longhaired offspring of the ancient Japanese breed Shiba Inu, larger and more robust than the woolly-dog has previously been supposed. In its size and build, but not its coat, it also resembles USNM 3512, an Indian "village dog" from Semiahmoo Bay, about 75 km distant from the origin attributed to USNM 4762. The hair of USNM 4762, but not the hair of USNM 3512, is consistent with the fibers found in the Smithsonian Institution examples of dog-hair blankets woven in the same geographic area in the 1840s and 1850s. Genetic comparison of USNM 4762 with living dog breeds may confirm its close relationship with northern spitz-like dogs such as the American Eskimo and Shiba Inu, which produce individuals with similar coat characteristics. Only a population-level analysis based on DNA extracted from hairs in the earliest surviving examples of Coast Salish weavings will determine whether the woolly-dog was a distinct "breed," however, or simply a widely recurring coat-type phenotype crosscutting all aboriginal Coast Salish dogs.

Authors' affiliations and acknowledgements

Russel Barsh is the Director of KWIAHT: Center for the Historical Ecology of the Salish Sea, a nonprofit laboratory devoted to research in human palaeoecology, marine ecology and stewardship of the San Juan archipelago of Washington State. Joan Megan Jones is the Director of Research and Archives for the Samish Indian Nation, as well as an experienced weaver who raises dogs and spins their hair. Wayne Suttles, who passed away while this paper was awaiting publication, and to whose memory as a "Great Cedar" this study is fondly dedicated, was Professor Emeritus of Anthropology at Portland State University, and was the editor of the Northwest Coast volume of the Smithsonian Institution's revised *Handbook of North American Indians*. The authors gratefully acknowledge the assistance of the Repatriation Office, the Registrar, and the Archives of the Smithsonian Institution in rediscovering "Mutton" and his true identity.

References

American Kennel Club 2003. "Breeds." URL http://www.akc.org/breeds.

Baird, S. F. 1833–1887. Spencer F. Baird Collection. Smithsonian Institution Archives, Record Unit 7002. Box 26. Washington, DC: Smithsonian Institution.

Boas, F. 1921. *Ethnology of the Kwakiutl, based on Data Collected by George Hunt*. Bureau of American Ethnology, Annual Report No. 35, Parts 1–2. Washington, DC: Smithsonian Institution.

Carlson, K. T. (ed.) 2001. *A Stó:lo-Coast Salish Historical Atlas*. Vancouver, British Columbia: Douglas & McIntyre.

Crockford, S. J. 1997. *Osteometry of Makah and Coast Salish Dogs*. Burnaby, British Columbia: Archaeology Press (Simon Fraser University).

Crockford, S. J., and Pye, C. J. 1997. Forensic reconstruction of prehistoric dogs from the Northwest Coast. *Canadian Journal of Archaeology* **21**, 149–153.

Eaton, D., and Urbanek, S. 1995. *Paul Kane's Great Nor-West*. Vancouver, British Columbia: University of British Columbia Press.

Elmendorf, W. W. 1992. *The Structure of Twana Culture; With Comparative Notes on the Structure of Yurok Culture*. Pullman, WA: Washington State University Press.

Fitzhugh, E. C. 1858. Report No. 135, Bellingham Bay Agency (Washington Territory), June 8, 1857, of E. C. Fitzhugh, Special Indian Agent. *Report of the Commissioner of Indian Affairs for 1857*, 325–329. Washington, DC: Government Printing Office.

Gunther, E. 1972. *Indian Life on the Northwest Coast of North America, as Seen by Early Explorers and Fur Traders During the Last Decades of the Eighteenth Century*. Chicago: University of Chicago Press, and Vancouver, British Columbia: Douglas & McIntyre.

Gustafson, P. 1980. *Salish Weaving*. Seattle: University of Washington Press.

Howay, F. W. 1918. "The Dog's Hair Blankets of the Coast Salish." *Washington Historical Quarterly* **9(2)**, 83–92.

Ishiguro, N., Okumura. N., Matsue, A., and Shigehara, N. 2000. Molecular Genetic Analysis of Ancient Japanese Dogs, pp. 287–292, in Crockford, S. J. (ed.) *Dogs Through Time: An Archaeological Perspective*. Oxford: Archaeopress.

Jenness, D. 1934. The Saanich Indians of Vancouver Island. Canadian Ethnology Service Archives, MS No. VII-G-8M. Ottawa: National Museum of Civilization.

Kane, P. 1859. *Wanderings of an Artist Among the Indians of North America, from Canada to Vancouver's Island and Oregon*. London: Longmans, Brown, Green, Longmans, and Roberts. (Reprinted: C. E. Tuttle, Rutland, VT, 1967.)

Kendrick, J. S. 1991. *Voyage of* Sutil *and* Mexicana, *1792: The Last Spanish Exploration of the Northwest Coast of America*. Spokane: Arthur H. Clark.

Kennerly, C. B. R. 1858. Natural History N.W. Boundary Survey Zoology. [Leather bound notebook.] Caleb Burwell Rowan Kennerly Papers. Smithsonian Institution Archives, Record Unit 7202. Box 26. Washington, DC: Smithsonian Institution.

Kennerly, C. B. R. 1859. [Packing list.] Smithsonian Institution Accession File No. 83 of 1859. Washington, DC: Smithsonian Institution.

Koop, B. F., Burbridge, M., Byun, A., Rink, U., and Crockford, S. J. 2000. Ancient DNA evidence of a separate origin for North American indigenous dogs, pp. 271–285 in Crockford, S. J. (ed.), *Dogs Through Time: An Archaeological Perspective*. Oxford: Archaeopress.

Krieger, H. W. 1928. American Indian Costumes in the United States National Museum. *Annual Report of the Smithsonian Institution for 1928*, 623–647. Washington, D.C: Smithsonian Institution.

Lamb, W. K, (ed.) 1960. *The Letters and Journals of Simon Fraser, 1806–1808*. Toronto: MacMillan of Canada.

Lamb, W. K. (ed.) 1984. *A Voyage of Discovery to the North Pacific Ocean and Round the World, 1791–1795*. London: Hakluyt Society.

Leonard, J. A., Wayne, R. K., Wheeler, J., Valadez, R., Guillen, S. and Vila, C. 2002. Ancient DNA Evidence for an Old World Origin of New World Dogs. *Science* **298**, 1613–1616.

MacLachlan, M. 1998. *The Fort Langley Journals, 1827–30*. Vancouver, British Columbia: University of British Columbia Press.

Peale, T. R. 1846. U.S. Exploring Expedition Collection 1838–1885, Smithsonian Institution Archives Accession No. RU 7186, box 1, folder 8.

Pickering, C. [1841] Lists of specimens unpacked by C. Pickering. U.S. Exploring Expedition Collection 1838–1885, Smithsonian Institution Archives Accession No. RU 7186, box 2, folder 9.

Ryder, M. L. 2000. Breed Differences in Dog Hair, pp. 251–255 in Crockford, S. J. (ed.), *Dogs Through Time: An Archaeological Perspective*. Oxford: Archaeopress.

Schulting, R. 1994. The hair of the dog: the identification of a Coast Salish Dog-Hair blanket from Yale, British Columbia. *Canadian Journal of Archaeology* **18**, 57–76.

Suttles, W. P. 1951. The Economic Life of the Coast Salish of Haro and Rosario Straits. Ph.D diss., University of Washington, Seattle. (Reprinted: Garland Publishing, New York, 1974.)

Suttles, W. P. 1987. *Coast Salish Essays*. Seattle: University of Washington Press, and Vancouver, British Columbia: Talonbooks.

Suttles, W. P. 1990. Central Coast Salish, pp. 453–475 in Suttles, W. P. (ed.), *Handbook of North American Indians; Northwest Coast*. Washington DC: Smithsonian Institution Press.

Teit, J. A. 1930. The Salishan Tribes of the Western Plateaus. *Forty-fifth Annual Report of the Bureau of American Ethnology, 1927–28*, 23–396. Washington, D.C.

Wagner, H. R. 1933. *Spanish Explorations in the Strait of Juan de Fuca*. Santa Ana, CA: Fine Arts Press.

Wright, R. K. 1991. Masterworks of Washington Native Art, pp. 42–151 in Wright, R. K. (ed.), *A Time of Gathering; Native Heritage of Washington State*. Seattle and London: University of Washington Press.

Young, F. G. (ed.) 1905. "Dr. John Scouler's Journal of a Voyage to N.W. America." *Oregon Historical Quarterly* **6(2)**, 159–205.

KWIAHT: Center for the Historical Ecology
of the Salish Sea
PO Box 415
Lopez Island
WA 98261
USA

rlbarsh@gmail.com

Samish Indian Nation
P.O. Box 217
Anacortes, WA 98221

mjones@samishtribe.nsn.us

9th ICAZ Conference, Durham 2002
Dogs and People in Social, Working, Economic or Symbolic Interaction
(eds Lynn M. Snyder and Elizabeth A. Moore) pp. 12–23

2. A Dwarf Hound Skeleton from a Romano-British Grave at York Road, Leicester, England, U.K., with a discussion of other Roman small dog types and speculation regarding their respective aetiologies

Ian L. Baxter

In the course of an excavation outside the Roman town walls of Leicester in 1997 the complete skeleton of a small dog was found on the base of a full-sized human grave dating from the fourth century AD. The York Road specimen is of particular interest as a complete skeleton of a type of small dog frequently encountered on sites of the Roman period, more generally as scattered cranial and postcranial remains, typified by having short bowed legs and a superficial resemblance to the modern Dachshund. The skeleton is described and the cranial and appendicular morphology of this type is compared to those of modern Dachshunds and other dwarf Roman dogs with more rounded crania and straight limbs, which anatomically more closely resemble the modern terrier, Maltese and Pomeranian breeds. Methods of cranial analysis used to discriminate between modern chondrodystrophic and other breeds of small dogs are applied to the archaeological material and radiographs of limb bones belonging to both types illustrated in order to provide a more accurate and comprehensive description of the morphotype.

Introduction

Harcourt (1974) was the first author to note that small dogs do not become frequent archaeologically in Britain until the Roman period. In his opinion there were at this time "... two, possibly three, distinct populations and what were almost certainly house dogs were seen for the first time". Subsequently, Teichert (1987) investigated the spread of brachymel or dwarf dogs following the advance of the Roman Empire in the regions north of the Alps, but failed to adequately distinguish between the types of dogs involved. Like the aforementioned publications of Harcourt and Teichert, most studies of Roman dogs hereto have been of a general nature (e.g. Clark 1995; De Grossi Mazzorin & Tagliacozzo 2000; Bartosiewicz 2000). However, to date no full description of a complete skeleton of a Roman dwarf hound appears to have been published and neither has a clear distinction been made on anatomical and aetiological grounds between the two quite distinct Roman small dog morphotypes. This paper attempts to provide the basis for a greater degree of anatomical clarification.

In the summer of 1997 during a rescue excavation in advance of development at York Road, Leicester, the complete skeleton of a small dog was found on the base of a full sized human grave dating from the fourth century AD (Baxter 1997, 1998a; Gossip 1998; Musty 1998: 90; Richardson 1997). The York Road site forms part of an extensive extramural Roman inhumation cemetery previously identified from chance finds during building work earlier this century and a more recent excavation at Newark Street, situated south of the defences of *Ratae Corieltauvorum* between the Gartree and *Tripontium* Roads (Cooper 1996). It is uncertain if a human burial originally accompanied that of the dog (J. Gossip pers comm.); as only a few human cranial fragments were recovered in the upper levels of the grave fill.

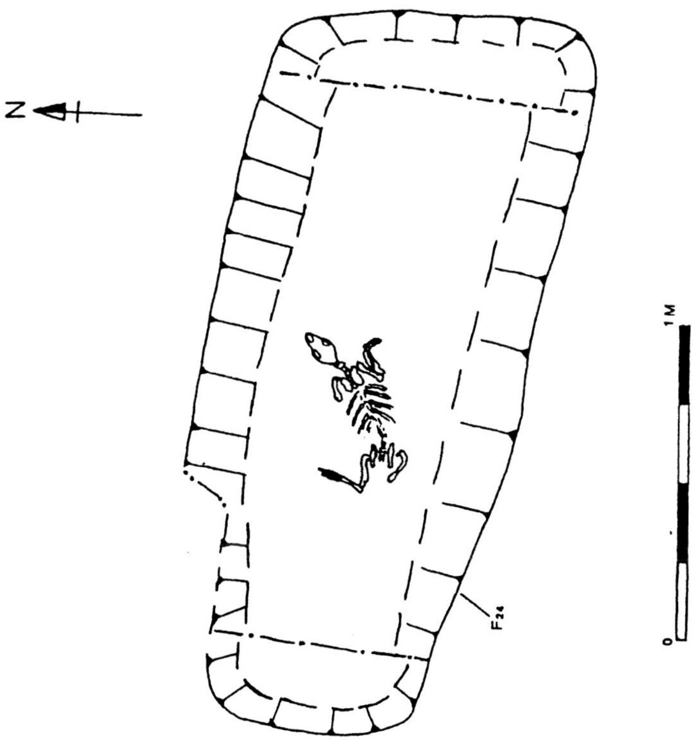

Fig.1. Plan of the York Road dog in its grave

The grave containing the York Road dog was a vertical sided quadrilateral feature orientated east-west. The grave appeared to have been cut through the backfill of a second century boundary ditch. The fill of the grave comprised a dark silt consistent with deliberate backfill, and contained several human cranial fragments in its uppermost areas. These may represent the remains of a disturbed burial, since the feature had been truncated by two subsequent shallow gullies. Three possible coffin nails were also recovered from the fill, but it is not clear whether these were from the lower or upper fills. The lower fill also contained fourth century pottery. The complete skeleton of a dog was found on the base and in the centre of the grave cut. The dog appeared to have been placed deliberately and was orientated northeast-southwest, with its head to the northeast (J. Gossip, pers. comm. and 1998; Figures 1–3). Originally thought to have cut marks on the basicranium (Gossip 1998; Musty 1998: 90), subsequent microscopic examination has revealed these marks to be natural in origin.

This paper largely replaces, though with a more anatomical slant, an earlier draft cited as "in press" in the literature (e.g. Cram 2000: 172) which failed to appear due to the demise of the original publisher (The Osteoarchaeological Research Group).

Anatomy and affinities of the York Road dog

All the permanent teeth were fully erupted and in wear and all the long bone epiphyses fused. The dog was probably over eighteen months old and adult but apparently not aged, as the teeth are in very good condition and the cranial sutures though fused are not obliterated. With the exception of I^{1-3}, I_{1-2} and to a much lesser extent $I_{3,}$ which are slightly worn, there is no appreciable wear on any of the teeth except the lower carnassial (M_1) which appears to have very slight wear on the metaconid (Horard-Herbin 2000: stage B). This suggests an age of between 6–24 months. An age of not less than 20–24 months is indicated by the fully fused state of the vertebral epiphyses (Habermehl 1961: 143). The unusual circumstances of deposition, in a full-sized human grave without, apparently, a human companion, within (by the fourth century AD) a dedicated human cemetery site suggest special treatment for this animal which may also have preceded its demise and included diet, hence possibly masking its apparent dental age.
The baculum or *os penis* was recovered indicating that this individual was male. This is also suggested by the morphology of the cranial base (The and Trouth, 1976).

The dental formula is: $2x \dfrac{I3\ C\ P4\ M2}{I3\ C\ P4\ M3}$

Fig. 2. The York Road dog in situ *within its grave viewed from the right front. Scale 0.3 m*

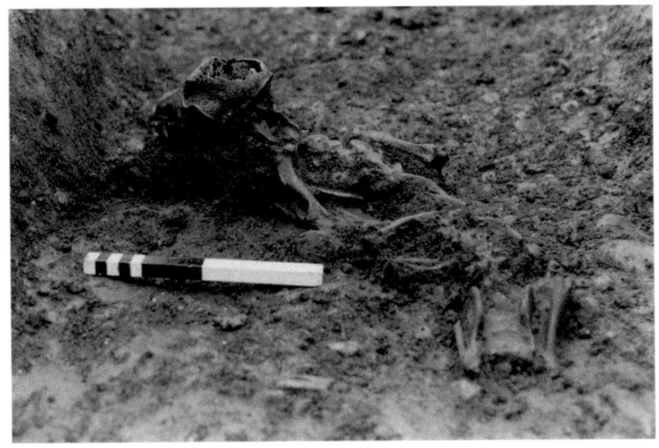

Fig. 3. The York Road dog in situ *within its grave viewed from the left rear. Scale 0.3 m*

Originally complete apart from some damage to the top of the braincase caused during excavation (Figs 2 and 3); the cranium has been temporarily restored to enable accurate measurements to be made (Table 1). The cranium has a relatively high cephalic index, but is mesaticephalic like most of the dogs in the Iron Age and Romano-British periods. The snout is very narrow and the parietofrontal crests are separated by an interval behind and diverge to the supraorbital process with only a slight sagittal crest on the interparietal. The occipital crest is well developed. In the mandible the P_1, P_2, P_4 and M_1 are crowded and the M_3 alveolus encroaches on the vertical ramus. The lower M_1 (carnassial) is large in proportion to the rest of the mandibular cheek tooth row.

The present author has also studied similar, but slightly smaller, crania of similar type from Little Lane and Great

Table 1. Selected measurements of the York Road dog (after Harcourt 1974, Nussbaumer 1976 and von den Driesch 1976)

Skull		
I	Occipital protuberance to anterior margin of the incisor alveoli	149.0 mm
HB(1)	*Hirnstammbasis* (brain stem base)	41.5 mm
II	Occipital protuberance to junction of nasal and frontal bones	82.1 mm
MX(2)	*Maxillarlänge* (maxillary length)	46.8 mm
III	Posterior junction of the nasal bones to anterior margin of the incisor alveoli	73.1 mm
PL(3)	*Palatinumlänge* (palatal length)	43.7 mm
IV	Bizygomatic breadth	85.4 mm
BL(5)	*Basilarlänge* (basal length = VDD 3)	132.0 mm
IX	Palatal length	71.4 mm
X	Palatal breadth	50.8 mm
XI	Maxillary cheek tooth row length	55.9 mm
XII	Width of snout between the outer margins of the canine alveoli	26.8 mm
13	Length of the lower carnassial	19.7 mm
XV	Mandibular cheek tooth row length	60.5 mm
	Bicondylar width of mandible	66.7 mm

Cranial Indices		
	Cephalic Index (IV.100/I)	57.3
	Snout Index (III.100/I)	49.1
	Snout Width Index (XII.100/III)	36.7
	Palatal Index (X.100/IX)	71.2

Postcranial skeleton	Length	Midshaft diameter	msd Index (msd.100/tl)
Humerus	90.3 mm	8.6 mm	9.5
Radius	77.4 mm	10.0 mm	12.9
Ulna	94.1 mm	-	-
Femur	92.7 mm	8.9 mm	9.6
Tibia	85.4 mm	9.8 mm	11.5

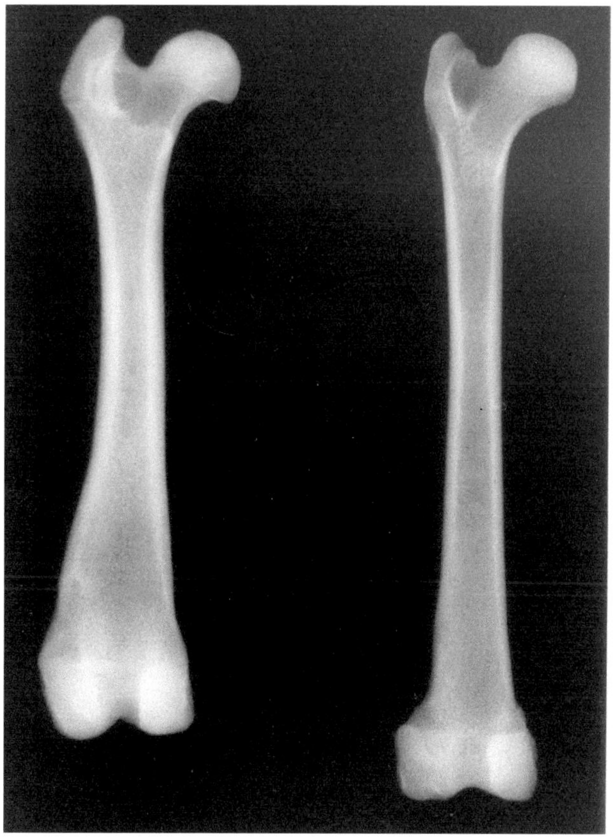

Fig. 4. Radiographs of the femur. Left: York Road. Right: High Street

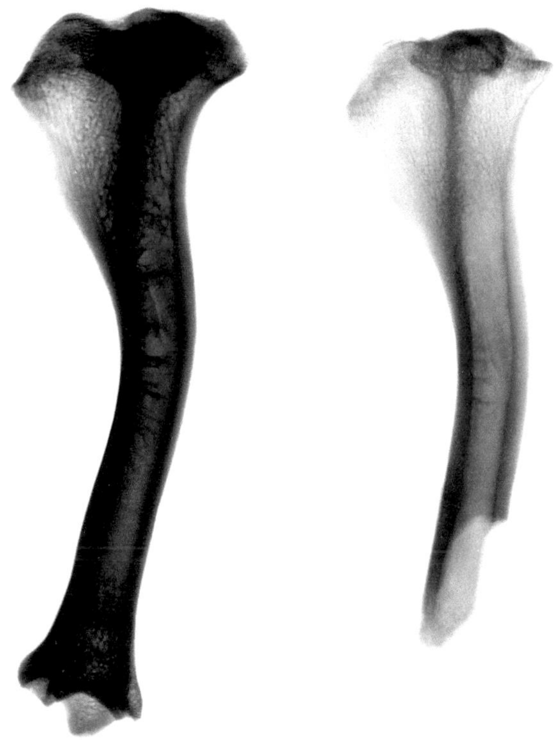

Fig. 5. Radiographs showing trabecular struts in the tibia shaft. Left: Silver Street. Right: Causeway Lane

Holme Street in Leicester. They occur on Iron Age and Roman sites in Europe, e.g. Manching (Petri 1961: cranium no. 11) and Classe (Farello 1995: nos 2, 3, 5). In smaller dogs of this sort the M_3 may be congenitally absent or the M_2 and M_3 alveoli may be situated in the vertical ramus of the mandible. The York Road specimen is of particular interest as a complete skeleton of a type of small dog frequently encountered on sites of the Roman period only as scattered cranial and postcranial remains. Both the radius and the tibia are bowed, and both bones have very high midshaft diameter (msd.100/tl) indices of 12.9 and 11.5 respectively. All the limb bones are short and very robust. The proximal and distal femur are both expanded and radiographs show that the femur and tibia shafts are up to 3 mm thick in section (Fig. 4 left). The tibia is shorter than the femur. The estimated shoulder height of the York Road dog is very approximately 27 cm, with a range between 26–28 cm based on the multiplication factors of Harcourt (1974). The mean figure is based on the average of the available long bones (humerus, radius, ulna, femur and tibia), and based on factors that do not take account of the angle of the shoulder joint (Scott 2002) and the bowed nature of some elements. The resultant error factor would appear to be relatively insignificant, however.

Only one coccygeal vertebra was recovered (Cy 1) and therefore no information is available regarding the tail. It may possibly have been docked, the Romans apparently believed that docking the tail gave protection against rabies (Clutton-Brock and Jewell 1979: 27), or more probably these bones were lost during excavation along with most of the wrist and anklebones. With a head length of 15 cm, estimated neck length of 12 cm, body length in the region of 30 cm, and live weight of around 10kg, this was a relatively heavy and powerful if short-legged animal which in life may have generally resembled the modern Dachshund in appearance and habits.

The specific shape of the Dachshund originates from a prenatal evolutionary disturbance, an endochondral ossification disorder known in human medicine as *chondrodystrophia fœtalis* or achondroplasty, a disorder resulting in disproportionately short limbs. Such bones differ from normal ones mainly in the coarse-meshed structure of the spongiosa, the earlier fusion of the epiphyses and the heavy curving of the diaphyses (Hilzheimer 1926: 97). Comparisons of cranial dimensions in the York Road dog (Figures 6–8) with those of modern breeds support the contention of Nussbaumer (1976: 13) that shortening of the brain stem base is also part of the chondrodystrophic syndrome. In scatter plots the York Road dog is more extreme in the relation of the upper carnassial (Fig. 7) and palatal length (Fig. 9)

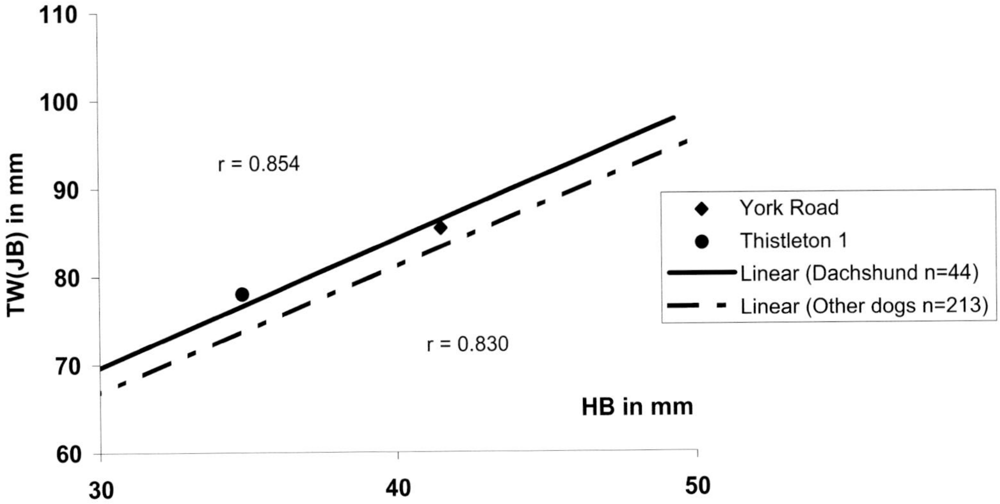

Fig. 6. The York Road dog compared with trendlines for dachshunds and other modern dogs: Bizygomatic breadth (TW/JB)/Brain stem base (Hirnstammbasis)

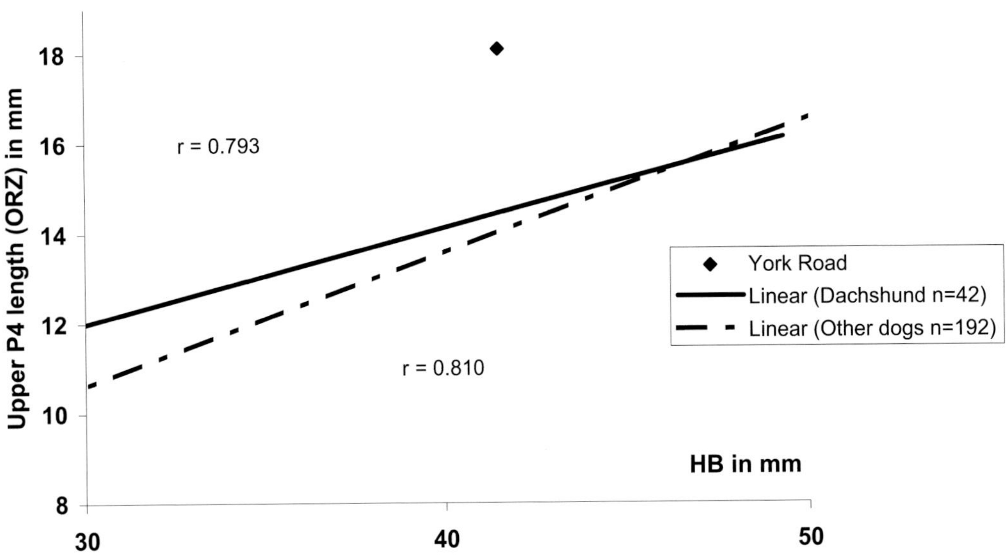

Fig. 7. The York Road dog compared with trendlines for dachshunds and other modern dogs: Upper P4 length (ORZ)/Brain stem base (Hirnstammbasis)

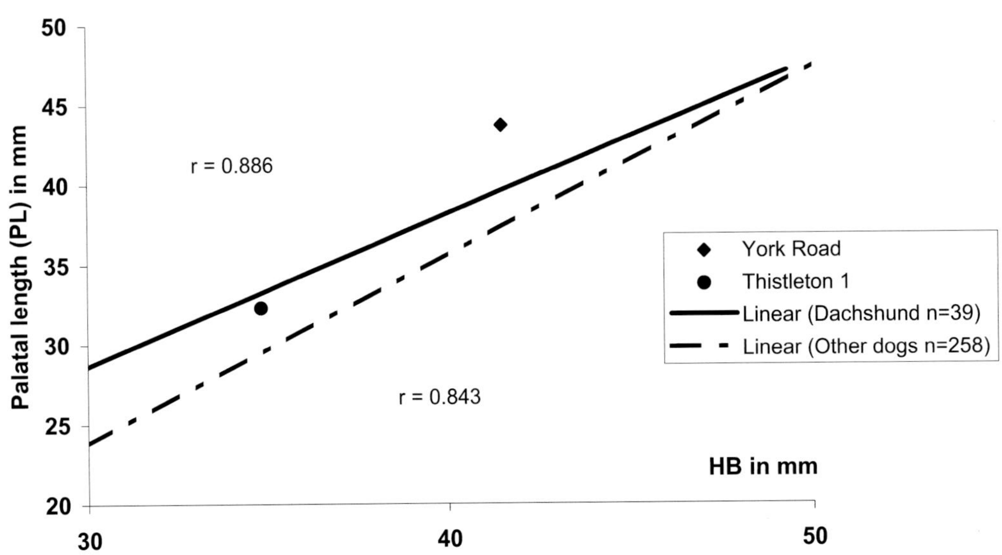

Fig. 8. The York Road dog compared with trendlines for dachshunds and other modern dogs: Maxillary length (MX)/Brain stem base (Hirnstammbasis)

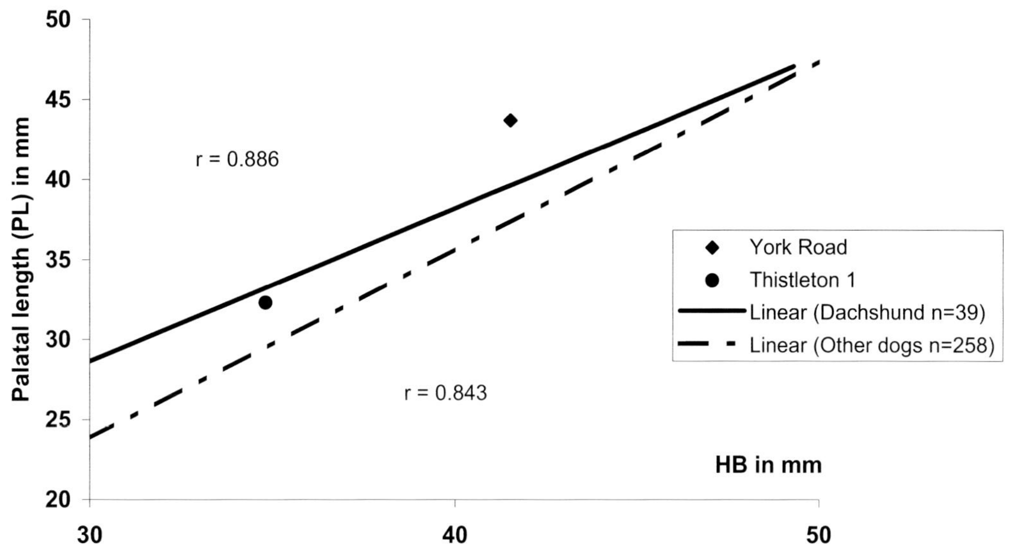

Fig. 9. The York Road dog compared with trendlines for dachshunds and other modern dogs: Palatal length (PL)/Brain stem base (Hirnstammbasis)

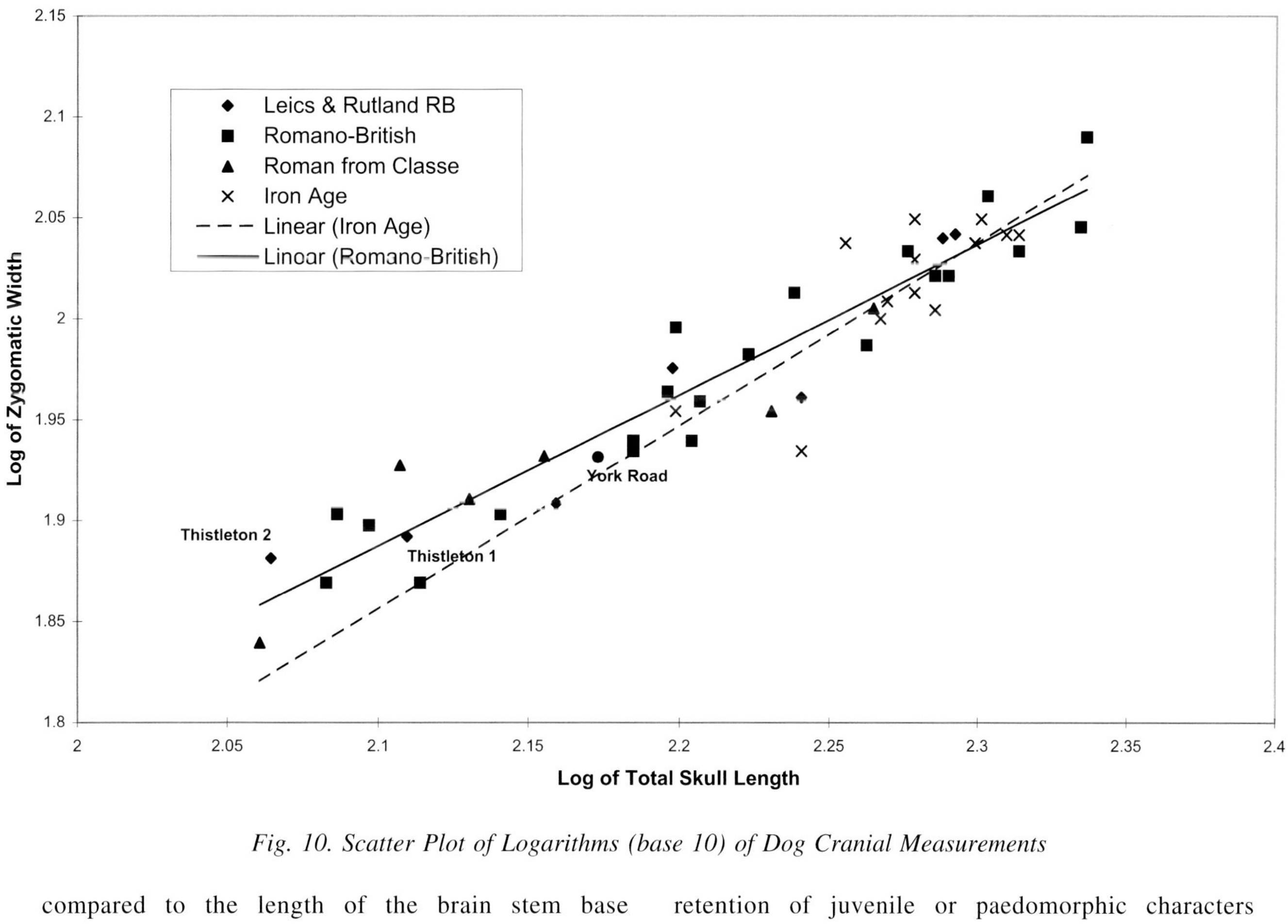

Fig. 10. Scatter Plot of Logarithms (base 10) of Dog Cranial Measurements

compared to the length of the brain stem base (*Hirnstammbasis* = length oral edge of foramen magnum (Basion) to boundary of the Pterygoid & Palatine where it joins the Presphenoid) than the regression lines for a significant sample of modern Dachshund crania (39–42 specimens). In terms of bizygomatic breadth (Fig. 6) it is closer to the Dachshund, but the relative maxillary length (Fig. 8) is closer to that of non-chondrodystrophic breeds. The aetiology of the form of dog represented by the York Road animal appears to be very different from the retention of juvenile or paedomorphic characters displayed by other types of Roman and modern non-chondrodystrophic dwarf dogs and whose crania are typified by a shortening of the palatine (see below). Plots based on the standard cranial measurements suggested by Harcourt (1974) and von den Driesch (1976) commonly used by archaeozoologists (e.g. Brothwell *et al.* 1979 and Churcher 1993), while suggesting some difference in the relationship of cranial length to breadth, are inadequate to discriminate between these two very different forms of small dogs (Fig. 10) and should be replaced with the more sophisticated system of Nussbaumer (Appendix 1), the efficacy of which is well documented for modern dog breeds (Nussbaumer 1976 & 1978).

Comparison of the York Road hound with radiographs of the modern Dachshund (Figs 11 and 12) indicate that the Roman femur is not as short and has less massively expanded ends than the Dachshund. Also, while the Dachshund femur has a midshaft diameter index of 14.4 (Table 2), the York Road specimen's index is only 9.6. The Roman bone has equally thick walls. In the tibia, although this is bowed in both the Roman and modern specimens, the York Road, Silver Street and Causeway Lane tibias are not only longer but also more massively constructed and have thicker walls than that of the Dachshund (Fig. 5). The msd index for the Dachshund tibia is 12.5 which is more closely comparable with the York Road dog's 11.5. The highest index recorded by the author for a Roman dwarf hound tibia is 12.0 for a specimen from New Bond Street, Leicester (Baxter, 1993). The author has also seen radiographs of the Basset Hound femur and tibia (not illustrated), that are similar in their conformation to those of the Dachshund but generally more massive. The msd indices for the Basset Hound specimen are 14.3 for the femur and 12.3 for the tibia.

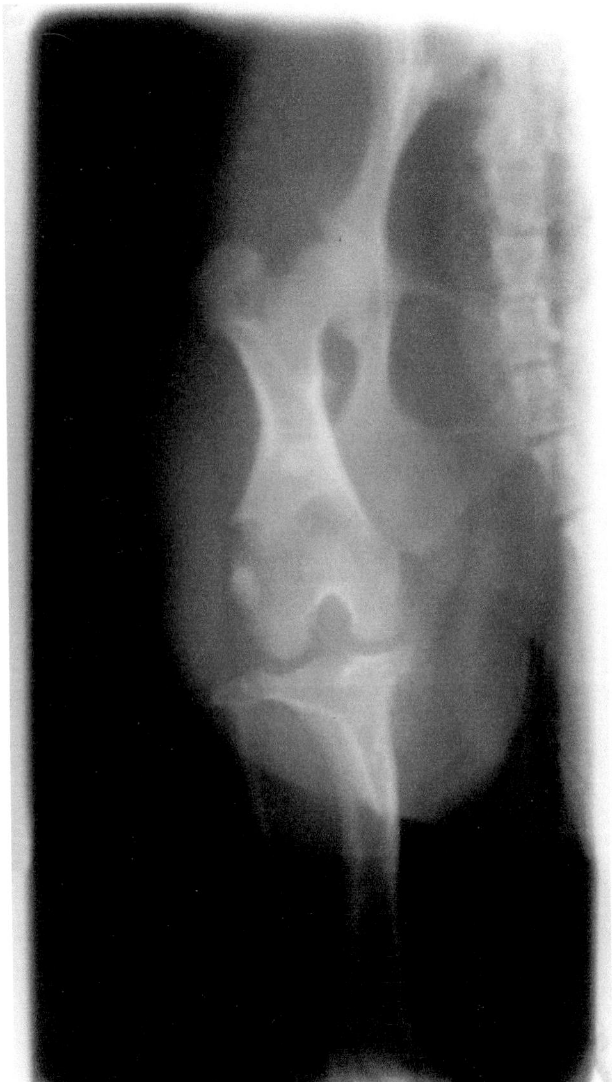

Fig. 11. Radiograph of a modern Dachshund (C98 786) femur and tibia (cranio-caudal aspect).

Less complete remains of dwarf hounds have been recovered from Little Lane (Gidney 1991), New Bond Street (Baxter 1993), Silver Street (Gouldwell nd), Causeway Lane (Gidney 1999: 317), and Bonners Lane (Baxter 1994) in Leicester and Thistleton in Rutland (THZ 128) dating from the 2nd to 4th centuries. Similar dogs have also been recovered from Late Roman deposits at Classe in Italy (Farello 1995), and are quite common on sites of the Roman Imperial period in both Britain and Central Europe (Bartosiewicz 2000; Bökönyi 1974; Teichert 1987). Earlier occurrences of such animals occasionally appear both in Britain and on the Continent either due to random mutation, breeding selection or import from the Roman Empire (Bökönyi 1974: 320–3; Teichert 1987; Hamilton-Dyer 2001). The York Road specimen falls near the middle of the range for such animals of approximately 22 to 37 cm shoulder height. A brachymel or dwarf hound rather than a lap dog (Teichert 1987), animals of this type occur quite frequently on Roman sites in Leicester and elsewhere in Britain, although this specimen is the most complete described so far. In some specimens, but not the York Road individual or the modern Dachshund and Basset Hound specimens, the bowed tibiae are strengthened by trabecular struts (Fig. 5). This suggests that relatively more of the body weight stresses were being supported by this bone in the Roman animals.

The recent Dachshund ("badger hound"), which this sort of Roman dog anatomically resembles, was originally used not only for badger hunting but also to track wounded

Table 2. Measurements of the modern Dachshund (C98 786) femur and tibia. (after Harcourt 1974 and von den Driesch 1976)

	Length	**Midshaft diameter**	**msd Index (msd.100/tl)**
Femur	65.2 mm	9.4 mm	14.4
Tibia	61.6 mm	7.7 mm	12.5

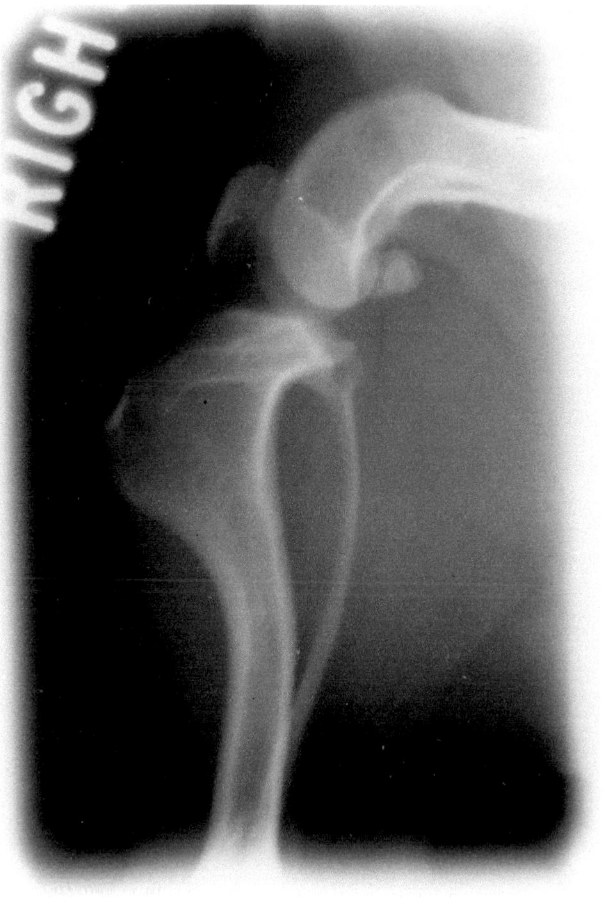

Fig. 12. Radiograph of a modern Dachshund (C98 786). Distal femur and proximal tibia (lateral aspect)

game and worrying wild boar in the forests, where being so low to the ground they could get about in undergrowth more easily when escaping the charges of their formidable antagonist (Sadler 1994; Adelman 1997: 154). The Basset Hound was also bred for slow trailing by scent (Adelman 1997: 137). There is very little evidence for hunting in Roman Britain where the remains of wild species, with the exception of deer antlers seasonally collected for use as raw material (MacGreggor 1985), are generally scarce on archaeological sites. Possibly dwarf hounds were in practice primarily used as herding dogs in similar fashion to the recent Corgi, although they were also probably kept as pets and watch-dogs, especially in urban areas. It is possible that the bronze statuette from Coventina's well at Carrawburgh on Hadrian's Wall may represent a dwarf hound (Toynbee 1973: Figure 45). This animal has a large head that is held erect, erect pointed ears, a long neck and body, short legs and a curly tail.

Other types of Roman dwarf dogs

The type of Roman dwarf dog exemplified by the York Road specimen is quite different in its morphology and aetiology to other types of dwarf dog less frequently encountered on Roman sites and typified by a more neotonous brachycephalic and rounded cranium and straight, thin-walled, long bones with low msd indices. The present author has not seen a complete skeleton of this type of dog and the following is largely based on a re-examination of the 3rd (?) century Thistleton 2 (THZ

Table 3. Selected measurements of the Thistleton 2 (THZ 1441) skeleton and High Street (A112.1991/237) femur (after Harcourt 1974, Nussbaumer 1976 and von den Driesch 1976)

Thistleton 2				
Skull				
I	Occipital protuberance to anterior margin of the incisor alveoli			116.0 mm
II	Occipital protuberance to junction of nasal and frontal bones			69.9 mm
III	Posterior junction of the nasal bones to anterior margin of the incisor alveoli			50.3 mm
IV	Bizygomatic breadth			76.1 mm
IX	Palatal length			*not measurable*
X	Palatal breadth			45.4 mm
XI	Maxillary cheek tooth row length			35.5 mm
XII	Width of snout between the outer margins of the canine alveoli			*not measurable*
13	Length of the lower carnassial			16.0 mm
XV	Mandibular cheek tooth row length			44.1 mm
	Bicondylar width of mandible			57.5 mm
Cranial Indices				
	Cephalic Index (IV.100/I)		65.6	
	Snout Index (III.100/I)		43.4	
	Snout Width Index (XII.100/III)		36.7	
	Palatal Index (X.100/IX)			
Postcranial skeleton				
	Length	Midshaft diameter	msd Index (msd.100/tl)	
Humerus	101.0 mm	6.7 mm	6.9	
High Street				
Postcranial skeleton				
	Length	Midshaft diameter	msd Index (msd.100/tl)	
Femur	98.1 mm	7.1 mm	7.2	

Table 4. Selected measurements of the Thistleton 1 (THZ 128) cranium. (after Harcourt 1974, Nussbaumer 1976 and von den Driesch 1976)

Skull		
I	Occipital protuberance to anterior margin of the incisor alveoli	128.7 mm
HB(1)	*Hirnstammbasis* (brain stem base)	34.8 mm
II	Occipital protuberance to junction of nasal and frontal bones	75.0 mm
MX(2)	*Maxillarlänge* (maxillary length)	39.8 mm
III	Posterior junction of the nasal bones to anterior margin of the incisor alveoli	62.2 mm
PL(3)	*Palatinumlänge* (palatal length)	32.3 mm
IV	Bizygomatic breadth	78.0 mm
BL(5)	*Basilarlänge* (basal length = VDD 3)	101.9 mm
IX	Palatal length	64.6 mm
X	Palatal breadth	44.4 mm
XI	Maxillary cheek tooth row length	46.5 mm
XII	Width of snout between the outer margins of the canine alveoli	26.8 mm

Cranial Indices		
	Cephalic Index (IV.100/I)	60.6
	Snout Index (III.100/I)	48.3
	Snout Width Index (XII.100/III)	43.0
	Palatal Index (X.100/IX)	68.7

1441) material originally described by Harcourt (1971) and an isolated femur from a 2nd century feature at the High Street, Leicester (Baxter 1991) apparently belonging to this morphotype (Table 3).

These gracile, straight-limbed small dogs are typified by having relatively shorter and broader faces, and a rounded cranium without sagittal crests. The palatine, but not the brain stem base, is reduced (Nussbaumer 1976, 1978). The cranial morphology is, therefore, more paedomorphic and closely resembles that of an immature animal. The cranial shape has a general resemblance to that of the modern Maltese. In Thistleton 2, M^2 seems to have been absent from the palate and M_3 was also absent in the mandible. The mandibular teeth are crowded, particularly P_4 and M_1 (Fig. 14 right). An associated humerus has a msd index of 6.9 and indicates a withers height in the region of 32 cm. The High Street femur is straight and very gracile with a msd index of 7.2 and came from a dog approximately 30 cm high at the shoulder (Figure 4 right). The msd indices for the York Road dog are much higher at 9.5 and 9.6 respectively. But it is particularly in the short and wide bowed radius and tibia and the expanded femur ends that the morphotype exemplified by the York Road animal is postcranially most distinct. Harcourt (1974) described a gracile straight tibia, anatomically indistinct from that of a modern Pomeranian, from Hemel Hempstead with an estimated msd index of 7.1. By comparison, the York Road tibia msd index is 11.5. While these dogs would appear from their size and gracility to be pets, and it is known from the writings of several Roman authors that pets were kept at this time, and are perhaps appropriately described as toy or lapdogs, some at least may also have been originally bred for a specific function in some region of the Empire. Perhaps like the recent *Griffons D'Ecurie* they were efficient destroyers of vermin (Adelman 1997: 396). Clark (2000) has recently drawn attention to the sporadic occurrence of small dog remains on pre-Roman British sites. These include chondrodystrophic and paedomorphic types (see above). A distal femur apparently belonging to a small straight limbed dog around 30 cm high has been described by the author from an Early Iron Age site at Landwade Road, Fordham in Cambridgeshire (Baxter 1998b).

One of the smallest of these straight legged dogs discovered thus far in Europe was found in a human cemetery at Neuenheim in Germany (Lüttswager 1965). This was certainly a lapdog, appears to have been relatively short-faced, and may be of the type called *Melitaei* by Pliny (Clutton-Brock 1987; Turner 1962), possibly related to the so-called "comforters" documented in medieval Europe (MacDonogh 1999) and the modern Maltese (see also MacKinnon, this volume). An isolated radius from an animal 22 cm high at the shoulder found at Causeway Lane in Leicester (Gidney 1999: 317) probably represents this type.

These straight limbed dwarfs would appear to originate from imbalance in the endocrine system and particularly thyroid hormone production patterns (Crockford 2000a) resulting in allometric dwarfing.

Summary and conclusion

The York Road dog is a good example of a widespread Roman morphotype, possibly represented by the Carrawburgh bronze figurine and superficially similar in its proportions to the modern Dachshund. It is, therefore, suitable to act as a paradigm for this kind of dwarf hound whose aetiology appears to be based on a prenatal evolutionary disturbance, a chondrodystrophic syndrome,

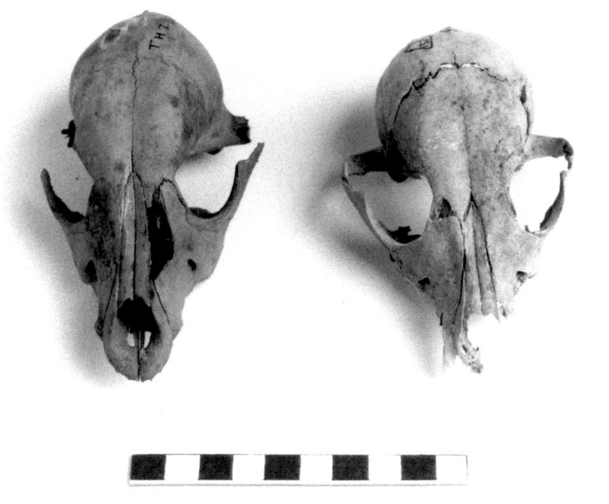

Fig. 13. A) The Thistleton 1 (THZ 128) and B) the Thistleton 2 (THZ 1441) crania viewed from above. Scale in centimetres

Fig. 14. A) The Thistleton 4 (THX 4289) and B) Thistleton 2 (THZ 1441) mandibles. Scale in centimetres

rather than the retention of juvenile or paedomorphic characters based on endrochrine (thyrozine) imbalance. The skull is long and the teeth large relative to the size of the jaws. There are sagittal and nuchal crests suggesting a powerful bite. In the Roman dog the femur is longer and less massive with less pronounced expansion of the epiphyses than in the modern Dachshund. The tibia is also longer but more massively constructed than in the Dachshund and sometimes appears to possess reinforcing trabecular struts. Both the radius and tibia are bowed and have high midshaft diameter indices indicative of short but very robust bones. This type of dog was a dwarf or brachymel hound and may have been originally bred as a working animal of some kind, possibly as a scent hound. The precise area of the empire from which dwarf (brachymel) hounds originate as a Roman "breed" is presently unknown. Possibly, as with the *Melitae,* an island. In island ecologies there is often a tendency towards dwarfism (Davis 1987: 118–125). They may even be identical to the small and lean rough-haired *Agassaeans* described by Roman authors as imports from Britain (Toynbee 1973: 104). The precise relationship of the Roman dwarf hound to the modern Dachshund or other Roman and modern breeds is unknown, and is unlikely to be clarified without a thorough program of DNA analysis. It seems most likely, primarily on the basis of differences in postcranial morphology, that the Roman dwarf hound represents an analogous rather than a homologous form ancestral to modern dachshunds.

Whereas the chondrodystrophic or achondroplastic dwarfism exemplified by modern Dachshunds and Basset hounds, together with otherwise genetically unrelated European prehistoric and Roman specimens and "breeds" such as the York Road dog and the Meso-American *Tlalchichi* (Valadez 2000: 198–200; Crockford 2000b: 306), probably inherits as a simple dominant trait as it does in humans (Weaver & Hedrick 1992); the straight limbed dwarfs (including modern Toy breeds) would appear to originate from imbalance in the endocrine system and particularly thyroid hormone production patterns (Crockford 2000a and pers. comm.) resulting in allometric dwarfing. The biological mechanisms involved in the production of these two distinct types of dwarf dogs are therefore quite different, and while both could occur, they would not have been perpetuated so successfully without an element of human selection and intention, i.e. breeding. The proliferation of both types of dwarfs in the Roman period, particularly in towns, may be largely influenced by cultural factors, and in particular the increased importance of pets in comparison with working animals and the spatial constraints of an urban environment.

Acknowledgements

I would like to thank James Gossip, formerly of University of Leicester Archaeological Services, for allowing me to study the remains of the York Road dwarf hound and for his help with details of the archaeology of the site; Sheila Hamilton-Dyer for helpful comments and access to forthcoming publications; Nadja Pöllath of Munich University for the Habermehl reference; Anthony Gouldwell of the University of Leicester for the Silver Street and Causeway Lane radiographs; the staff of the radiology department of Leicester Royal Infirmary N.H.S. Trust for the York Road and High Street radiographs; Gilly Thorp of The Queen's Veterinary School Hospital, University of Cambridge, for the modern Dachshund and Basset Hound radiographs and John Lucas, Keeper of Archaeology at the Jewry Wall Museum, Leicester for additional measurements of the Thistleton 1 cranium. I would particularly like to thank Marc Nussbaumer of the Albert Heim Foundation for Canine Research, Naturhistorischen Museums der Stadt Bern, Switzerland for helpful suggestions, drawing my attention to his studies of modern dog crania and kindly supplying a plethora of comparative cranial data. Helpful discussions with colleagues at the 9th ICAZ Conference in Durham, particularly Susan Crockford and Lynn Snyder are also appreciated.

References

Adelman, B. 1997. *The Complete Dog Book. 19th edn. Official Publication of the American Kennel Club*. New York: Howell Book House.

Bartosiewicz, L. 2000. Metric variability in Roman period dogs in Pannonia Provincia and the Barbaricum, pp. 181–9 in Crockford, S. J. (ed.) *Dogs Through Time: An Archaeological Perspective*. Oxford: BAR International Series 889.

Baxter, I. L. 1991. The Animal Bones from 33–47 High Street, Leicester. Report prepared for Leicestershire Archaeological Unit.

Baxter, I. L. 1993. Report on the Animal Bones from New Bond Street, Leicester. Report prepared for Leicestershire Archaeological Unit.

Baxter, I. L. 1994. The Human and Animal Bone at Bonners Lane, Leicester. Report prepared for Leicestershire Archaeological Unit.

Baxter, I. L. 1997. Report on the skeleton of a Roman dog from York Road, Leicester. Report prepared for University of Leicester Archaeological Services.

Baxter, I. L. 1998a. Small Roman Dogs. *Organ* **17**, 6–8.

Baxter, I. L. 1998b. Landwade Road, Fordham (FOR LR 96) Report on the Mammal, Bird and Amphibian Bones. Report prepared for Cambridgeshire County Council Archaeological Field Unit.

Bökönyi, S. 1974. *History of Domestic Mammals in Central and Eastern Europe*. Budapest: Akademiai Kiado.

Brothwell, D. Malaga, A. and Burleigh, R. 1979. Studies on Amerindian Dogs, 2: Variation in Early Peruvian Dogs. *Journal of Archaeological Science* **6**, 139–161.

Churcher, C. S. 1993. Dogs from Ein Tirghi Cemetery, Balat, Dakhleh Oasis, Western Desert of Egypt, pp. in Clason, A., Payne, S. and Uerpmann, H-P. (eds) *Skeletons in Her Cupboard: Festschrift for Juliet Clutton-Brock*. Oxford: Oxbow Monograph 34.

Clark, K. M. 1995. The later prehistoric and protohistoric dog: The emergence of canine diversity. *Archaeozoologia* **7(2)**, 9–32.

Clark, K. M. 2000. Dogged Persistence: the phenomenon of canine skeletal uniformity in British prehistory, pp. 163–169 in Crockford, S. J. (ed.) *Dogs Through Time: An Archaeological Perspective*. Oxford: BAR International Series 889.

Clutton-Brock, J. 1987. *A Natural History of Domesticated Mammals*. C.U.P./British Museum (Nat. Hist.).

Clutton-Brock, J. and Jewell, P. 1979. Origin and Domestication of the Dog, pp. 21–31 in Evans, H. E. (ed.) *Miller's Anatomy of the Dog*. 3rd edition, pp. 21–31. London: W.B. Saunders.

Cooper, L. 1996. A Roman Cemetery in Newarke Street, Leicester. *Transactions of the Leicestershire Archaeological and Historical Society*. **70**, 1–90.

Cram, L. 2000. Varieties of Dog in Roman Britain, pp. 171–189 in Crockford, S. J. (ed.) *Dogs Through Time: An Archaeological Perspective*. Oxford: BAR International Series 889.

Crockford, S. J. 2000a. Dog evolution: a role for thyroid hormone physiology in domestication changes, pp. 3–20 in Crockford, S. J. (ed.) *Dogs Through Time: An Archaeological Perspective*. Oxford: BAR International Series 889.

Crockford, S. J. 2000b. A commentary on dog evolution: regional variation, breed development and hybridisation with wolves, pp. 295–312 in Crockford, S. J. (ed.) *Dogs Through Time: An Archaeological Perspective*. Oxford: BAR International Series 889.

Davis, S. J. M. 1987. *The archaeology of animals*. London, Batsford.

De Grossi Mazzorin, J. and Tagliacozzo, A. 2000. Morphological and osteological changes in the dog from the Neolithic to the Roman period in Italy, pp. 141–161 in Crockford, S. J. (ed.) *Dogs Through Time: An Archaeological Perspective*. Oxford: BAR International Series 889.

von den Driesch, A. 1976. *A Guide to the Measurement of Animal Bones from Archaeological Sites*. Cambridge: Peabody Mus. Bull. 1. Harvard.

Farello, P. 1995. I Cani Tardo-Antichi Rinvenuti in un Condotto Fognario di Classe (RA). Atti del I Convegno Nazionale di Archaeozoologia, Rovigo (marzo 1993). *Padusa Quaderni 1*, 295–308.

Gidney, L. J. 1991. *Leicester, The Shires 1988 Excavations. The Animal Bones from the Roman Deposits at Little Lane*. London: English Heritage AML Report 56/91.

Gidney, L. J. 1999. The Animal Bones, pp. 310–318 in Connor, A. and Buckley, R. *Roman and Medieval Occupation in Causeway Lane, Leicester. Excavations 1980 and 1991*. Leicester: Leicester University Press.

Gossip J. 1998. Excavations at York Road/Oxford Street (SK585039). *Transactions of the Leicestershire Archaeological and Historical Society*. **72**, 159–160.

Gouldwell, A. J. (nd). The Animal Bones from Silver Street, Leicester. Report prepared for Leicestershire Archaeological Unit.

Habermehl, K-H. 1961. *Alterbestimmung bei Haustieren, Pelzitieren und beim jagdbaren Wild*. Berlin and Hamburg.

Hamilton-Dyer, S. 2001. Animal bone. In (J. McKinley) Excavations at Ham hill, Montacute, Somerset 1994 and 1998. *Somerset Archaeology and Natural History*. **142**, 125–127.

Harcourt, R. 1971. *Animal Bones from Thistleton*. London: English Heritage AML Report 1539.

Harcourt, R. A. 1974. The Dog in Prehistoric and Early Historic Britain. *Journal of Archaeological Science* **1**, 151–175.

Hilzheimer, M. 1926. *Naturaliche Rassengechichte der Haussaugetiere*. Berlin.

Horard-Herbin, M-P. 2000. Dog management and use in the late Iron Age: the evidence from the Gallic site of Levroux (France), pp. 115–121 in Crockford, S. J. (ed.) *Dogs Through Time: An Archaeological Perspective*. Oxford: BAR International Series 889.

von Lüttschwager, J. 1965. Ein Zwerhund aus dem römischen Gräberfeld an der Berliner Straße zu Heidelberg-Neuenheim. *Zeitschrift für Säugetierkunde* **30**, 24–30.

MacDonogh, K. 1999. *Reigning Cats and Dogs*. London: Fourth Estate.

MacGregor, A. 1985. *Bone, Antler, Ivory and Horn. The Technology of Skeletal Materials Since the Roman Period*. London: Croom Helm.

MacKinnon, M. 2002. In Sickness and in Health: Care for an Arthritic Maltese Dog from the Roman Cemetery of Yasmina, Carthage, Tunisia. Presented paper, 9th International Council of Archaeozoology Conference, Durham.

Musty, J. 1998. Science Diary. *Current Archaeology* **159**, 90.

Nussbaumer, M. 1976. *Das Problem der Hirnstammbasis bei den Dachshunden*. Separatdruck aus dem Jahrbuch des Naturalhistorischen Museums der Stadt Bern BD. 6, 1975–1977.

Nussbaumer, M., 1978. Biometrischer Vergleich der Topogenesmuster an der Schädelbasis kleiner und mittelgroßer Hunde. *Sonderdruck aus Zeitschrift für Tierzüchtung und Züchtungsbiologie* **95(1)**, 1–14.

Petri, W. 1961. *Neue Funde des Hundes aus dem keltischen Oppidum von Manching. Studien an vor- und frühgeschichtlichen Tierresten Bayerns X*. Munich: Verlag Kiefhaber Kiefhaber & Elbl.
Richardson, A. 1997. It was a dog's life in Roman times. *Leicester Mercury* **January 28th**.
Sadler, P. 1994. Useful small dogs. *Circaea* **11(1)**, 6.
Scott, D. 2002. Dogs and bones... can living dogs give us clues about the dogs of archaeology? Poster presented at the 9th International Council of Archaeozoology Conference, Durham.
Teichert, M. 1987. Brachymel dogs. *Archaeozoologia* **1(1)**, 69–75.
The, T. L. and Trouth, C. O. 1976. Sexual dimorphism in the basilar part of the occipital bone of the dog (*Canis familiaris*). *Acta Anatomica* **9**, 565–571.
Toynbee, J. M. C. 1973. *Animals in Roman Life and Art*. London: Thames & Hudson.
Turner, P. (ed.) 1962. *Pliny's Natural History in Philemon Holland's Translation*. London: Centaur Press.
Valadez, R. A. 2000. Prehispanic dog types in Middle America, pp. 193–204 in Crockford, S. J. (ed.) *Dogs Through Time: An Archaeological Perspective*. Oxford: BAR International Series 889.
Weaver, R. F. & Hedrick, P. W. 1992. *Genetics*. Dubuque, IA: Wm. C. Brown, Publishers.

Ian L. Baxter
4 Moor View
Newbiggin-by-the-Sea
Northumberland
NE64 6DH
UK

Ilbaxter@aol.com

Appendix 1

Measurement system for canid crania originated by Dr. Marc Nussbaumer of the Albert Heim Foundation for Canine Research, Naturhistorischen Museums der Stadt Bern, Switzerland (Nussbaumer 1976, 1978) with von den Driesch (1976) equivalents (if any).

1) Brain stem base – Basion to boundary of the Pterygoid & Palatine where it joins the Presphenoid (HB = *Hirnstammbasis*)

2) Maxillary length – Palatinoorale to Prosthion (MX = *Maxillarlänge*)

3) Palatine length – boundary of the Pterygoid & Palatine where it joins the Presphenoid to Palatinoorale (PL = *Palatinumlänge*)

4) Zygomatic breadth – Zygion to Zygion (JB = *Jochbogenbreite*) = VDD 30

5) Basal length – Basion to Prosthion (BL = *Basilarlänge*) = VDD 3

6) Upper Carnassial length (ORZ = *obere Reisszahnlänge*)

9th ICAZ Conference, Durham 2002
Dogs and People in Social, Working, Economic or Symbolic Interaction
(eds Lynn M. Snyder and Elizabeth A. Moore) pp. 24–31

3. Food, Rituals? The Exploitation of Dogs from Eretria (Greece) During the Helladic and Hellenistic Periods

Isabelle Chenal-Velarde

The site of Eretria, situated on the island of Euboea (ancient Euboia), was occupied from the end of the Neolithic to the palaeo-Christian Period. The dog remains from five archaeological contexts within the ancient city are considered here. These samples can be separated in two principal types of deposit: dog bone fragments associated with the remains of other species and interpreted as butchered debris; and complete, or almost complete, unmodified dog skeletons found in wells, without any anthropic marks. The dog remains from each archaeological context are described and interpreted in relation to the type of deposit from which they came, their association with other remains, and the presence/absence of anthropic signs of exploitation.

Introduction

The ancient city of Eretria is situated on the island of Euboea (ancient Euboia), which lies east of the Attic coast of Greece, some 50 km north of Athens (Fig. 1).

The site (Fig. 2) was occupied from the Meso-Helladic (17th to 15th centuries BC) to the palaeo-Christian periods, through Geometric, Archaic, Classic, Hellenistic and Roman occupations (Table 1). Since the 1830s, the modern town of Eretria has partially covered the ancient city. A number of archaeological studies, most of them rescue excavations, have been conducted in the area of the ancient city. These punctual investigations, conducted by Greek teams and the Swiss School of Archaeology in Greece (ESAG) (*cf.* Ducrey 1985) have contributed to our understanding of the organisation of the ancient city from the Helladic through Roman occupations.

Archaeozoological investigations have been conducted on materials from a number of geographical and chronological contexts in Eretria since 1994 (see for example Chenal-Velarde 2001; Chenal-Velarde and Studer 2003), in different geographical and chronological contexts of the city. All these faunal materials come from excavations of the Swiss School of Archaeology in Greece. Dog remains have been identified in all the faunal samples studied. However, the quantity and state of preservation of the remains vary greatly, depending on the archaeological context. The presence of dog remains in these contexts takes on varying meanings according to both the characteristics of the bones themselves, and the nature of the archaeological deposit. Therefore, any interpretation of these materials must consider both the intrinsic and extrinsic characteristics of the sample, as this paper will show.

The dog remains from Eretria

The materials considered in this analysis were recovered from five archaeological contexts within the ancient city. The canid bone assemblages from these contexts range from a small number of fragments to "complete" individuals (Table 2).

The remains from the acropolis excavations

This portion of the city was in part excavated by P. Friedemann (Friedemann 1995).

The dog bones recovered from this context consist of two mandibles fragments from the same juvenile dog, one additional mandible fragment from a second individual, one canine tooth fragment, two metatarsals,

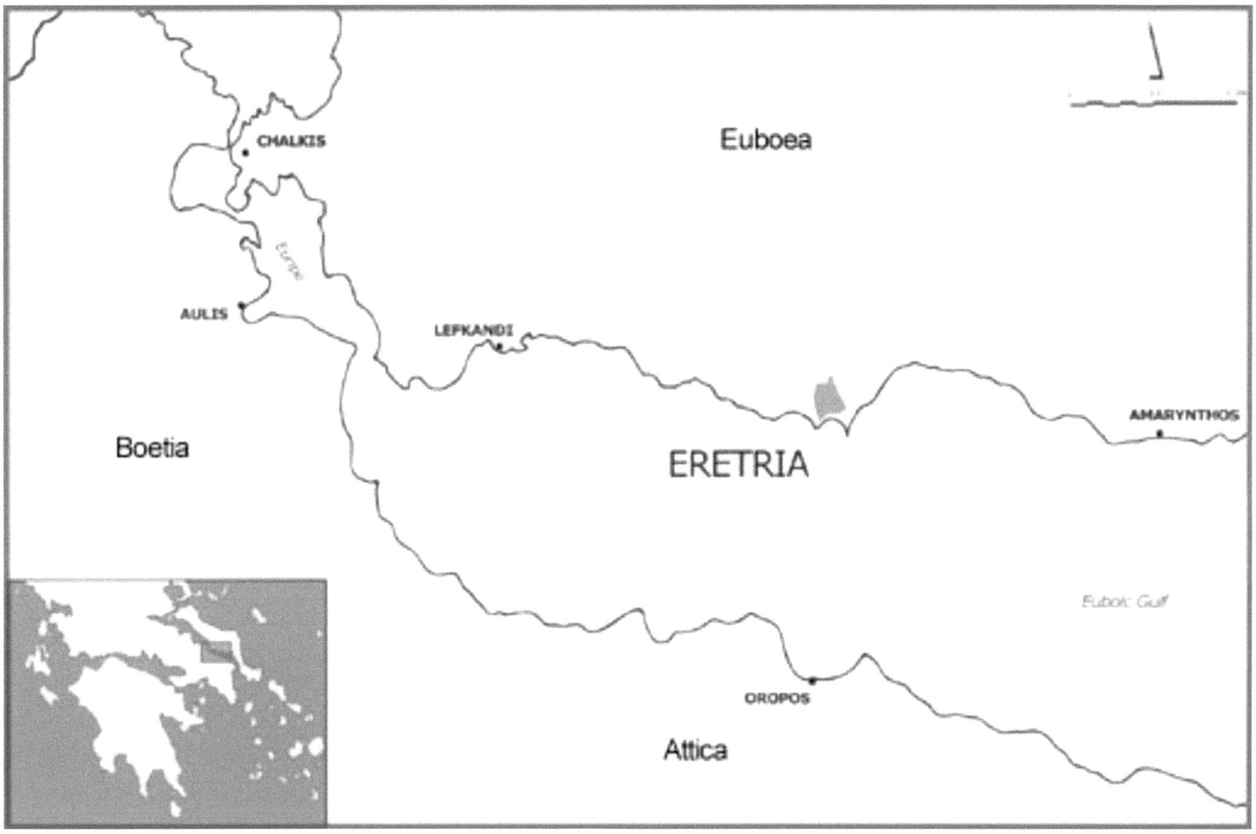

Fig. 1: The location of Euboia Island and Eretria (drawing ESAG)

and one rib. One of the mandible fragments was burned and the rib bore cut marks, indicating cooking or roasting (the mandibule) and butchering.

The remains from the excavation South-East of the sanctuary of Apollo

The dog remains from this context (see Huber 1993) consist of one mandible fragment, two premolars from a single adult found in a fire pit, one cervical vertebra, one metacarpal, and one metatarsal. These materials have been described elsewhere (Chenal-Velarde 2001). The two teeth from the fire pit are burnt, suggesting possible intentional cremation. The metatarsal has cut marks on it's dorsal surface, indicating skinning.

The remains from the Archaic pit in the sacrificial area

The sacrificial area was excavated by S. Huber (Huber 2003). Nevertheless, the Archaic pit found in this part of the site is not related to any sacrificial remains. The scattered dog bones from this context were found mixed with the remains of other butchering and food debris (Studer and Chenal-Velarde 2003). They consist of one atlas and one cervical vertebra, one fragment of coxal bone, one complete femur, one carpal bone, one canine tooth and five additional tooth fragments. Both the atlas and cervical vertebra show cut marks, possibly suggesting cutting of the throat, and removal of the skin. The cut mark on the coxal may have been inflicted during removal of the intestines.

The West housing district of Eretria

In this area, dog bones were recovered from a well associated with a domestic structure (House 4, see Reber 1993). The well was excavated in seventeen strata (Reber, Chenal-Velarde and Metzger 2001) designated I (latest) to XVII (oldest). In stratum IV, left and right mandibles from an adult individual were found. In stratum V, 169 fragments from a single animal at least 10 months of age were found, and in stratum IX, seven bone fragments and a mandible were recovered, which appear to come from a single individual approximately 7 months of age. The two mandibles from stratus IV were burned while no cut marks or burning were noted on the individuals from strata V and IX.

A particular case: the dogs remains from the Hellenistic well of the Sebasteion

The archaeological context

This well was located beside a Hellenistic street in the northern part of the site (Fig. 3). The well was excavated

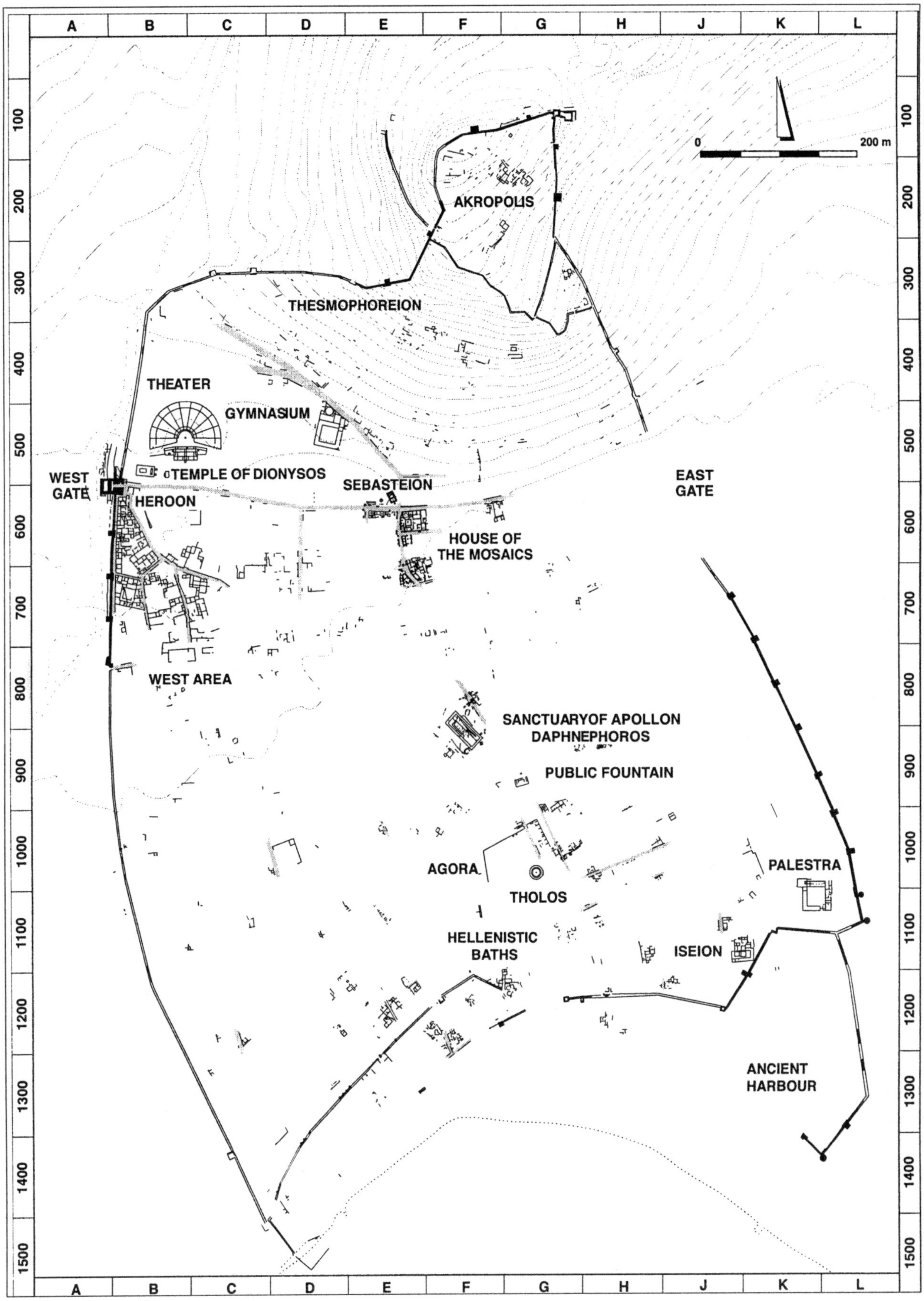

Fig. 2: The ancient city of Eretria, showing the various areas and monuments of the site (drawing ESAG)

Table 1. Some dates in Eretrian history (from Ducrey 1985)

	Eretria in Greek History
17th–15th c. BC	Helladic occupation
8th c. BC	Colonisation. Geometic occupation. First temples
8thth c. to 480 BC	Archaïc Period
490 BC	Destruction of Eretria by the Persians
480–336 BC	Classic Period
336–146 BC	Hellenistic Period
198 BC	Taking of the city by the Romans

Table 2. Frequency of dog remains in the archaeological contexts studied

Place	Acropolis	SE Apollo temple	Sacrificial Area	West District Well	Sebasteion Well
Period	Helladic to Archaïc/Classic	Geometric	Archaïc pit	Hellenistic	Hellenistic
NR or NMI	7 bone fgts	6 bone fgts	11 bone fgts	-1 complete ind. -10 bones in dif. layers	26 complete ind.

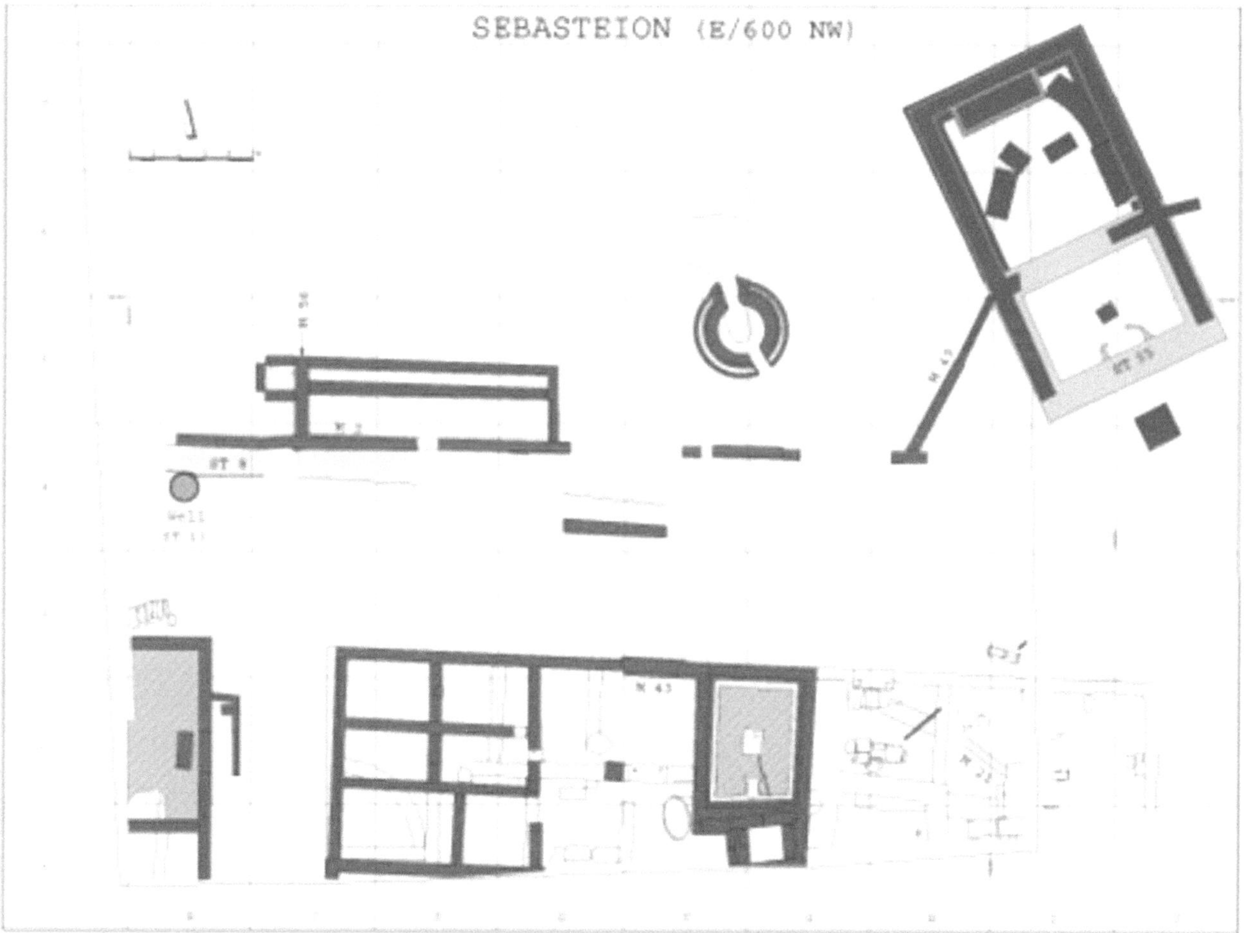

Fig. 3. The Sebasteion *in Eretria and the location of the well (st.13) studied here (drawing ESAG)*

by S. Schmid (1997) under difficult conditions, due to the depth of the structure (more than five meters) and the presence of underground water. The filling of the structure began with the deposit of a coin hoard, associated with an important quantity of well-preserved bones. The silver and bronze coins help to date this event to the first half of the third century BC, possibly corresponding to the war of Chremonides, between 267 and 261 BC (study by M. Brunner, see Schmid 2000). It seems that the coins and the bones (both dog and human bones, see below) were part of the same layer. The upper levels of the well contained pottery and isolated bones of caprines, cattle, pig, birds and dogs.

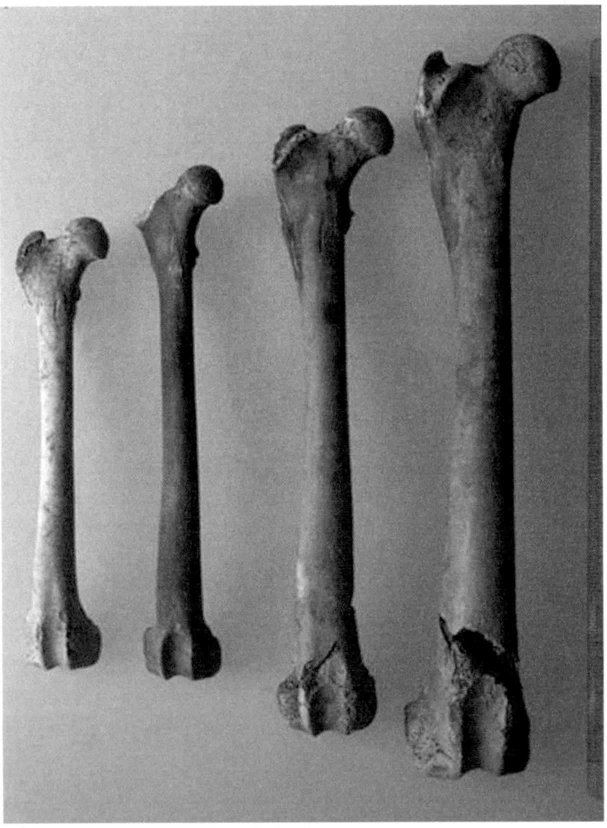

Fig. 4. Adult femurs from the dogs (FK153) in the Hellenistic well associated with the Sebasteion *(photo I. Chenal-Velarde)*

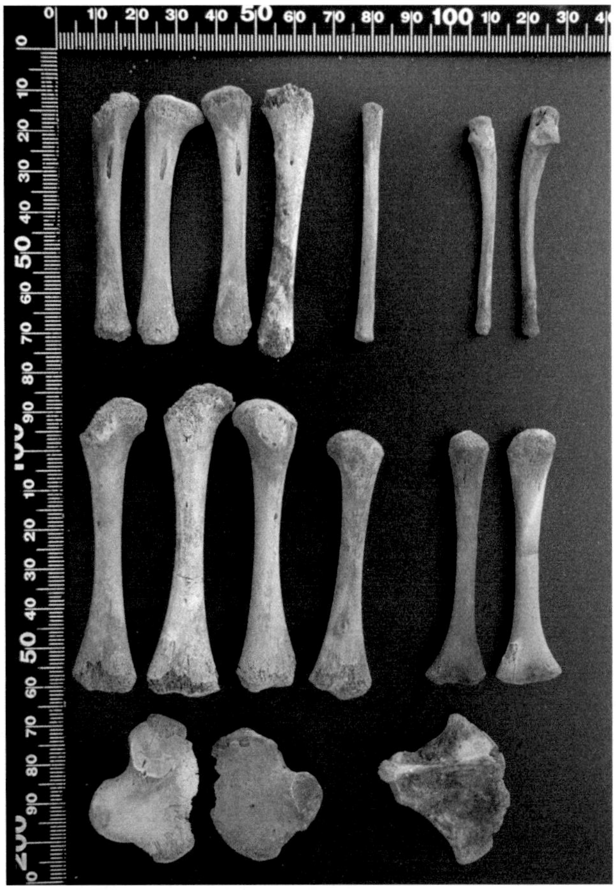

Fig. 5. A sample of human infant bones (FK153) from the Hellenistic well of the Sebasteion *(photo I. Chenal-Velarde)*

The initial deposit (FK 153)

This initial deposit is notable and unique in that it contained a concentration of over 1100 dog bones in apparent association with the remains of a number of human infants, plus the hoard of coins described above.

The dog remains

A close examination of the dog remains from this assemblage revealed no evidence of human modification of the bones, indicative of butchering, skinning or cooking. Based on element pairing and age assessment, a minimum number of 26 individuals are represented in this assemblage. All anatomical portions of the skeletons are present, although elements of the lower leg (carpals, tarsals, metapodials, phalanges) are underrepresented, probably due to the difficulties of collecting these small elements during excavation of the well deposit. Based on epiphyseal fusion of the femora (the most commonly occurring long bone in the assemblage) three of the animals represented were neo-natal or foetal, seven were less than 6 months of age, one was between 6 and 12 months, two were approximately one year old, and 13 were adults. Estimations of stature for the better preserved adult femora (Table 2) suggest a range of wither heights between 36 and 62 cms (Koudelkha 1885).

The human infant remains

In the same deposit, and in direct association with the dog skeletons and coin hoard, the skeletal remains of at least 19 human infants were found (Fig. 5). Evaluation of age, based on an analysis of the femora (Adallian *et al.* 2003), suggests that these infants were between 31 weeks gestational development and neo-natal or newborn at death.

The dog remains from the upper levels of the well

The upper levels of the well were filled with a mixed deposit of butchering or food debris, including bones of sheep, goat, pig, cattle and birds. Several of these stratigraphic levels also contained interesting dog remains. These included, proceeding from the lower to

*Fig. 6. Deep cut marks on a radius from an adult dog (*Sebasteion*, St.13) (photo I. Chenal-Velarde)*

upper levels: two vertebrae which showed no evidence of human modification; 38 bone and tooth fragments (cranial elements, metapodials and some fragments from long bones and vertebra) without any evidence of anthropic modification;one vertebra, one radius fragment which has been chopped and broken (Fig. 6) and one metatarsal;10 elements, including one mandible from a single adult animal, which show no modification; and 4 long bone fragments, including a distal humerus, which exhibits cut marks on it's cranial and caudal surfaces.

Synthesis and interpretation

Elements of synthesis

At the ancient site of Eretria dog remains have been found in all archaeological contexts, and through all chronological periods. These assemblages differ in quantity and in the nature of the deposits in which they occur, but can be divided into two general categories. The first are those assemblages which contain the scattered and broken remains of a number of species,

Table 3. Extrinsic characteristics of the dog remains from the archaeological contexts studied

Dog remains / **Archaeol. context**	*Association with butchery remains*	*Association with particular remains*	*Open context*	*Closed context*
Acropolis (Helladic to Archaïc-Classic)	Yes		Yes. Embankment, fault...	
SE Temple Apollo (Geom.)	Yes. Consumption type remains		Yes. Fire pits + soils (+ layers)	
Sacrificial Area, (Archaïc pit)	Yes. Butchery and consumption remains	Miniature hydries		Yes (pit)
Hellenistic Well West district	Yes	Yes (complete chicken)		Yes (well)
Hellenistic Well Sebasteion	Yes (other layer?)	Yes (12 human babies)		Yes (well)

Table 4. Intrinsic characteristics of the dog remains from the archaeological contexts studied

Dog remains / **Archaeol. context**	*Complete skeletons*	*Remote and burnt bones*	*Bones with cut marks*	*Remote bones*
Acropolis (Helladic to Archaïc-Classic)		1 mandible	1 rib	5 (2 mandibles + 1 tooth + 2 métatarsals)
SE Temple Apollo (Geom.)		2 teeth	1 métatarsal	2 (1 cervical vert. + 1 métacarpal)
Sacrificial Area, (Archaïc pit)			1 cervical vert, 1 coxal, 1 atlas?	8 remains, 1 complete femur
Hellenistic Well West district	-1 complete individual -1 half-individual	2 hemi-mandibles		1 humérus fgt
Hellenistic Well Sebasteion	26 "complete" individuals			

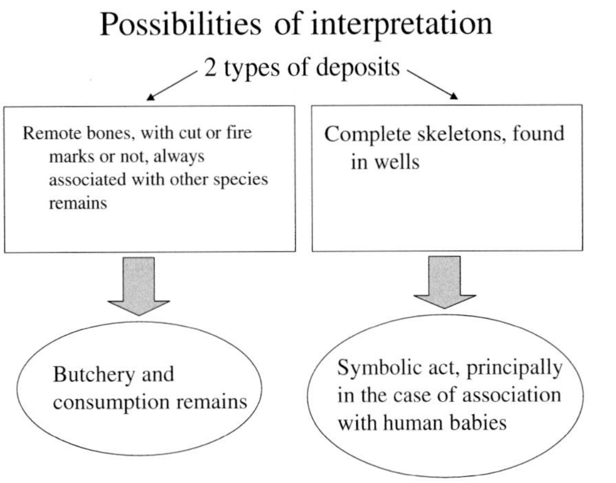

Fig. 7. Interpretation of the different types of samples of dog remains in accordance with the types of deposit

including dogs. The second type of assemblage, found exclusively in wells, consists of complete dog skeletons, or portions of individual skeletons. The interpretation of these quite different and unique assemblages of dog bones must therefore take into consideration both extrinsic (Table 3) data or factors (location, archaeological context, association with other remains) and the intrinsic data or characteristics (cut marks, burning, fragmentation patterns) on the bones themselves (Table 4).

Propositions for interpretation

The possibilities of interpretation are related to two principal types of deposit and their related bone assemblage characteristics (Fig. 7). In the first type of assemblage, the scattered and broken bones of dogs, some bearing cut marks or signs of burning, may be interpreted as the remains of animals which were killed or sacrificed, butchered, skinned and perhaps eaten. In at least one case (the burned dog teeth found in the fire pit southeast of the sanctuary of Apollo) the teeth may represent the remains of a dog deliberately cremated. The scattered and broken dog bones from the upper levels of the well associated with the Sebasteion also appear to represent this type of deposit.

In the second type of assemblage, the more complete and well preserved skeletons found in restricted contexts such as the lowest level of the Sebasteion well, dog remains are probably present as the result of deliberate and symbolic acts. The presence of a single dog skeleton in the fill of an abandoned well is not unusual, but the number of dog skeletons, and their association with the human infants suggest a possible association with a specific historical event, the war of Chremonides.

Conclusions

It is interesting to observe that dog remains are present in all the archaeozoological samples studied in Eretria, although generally in low quantity. The interpretations that can be made of these remains depend on the archaeological context in which they were found and the nature of the remains themselves. The widespread presence of scattered dog elements mixed with those of other species in the archaeological deposits of Eretria suggests that throughout the history of ancient Eretria, dogs were at least occasionally slaughtered and eaten. In contrast, the ancient texts would suggest that it was not a tradition to eat dog meat in Classical Greece. Dog meat is never cited in the lists of "consumable" animals (see for example Detienne and Vernant 1979). Dog bone fragments associated with the bones of other species' bones, and identified as the remains of butchering and/or consumption, indicate dogs which have been slaughtered and eaten. This interpretation can be applied to all the strata studied, from Geometric to Hellenistic Periods. It is particularly interesting to note that archaeozoological evidence clearly shows that dogs have probably been consumed, although it was not a tradition to eat dog meat in Classical Greece.

In the case of the unique and compelling deposit found in the Sebasteion well, the skeletons of complete or almost complete individuals, we must seek the help of ancient texts to interpret the significance of their presence, and their association with the infant skeletons. Nevertheless, the precise dating possible for the deposit of dogs and infants in the well of the *Sebasteion*, as evidenced by the coin hoard dating to the first half of the third century BC, closely corresponds to the war of Chremonides. The apparent association in time between these two events suggests a tradition that requires further investigation and clarification.

Acknowledgements

I would like to thank the Swiss School of Archaeology in Greece (ESAG), and in particular its director P. Ducrey, for making possible these archaeozoological investigations in Eretria. The archaeozoological studies of dog remains were conducted in collaboration with the archaeologists responsible for each excavation: P. Friedemann, S. Huber, K. Reber and S. Schmid. S. Schmid and L. Snyder kindly agreed to read and correct the English version of this paper.

References

Adallian, P., Lalys, L., Leonetti, G., Dutour, O. 2003. Détermination de l'âge fœtal: evaluation des formules "classiques". Résumé des communications des 8e journées anthropologiques de Valbonne, 5–7 juin 2003. Centre d'études Préhistoire, Antiquité, Moyen-Âge (CEPAM).

Chenal-Velarde, I. 2001. Des festins à l'entrée du temple? Sacrifices et consommation des animaux à l'époque géométrique dans le sanctuaire d'Apollon à Erétrie, Grèce. *Archaeofauna*, **10**, 25–35.

Chenal-Velarde, I. and Studer, J. 2003. Archaeozoology in a ritual context: the case of a sacrificial altar in Geometric Eretria (Greece), pp. 215–220 in Kotjabopoulou, E., Hamilakis, Y., Halstead, P., Gamble, C. and Elefanti, P. (eds), *Zooarchaeology in Greece: recent advances*. Athens: The British School at Athens. (British School at Athens, studies 9).

Detienne, M. and Verant, J. P. (eds) 1979. *La cuisine du sacrifice en pays grec*. Paris: Gallimard.

Ducrey, P. 1985. Erétrie, une cité de la Grèce antique. *Les dossiers histoire et archéologie*, 94, mai 1995, 8–11.

Friedmann, P. 1995. Nouvelles données sur la préhistoire d'Erétrie: l'apport des investigations 1994 sur l'acropole. *Antike Kunst* **2**, 108–119.

Huber, S. 1993. Les fouilles dans le sanctuaire d'Apollon à Erétrie 1992. *Antike Kunst*, **2**, 122–125.

Huber, S. 2003. *L'Aire sacrificielle au nord du Sanctuaire d'Apollon Daphnéphoros. Un rituel des époques géométrique et archaïque*. Gollion: Infolio. (Erétria, fouilles et recherches; XIV).

Koudelka, F. 1885. Das Vorhältnis der Ossa longa zur Skeletthöhe bei den Säugetieren. *Verhandlungen der Naturvorch. Ver. Brünn*. **24**, 127–153.

Reber, K. 1993. Die Grabungen in Haus IV von Eretria. Kampagne 1992. *Antike Kunst* **2**, 126–131.

Reber, K., Chenal-Velarde, I., and Metzger, I. R. 2001. Ein Hellenistischer Brunnen im Bezirk B von Haus IV in Eretria, pp. 115–153 in Frei-Stolba, R. and Gex, K. (eds) *Recherches récentes sur le monde hellénistique*. Actes du colloque international organisé à l'occasion du 60e anniversaire de P. Ducrey. Lausanne, 20–21 nov. 1998. Berne: Peter Lang.

Schmid, S. G. 1997. Vorbericht über die Grabung in E/600 NW. *Antike Kunst*, **2**, 104–107.

Schmid, S.G. 2000. A group of early Hellenistic pottery from a well in Eretria, pp. 361–372 in *E' Episthmoniki Sunantisi gia tin Ellinistiki Kerameiki (5th Scientific Colloquium on Hellenistic Pottery)*. Athèns.

Studer, J. and Chenal-Velarde, I. 2003. La part des dieux et celle des hommes: offrandes d'animaux et restes culinaires près du temple d'Apollon à Erétrie, Grèce (périodes géométrique, archaïque, classique et hellénistique), pp. 175–184 in Huber, S. (ed.) *L'Aire sacrificielle au nord du Sanctuaire d'Apollon Daphnéphoros. Un rituel des époques géométrique et archaïque*. Gollion: Infolio. (Erétria, fouilles et recherches; XIV).

Isabelle Chenal-Velarde
Muséum d'histoire naturelle
Dpt d'archéozoologie
C.P. 6434
CH-1211 Genève 6
Switzerland

Isabelle.chenal-velarde@mhn.ville-ge.ch

9th ICAZ Conference, Durham 2002
Dogs and People in Social, Working, Economic or Symbolic Interaction
(eds Lynn M. Snyder and Elizabeth A. Moore) pp. 32–37

4. Artemis Pit? Dog Remains from a Well in the Ancient Town of Siracusa (Sicily)

Salvatore Chilardi

In 1998, a well was discovered in Duomo Square on the island of Ortigia, the historical centre of Siracusa and first nucleus of the Greek colony. Excavations in the square, started in 1996, brought to light the foundations of a sacred building dating to the 8th century BC, which was transformed into an actual temple in the 7th century. The well was located near the north wall of the temple. Pottery found in this structure spans a chronological range from the 7th through the 4th centuries BC, and consists primarily of typological classes usually related to ritual offerings. Dog remains from the pit consisted of the elements of two individuals. The remains of swine, sheep or goat, cattle and fish were also found. Cut marks on several of the dog bones suggest dismemberment of the bodies, and some of the fragments are burnt. The context in which these materials were found suggests a relationship between the dog remains and the religious rites which took place in the nearby temple.

The archaeological context

Siracusa is well known as one of the most important Greek colonies in the Mediterranean (Finley 1968; Manfredi 1996). The first nucleus of the colony was the island of Ortigia (Fig.1), now the historical centre of the modern town. Piazza Duomo is the most beautiful and important square of Ortigia. The baroque Cathedral (the Duomo), formerly the temple of Athena (5th century BC), and the town hall, built over the foundation of an Ionic temple (6th century BC), overlook the square. Despite being located behind the two principle temples of the island, the square historically played a leading role in the spiritual life of the colony.

During the first decade of the 20th century the excavations of Paolo Orsi uncovered in Via Minerva, between the Town Hall and the Cathedral, an archaic altar, remains of sacred buildings, *stelai*, sculptures and a stratigraphic sequence ranging over one thousand years of history, from the 7th century BC through the Byzantine period (Orsi 1919). In 1996, after preliminary survey (1992/93), new archaeological investigations began, in advance of planned repaving of the square. These excavations, directed by Giuseppe Voza, Superintendent for

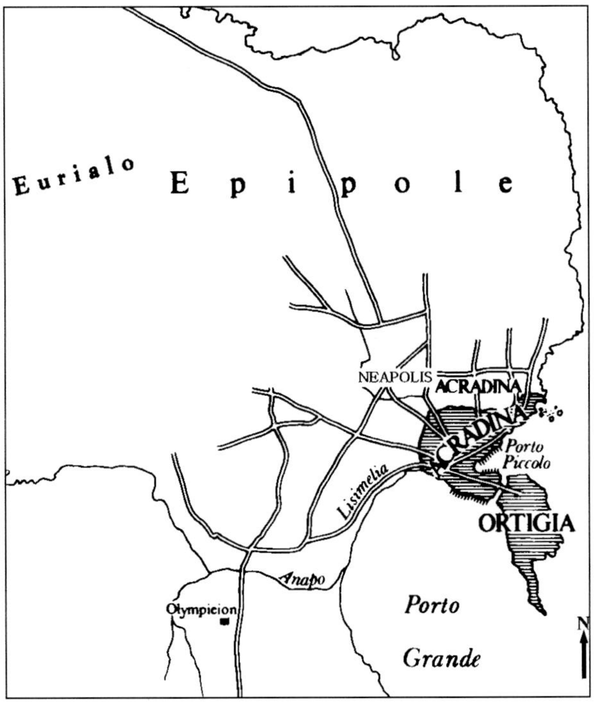

Fig. 1. Plan of the ancient town of Siracusa. The island of Ortigia was the first nucleus of the greek colony during the 8th century BC

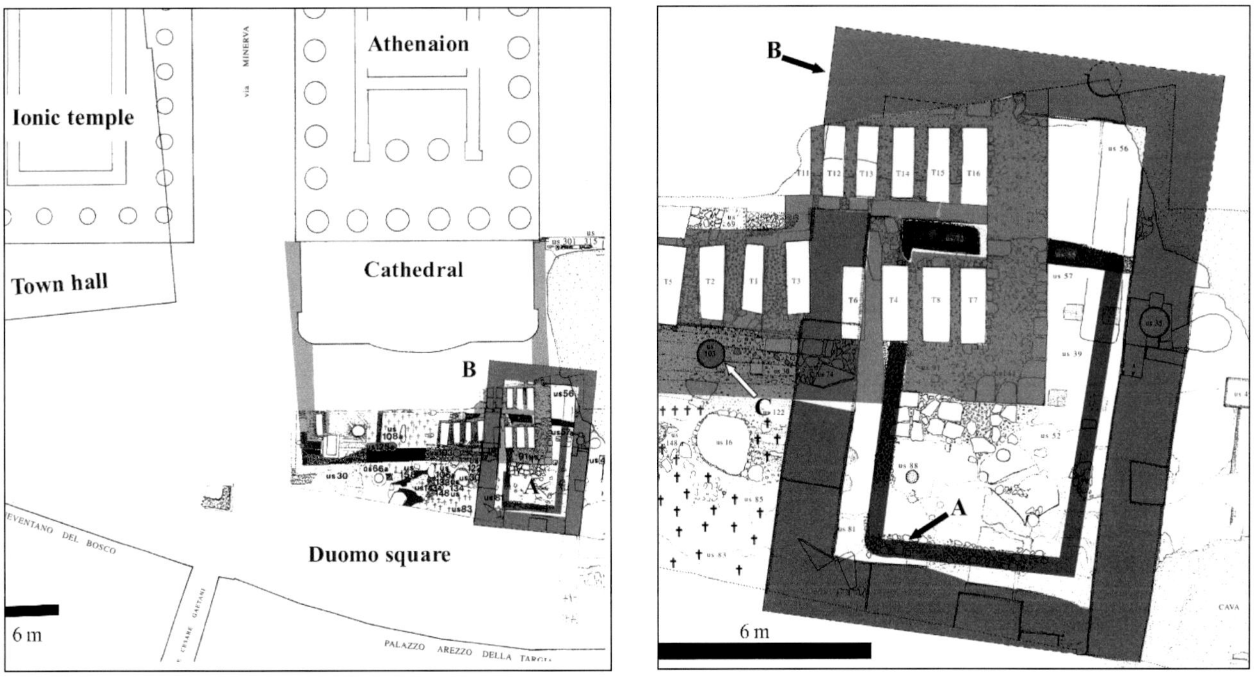

Fig. 2. On the left: plan of the central area of the excavation of the Duomo square with the former Athenaion *(now the Cathedral) and the Ionic temple under the town hall. On the right: the sacred* oikos *(A), the temple (B) and the well (C) described in the text*

the Arts and the Environment, brought to light the foundations of an older sacred building (an *oikos*) dating to the end of the 8th century BC, which was transformed into a temple in the 7th century (Fig. 2). This ancient temple lay just in front of the modern Cathedral, at the centre of the square. Several small sacred pits (*thysiai*), exposed through excavations in the area, contained fictile offerings demonstrating the sacred character of the entire space around the buildings (Voza 1999).

Close to the northern side of the temple a well was found (Fig. 2). It was excavated to a depth of 17 meters below ground level, and then the presence of water and safety problems stopped any further exploration. Pottery found in this well spans a chronological range from the 7th through the 4th century BC, and consists primarily of typological classes often found as ritual offerings or related to ritual banquets, including small *lekythoi*, globular *aryballoi*, *amphoriskoi* and libation pots (Ciurcina and Amato 1999).

Dog remains from the well

A concentration of animal remains was found in this well, at a depth of 12.22 m. This deposit was dated by the ceramics it contained to the late 6th through 5th centuries BC. A total of 491 bones or bone fragments were identified to species, including sheep or goat, cattle, pig, dog and two species of fish, the bonito (*Sarda sarda*) and the false albacore (*Euthynnus allitteratus*). Figures 3 and 4 present the percentages of taxa by number of identified

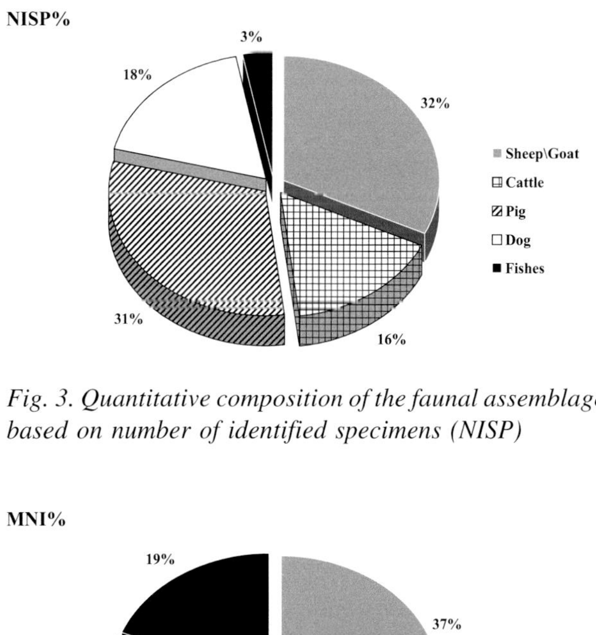

Fig. 3. Quantitative composition of the faunal assemblage based on number of identified specimens (NISP)

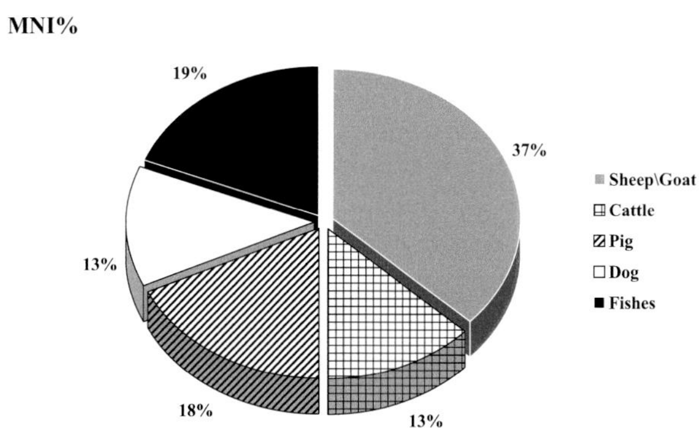

Fig. 4 Quantitative composition of the faunal assemblage based on minimum number of individuals (MNI). Note the increased importance of fish as compared with NISP

Table 1. Summary of dog bones recovered from the Duomo square well

Ind. A (Adult)	Ind. B (Young)
Incomplete skull	9 skull fragments
	3 isolated upper teeth
Complete mandible	Complete mandible
1 fragment of left scapula	1 fragment of left scapula
1 fragment of right scapula	1 fragment of right scapula
1 complete left humerus	1 complete left humerus diaphysis
	1 proximal left humerus epiphysis (unfused)
	1 proximal right humerus epiphyses (unfused)
2 fragments of left radius	1 fragment of right radius
1 fragment of left ulna	1 fragment of right ulna
1 complete right coxal bone	1 fragment of right coxal bone
1 proximal fragment of left femur	1distal right femur epiphyses (unfused)
	1 left tibia
	1 right tibia
1 left talus	
11 incomplete metapodials	13 incomplete metapodials
	3 first phalanges
12 rib fragments	
1 incomplete atlas	
4 cervical vertebrae (with disks unfused)	
3 thoracic vertebrae (with disks unfused)	
4 lumbar vertebrae (with disks unfused)	

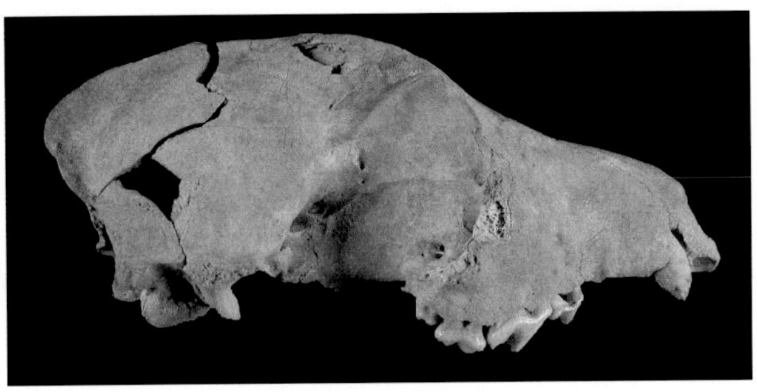

Fig. 5. Skull of the adult individual in right lateral view

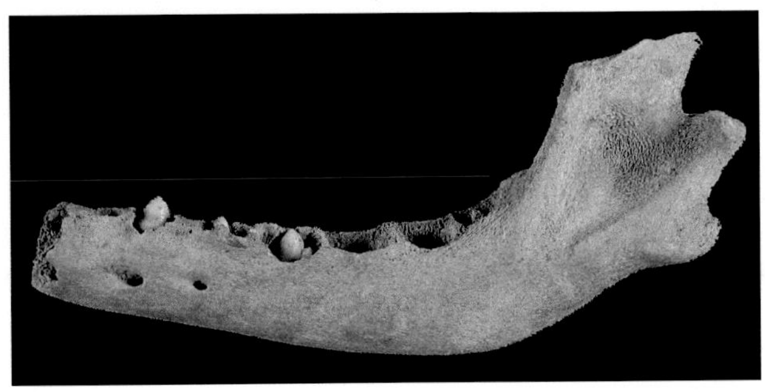

Fig. 6. Left hemimandible of the younger individual showing the eruption of the permanent teeth

specimens (NISP) and minimum number of individuals (MNI). Burned and calcined bones were not common, but frequent butchering marks were noted.

Dog remains from this deposit consisted of the partial skeletons of two individuals (Table 1). These two animals differed in age and stature. The first was less than one year, probably 6–7 months of age at death, based on dental eruption data (Hillson 1986). The other was an adult, based on tooth eruption and wear, and epiphyseal fusion (Barone 1986). The younger individual (Ind. B) was represented by fragments of the skull, the complete mandible (Fig. 6), a number of vertebrae, fragments of both scapulae and both humeri, a fragment of the right radius and ulna, a portion of the right coxal bone, the distal epiphysis of the right femur, both tibiae, 13 metapodials and three first phalanges. The adult is represented by an incomplete skull and mandibles (Fig. 5), fragments of both scapulae, a left humerus with both distal and proximal epiphyses fused, fragments of the left radius and ulna, a portion of the right coxal bone, a proximal fragment of left femur, the left talus and 11 metapodials.

In stature, the younger animal (Ind. B) was larger than the older (Ind. A), although fragmentation of the majority of skeletal elements allowed few whole bone measurements. Based on the two complete left humeri (Fig. 7), however, it was possible to calculate the withers height of both individuals (Koudelka 1885). The younger dog stood approximately 56.3cm at the shoulder; the older animal 49.6cm. Thus, both animals appear to have been medium-sized dogs.

Butchery marks (Fig. 8) were present on long bones and the innominates, most of which are related to dismemberment. Humeri and radii of both individuals have cut marks close to both their proximal and distal ends (Fig. 9), whereas the ulnae have cut marks near

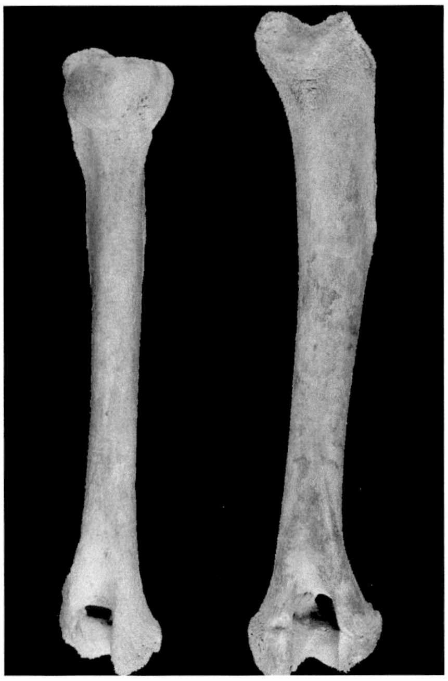

Fig. 7. Dog humeri in caudal view. The humerus of the larger, younger dog is on the right

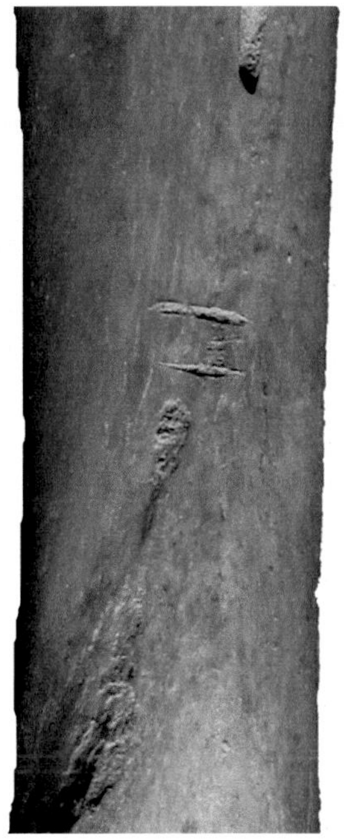

Fig. 8. Cutmarks on the caudal face of the older dog humerus

Fig. 9. Cutmarks associated with dismemberment on the younger dog humerus situated just under the unfused articular head

Fig. 10. Deep cutmarks on the dorsal surface of the younger dog coxal bone

their trochlear notches. In summary, it appears that the forelegs were cut into three segments, which were the upper limb, the forelimb and the foot (Binford 1981; Lyman 1994). Little can be said about the hind limbs of these animals because of the fragmentary nature of the remains. Although no cut marks were found on the tibiae or femora fragments, several deep cut marks were found on the innominate of the older individual. These consisted of deep, chopping cuts on both the dorsal and ventral faces of the element (Fig. 10). The action which produced these marks could be related to the segmentation of the carcass at the hip. The unfused distal epiphysis of one femur was burned and blackened, while faint reddish traces of fire were visible on the distal third of one tibia and on the diaphyses of a number of metapodials. Both the burning on the tibia and on the femur could be interpreted as roasting of a meat joint; in this case the exposed bone on the extremities is directly exposed to the fire used for cooking (Gifford Gonzales 1989).

Discussion

The faunal assemblage of the well could be associated with some kind of ritual and/or to a ritual banquet related to the sacred buildings of the excavated area and it is unlikely that the bones were just common rubbish discarded in the well. The sacred nature of the area in which these remains were found, the ceramic vessels found with them, and the position of the well, close to

Fig. 11. Painted oinochoe *found in Duomo square. Close up of Artemis depicted as the* Potnia theron

the walls of the temple, suggests that they played a role in some form of ritual, but if this is so, is it possible to identify that ritual? A painted *oinochoe* (Fig. 11) was found in one of the excavated *thysiai*. The painted scene depicts a woman, her hands on the heads of two lions, followed by a procession of beasts. This scene was interpreted by Pelagatti (1999) as the "*Potnia theron*" (Lady of the beasts), the name used by Homer for "*Artemis Agrotera*" in the Iliad (*Iliad*, XXI) and it corresponds to a description of the goddess given by Pausanias: "[Depicted on the chest of Kypelos at Olympia] *Artemis has wings on her shoulders ... in her right hand she grips a leopard, in her left a lion"* (Pausanias, Guide to Greece, 5.19.5). The archaeologists who excavated the site hypothesized that first the *oikos*, then the temple were consecrated to Artemis as was the whole area (Voza 1999). The *oinochoe* is dated to the first half of the 7th century and it is the oldest witness of the cult of Artemide, the first goddess worshipped in the ancient colony (Pelagatti 1999).

Consequently the bones found in the well could be interpreted as offerings to Artemis, but the dogs are a quite odd presence among the victims. It is true that hounds are closely connected with Artemis, as in the Homeric Hymn to the goddess: "*I sing of Artemis, whose shafts are of gold, who cheers on the hounds, the pure maiden....*" (Homer, Hymn to Artemis). Conversely, dogs were considered as impure animals by the Greeks, and they were not involved in ritual ceremonies dedicated to the Olympians but used as victims of rituals connected to the cthonian gods (Bodson 1980; Zaganiaris 1975). However, dogs were used as victims in the sacrifices offered to Hekate whose apparition was announced by their barking. "*Zerynthos* [on the island of Samothrake], *cave of the goddess to whom dogs are slain"* (Lycophron 74). *"I know of no other Greeks* [than the Spartans' sacrifices to Enyalios] *who are accustomed to sacrifice puppies except the people of Kolophon; these too sacrifice a puppy, a black bitch, to Enodio* [the wayside goddess Hekate]. *Both the sacrifice of the Kolophonians and that of the youths at Sparta are appointed to take place at night"* (Pausanias, Guide to Greece, 3.14.9–10).

It seems that we are talking about two different goddesses, each one related to a different world and perhaps with a different set of victims, as only Hekate could accept dogs as victims. But if we examine in detail the nature of both goddesses there is no contradiction between the Olympic Artemis and the cthonian Hekate as both were related to the moon, the night, and the world of darkness, magic and childbirth. Hekate, the Goddess of the Crossways, was also known as *"Trimorfos"*, or the goddess with three forms. These forms were interpreted also as Selene in the sky, Artemis on earth, and Hekate in the underworld as well as the world above when it is wrapped in darkness (Kraus 1980; Usener 1896). Further, Artemis was sometimes identified with Hekate, called *"Artemis Hekate"*, while her brother was known as *"Phoebus Hekatos"* (Kraus 1980). The temple and the well discovered in Piazza Duomo are located in the very sacred heart of the colony, the acropolis of the Island of Ortigia, and Ortigia was the name of the mythic island where Artemis was born. Moreover, Artemis was the principle goddess worshipped in Siracusa until 5th century BC when she was replaced by Athena. It is probable that the ritual in which the dogs (and the other animals whose remains were discarded in the well) were involved was a cthonian one, celebrating the dark side of the first patron deity of the town.

Thus, based on archaeological, iconographic and bibliographical evidence it can be suggested that the dogs found in the well in the Piazza Duomo may be related to a ritual in honour of "*Artemis-Hekate*", which may have taken place at night.

Acknowledgements

I am grateful to Dr. Giuseppe Voza, Superintendent for Arts and Environment of Siracusa for allowing me to study the archaeozoological remains from Piazza Duomo. My sincere thanks to Dr. Alfredo Carannante of the Laboratory of Bioarchaeology of the University Suor Orsola Benincasa of Naples for his help with the identification of fish remains.

References

Barone, R. 1986. *Anatomie comparée des Mammifères doméstiques. Tome I Ostéologie*. Paris: Vigot.

Binford, L. R. 1981. *Bones: Ancient Men and Modern Myths*. New York: Academic Press.

Bodson, L. 1980. Place et fonction du chien dans le monde antique. *Ethnozootechnie* **25**, 13–21.

Ciurcina, C. and Amato, R. 1999. I materiali dai pozzi votivi, pp. 36–41 in Voza, G. (ed.), *Siracusa 1999 – Lo scavo archeologico di Piazza Duomo*. Siracusa: Arnaldo Lombardi Editore.

Finley, M. 1968. *A history of Sicily, from ancient Sicily to the Arab Conquest*. New York: Viking Press.

Gifford Gonzales, D. 1989. Ethnographic analogues for interpreting modified bones: some cases from east Africa, pp. 179–246 in Bonnichsen, R. and Sorg M. *Bone modification*. Orono, Center for the Study of the First Americans: University of Maine.

Hillson, S. 1986. *Teeth*. Cambridge, Cambridge University Press.

Koudelka, F. 1885. Das Verhältnis der Ossa longa zur Skeletthöhe bei den Säugetieren. *Verhandl. D. Naturforsch. Ver. Brünn* **24**, 127–153.

Kraus, T. 1960. *Hekate: Studien zu Wiesen und Bild der Gottin in Kleinasien und Griechenland*. Heidelberg: Winter.

Lyman, R. L. 1994. *Vertebrate Taphonomy*. Cambridge: Cambridge University Press.

Manfredi, V. M. 1996. *I Greci d'Occidente*. Milano: Mondadori.

Orsi, P. 1919. Gli scavi intorno a l'Athenaion di Siracusa negli anni 1912–1917. *Memorie dell'Accademia dei Lincei*, XXV.

Pelagatti, P. 1999. L'*oinochoe* di Artemide, pp. 29–35 in Voza, G. (ed.), *Siracusa 1999 – Lo scavo archeologico di Piazza Duomo*. Siracusa: Arnaldo Lombardi editore.

Voza, G. 1999. Le opere di scavo, pp. 7–20 in Voza, G. (ed.), *Siracusa 1999 – Lo scavo archeologico di Piazza Duomo*. Siracusa: Arnaldo Lombardi editore.

Usener, H. 1896. *Götternamen: Versuch einer Lehre van der religiosen Begriffsbildung*. Bonn.

Zaganiaris, M.J. 1975. Sacrifices de chiens dans l'Antiquité classique. *Platon* **27**, 322–329.

Laboratorio di Bioarcheologia
Università degli Studi
Suor Orsola Benincasa
Via S. Caterina da Siena 37
80135 Napoli
Italy

labtechnie@unisob.na.it

9th ICAZ Conference, Durham 2002
Dogs and People in Social, Working, Economic or Symbolic Interaction
(eds Lynn M. Snyder and Elizabeth A. Moore) pp. 38–43

5. In Sickness and in Health: Care for an Arthritic Maltese Dog from the Roman Cemetery of Yasmina, Carthage, Tunisia

Michael MacKinnon and Kyle Belanger

Many have had strong relationships with pets. We are certain that such deep ties between humans and pets existed in the past as well, and would like to illustrate this using an example from a Roman context in Carthage, Tunisia. It is a tale of a very ill and pathologic dog that survived to an elderly age only because of human care. Moreover, this was a special dog, because it was not like most other canids recovered from ancient sites around the Mediterranean. Rather this was a toy breed of dog – and, based on osteological attributes, most likely a Maltese.

Introduction

The cemetery of Yasmina lies in the SW quadrant of the ancient city of Carthage, Tunisia (Fig. 1), just outside the south gate. The area was first recognized as an archaeological site in 1981 during bulldozing operations for a road. At that time, the bulldozer churned up several ashlar blocks from a substantial rectangular tomb, as well as a magnificent early 3rd century AD marble portrait statue of a charioteer. The location of this necropolis sparked interest among archaeologists who were excavating at the nearby Roman circus in Carthage, and in 1992 the University of Georgia (under the direction of Dr. Naomi Norman), with the gracious support of Tunisian authorities, undertook the first of a five-year excavation campaign at the Yasmina cemetery. The necropolis underwent numerous phases, beginning with the erection of stucco monuments, such as the Tertullus burial monument for cremation burials, in the 2nd century AD, at a period coincident with some modest inhumation burials. This phase was followed by construction of ashlar funerary monuments during the early 3rd century AD, and destruction of these about a century later. Phases of both less elaborate inhumation and cremation burials occurred next, with most concentrated in the 5th century; however, there seems to have been little activity at the site after the late 5th century AD (Norman and Haeckl 1993).

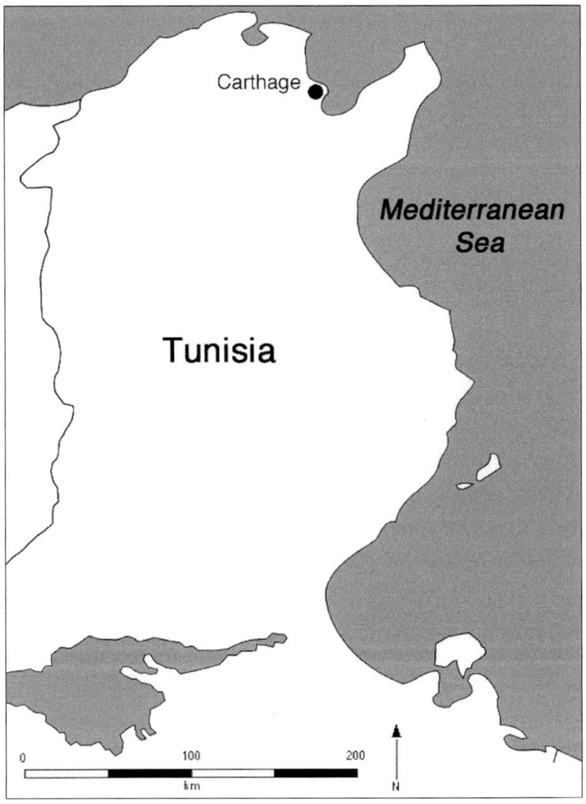

Fig. 1. Location of Carthage, Tunisia

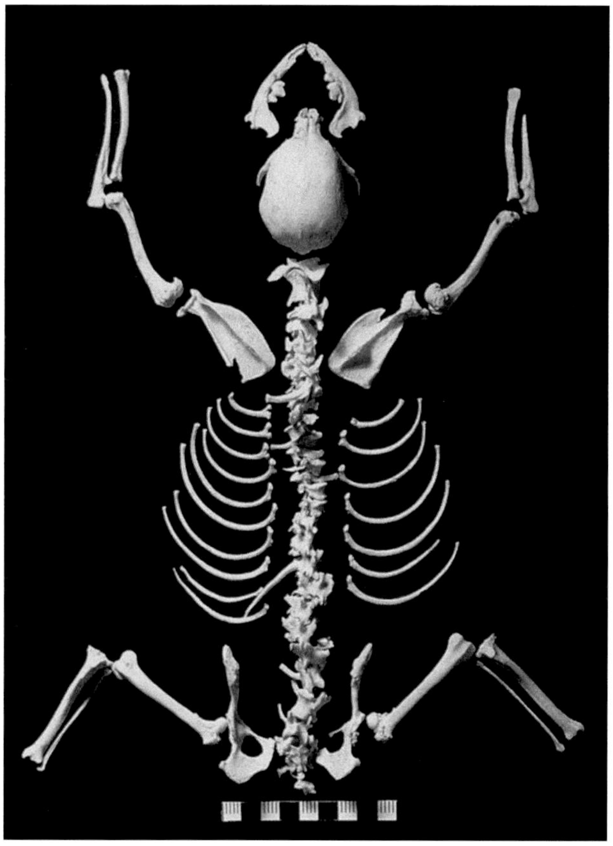

Fig. 2. Reconstructed dog skeleton from Yasmina necropolis – dorsal view

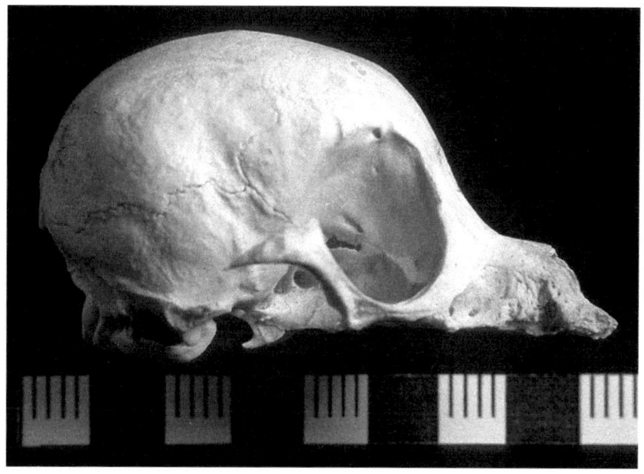

Fig. 3. Cranium – right side view

The Yasmina Dog

Although each of the burials excavated at Yasmina is important, one is unique in that it contained the skeleton of a dog. While others yielded various grave goods and accoutrements, including charred pig remains, presumably a ritual meal for the dead, this is the only burial associated with an animal companion. This special inhumation burial – that of a young adolescent, between approximately 10-15 years of age and located along the north precinct wall – was excavated in 1997. It was a rather carefully-made grave, capped with cobbles and tiles, and dates to around the 3rd century AD, in terms of its stratigraphic relationship to other monuments and burials, as well as through the stylistic analysis of a glass vessel that accompanied the adolescent.

At the foot of the adolescent was the skeleton of a dog. MacKinnon initially examined the faunal material from Yasmina during May 1998 and June 1999, while Belanger performed further analyses of the canid remains in 2001. This dog skeleton (displayed in Fig. 2) was recovered in a relatively complete state, which included small elements such as phalanges, carpals and tarsals, indicating that it was interred whole. All elements exhibited uniform taphonomic conditions, free of alterations from most natural and cultural agents, save for some evidence of root etching. At first the skeleton was puzzling; its dentition was clearly canid, as were its post-cranial elements. The cranium, however, was highly brachycephalic and very bulbous, with a short snout (Fig. 3). This shape was atypical of most of the comparative dog skulls examined from other ancient sites in the Mediterranean for which we were familiar, many of which were more elongated in shape, with relatively longer muzzles and a distinct sagittal crest. This is supported in Harcourt's (1974) survey of dog breeds in Iron Age and Roman Britain, where brachycephalic individuals represent less than 5% of the archaeological specimens included.

Measurements for stature, following Harcourt's (1974) formulae, estimated the dog to be between 20–21 cm at the withers. This height, coupled with a morphometric analysis of each element, especially the cranium, placed the dog into the midget or toy dog range, most securely within estimates for the Maltese breed.

The sex of the dog could not be determined conclusively. Excavation methods or taphonomic factors may be responsible for the loss of the bacculum (if it was present); however, given the careful excavation and good preservation state of the skeleton, it is likely that, in the absence of a recovered bacculum, it was female.

As for age, permanent dentition had erupted with teeth in wear, while all epiphyses and sutures were fused. The latest epiphyses to fuse in the dog are those of the vertebrae, at around 2 years of age (Schmid 1972). The Yasmina dog was certainly older than this. Fragments of ossified costal cartilage suggested an elderly dog; however, this may not be a good indicator given the pronounced presence of osteoarthritis on the skeleton. The advanced state of pathological conditions evident on the skeleton (which we shall describe in depth shortly) also implied an elderly animal. The life expectancy for a modern Maltese is between 15 and 18 years (www.dogbreedinfo.com/maltese.htm). This individual seems to have attained a comparable age.

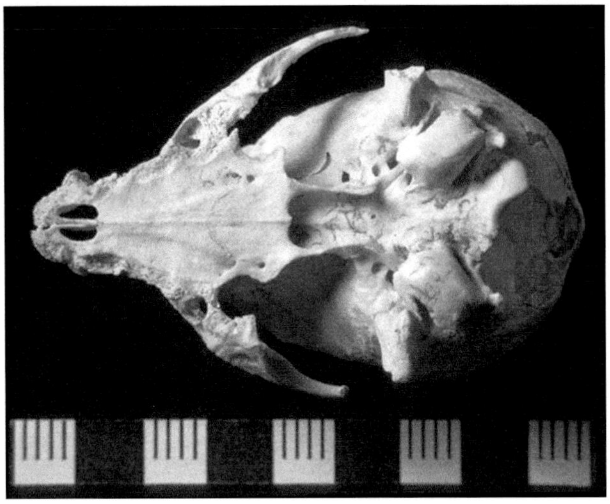

Fig. 4. Cranium – basal view.

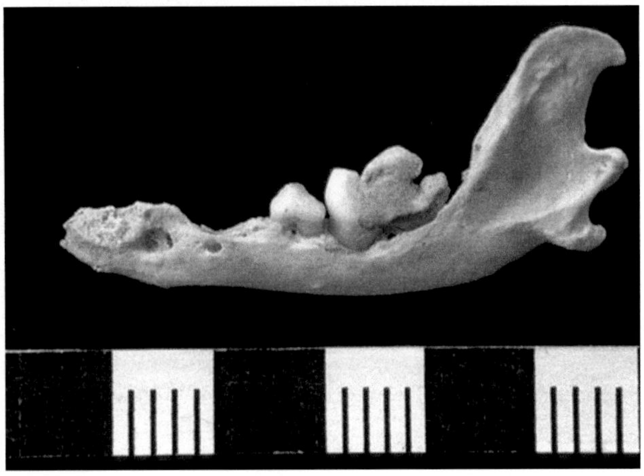

Fig. 5. Left mandible – lateral view

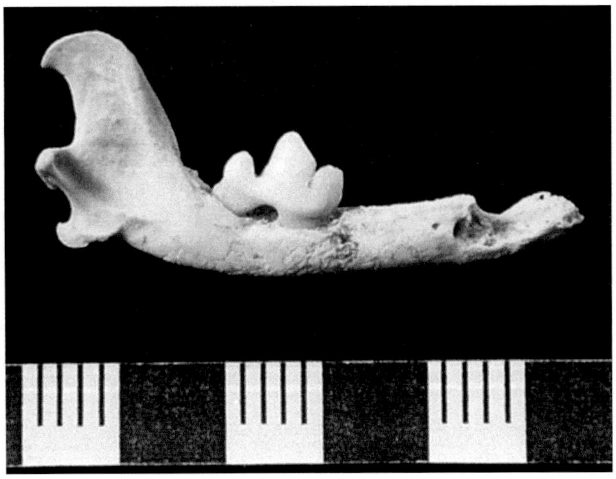

Fig. 6. Right mandible – lateral view

This dog was not healthy, but lived with a variety of dental and skeletal ailments for quite some time. There were no maxillary teeth present – all had been lost antemortem, and some, such as the incisors and molars, perhaps years before the animal's death, given that the tooth sockets here had been obliterated by bony remodeling (Fig. 4). Although oligodontia (several missing teeth) and hypodontia (a few missing teeth) of the incisor teeth are common in Maltese breeds of dogs (Ackerman 1999: 42), the presence of new bone growth in the incisor area suggests that these teeth had formed and erupted but were lost during the dog's life. Two alveoli marked the root position for the 4th premolars. The right example contained a remnant of a tooth root, heavily destroyed due to infection.

The mandibular dentition fared slightly better than its maxillary equivalent. The left mandible (Fig. 5) retained the 4th premolar and 1st molar, while only the 1st molar remained in the right mandible (Fig. 6). All other teeth had been lost antemortem, and again probably many years before death given the state of bone development filling in each tooth socket. Abscessing is indicated in two distinct cases, with one prominent infection draining out of the left mandible body under the 2nd premolar. Alveolar resorption had occurred in numerous cases with bone loss at the base of each tooth. The dog likely suffered from advanced stages of periodontal disease, with the subsequent infection eating away the bone at the neck of each tooth. No doubt this was exacerbated by the heavy build-up of calculus, clearly evident as a thick greenish deposit on the left 1st molar. Calculus accumulated here along all surfaces of the tooth, and even on root surfaces below the gum line. The presence of calculus on the occlusal margin of this molar indicates some form of masticatory dysfunction. Antemortem loss of maxillary teeth would have negated any counter friction during chewing. Consequently, there would be no natural dental cleaning from mastication, and an opportunity for quick accumulation of calculus.

Human care may have been required for feeding this dog. Tooth loss may have caused the dog to reject hard foods, which it would not be able to crunch effectively. Consequently, the dog probably relied on its human caregiver to provide it with soft foods to consume. Such a diet, in turn, may have led to further bacterial-related troubles such as calculus build up, infection, and caries in the dog (although there are no visible signs of the latter).

Practically all limb articulations in the Yasmina dog are disfigured due to osteoarthritis. Both eburnation and porosity are present on most articular surfaces, while osteophytes surround the periphery of the joint margins in multiple cases. The medial shaft of the left humerus has stimulated excess bone deposition around the glenoid fossa of the left scapula. Nearly half of the left humeral head is polished through eburnation, with projections of new bone jutting around the proximal surface of this bone (Fig. 7). The right humerus and scapula, by contrast, exhibit less severe stages of osteoarthritis.

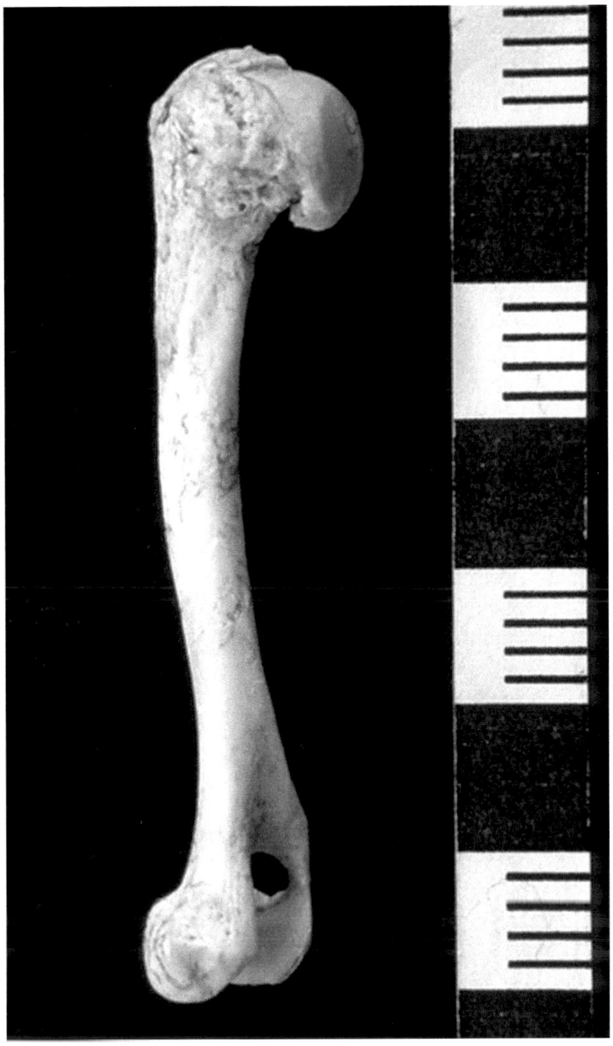

Fig. 7. Left humerus

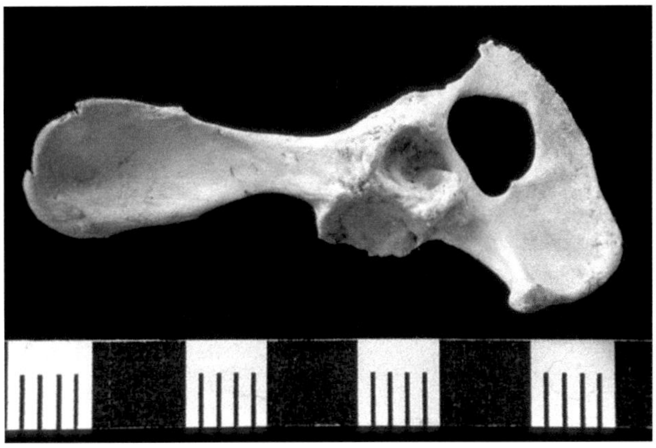

Fig. 8. Right pelvis

In the hind legs, a definite dislocation of the right femur is noted, which has shifted cranially and dorsally from the original pelvic acetabulum to form a totally new acetabular pit (Fig. 8). This new hip socket continued to deform until the dog's death – the femur does not appear to have shifted back to its original position. The new acetabular surface also affected the shape of the right femoral head. As a consequence of its placements in the new acetabulum the femoral head became distorted, and oval in shape, flattened dorsally and ventrally (Fig. 9). The right femur also lacks a neck, the region given over to osteophyte formation as the bone adjusted to its new position. Eburnation is only present on the ventral surface of the femoral head, which suggests that it rested on the reformed bone just above the original acetabulum.

The left pelvis and femur also display marked stages of osteoarthritis, but here there is no trace of a dislocation and radical acetabulum deformation. The left femur exhibits marked eburnation – over 80% of the head was affected. Osteophytes also surround the joint margin and trochanters and have completely obliterated the femoral

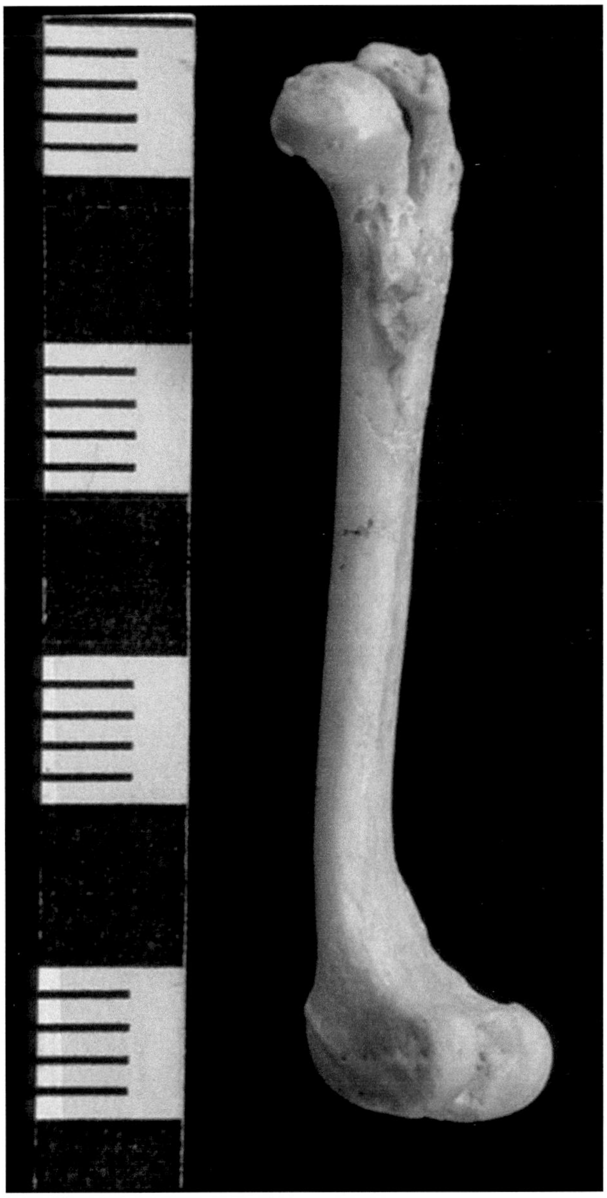

Fig. 9. Right femur

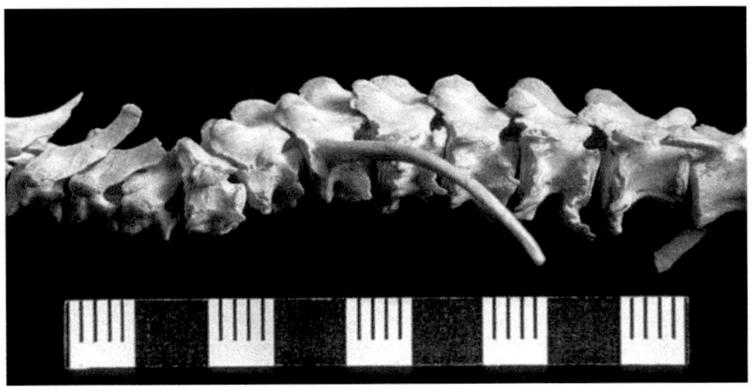

Fig. 10. Section of the vertebral column, showing progression of spondylosis deformans and fused rib.

neck. The left acetabulum has osteophytes surrounding the entire articulation, as well as within the acetabular fossa itself.

The vertebral column of the dog exhibits a host of pathological conditions. Most prominent is spondylosis deformans, a disorder characterized primarily by the presence of osteophytes on the borders of the vertebral bodies at the intervertebral spaces (Morgan 1967; Morgan *et al.* 1967). Spondylosis deformans is distinguished from vertebral or spinal osteoarthritis in that the latter involves the joints between the articular processes of the vertebral column as opposed to the intervertebral spaces that are affected in spondylosis deformans, even though osteophyte development is a symptom of both conditions (Morgan 1967; Morgan *et al.* 1967). Osteophytes are most marked on the last four cervical vertebrae (C4–C7) of the Yasmina example, then again along the posterior four thoracic vertebrae (T10–T13) and the first four lumbar vertebrae (L1–L4). In one instance (T13), the degree of osteophyte formation here is so marked as to cause fusion of rib to vertebrae (Fig. 10). In no cases are the vertebrae themselves fused to one another.

Although spondylosis deformans is clearly visible on the vertebral column of the Yasmina dog, the animal was also affected by spinal osteoarthritis and osteoporosis. Articular surfaces of vertebral discs themselves show variable signs of pitting, porosity, and eburnation in a number of cases.

A cursory glance at the advanced stages of spondylosis deformans and spinal osteoarthritits on the Yasmina dog brings questions about the animal's range of movement. Although the conditions may seem debilitating, while researching similar situations in red fox, Harris (1977) concluded that many animals from his sample functioned while alive without any physical handicap. Still, with restricted vertebral movement, one has to wonder how active the Yasmina dog was. Could it walk or run?

We argue that the marked spondylosis deformans and osteoarthritis exhibited did not prevent the Yasmina dog from moving. Maltese dogs, like many toy dogs, have a high temperament and are generally very active. Marked eburnation at joint surfaces of the Yasmina dog indicates that movement was taking place, no matter how painful this might have been. Moreover, the placement and condition of the osteoarthritis denotes movement. Recall that the front left limb and the hind right limb (with its reformed acetabulum) were most affected by this pathological condition. Dogs have a three-point and a two-point suspension when moving (Smythe 1970). During walking, a dog will be balanced on its left front limb at the same time as its right hind limb. After the Yasmina dog suffered a dislocation at its right hind limb, the dog likely compensated by trying to walk as much as possible on three legs, predominantly favouring its front left limb while the dislocated back right limb healed itself by reforming the acetabulum. With the limbs already arthritic, the left front limb could have been more vulnerable to inflammation with the increased stress.

The right front and right hind limb are also two points of suspension when in locomotion for a dog (Smythe 1970). So, why didn't the right front leg also display as severe an accumulation of arthritis as did the left? When walking, an animal's body falls towards the unsupported side as a counter balance. This suggests that the right front limb may not have taken on extra weight since the load shifted away from it before the left limb landed to take on weight and suspension for movement.

The modified three-legged walk on the Yasmina dog may have led to further complications in the spine. Dogs with a sore, broken or otherwise injured leg often develop what is known as a "tart-walk" (Dr. A. Cooksley [Veterinarian, Calgary, AB], personal communication). The dog tries to relieve stress on the leg joints by swaggering the spine laterally, back and forth, to assist in forward movement. The increased strain on the vertebrae could easily have led to augmented states of spondylosis deformans and spinal osteoarthritis.

Although there are numerous causes noted for joint diseases or arthropathies, in the case of the Yasmina dog, most examples seem to be more proliferative rather than erosive in nature, with accumulation processes such as osteophyte formation predominating over erosive symptoms such as pitting at the joint surfaces. It would appear that old age and aggravated joint stress from an awkward walk or hip displacement contributed to the osteoarthritis in this dog. The loss of bone density due to osteoporosis is not visually apparent as a cause, and seems unlikely given the near absence of signs of osteoarthritis in all articulations further down the dog's legs (i.e., from the distal humerus down, and from the distal femur down).

Discussion

That this dog survived to an elderly age with such a suite of pathological conditions – and many of these at advanced stages – suggests that it received great care from its provider. This begs the question: why? According to Roman pagan religion (Soren 1999, 621), dogs were believed to have healing powers, a belief that may have derived from the observation that dogs lick their owns wounds and seem to recuperate thereafter (Stager 1991:

39). The ancient Greek author Callimachus, in 264 BC, was the first writer to make note of a specific use of a Maltese in this respect. He wrote that this breed was laid upon the stomach of an ill individual to draw out and ease pain (Cutillo 1986: 15). Hence, the fashion was to carry Maltese dogs close to one's chest. Could it be that the people who interred the Yasmina dog did so because they believed it would protect the child in the afterlife? The dog did, after all, overcome a crippled state, and would be a perfect candidate as a healer. Or, did the family sacrifice the dog with the child for companionship in the afterlife? According to the ancient author Pliny, the Younger, Roman children sometimes were buried with a beloved pet or pets (*Ep*. 4.2) The Yasmina dog was certainly a well cared for and treasured pet. Even death may not have been a deterrent to keep the child from its cherished dog. Ancient authors such as Martial, Strabo and Pliny discuss the beauty, intelligence, and lovable qualities of Maltese dogs. Martial (in the 1st century AD) writes of one:

> Issa is more frolicsome that Catulla's sparrow. Issa is purer than a dove's kiss. Issa is gentler than a maiden. Issa is more precious than Indian gems...Lest the last days that she sees light should snatch her from him forever, Publius has had her picture painted (*Ep*. 1.109)

We know little about the origins and spread of the Maltese dogs in antiquity. The name itself is misleading, because the breed likely does not originate from the island of Malta (Cutillo 1986, 14). Arguments linking the Maltese to the town of Melita in Sicily, or the island of Melita in the Adriatic are also deceptive. Rather, the dog is probably descended from spitz-type dogs bred by people inhabiting south-central Europe (Cutillo 1964: 190, 199; Fiennes 1970: 48). Early Maltese, therefore, probably resembled Pomeranian breeds of dogs in having a short snout, prick ears, and a rather bulbous head. The exact division between these two types is sketchy, at least in antiquity. True Pomeranian dogs were bred from sled dogs of northern Europe and Iceland (Jones and Rendel 1964: 199). Images of toy dogs on Greek vases from as early as 500 BC resemble Pomeranian-type dogs; however, most references in ancient texts and inscriptions speak of the Maltese breed (Cutillo 1986: 15). The introduction of pug dogs (such as the early Pekingese) from the Far East, brought to the Mediterranean from Roman trading expeditions, would have further confused the picture since these toy breeds interbred (Fiennes 1970: 48). The Maltese may have served as the foundation for toy-type dog breeds in antiquity. The name "Maltese" may have derived from the use of Malta as an ancient trading center through which the breed of dog spread around the Mediterranean (Cutillo 1986: 14). Carthage too was a major port in antiquity, and one close to Malta, so it is not unexpected that Maltese dogs eventually made their way to North Africa.

Conclusion

Animals fulfill numerous roles in antiquity, as they do today. The Yasmina dog provides us with a case of special care taken for a pet. This dog is important in that it is a rare example of a toy-breed, one of the earliest cases of a Maltese. Moreover, it exemplifies the care humans provided to their cherished pets. The Yasmina dog was not well, it had only a few teeth and certainly required ground-up food; it had a dislocated hip and was highly arthritic, but it lived to an elderly age with these pathological conditions, again no doubt a factor of human concern. We have no doubt that the bond between the Yasmina Maltese dog and its owner was strong. This aspect of human culture does not seem to have changed since Roman times.

References

Ackerman, L. 1999. *A Guide to Health Problems in Purebred Dogs*. Lakewood, Colorado: AAHA.

Cutillo, N. 1986. *The Complete Maltese*. New York: Howell.

Fiennes, R. A. 1970. *The Natural History of Dogs*. Garden City: Natural History Press.

Harcourt, R. 1974. The dog in prehistoric and early historic Britain. *Journal of Archaeological Science* **1**, 151–75.

Harris, S. 1977. Spinal arthritis (Spondylosis deformans) in the Red Fox, *Vulpes vulpes*, with some methodology of relevance to zooarchaeology. *Journal of Archaeological Science* **4**, 183–95.

Jones, A. F. and Rendel, J. 1964. *The Treasury of Dogs*. New York: Golden.

Morgan, J. P. 1967. Spondylosis deformans in the dog. *Acta Orthopaedica Scandinavica. Supplementum* **96**, 1–88.

Morgan, J. P., Ljunggren, G. and Read, R. (1967) Spondylosis deformans (vertebral osteophytosis) in the dog. *Journal of Small Animal Practice* **8**, 57–66.

Norman, N. and Haeckl, A. 1993. The Yasmina necropolis at Carthage, 1992. *Journal of Roman Archaeology* **6**, 238–50.

Schmid, E. 1972. *Atlas of Animal Bones*. Amsterdam, Elsevier.

Smythe, R. 1970. *The Dog: Structure and Movement*. New York: Arco.

Soren, D. 1999. Hecate and the infant cemetery at Poggio Gramignano. In D. S. Soren and N. Soren (eds.) *A Roman Villa and a Late Roman Infant Cemetery: Excavation at Poggio Gramignano Lugnano in Teverina*, 619–31. Rome: L'ERMA di Bretschneider.

Stager, L. 1991. Why were hundreds of dogs buried at Ashkelon? *Biblical Archaeology Review* (March/April 1991) 39.

Michael MacKinnon
Department of Anthropology
University of Winnipeg
Winnipeg, MB R3B 2E9
Canada

m.mackinnon@uwinnipeg.ca

Kyle Belanger
Department of Archaeology
University of Calgary
Calgary, AB
Canada

kbelange@ucalgary.ca

9th ICAZ Conference, Durham 2002
Dogs and People in Social, Working, Economic or Symbolic Interaction
(eds Lynn M. Snyder and Elizabeth A. Moore) pp. 44–48

6. What did the Bronze Age Dogs Eat? Coprolithic Analyses

Liina Maldre

Asva is a fortified settlement dated to the Late Bronze Age, but there were also finds dating to the Iron Age. In this paper only the dog's coprolites are analysed, collected during the excavations in 1939 (directed by Richard Indreko). These coprolites contain many bone fragments, including well preserved phalanges and other small bones of sheep or goat, and fish bones, especially vertebrae and scales.

Introduction

The fortified settlement of Asva is situated in South-eastern Saaremaa Island, West Estonia. This settlement is located on the eastern part of a ridge by a former bay (Fig. 1). Archaeological excavations in Asva were carried out in 1934 and 1938–1939 under the direction of Richard Indreko (Indreko 1939a, Indreko 1939b), in 1948–1949 under the direction of Artur Vassar and Marta Schmiedehelm (Vassar 1955) and in 1965–1966 under the direction of Vello Lõugas (Lõugas, V. 1970).

The Asva fortified settlement dates primarily to the Late Bronze Age (9th-6th centuries BC), but also contains some Iron Age components. In 1939 investigations of excavation Unit A from the year before were finished and new excavations (B, C, and D) were begun (Fig. 2). From excavation A were found The remains of burned logs and fireplaces were found in Unit A, but no buildings locations were located (Indreko 1939b). Results of excavations show that buildings were placed near the walls of the site; while the middle part of settlement was not built upon. Since the settlement had continued in existence for a quite long time, chronologial strata were not easily differentiated (Vassar 1955: 116–117). The only excavation unit in which the earliest open settlement layer, dated into the first millennium BC, was recognisable, was excavation A (Lõugas, V. 1970). All of the found coprolites originate from this excavation. Since in 1938 all upper layers above this were removed, it may be supposed that for the most part the materials found in 1939 originate from the Bronze Age or, in extreme cases, from the Early Iron Age. Some coprolites have been discovered in the 1938 materials which is not

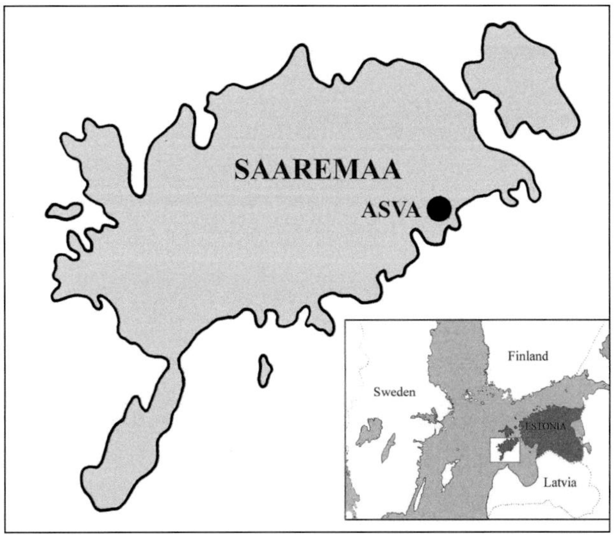

Fig. 1. Location of the fortified settlement of Asva

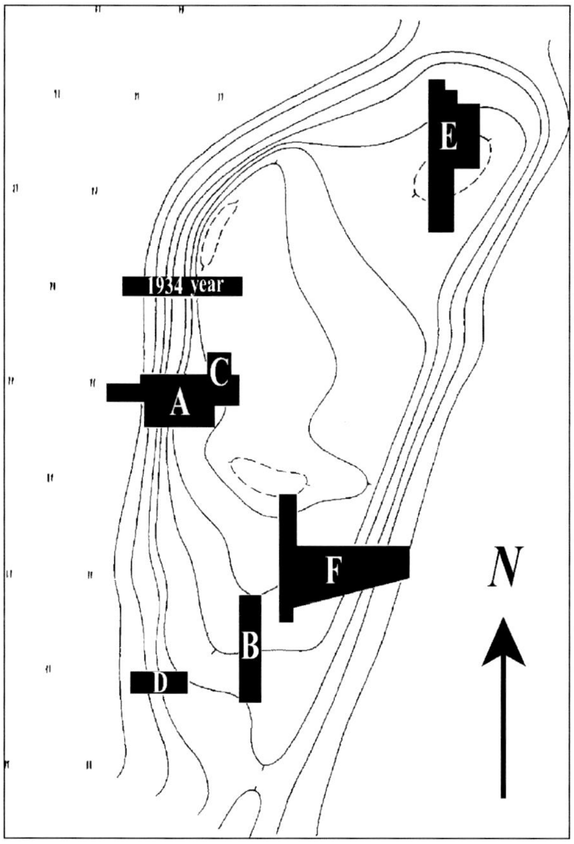

Fig. 2. Sketch-map of the excavated area at Asva (after Jaanits et al. *1982, fig. 92)*

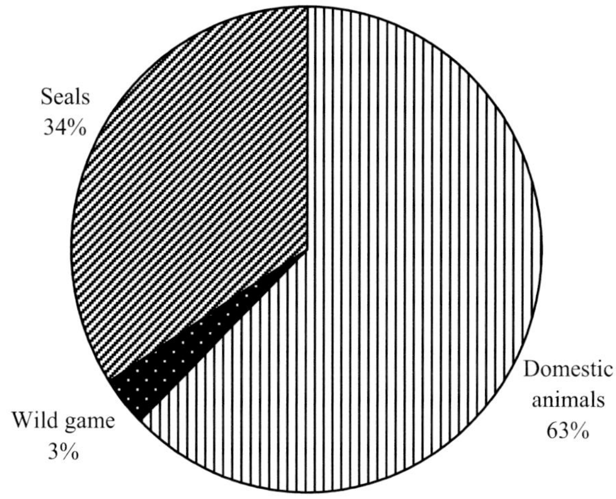

Fig. 3. The structure of archaeozoological material recovered from Asva in 1939

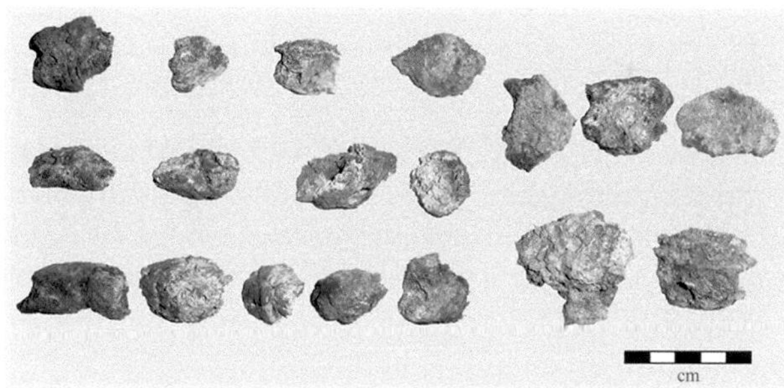

Fig. 4. The dog coprolites from Asva

yet fully analyzed, so the exact number of speicmens from the site is not yet clear. There is no information about coprolites from other excavations at present.

About 60% of the archaeozoological material of Asva excavation A of 1939 comes from domestic animals (Fig. 3), other remains are from seals (34%) and wild game (3%). Of the domestic animals sheep and/or goats *(Ovis aries/Capra hircus)* are dominant (51% of domestic animal bones). Cattle *(Bos taurus)* and pig *(Sus scrofa dom.)* bones are also quite common, each species contributing 18–19% of domestic species. The role of horse *(Equus caballus)* is considerably smaller, only 12% of domestic animal bones belong to this species. The most commonly occuring wild or game species is the elk *(Alces alces)*. Wild boar *(Sus scrofa ferus)*, beaver *(Castor fiber)*, brown bear *(Ursus arctos)*, pine marten *(Martes martes)* and mountain hare *(Lepus timidus)* are represented by only a few bones each. Materials from different areas of the excavations vary somewhat in species distribution; the percentage of domestic animal bones varies from 60–80%, seals form 15–40%, while in all contexts wild animal bones are scarce (Lepiksaar 1940; Tsalkin 1952; Paaver 1965; Lõugas, L. 1991; Maldre 2004).

Fish bones were recovered from all excavations as well. Identified species include common sturgeon (*Acipenser sturio*), pike (*Esox lucius*), orfe (*Leuciscus idus*), tench (*Tinca tinca*), vimba bream (*Vimba vimba*) and perch (*Perca fluviatilis*) (Lõugas 1997, 25).

Material and methods

In this study only the dog coprolites recovered during the 1939 excavations are considered. The total amount of material is over 2 kg, of which about 800 g of material was studied. Coprolites were recovered from all excavated squares of the excavation, but unfortunately exact locations were not fully recorded.

Collected coprolites vary greatly in shape and size; some are compact while others are quite diffuse and irregular in shape (Fig. 4). To dissolve the coprolites, the specimens were soaked for 24 hours in a 35% acetic acid (CH_3COOH) solution. The material was then washed through a sieve, using water, and all bone fragments were picked from the screen. Specimens which resisted this initial treatment were resoaked up to three times. Following three soakings, still resistant clumps were broken up mechanically, but care was necessary, since the long soaking in the acid solution had affected the

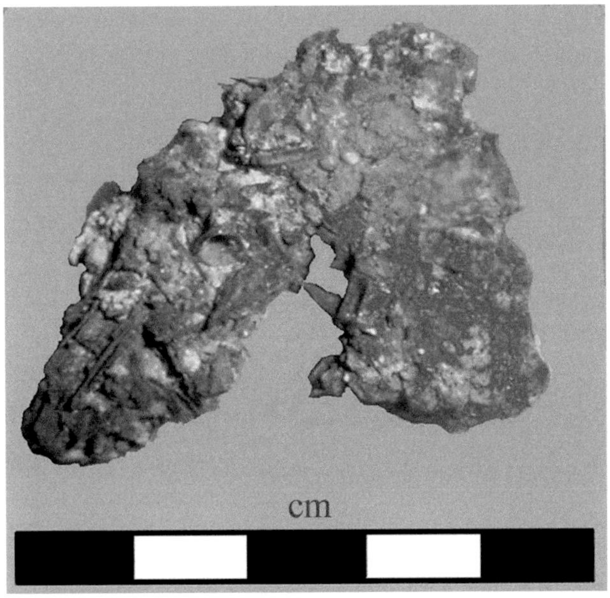

Fig. 5. A cluster of fish bones in a coprolite

Fig. 6. Sheep or goat bones from coprolites

inorganic component of the bone. Coprolites containing fish bones and scales (Fig. 5) were particuarly difficult to dissolve, due to their high phosphorus content (J. Peets, pers. comm.). They were also difficult to break apart by mechanical means, for the same reason. In these specimens, the majority of fish bones could not be identified, nor was it possible to determine the number fish bones contained in these specimens.

Results

Mammals

The majority of mammal bone recovered consisted of small fragments of spongy cancellous or compact tissue. These small, broken and heavily digested fragments were impossible to identify. Identifiable specimens were limited primarily to small elements which the dogs had swallowed whole, after only minimal chewing and breakage (Fig. 6). Twenty-five sheep or goat bone fragments, two pig bones, and one harp seal element were identified. The anatomical elements represented by these fragments are presented in Table 1.

Fish

The dogs at Asva apparently did like to eat fish (Fig. 7). The majority of the identified fish remains (identified by L. Lõugas) from the coprolites were scales of perch *(Perca fluviatilis).* Vertebrae and cranial elements from the same species were also recovered. A few scales and skull fragments come from pike (*Esox lucius*) and cyprinids (*Cyprinidae*). Fragments of fish ribs and spines were also identified. An exact number of fish elements could not be determined due to the clumping and compaction of many of the coprolites containing fish elements. The approximate magnitude of fish bones is as follows: 200 scales of perch, 20 skull fragments of perch, 50 vertebrae of perch; 3 scales of pike, 2 vertebrae of pike, and from cyprinid one scale and one vertebra.

Plants

An interesting discovery was made when one hard aggregation was broken: an impression of a cereal blade (Fig. 8). Certainly dogs ate grass more frequently, but in coprolites soaked in acid any remaining plant materials were destroyed. Comprehensive palebotanic investigations have regrettably not been conducted at Asva, but a score of potsherds have been found which bear the impressions of grains, primarily barley (Jaanits *et al.* 1982). Is likely that the impression of a cereal leaf blade found in this coprolite is not from a cultivated plant.

Discussion

Additional evidence of the presence of dogs at the site is shown by the occurance of dog gnawing on the mammal bones recovered (Table 2). However, the rare occurrence of seal bones in the coprolites should be remarked upon. In addition to one calcaneus of a harp seal one or more bone fragments could belong to seals, but they were too fragmentary to allow exact identification. Considering the composition of faunal remains from the site, a larger number of seal bone fragments would be expected in the coprolites. Seal bones were mixed with other animal bones in this cultural layer and all elements of the seal skeleton were represented, so it is unlikely that dogs did not have access to the discarded seal bones.

Table 1. The specific and anatomical structure of mammal bones recovered from coprolites

Species	***Cranium, dentes***	***Vertebrae***	***Costae***	***Ossa metapodiale***	***Ossa carpi***	***Ossa tarsi***	***Phalanges***
Ovis aries/Capra hircus	4	4	3	1	2	3	8
Sus scrofa domesticus	–	2	–	–	–	–	–
Phoca groenlandica	–	–	–	–	–	1	–

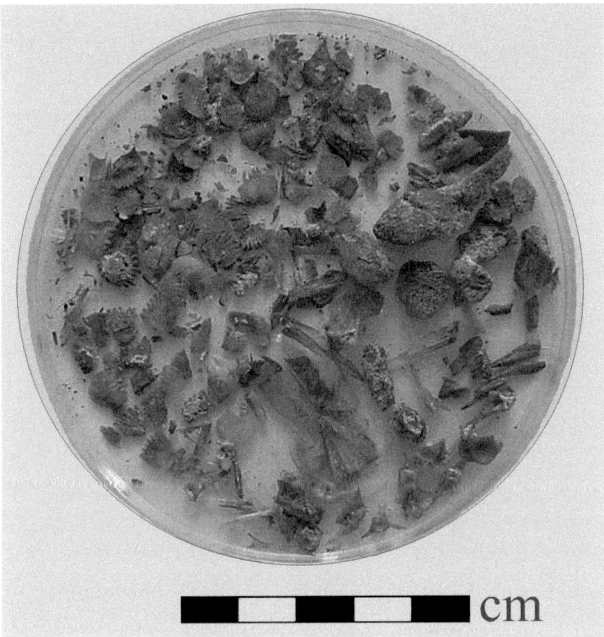

Fig. 7. Fish bones from coprolites

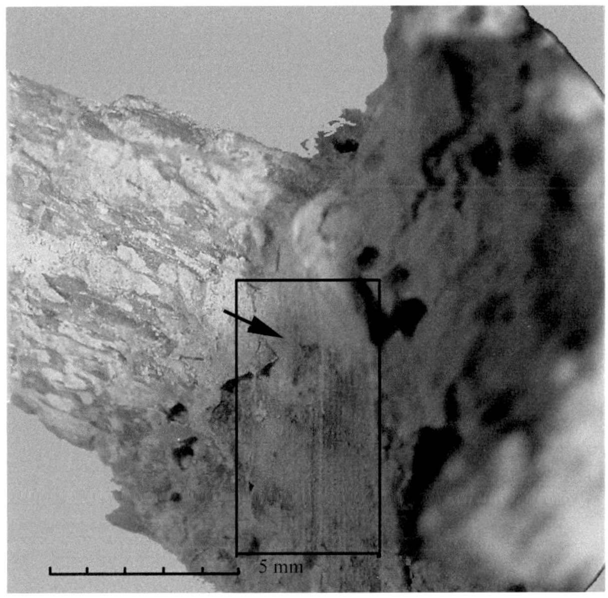

Fig. 8. Impression of a cereal blade in a coprolite

Table 2. Mammal bones gnawed by dogs in the archaeozoological materials from Asva

Species	***Scapula***	***Humerus***	***Ulna***	***Radius***	***Ossa carpi***	***Ossa metacarpalia***	***Ossa coxae***	***Femur***	***Patella***	***Tibia***	***Ossa tarsi***	***Ossa metatarsalia***	***Ossa metapodiale***	***Phalanges***
Bos taurus	1	3	1	–	1	2	1	–	1	1	6	1	–	1
Capra hircus / Ovis aries	–	3	2	9	–	2	–	1	–	–	2	2	–	–
Sus scrofa domesticus	3	2	3	–	–	–	–	1	–	1	–	–	–	–
Equus caballus	2	–	–	–	1	2	–	–	–	–	3	–	2	4
Alces alces	–	–	1	–	–	–	–	–	–	–	–	–	–	1
Sus scrofa ferus	–	–	–	–	–	–	–	–	–	–	–	1	–	–

Certainly, we could possibly conclude that the analysed coprolites incidentally originate from a season when no seal hunting took place, but the seal bone remains found at the site were also without marks from dog's teeth. It is possible that dogs did not like oily seal meat, but preferred some *terrestrial* animal. As shown in Table 2, in the Asva assemblage there were cattle, horse and elk bones, as well as long bones from sheep/goat and pig, which were marked by dogs teeth. Surely, parts of these bones, especially fragments of epiphyses, were present in the coprolites, but in the process of chewing and digestion they were shattered into small pieces and were therefore unidentifiable. While fish bones collected from Asva during excavation belong mainly to bigger fish, analyses of coprolites shows that smaller fish species were caught and brought to the site as well.

Acknowledgments

The author wishes to thank Estonian Science Foundation (grant no 5098), target-financed project no. AI0042476s03 and Liis Soon who translated the paper.

References

Indreko, R. 1939a. Asva linnus-asula. *Muistse Eesti linnused*, 17–52.

Indreko, R. 1939b. Aruanne kaevamiste kohta Asva linnus-asulal **10**. VI–15. VIII 1939. *Manuscript in Institute of History*, Tallinn.

Jaanits, L., Laul, S., Lõugas, V. and Tõnisson, E. 1982. Eesti Esiajalugu: Tallinn.

Lepiksaar, J. 1940. Gröõni hüljesest, *Phoca groenlandica* Erxl., Läänemeres tema uue leiu puhul pronksiaegsest asulast Asvas, Saaremaal. *Eesti Loodus* **2**, 87–90.

Lõugas, L. 1991. Sekundaarne tanatotsönoos Asva (Saaremaa) muistses asulakohas. Diploma Thesis. Manuscript in Institute of Zoology and Hydrobiology, University of Tartu.

Lõugas, L. 1997. Post-glacial development of vertebrate fauna in Estonian waterbodies. A palaeozoological study. *Dissertationes Biologicae Universitatis Tartuensis*, **32**.

Lõugas, V. 1970. Eesti varane metalliaeg (II a.-tuh. keskpaigast e.m.a.–1. sajandini m.a.j.). Dissertation. Manuscript in Institute of History, Tallinn.

Maldre, L. 2004. Aruanne Asva asulast 1939. aastal kogutud loomaluudest. Manuscript in Institute of History, Tallinn.

Paaver, K. L. 1965. Formirovanie teriofauny i izmenchivost mlekopitajuschih Pribaltiki v golotsene. Tartu.

Tsalkin, V. I. 1952. Novye dannye o rasprostranenii grenlandskogo tjulenia. *Bull. MOIP, biol.* **57/9**, 81–83.

Vassar, A. 1955. Ukreplennoje poselenie Asva na ostrove Saaremaa. In: *Muistsed asulad ja linnused*, 113–137.

Liina Maldre
Institute of History
Rüütli 6
EE-10130 Tallinn
Estonia

liina17@mail.ee

9th ICAZ Conference, Durham 2002
Dogs and People in Social, Working, Economic or Symbolic Interaction
(eds Lynn M. Snyder and Elizabeth A. Moore) pp. 49–61

7. What Do Dogs Mean? What Do Dogs Do? Symbolism, Instrumentality, and Ritual in Afro-Cuban Religion

Michael Atwood Mason and Lynn M. Snyder

Many African and African-based religions rely on animals and animal symbolism as key constituents of their rituals. Taking a contemporary Washington, D.C. ritual installation as a starting point, the role of animals, and particularly dogs, in religious ritual is explored as well the potential archaeological signatures of these rituals. Starting with a single dog skull and tail, plus the bones of a number of other animals found in the Washington deposit, this paper reviews similar historical deposits documented in the archaeological literature of the African Diaspora and several modern contemporary ngangas *(religious altar assemblages), then explores their meanings via ethnographic data on Afro-Cuban religion. In their many rituals, Afro-Cuban religions, with their origins in Central and West Africa, routinely employ a wide range of animals, both as sacrifices whose blood feeds the spirits and as ingredients in magical "works" designed to direct the spirits and influence human behavior. Closely associated with deities of the forest, dogs appear frequently both in offerings and in "works". While exploring the meanings assigned to dogs can provide interesting information, the importance of dogs only becomes clear when their instrumentality comes to the fore. For practitioners of Afro-Cuban religions, it is the dog's agency – as a living animal or as a spiritual presence maintained through remains – that makes the difference.*

Introduction

Beginning in the 16th century, and continuing until the legal end of slavery in the United States at the end of the American Civil War, as many as 15 million people from West and Central Africa were forcefully removed from their homes and sent to the Americas as slaves (Joyner 2003: 11; Singleton and Bograd 1995: 5–12). These peoples, coming from many different areas of the African continent, from different homelands and cultures, brought with them diverse but often related belief systems, complete with rituals and iconography.

During the Atlantic Slave Trade, nearly one million of these enslaved Africans were carried to Cuba, close to half of them arriving between 1780 and 1840. Because of laws and social practices in the Cuban Colony, African peoples congregated according to roughly defined African ethnicities and continued their religious traditions. With time, their religions became widespread in Cuba. "Congo" people from Bantu-speaking groups brought heterogeneous traditions which they forged into the religion now called Palo Monte or Palo Mayombe. Yoruba-speaking people's traditions took the form of Santería, also known as the *Regla de Ocha*. Together with the secret society known as Abakuá, Roman Catholic beliefs and symbols, and the symbols of nationhood deployed first by Spain and later the Cuban republic, these religions are mutually constitutive (Brown, D. 2003: 3–8). So long have these traditions coexisted that they make constant reference to each other's symbols and divinities, and many practitioners today actively embrace both traditions (see Bettelheim 2001). These Afro-Cuban religious traditions have continued to exist and evolve, and as Afro-Cuban peoples moved on to North, South and Central America, they have carried with them their cultures and belief systems.

Recovery and study of the archaeological manifestations of these belief systems in historical contexts, often enigmatic and subtle elements in the larger context of African-American archaeological locations, have been generally recognized only relatively recently. The interpretation of these materials and contexts have also developed relatively recently, as archaeologists, anthropologists and ethnologists have looked to the traditions and literature of groups of the African diaspora as well as traditions in their original African homelands. In this paper, we also explore an additional source of contextual meaning, through the analysis of a number of modern religious installations, or *ngangas*, from the eastern United States. Originally unintentionally discovered and reported, these installations were carefully removed from their original and active contexts, studied, and conserved by anthropologists and archaeologists. Dogs remains are often a part of these installations, and the rich iconography and material aspects of these deposits, plus a consideration of the religious belief systems of modern practitioners of Afro-Cuban religions allows us to explore in depth the complex relationships between these belief systems and their natural environments, including the symbolic importance, instrumentality and agency of domestic dogs.

Archaeological evidence of African and African-American religions

In a reflective consideration of African-American archaeology, Singleton and Bograd (1995) noted that from an early interest in "descriptive studies of living conditions" of enslaved African-Americans, often in plantation settings, there has been a shift in more recent scholarship toward "addressing questions concerning class relationships, planter dominance and slave resistance" and wider studies of ethnicity, landscape interpretation and use, and gender studies. Previous archaeological research concerning Africans in America and the African Diaspora had concentrated primarily on materials analysis, exploration of plantation life and labor, living conditions, housing and spatial relationships, foodways, and artifact patterns. More recently, they note, studies have expanded to include exploration of belief systems though the analysis of "the social and symbolic contexts of artifacts," (Singleton and Bograd 1995: 13–34). Included in this re-focus has been a developing recognition of the role of religion in the lives of African-Americans, carried to the Americas as part of the living culture and belief systems of enslaved Africans, as well as archaeological recognition of the material manifestations of these evolved and evolving belief systems (see, for example, such studies as Fennell 2000, 2003; Wilkie 1995, 1997; and the papers in Franklin and McKee (eds) 2004). In an effort to move these research agendas forward, many archaeologists have focused on material evidence of different ethnic identities among enslaved Africans and their descendants and of ritual and religious activity, as one of the most material manifestations of belief systems.

In these studies, attention has often focused on contexts and material objects which appear to have religious or ritual significance. Materials often identified as related to ritual and religious expressions by enslaved Africans or African-Americans include cowrie and other shells, glass and natural crystals, pierced, etched and unmodified coins, reshaped ceramic sherds, European crystal and glass beads, Native American chipped and ground stone objects, small pebbles, and a number of common household items such as spoons and marbles, etched with "Xs" or other symbols (Davison 2004; Ferguson 1992; Leone and Fry 1999; Orser 1994; Patten 1992; Pearce 1993; Russell 1997; Singleton 1991, 1995; Wilkie 1997; Young 1996). In most instances, these objects have been attributed to ritual use based on locational and contextual evidence and comparison with ethnographic and ethnohistoric and contemporary accounts of ritual and religious practices in West Africa and among enslaved and freed African Americans and modern religions of the African diaspora (c.f. Brown, K. 2004; Davidson 2004; Fennell 2000, 2003).

A conjurers/healers house, Bazoria County, Texas, 19th Century

One of the most thoroughly studied sites at which material evidence of the ritual activities and material symbolism of enslaved and free African Americans has been recognized is the Levi Jordan Plantation in Brazoria County, Texas (Brown and Cooper 1990; Brown, K. 1994, 2003, 2004; Bruner 1996; Garcia-Herreros 1998; Barnes 1999; Harris 1999). At its production height, this large sugar and cotton plantation, founded by Jordan in 1848, had a slave population of over 140 individuals. In addition, from 1865 through 1891, as many as 100 Freedmen lived and worked on the plantation as tenants and sharecroppers, many of them continuing to occupy the former slave quarter buildings. Individual buildings or portions of buildings in the area of the slave and tenant community have produced evidence of the presence of a number of occupation specialists including "a conjurer/mid-wife, carver, hunter, seamstress, blacksmith, and carpenter" (Brown, K. 2003: 100). In one of these buildings, the conjurer/midwife's cabin, deposits were found which have been interpreted as remains of a "curing kit", and an "*Nkisi*", the latter being a collection of objects used in religious rituals by the BiKongo peoples of West Africa (Brown, K. 2003, Fennell 2003). Along with two other small distinct deposits of objects found in the same cabin, they physically form the four cardinal points of a cosmogram, again conforming to ritual symbolism and practices with parallels in West Africa.

On the west side of the cabin, in the area of the doorway, two cast iron kettles were found standing upright, one inside the other, with parts of a third, broken kettle placed on top. The bottom most kettle contained a layer of ash, the upper one objects of metal, shells, glass, small bone fragments and soil. Wrapped around these kettles was a length of heavy iron chain. The excavators also recognized what they have characterized as "two 'lines' of artifacts" which "radiated out" from the kettles

Fig. 1. Location of the nganga *in Rock Creek Park, Washington, D.C. Palo Monte practitioners often bury their altars in wooded areas like this one. This location, however, is somewhat indiscrete as it is located very close to the Park's Nature Center and Equestrian Center. Photograph by Malcolm L. Richardson for the Smithsonian Institution*

(Brown, K. 2003: 102). Included in these lines, which extended to the northeast and southeast, were a number of heavy iron or metal objects (hinge, spikes, bolt, plow fragment, chain, bayonet), Confederate military buttons, shells, a quartz crystal and large bone fragments. While these radiating lines and the kettles appear to form parts of the cosmogram, the contents of the kettles and radiating lines (particularly the many metal objects), as well as the use of the cast iron kettles as ritual containers, suggests that this may represent an *amula* (Brown, K. 2003) or *nganga* composed of objects associated with the Afro-Cuban deity of Yoruba origins known as Orisha Ogún. Thus, the excavators note, the deposits in this cabin may represent a mixture of materials, symbolism and ritual from two West African traditions, the BiKongo and the Yoruba. Although animal bones are noted in this and other religious contexts at Levi Jordan, their identifications are not reported, nor is the possible ritual significance of the animal bones discussed.

Havana, Cuba latrine deposit, 16th century

A singular archaeological deposit containing human bones has been reported from Havana, Cuba. In 1997, archaeologists from the Archaeology Department of the Office of the Historian of the City of Havana excavated a property dating to the sixteenth century located at Calle Obrapía No.55. Lisette Roura Álvarez lead the team under the direction of Roger Arrazcaeta Delgado, the director of the Department. In their very diverse excavations, they discovered an intriguing deposit in a latrine in the house: three infant skeletons, five adult crania, and 2 mandibles were clearly buried together at the same depth and in an obvious cruciform pattern. The latrine had evidence of use in the mid-nineteenth century, and the American Commission ordered their cleaning and sealing in 1900. These human remains were deposited with two large iron rods, one approximately 90 cm and the other 43 cm in length. They were also accompanied by small bird bones, but no other animal bones were reported. Among their hypotheses about this deposit, the archaeologists included the possibility that it represented some sort of religious activity linked to the Bantu-based Afro-Cuban religion Palo Monte. (Roura Álvarez 2003).

Modern ritual installations, *ngangas*

The literature on archaeological deposits of African-American religious significance rarely reports the presence of associated animal bone. This may well be

Fig. 2. Cauldron found in the Rock Creek Park nganga, *Washington, D.C. The three-footed cauldron is a widespread and powerful symbol in Afro-Cuban imagery. Its domestic qualities of enduring fire and heat, containing important substances, and transforming the raw into the cooked all come into play in Palo Monte. Photograph by Kari Bruwelheide, Smithsonian Institution*

because of the very enigmatic nature of the deposits themselves, which are often found within homes, slave quarters or other structures, contexts which may contain a mix of non-related faunal debris. In contrast, historical and contemporary *ngangas* from Central Africa, Cuba and the United States make extensive use of birds, wild animals, domesticated animals and especially dogs. In these deposits, both the physical remains of the animals, in the form of select skeletal remains, and material representations of dogs document their importance.

The Rock Creek Park Nganga, *Washington, D.C., 2000*

Rock Creek Park is a narrow ribbon of public park land along both sides of a perennial creek which runs through the northern sections of Washington D.C. On April 29, 2000 a woman reported to the metropolitan police department that while walking in the park her dog had detected and unearthed bones which she believed were human, as well as a number of metal objects. After inspecting the site (Fig. 1), a narrow erosional gully leading to the creek bed itself, police investigators asked the Smithsonian Institution's Department of Anthropology for help in recovery and documentation of the human bones and associated deposit. Field investigations by Dr. Doug Owsley and a Smithsonian scientific crew consisted of surface survey and recovery, plus screening of all soil removed during excavation of the remainder of the deposit. Following excavation the entire contents of the deposit were taken to the Anthropology Department of the Smithsonian Institution, National Museum of Natural History, where they were cleaned, examined and identified (Owsley and Richardson 2000, Owsley and Bruwelheide 2000).

The majority of objects associated with the deposit were contained in a large iron pot or cauldron (Fig. 2) with embossed lettering reading "FABRICO PORTUGAL". A number of objects, and one human tibia segment were recovered from the area near the deposit; careful excavation and water-screening of the soil in the area also produced a human skull fragment, coins, beads, candles and metal objects. Placed near the pot were one large and one small terracotta saucer, both containing additional items, and a machete. The pot itself was also filled with

Fig. 3. A manufactured bow and arrow "tool" form from the Rock Creek Park nganga, *Washington, D.C. This form has been enhanced with string in some kind of "spiritual work". Photograph by Kari Bruwelheide, Smithsonian Institution*

Fig. 4. Iron objects from the nganga *in Rock Creek Park, Washington, D.C. Photograph by Kari Bruwelheide, Smithsonian Institution*

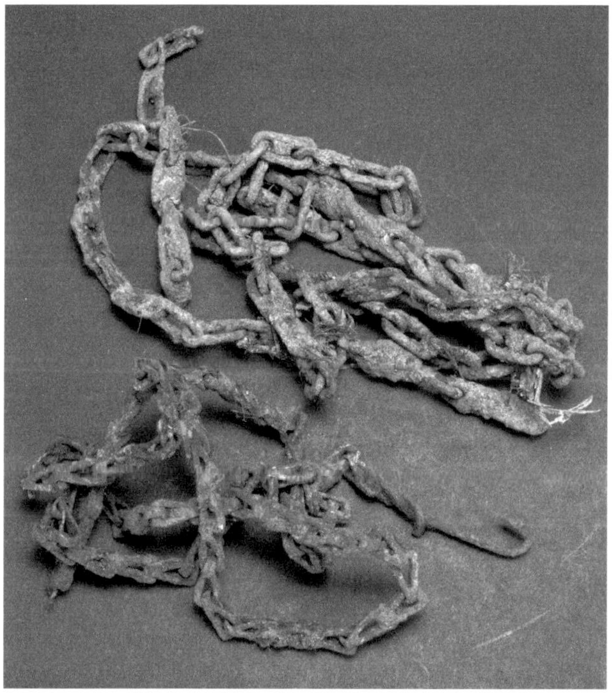

Fig. 5. Chains from the nganga *in Rock Creek Park, Washington, D.C. These chains are encrusted with dirt, but they and other ordinary iron objects were originally placed in the assemblage to enhance the presence of Sarabanda, the deity associated with all things iron. Photograph by Kari Bruwelheide, Smithsonian Institution*

Fig. 6. Massed coins from the nganga *in Rock Creek Park, Washington, D.C. Palo Monte practitioners place coins in their altar assemblages because as metal objects they reflect durability and because their presence is thought to draw money and wealth. Photograph by Kari Bruwelheide, Smithsonian Institution*

objects, including bones (human and animal), feathers, iron fragments and objects (Fig. 3), coins, strings of beads and metal jewelry, modified and unmodified shells, wooden sticks and lengths of bamboo, cloth and cloth pouches, strings, bundles of thread, and candles. Beads of mercury were also observed. Metal objects, primarily of iron, included a number of horseshoes and railroad spikes (Fig. 4), lengths of chain (Fig. 5), nails, keys, switchblades and razor blades. Over 300 coins were found (Fig. 6). The majority were small denomination US currency, with lesser numbers of Mexican, Nicaraguan, Canadian, Barbadian, French, Italian and Haitian issue. A single Metro-Dade County transit token was also found. Several strings of yellow, blue and black beads were recovered, as well as one thin gold chain necklace and two finger rings.

Fig. 7. Cut sticks from the nganga *in Rock Creek Park, Washington, D.C. Giving specific natural powers to the* nganga, *different kinds of woods and herbs are placed inside the container. In fact, the religion gets its name from these sticks (*palos *in Spanish). Photograph by Kari Bruwelheide, Smithsonian Institution*

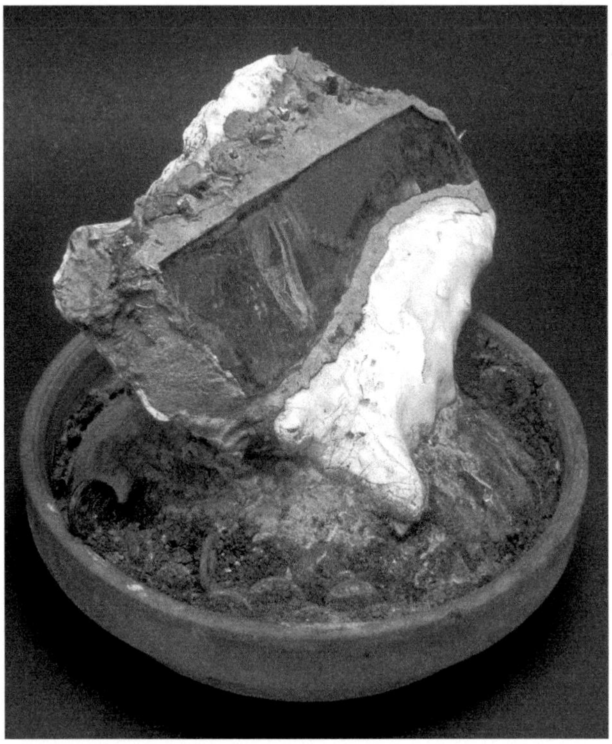

Fig. 8. Conch shell compound object from the nganga *in Rock Creek Park, Washington, D.C. This conch shell, "charged" with natural ingredients and sealed with cement, is a manifestation of the Palo Monte trickster and messenger deity called Lucero Mundo. The mirror is a common element in Palo, thought to facilitate vision into the spirit world. Photograph by Kari Bruwelheide, Smithsonian Institution*

Other perishable objects included a number of cut sticks (Fig. 7) and a halved and inscribed gourd of the calabash family (*Crescentia* sp.), which had been lined with paper and contained a concreted mass of coins. The human bones contained in this deposit (including one complete and one partial skull and several limb bone segments) were all non-associated skeletal elements apparently gathered from previous burials and/or autopsy specimens. Two metal femoral head hip replacements had also been placed in the *nganga*. Although the precise origins of these elements could not be determined, none appeared to represent recent burials or deaths (Owsley and Bruwelheide 2000).

Animals were well represented in this assemblage. Several small clam (*Linga pennsylvanica*) valves were found. Two larger shells, both conches (*Cymbiola vespertilio*, and *Strombus gigis*) formed the bases of larger compound objects (Fig. 8). The bones and feathers of a number of birds were found in the deposit. At least 11 domestic chickens (*Gallus gallus*) skulls were found. Feathers of domestic chickens were found adhering to a number of items in the *nganga*, and a number of helmeted guineafowl (*Numida meleagris*) primary feathers were also recovered. Three fighting cocks or roosters were represented by the nearly complete skeletons of two animals with fully developed, spurred tarsometatarsi, plus a third paired of isolated tarsometatarsi. Two additional, non-domestic birds were represented by single elements. These included a right proximal humerus of a turkey vulture (*Cathartes aura*) and the left distal femur of a crested caracara (*Polyborus plancus*). The turkey vulture has a wide distribution throughout the Americas, where it is considered a common scavenger. The crested caracara, an opportunistic feeder on both carrion and smaller live prey, is widespread in Central and South America, but has a much more restricted North American range, occurring in only limited areas of the Texas gulf coast and southern Florida where conservation programs have been instituted (Del Hoyo *et al*. 1994; Dove and Banks 1999; Morrison 2001).

A number of mammals were represented in the assemblage primarily by head and foot elements. White-

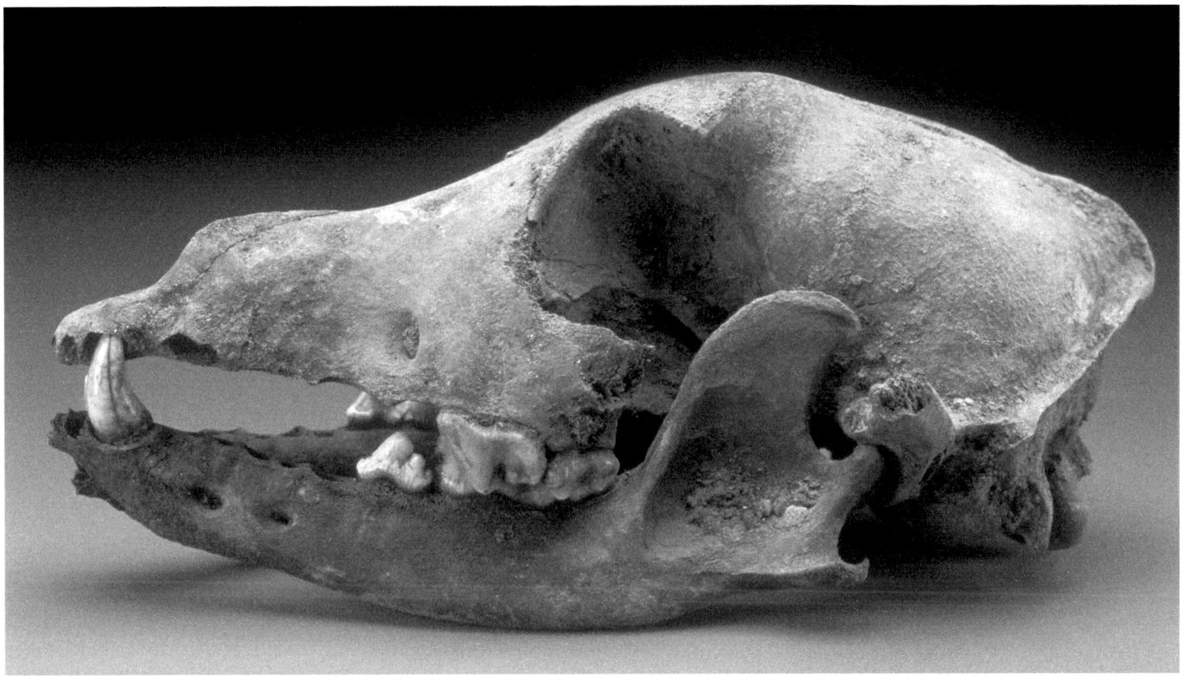

Fig. 9. Dog skull from the nganga *in Rock Creek Park, Washington, D.C. This skull was accompanied by associated mandibles, and articulating vertebrae of the tail. No cut marks indicating death by decapitation were found on the skull, however this animal may have been sacrificed and offered as food for the entities of the* nganga. *Photograph by Kari Bruwelheide, Smithsonian Institution*

tailed deer (*Odocoileus virginianus*) elements were limited to four sets of antlers, three of which had been sawn free of the skull. The fourth pair were still articulated by a portion of the frontal, and appear to have been professionally mounted for wall display. One set of deer lower legs and feet (left and right carpals/tarsals, metapodials and phalanges) had also been placed in the pot. A single domestic goat (*Capra hircus*) toe (articulating 2nd and 3rd phalanges) was found, as was an unsided deer, sheep or goat hyoid which appeared to have been cut through the distal portion of the diaphysis. Several smaller mammals were represented in the *nganga* by cranial materials only. These included a young domestic cat or kitten (*Felis domesticus*), a woodchuck (*Marmota monax*) and a long-tailed macaque (*Macaca fascicularis*). Elements of a small mammal foot, consistent in size with the young cat or kitten were also recovered, suggesting that one paw of the kitten may also have been included in the deposit. While the skulls of the kitten and woodchuck were whole and unaltered, the macaque skull had been sectioned, and appeared to be from an animal which had been necropsied.

One domestic dog (*Canis familiaris*) was represented by the skull (Fig. 9) and mandibles of a medium sized animal, plus eight articulating caudal vertebrae. The caudal vertebrae are consistent in size with the skull and mandibles, suggesting that both the head and tail of a single adult dog were placed in the deposit.

After cleaning and examination of the deposit's contents it was concluded that this installation was an *nganga*, constructed within the parameters of the contemporary Afro-Cuban tradition known as Palo Monte (discussed in more detail in the next sections of this paper). The *nganga* is a container of myriad natural forces, the focus of ritual attention, the seat of a divinity and associated ancestral spirits, and an icon of Palo Monte. The characteristic large iron cauldron contains small samples of natural forces like plants, animals, earths, and metals. The central figure within Palo Monte is Sarabanda, who rules all things iron. Thus the many metal implements and the coins link this deposit to him. As an initiate accumulates knowledge and power in the tradition, he or she will gather small but important bits of the natural world and deposit them into the *nganga*. The many animals represent just these sorts of additions. Over time, the *nganga* becomes a microcosm of the entire natural world.

Potomac River nganga, *Washington, D.C. 2001*

In the spring of 2001, the Park Police contacted Mason about an assemblage of objects deposited in the Potomac River near the 14th Street bridge. A National Park Service work crew removing trash and other debris from the edge of the river noticed a skull in the water and called

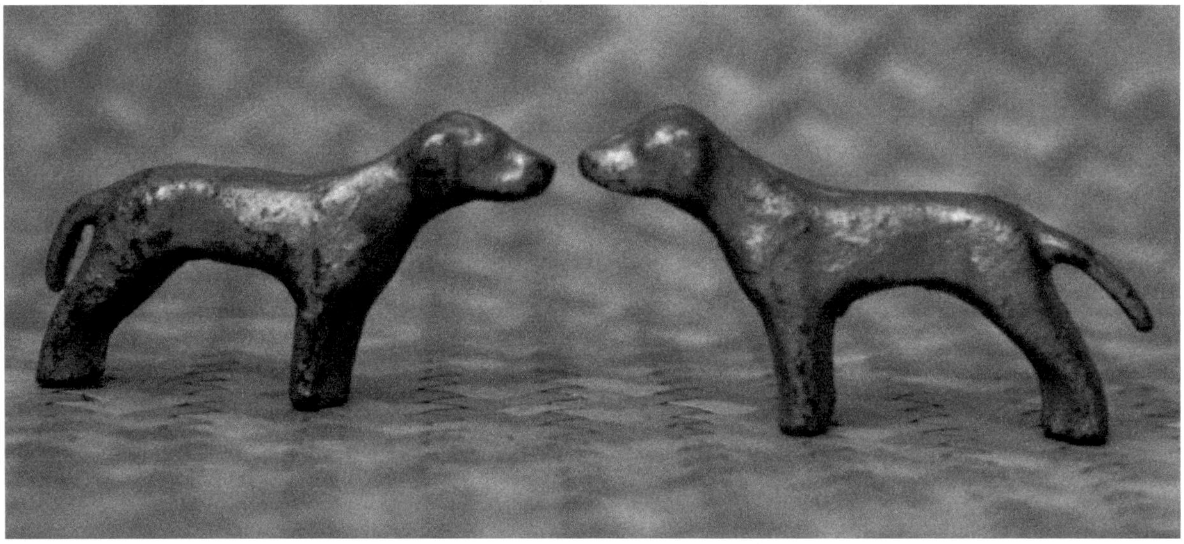

Fig. 10. Small dog sculptures of an unidentified "white metal". Such figures are often placed in the sacred vessels of the Afro-Cuban deities Ochosi and Babalú-Ayé. Photograph by Michael Atwood Mason, 2002

the Park Police. They in turn called in divers to retrieve the skull and the objects around it. These objects included: a human long bone; a large cast-iron cauldron; hundreds of nails, railroad spikes, coins, knives, chains, and other pieces of iron; cowry shells; lead dog figurines; white metal figurines; polished stones; chunks of white coral; a beaded horn; multicolored beaded necklaces; several small metal vessels topped with metal rooster figurines and one with a dog figurine; and a dead rooster with its neck cut but its head not removed. The District of Columbia Medical Examiner took possession of all skeletal remains and Mason retrieved the other objects. The cauldron, iron pieces, and knives strongly suggest a *prenda* or *nganga*. The necklaces, stones, white coral pieces, metal figurines, and vessels all play a role in the Afro-Cuban religion the *Regla de Ocha*, better known as *Santería* (see below for more discussion of these traditions). The vessels with the figurines each represent a single individual in that religion, so they suggest a whole family's altar is included here. The exsanguinated rooster with its head attached reflects common sacrificial practices for the ancestors in Santería. Despite these facts, it is difficult to make sense of how and why this installation was deposited in the river. To date, the skeletal remains found with this *nganga* have not been examined in detail, but the possible or probable inclusion of animal bones cannot be excluded.

Lindhurst, N. J. nganga, *1985*

In October of 1985, the Chief of Enforcement for the Bergen County Society for the Prevention of Cruelty to Animals notified researcher David H. Brown of an assemblage in Lindhurst, N.J. Someone walking a dog through the Meadowlands discovered a muddy hole in which were deposited a great many objects. The assemblage in this hole had been covered with several dead chickens, and a box found nearby contained evidence which suggested that it had been used to transport and store the birds. After discussions with Brown in which he explained the workings of the *nganga* in Palo Monte, the SPCA misguidedly staked out the site on Halloween night, but no sacrificers appeared. Brown returned to the site in November and over two days recovered the major elements of the deposit. The assemblage included chains, iron balls, railroad spikes, horseshoes, magnets, and a myriad of coins. Two bovid horns were also recovered. One white horn was wrapped in red cloth; a black horn had 7 scalpels embedded around the open proximal end of the cut element. The deposit also contained many cut sticks, abundant bird skulls, the long bones of domestic farm animals, and one dog skull. The only human bone was a human skullcap. Cigar butts, candle stubs, and tourist statues with candles burned on top as well as the dead chickens evidenced regular sacrifice. Based on his knowledge of Palo Monte, Brown is convinced that this assemblage was an *nganga* belonging to Sarabanda, the leading deity in Palo Monte.

What Do Dogs Mean in Afro-Cuban Religion?

Religions of the African diaspora

The primary religions of the African diaspora in Cuba, and their later expressions in the United States, Palo Monte or Palo Mayombe of the Bantu-speaking Congo groups, and Santería of the Yoruba, are symbolically complex and philosophically subtle. Practitioners worship a Supreme God who created the universe. Called

Olodumare, Olofi, or Olorun in the *Regla de Ocha*, he is thought to be essentially uninvolved in human affairs, but left the universe in the hands of a vast pantheon of divinities, called *orichas* or *santos* (saints). Along with these deities are ancestors and spirits of the dead, called *espíritus* or *egun*. Palo too imagines the universe as comprised of a Supreme God called Nsambi, Nsambia, or Sambia; a large number of divinities associated with nature, called *npungus* or *mpungus*, and ancestral spirits. Palo ceremonies move between the *npungus* and the ancestors, often seeming to fuse the two in practice. In Afro-Cuban religion the various beings constantly influence people as they live in the world, and many ceremonies focus human worship upon them. These ceremonies focus on exchange and communication between spirits and people. In spirit possession, spirits briefly inhabit human bodies. In divination, spirits speak to people to orient them and guide their actions.

In sacrifice, people respond to the spirits, giving them food, drink, and not infrequently animal blood. A number of animals are considered appropriate for sacrifice to the deities or orishas of Santeria, Palo Monte and other religious sects of the Caribbean/American Africa diaspora, including sheep, goats, and a number of birds of which chickens and fighting cocks are by far the most common (Bascom 1952; Murphy 1993; Pollak-Eltz 1993).

Fig. 11. Image of San Lazaro. This statue of St. Lazarus graces the dining room of an Afro-Cuban religious house in Washington, D.C. One dog can be seen licking the sores of the mendicant saint. Photograph by Michael Atwood Mason, 2002

The role of dogs in these religions

While animals figure prominently in sacrifice, they also play an important role in the iconography of many of the divinities in both traditions. These animals frequently include dogs. It should be noted from the outset that Afro-Cuban religion tends to use animals in much the same way as many African cultures. "By close observation and study of animal habits and conduct" (Reinhardt 1982), Africans have used the natural world as a model for their own. Like many traditionally minded Africans, Afro-Cuban religious "see animals as teachers of useful arts and crafts, as models for faithful family behavior and social conduct, and as metaphors of magical transformation and the manipulation of supernatural powers" (Lifschitz 1982:2).

Of special importance, animals that move effortlessly through different realms are thought to have strong spiritual connections (Lifschitz 1982: 3). The dog is one of these spiritually connected animals. Afro-Cuban "lived religion" marks off a series of interrelated but distinct domains (Brown D. 1999; see Hall 1997 passim). The *casa* – house – is contrasted with the street, *la calle*. The house represents the most intimate domain, where families are formed and nurtured and where tranquility ideally rules. Beyond the house lies the street, the more active and dangerous space where people make and lose their fortunes. The street also carries one to other houses, and beyond to the forest, the *monte* where sacred plants, wild animals, and strong spirits dwell. In fact, these domains have names in the African-based ritual lexicons used in Cuba. For example, in the *Regla de Ocha*, the house is called the *ilé*, the street *ona*, and the forest *odé*. The dog moves with relative freedom between these domains, living in the house as a pet but never losing its instinctual gregarious urge to be exploring out in the street. Similarly, the dog roams out into the *monte* to seek food and to assist human hunters. In the Afro-Cuban religious imagination, dogs live anywhere, but rule the street and accompany important spirits into the forest.

Practical and scholarly students of Afro-Cuban religion both benefit from the very elaborate corpus of sacred stories, legends, and proverbs deployed in Santería divination rituals (Mason 2002, chapter 2). There are many proverbs in the corpus that refer to dogs and their qualities. Many refer to their loyalty; for example, the divination sign called Osá-Odí says, "If you feed someone else's dog, you lose the bread and the dog." This proverb suggests that a person should attend to his or her own issues and relationships before focusing outside the home. The sign Iroso-Odí says, "The dog is loyal but betrays its master." This and other proverbs refer to loyal followers or family members encumbering a person despite their

Fig. 12. Palo Monte altar, Havana, Cuba. This altar shows the variety of containers and offerings which compose such installations. Photograph by Michael Atwood Mason, 2003

good intentions. Still another sign says, "He who knows the guard dog will not be discovered." Another sign, Ogunda-Eyioco, says, "A dreaming dog will remain a dog" and the sign Obara-Odí says "A dog has four legs but takes a single path." This last proverb is by far the most common evocation of the dog in the religion and in daily life in Cuba. These proverbs evoke the focus, or lack thereof, that dogs exhibit in different contexts. Taken together, they portray dual aspects of the dog: The dog can be a loyal companion or a betrayer. The dog can dream or be focused.

More naturally, the normal physical characteristics of the dog also augment this more culturally based representation. The dog has strong, sharp teeth. The dog can follow strong scents. The dog has a voracious sexual appetite when the time is right. Dogs show remarkable loyalty to the strong animals and people in their lives, and dogs are often docile and just as often fierce.

Dogs in Santería iconography and sacrifice

In Santería's religious iconography, dogs are exclusively associated with male orichas with strong connections to the outdoors. Always first comes the oricha Echu-Elegguá, the trickster and messenger of the other orichas. He owns the street and the road, the *camino*, a key metaphor for the individual's movement through social circumstances and life more generally. An open road carries blessings and a closed road suggests little progress and ultimately stagnation and death. There are many ritual cleansing rituals done with the authority of Echu which directly implicate dogs. In these rituals, a priest will place meat and other ingredients in paper and then rub a person with the package to cleanse him or her of negative forces. This bundle is then thrown into to the street with the express understanding that a dog will carry it away, thus carrying away the negativity. Similarly, after ritual meals—and even after family dinners in some houses—a little bit of all the food remaining on the table is placed on a plate. This food is then carried out to the street and dumped in the gutter to feed Echu. As a Havana elder recently explained to Mason, "We feed the dog and thus feed Echu, so Echu will also give us food." These laconic interpretive remarks are common in Santería and show the logic of the religious act. By sharing with the oricha, people seek the oricha's favor and future blessings.

Echu's brother Ochosi is the quintessential hunter and always has dogs on his altars. As a hunter, he moves from the house into the street and then into the woods and his dogs move with him. He is famous for his ability to sense changes in the natural environment. He is calm and focused and embodies the proverbial wisdom: A dog has four legs but takes only one path.

Similarly, his other brother Ogún is a blacksmith who also uses dogs to hunt. At various times, he has disappeared in the forest and he is thought to know its secrets. The dogs that accompany him can be seen as a manifestation of his brother or as normal companions for a hunter who must find, flush out, and retrieve game in the dense tropical forest. Here the street has led to the world of the forest. The dogs are functional, almost like the metal tools for which Ogún is famous, but at the same time they remind people of the oricha's loyal character. The dogs sleep in the forge, but then follow their master Ogún out on the hunt and help him successfully negotiate the forest. Again, dogs move through different realms and in close relationship with a male oricha.

Interestingly, Ogún is associated with dogs but his iconography does not include them. There is one mythic narrative, or *patakí* (a word from Lucumí, the ritual dialect of Yoruba spoken in Cuba), that explains his loss of ownership over dogs. It is said that Ogún lost his dogs when Changó, the regal oricha, took them from him and gave them to Babalú-Ayé, the wandering oricha of infectious disease and healing.

Unlike Ogún, Babalú-Ayé always has dogs with him. There are two small lead dogs that are among his sacred objects (Fig. 10), whether visible or not. He is closely associated with the Roman Catholic St. Lazarus (Fig. 11), and his image includes this same pair of canines. While the iconography comes from the mendicant saint, it serves clear functions in the world of the orichas. Babalú wanders the roads for years in near solitude, accompanied only by his dogs. Here again, the dogs points to loyalty, but also to a survival instinct, as they live in the street and journey the road. They suffer the injustices of their master, but they remain true. Similarly, the dogs lick his wounds and are thought to provide some solace to his painful lesions, be they from leprosy or smallpox, a detail on which the myths do not agree. With Babalú, another aspect of the dog's behavior comes to the fore: the licking of wounds to heal them. This healing function is Babalú's primary responsibility in the pantheon. Here again the dog echoes the character of the oricha with whom it is associated.

So close, in fact, is the relationship between Babalú-Ayé and dogs that one manifestation of the oricha is thought to have the body of a person and the head of a dog. Called Adú-Kaké, this Babalú is said to bite people when he possesses a follower. Babalú-Ayé priest Pedro Abreu of Havana claims this Babalú cannot be consecrated without sacrificing a dog to him.

As the leading priest of Babalú in Havana, Abreu represents Babalú in the social world, and once a year Abreu impersonates a dog in a key public ritual. On December 31st, the senior diviners of Cuba gather in Havana to divine the will of the orichas for the coming year. As part of this ritual, Abreu orchestrates a cleansing ritual with Babalú for all present. At a key moment before the sacrifice, Abreu gets down on his hands and knees and uses his head to nudge the vessel containing the sacred objects of Babalú into the middle of the floor where they will partake of the sacrifice. He is clearly canine in this moment and assumes the role of the attending dog for his master, Babalú-Ayé. "The dog can move Babalú this way or that way with his snout. Babalú loves his dog and so his dog can influence him," Abreu explained in 2001.

As mentioned earlier, dogs are used as sacrificial animals in Santería and in other Afro-Cuban religious traditions as well. In Santería, the smithing and hunting Ogún is the oricha who most commonly requires dogs as part of his sacrifices. In fact, the consecration of a priest of Ogún routinely involves the sacrifice of three dogs. First, the initiate and initiators travel to a railroad and feed the tracks with a dog and roosters. Second, they enter the woods and feed a dog to the sacred objects of Ogún in his sylvan abode. Finally, those objects are returned to the house where the principal initiation rites will transpire, and as part of those ceremonies, Ogún eats another dog. The skulls of these animals often hang around the shrine and altar objects of Ogún. Ironically, these rituals identify Ogún more closely with the dog than any other oricha, despite the fact that they are excluded from his official iconography.

There is an interesting entry in one typescript treatise on the secrets of the religion. This treatise – *tratado* – explained in great detail the ceremonial process for offering a dog sacrifice to the oricha Erinle. Erinle is another hunter who was displaced from the woods to the riverside by Ochosi. Erinle's iconography revolves around fish, but the tratado stresses that priests of Erinle and other knowledgeable practitioners used to perform this dog offering to Erinle quite commonly. It further explains that this was done because of Erinle's links to Ogún in a particular divination sign, Iroso-Ogunda. Research on this sign reveals no paradigmatic mythic story to explain this sacrifice, but several stories suggest that sacrificing a dog to Ogún in this sign is a common way to redress illness and social disorder.

Linkages between Santería and Palo Monte

In the Afro-Cuban religious sphere, practitioners frequently link Ogún with the most central *npungu* of Palo Monte know as Zarabanda. Both are fierce deities linked with the transformative and violent powers of iron and dogs. But what is going on when people offer dogs to orichas who already partake of their qualities? For some years, colleagues David H. Brown and Mason have been theorizing Afro-Cuban religion with an eye to exploring how ritual practices maintain the social presence of the orichas in the daily life of practitioners and how the altar objects become the central focus of the subjectivity of the orichas (Brown, D. 1996; Mason 2002).

By expanding the interpretive material we use to understand altar objects and installations beyond mythic narratives, Brown has presented the interrelationship between spiritual devotion and making altars. Mason has laid out how initiation in the religion creates long-term intersubjective experiences with spirits and orichas and changes individuals both psychologically and socially. Together they have articulated the idea that through ritual layering of specific items associated with the orichas – syndesis – their presence is instantiated in daily life. These presences represent highly valued moral persons within the social lifeworld, and people create intense, often connective, relationships with them. Another colleague working with Yoruba religious, David Doris has developed a provocative idea about Yoruba portraiture. Building on the widespread notion that much of Yoruba art represents moral personhood, he suggests that certain kinds of ritual works called *aalé* can be seen as portraits of people who embody the antithesis of Yoruba moral persons. These objects remind people what will befall them should them become thieves or criminals (Doris 2002).

It is suggestive and edifying to consider sacrifice as a part of an ongoing process of portraying the presence of the oricha. Ogún has the canine qualities of loyalty, focus, and dominion over several realms. To offer a dog – or three – serves to remind people of those qualities and to intensify the canine aspects of the oricha. The sacrifice makes Ogún – or Babalú or Erinle – more focused, more fierce, more aggressive. The oricha is more capable of sensing what cannot be seen, and thus the person serving the oricha benefits from these new powers.

Dogs in the ngangas *of Palo Monte*

In Palo Monte, the dog is an essential image of the power of the spirits. Every fully constituted altar (Fig. 12), called an *nganga* or *prenda* within the religion, takes the form of a large cauldron or terracotta pot filled with a wide variety of metonymic and syndetic objects and substances that practitioners say empower and direct the spirits living in the *nganga*. These ingredients inevitably include "a relic of the dead" like a skull, a tibia, some other human bone or dirt from a grave or cemetery; this "relic" locates the spirit within the *nganga* and provides its human caretaker with a way to interact with it. A great many sticks – the *palos* from which the tradition takes its name – are also indispensable. Cubans generally consider these altars and spirits aggressive and often turn to them for antisocial desires, commonly termed "*brujería*" or "witchcraft."

Another extraordinarily common ingredient is a dog or some part of its body – most commonly the head, paws, heart, and tail. In at least two of the modern installations described above, dog bones were present. By placing the dog's body parts into the *nganga*, the spirits therein take on its character. One Palo priest described the creation of an *nganga* this way more than 30 years ago:

> I put in ...the whole, dry head of a small, black, male dog so the *prenda* can smell, follow trails. The dog head is seated on top of the earths [from graves and other places] in the middle of the container... The jaw bone of the dead person is fitted inside the dog's head and around it sit the fingers of the hands and the toes of the feet... (Quoted in Cabrera 1983: 123; see also p. 125 for another account.)

Thus by intermingling the physical remains of the dog and the human being, the dog's attributes and those of the ancestor empowering the *nganga* merge. So important is the dog's head to the constitution of the *nganga* that specialty shops catering to these religious communities in the United States stock high quality dog skulls from osteological suppliers; for example, the popular online shop Folkcuba.com sells dog skulls purchased from Skulls Unlimited.

But some Palo practitioners insist that the dog used in the *nganga* should be sacrificed to it first. The thinking goes something like this: Just as the skull and other "essential" body parts contain the power of the dog and transfer it to the *nganga*, so too does the blood of the dogs convey its essential power. In fact, some practitioners go so far as to say that, before sacrificing the dog, it should be whipped into a rage and tormented. In this way, its rage and violence will go into the prenda and be available to the spirits therein and by extension their human colleague. "The head of raging dog...is very highly valued, 'so that it might attack' and torment the victim chosen by the priest" (Cabrera 1983: 130).

Starting with the material evidence from archaeological deposits – be they nineteenth century or twenty-first century – and using ethnographic data, it is possible to create a provisional interpretation of these African Diasporan assemblages. This interpretation responds to the larger issues in the discipline at present and gives some impression of the life ways and belief systems of diasporal peoples. Like the older excavations, the Rock Creek Park *nganga* has the classic form of a container filled with natural elements, but its recent interment also provides more data on its contents. In addition, the recent nature of the deposit, plus it's isolation, makes clearer the association and significance of the materials it contained, including the dog bones and other faunal remains. The contemporary nature of the deposit also makes it an ideal candidate for ethnographic investigation. Taken together these modern archaeological and ethnographic data provide some insight into the central importance of dogs as companions in everyday life, as symbols in religious iconography, and as sacrifices in ritual.

References

Bankoff, H. A. and Winter, F. A. 2005. The archaeology of slavery at the Van Cortlandt plantation in Bronx, New York. *International Journal of Historical Archaeology* **9(4)**, 291–318.

Barnes, M. K. 1999. *Church and Community: An Archaeological Investigation at the Levi Jordan Plantation, Brazoria County, Texas*. Master's thesis, Department of Anthropology, University of Houston: Houston, Texas.

Bascom, W. R. 1952. Two forms of Afro-Cuban divination, pp. 269–179 in Tax, T. (ed.), *Acculturation in the Americas. Proceedings and Selected Papers of the XXIXth International Congress of Americanists*. Chicago: University of Chicago Press.

Betelheim, J. 2001. Palo Monte Mayombe and its influence on Cuban contemporary art. *African Arts* **34(2)**, 36–49, 94–96.

Brown, D. H. 1996. Toward an ethnoaesthetics of Santería ritual arts: the practice of altar-making and gift exchange, pp. 77–146 in Lindsay, A. (ed.), *Santería Aestetics in Contemporary Latin American Art*. Washington, D. C.: Smithsonian Institution Press.

Brown, D. H. 1999. Altared spaces: Afro-Cuban religions and the urban landscape in Cuba and the United States, pp. 155–230 in Orsi, R. (ed.), *Gods of the City*. Bloomington: Indiana University Press.

Brown, D. H. 2003. *The Light Inside: Abakuá Society Arts and Cuban Cultural History*. Washington, D.C.: Smithsonian Institution Press.

Brown, K. L. 1994. Material culture and community structure: the slave and tenant community at Levi Jordan's plantation, pp. 95–118 in Hudson, L. E. (ed.), *Working Toward Freedom: Slave Society and Domestic Economy in the American South*. Rochester: University of Rochester Press.

Brown, K. L. 2003. Interwoven traditions: archaeology of the conjurer's cabins and the African American cemetery at the Jordan and Frogmore manor plantations, pp. 99–114, in *Places of Cultural Memory: African Reflections on the American Landscape*, on-line compilation of papers prepared for the conference held May 9–12 2001, Atlanta, Georgia, at http://www.cr.nps.gov/crdi/conferences/conflinks.htm

Brown, K. L. 2004. Ethnic analogy, archaeology, and the African diaspora: perspectives from a tenant community. *Historical Archaeology* **38(1)**, 79–89.

Brown, K. L. and Cooper, D. C. 1990. Structural continuity in an African-American slave and tenant community. *Historical Archaeology* **24(4)**, 7–19.

Bruner, D. E. 1966. *Hidden Power: Burial Practices from an African American Slave and Tenant Community*. Master's thesis, Department of Anthropology, University of Houston: Houston, Texas.

Cabrera, L. 1983. *El monte: Igbo finda, ewe orisha, vititi nfinda*. Miami: Colección de Chicherekú.

Davidson, J. M. 2004. Rituals captured in context and time: charm use in North Dallas Freedman's Town (1869–1907), Dallas, Texas. *Historical Archaeology* **38(2)**, 22–54.

del Hoyo, J., Elliot, A. and Sargatal, J. (eds) 1994. *Handbook of the Birds of the World. Volume 2. New World Vulture to Guineafowl*. Barcelona: Lynx Edicions.

Doris, D. T. 2002. *Vigilant Things: The Strange Fate of Ordinary Objects in Southwetern Nigeria*. PhD. Dissertation: Yale University.

Dove, C. J. and Banks, R. C. 1999. A taxonomic study of the Crested Caracaras (Falconidae). *Wilson Bulletin* **111(3)**, 330–339.

Fennell, C. C. 2000. Conjuring boundaries: inferring past identities from religious artifacts. *International Journal of Historical Archaeology* **4(4)**, 281–313.

Fennell, C. C. 2003. Group identity, individual creativity, and symbolic generation in a BaKongo diaspora. *International Journal of Historical Archaeology* **7(1)**, 1–31.

Ferguson, L. 1992. *Uncommon Ground: Archaeology and Early African America*. Washington, D.C.: Smithsonian Institution Press.

Franklin, M. and McGee, L. (eds.) 2004. Transcending Boundaries, Transforming the Discipline: African Diaspora Archaeologies in the New Millenium. *Historical Archaeology* **38(1)**.

Garcia-Herros, J. 1998. *A Munitions Maker's Cabin: An Archaeological Investigation at the Levi Jordan Plantation, Brazoria County, Texas*. Master's thesis, Department of Houston: Houston, Texas.

Hall, D. D. (ed.). 1997. *Lived Religion in America: Toward a History of Practice*. Princeton: Princeton University Press.

Harris, R. N. 1999. *Craft Specialization in a Nineteenth-Century African American Community: the Shell Carver's Cabin on the Levi Jordan Plantation, Brazoria County, Texas*. Master's thesis, Department of Anthropology, University of Houston: Houston, Texas.

Joyner, B. D. (ed.) 2003. *African Reflections on the American Landscape*. Washington, D.C.: National Park Service, U.S. Department of the Interior.

Leone, M. P. and Fry, G.-M. 1999. Conjuring in the big house kitchen: An interpretation of African American belief systems based on the uses of archaeology and folklore sources. *Journal of American Folklore* **112(445)**, 372–403.

Lifschitz, E. 1982. *Thinking with Animals: African Images and Perceptions*. [Exhibition catalogue] Washington, D.C.: National Museum of African Art, Smithsonian Institution.

MacGaffey, W. 1993. The eyes of understanding, pp. 21–103, in *Astonishment and Power: Kongo Minkisi and the Art of Renée Stout*. Washington, D. C.: National Museum of African Art, Smithsonian Institution.

Mason, M. A. 2002. *Living Santeria: Rituals and Experiences in an Afro-Cuban Religion*. Washington, D. C.: Smithsonian Institution Press.

Morrison, J. L. 2001. Conservation vale of private lands for Crested Caracaras in Florida. *Conservation Biology* **15(3)**, 675–684.

Murphy, H. M. 1993. *Santería: African Spirits in America*. Boston: Beacon Press.

Orser, C. E. 1994. The archaeology of African-American slave religion in the ante-bellum south. *Cambridge Archaeological Journal* **4(1)**, 33–45.

Owsley, D. W. and Richardson, M. L. 2000. *Field work report Picnic Site 14 Rock Creek Park Washington, D.C.* Report on file, Department of Anthropology, National Museum of Natural History, Simthsonian Institution: Washington, D.C.

Owsley, D. W. and Bruwelheide, K. 2000. *Osteological analysis of human remains from case SI-2000–5*. Report on file, Department of Anthropology, National Museum of Natural History, Smithsonian Institution: Washington, D.C.

Patten, D. 1992. Mankala and Minkisi: possible evidence of African American folk beliefs and practices. African-American Archaeology. *Newsletter of the African American Archaeology Network* **6**, 5–7.

Pearce, L. E. 1993. To whom do they belong?: cowrie shells in historical archaeology. African-American Archaeology. *Newsletter of the African-American Archaeology Network* **9**, 1–3.

Pollak-Eltz, A. 1993. The Shango cult and other African rituals in Trinidad, Grenada, and Carriacou and their possible influence on the Spiritual Baptist faith. *Carribean Quarterly* **39(3/4)**, 12–26.

Reinhardt, J. E. 1982. Preface, *Thinking with Animals: African Images and Perceptions*. [Exhibition catalogue] Washington, D.C.: National Museum of Art, Smithsonian Institution.

Roura Álvarez, L. 2003. *"Excavaciones arqueológicas en Obrapía No. 55, Habana Vieja" [Excavation report]*. Gabinete de Arqueología, Oficina del Historiador de la Cuidad de la Habana.

Russell, A. E. 1997. Material culture and African-American spirituality at the Hermitage. *Historical Archaeology* **31(2)**, 63–80.

Singleton, T. A. 1991. The archaeology of slave life, pp. 155–175 in Campbell, E. D. C. and Rice, K. S. (eds), *Before Freedom Came: African-American Life in the Antebellum South*. Charlotteville: University of Virginia Press.

Singleton, T. A. 1995. The archaeology of slavery in North America. *Annual Review of Anthropology* **24**, 119–140.

Singleton, T. A. and Bograd, M. D. 1995. *The Archaeology of the African Diaspora in the Americas. Guides to the Archaeological Literature of the Immigrant Experience in America, No. 2.* Tucson: Society for Historical Archaeology.

Thompson, R. F. 1983. *Flash of the Spirit*. New York: Random House.

Wilkie, L. 1995. Magic and empowerment on the plantation: an archaeological consideration of African-American world view. *Southeastern Archaeology* **14(2)**, 136–148.

Wilkie, L. 1997. Secret and Sacred: contextualizing the artifacts of African-American magic and religion. *Historical Archaeology* **31(4)**, 81–106.

Young, A. L. 1996. Archaeological evidence of African-style ritual and healing practices in the upland South. *Tennessee Anthropologist* **XXI(2)**, 139–155.

Michael Atwood Mason
Department of Public Programs
National Museum of Natural History
Smithsonian Institution
Washington, D.C. 20560–0112
USA

masonm@si.edu

Lynn M. Snyder
Department of Anthropology
National Museum of Natural History
Smithsonian Institution
Washington, D.C. 20560–0112
USA

snyderl@si.edu

9th ICAZ Conference, Durham 2002
Dogs and People in Social, Working, Economic or Symbolic Interaction
(eds Lynn M. Snyder and Elizabeth A. Moore) pp. 62–66

8. Dog Sacrifice in the Ancient World: A Ritual Passage?

Jacopo De Grossi Mazzorin and Claudia Minniti

This paper explores the ritual use of dogs in Italy from the Iron Age to the Roman Period. Recent excavations have revealed new evidence of dog burials and sacrifices in the pre-Roman and Roman worlds. Dogs were sometimes buried in pits in ancient cemeteries, separate from their masters. It is possible that they were intended to act as companions or guardians in the journey to the Underworld, although they may also have served a purification function. Dogs were also buried in votive bothroi near sanctuaries, probably as a ritual offering, or buried under the foundations of buildings. Finally, dogs were often sacrificed to a number goddesses, including Genita Mana and Hecate. Dogs were also companion animals to these goddesses, who were overseers of cyclical times, guardians of life and the awakening of vegetation. As dogs were also often linked with the underworld and death, their sacrifice can also be interpreted as part of a ritual passage.

Introduction

The sacrifice of dogs in ancient times took many ritual forms, although two general categories of symbolism can be identified (Bodson 1980; Zaganiaris 1975). The first connects the rites of animal sacrifice to Cthonic gods related to procreation and development. The second form appears to take its origin from the everyday role of dogs in human life as faithful companions and guardians of precious possessions. In some cases these two roles may overlap and interact.

Plutarch (*Quaest. Rom.*, 111, 290D) writes that the Ancient Greeks did not sacrifice dogs to the gods of Olympus and Pausanias (VI, 2, 2) notes that dogs were not sacrificed during divinatory rituals. In contrast, Plutarch notes that in Sparta young dogs were given as burnt offerings to Enialius, another name for Ares. This practice was also reported by Pausanias (III, 14, 5) who writes that some Spartans sacrificed dogs in a nocturnal ritual. Colophones also offered a black dog to the goddess Enodia at night (Pausanias, III, 14, 9). This divinity was associated with Hecate and through time became identified with Hecate herself. According to Plutarchus (*Quaest. Rom.*, 52, 277B), Socrates reported that the Argives sacrificed a bitch to Eiloneia to assure successful childbirth.

The Underworld

Dogs were also often connected with the Underworld (Jenkins 1957; Mainoldi 1981; Menache 1997). In the mythology of ancient Greece dogs played a part in three important phases of man's relationship with death. These phases were: 1) the passage from life to death; 2) the time spent in the Underworld; 3) the return to life as a spirit (Mainoldi 1984). This association was in fact common in a number of Indo-European cultures. In Germanic mythology, the goddess Holle escorted the deceased to the land of the dead, while her dog tore their flesh. Cerberus, the guard dog of Hades had to stop living persons from entering, but above all to prevent the souls of the dead from exiting. Homer speaks of a terrible dog of Hades (*Iliad*, VII, 368; *Odyssey*, XI, 623) but the first author to identify this animal as Cerberus is Hesiod in his Theogonia (310–312; 767–773). Other watch dogs performing similar tasks were Odin's wolf/dog Garm, and the Sarameyan dogs Cabala and Cyama (Majupuria 1991: 151). The first was the gigantic guard dog of the Germanic realm of Hel, while Cabala and Cyama were sons of Sarama the Indra's dog. The Vedic god of death, Yama, sent these two dogs out from the Underworld to fetch the errant and reluctant souls from the land of the living. In Etruscan culture dogs appear to have been associated with the cult of Calu, the god of the infernal regions. In fact, in the tombs of Golini at Orvieto and of Orco at Tarquinia (Italy) there are two paintings in which the god of the dead, Hades, is dog-headed (Markussen 1993). In all these instances, dogs are linked to the Underworld, as both guardians and symbols.

In Ancient Greece dogs were often associated with Hecate, a goddess of the Underworld. The origin of this entity is rather complex, but it is suggested that Hecate is the daughter of Tartarus and Demeter (Barthell 1973: 38). In the earliest representations of Hecate, she is depicted as dog-headed or as a bitch accompanied by the dog-like demons Lamia, Gello and Empusa. She is also accompanied by the souls of those who had died prematurely or had not been properly buried (Mainoldi 1984:47). The ancient writers said that for this reason young dogs were offered to her during purificatory ceremonies (Sofron. in *Scholastica*, *Lycophr.*, 77; Plutarch, *Quaest. Rom.*, III, 52, 68, 280C). In addition, it was believed that dogs bayed at her arrival and that these howls heralded death (Burriss 1935). Like the goddess they served, these dogs were believed to be the guardians of the cycle of time and life (Gimbutas 1989).

Other mythological figures of the Underworld associated with dogs were the Cherae who were traditionally identified with the wicked souls of the dead (Euripides, *Electra*: 1252–1253; Apollonius Rhodius, *Argonautica* IV, 1666) and the Erinys (Aeschylus, *Choephori*, 924, 1054; Sophocles, *Electra*: 1386–1388; Euripides, *Orestes*, 260–261; Aristophanes, *Ranae*, 472). In addition, Hecuba, another character related with Hecate, was turned into a ghost dog with eyes of fire (Euripides, *Hecuba*, 125 ss.).

Because dogs were associated with the Underworld, they were sometimes considered evil (Delort 1987). In ancient Delos (Greece), dogs were not allowed in the temples, nor were they allowed on the island (Strabo. X, 55). They were also excluded from the Acropolis of Athens (Plutarch, *Quaest. Rom*, 111, 290b). In Ancient Rome, they could not enter the temple of Hercules in the Forum Boarium (Pliny the Elder, *Nat. Hist.* X, 79). In contrast, dogs guarded the temple of Jupiter Capitolinus in Rome (Burriss 1935). In Sicily, they were consided sacred to the temples of Hephaestus on Mount Etna and in Adrano (Aelian, *De Nat. anim.*, 3, 11, 20).

Purification and rites of passage

Since dogs were considered impure, their sacrifice became cathartic and acted as a "purifying agent" (Mainoldi 1984; Rudhart 1958). In the ritual of περισκυλακισμοσ, purification was acomplished by rubbing one 's body against that of a dog (Plutarch, *Quaest. Rom.*, 68, 280C). Rituals in which an individual passes from a state of impurity to purity were also often involved in rites of passage. For instance, the young Spartans performed a dog sacrifice to Enialio, which purified them as they entered the new age group of ephebes. Hesychius (*Xanthica*, s.v.) describes a similar ritual practiced in Xanthus by the Macedonian army. In this instance, a dog was quartered and the forequarters were placed on the right side of the road, the hindquarters on the left. The army then marched down the road between the sections of the dog. This rite was also described by Quintus Curtius (X, 9, 12) regarding the *lustratio* in 323 BC and by Titus Livy (XL, 6, 1–2) for the *lustratio* in 182 BC.

In Ancient Greece one of the rites of passage involving dog sacrifice, was in honor of Eiloneia (or Eileithyia), another gamelic earth goddess. Eileithyia was a goddess who watched over birth and was sometimes identified with Hecate (Plutarch, *Quaest. Rom.*, 52) and surely with the Phoenician goddess Astarte. This ritual is documented in Italy by the bones of dogs found together with ceramic sherds dating to the late 4th/early 3rd centuries BC found in the well of temple A at Pyrgi (Caloi and Palombo 1980). The Pyrgian sanctuary was consecrated to the goddess Uni, who in turn was identified with the Phoenician goddess Astarte, and by the Ancient Greeks as Leukothea or Eileithyia, all goddesses strictly associated with the concept of birth and development. So too was the goddess Mater Matuta, to whom puppies appear to have been sacrificed in the sacred area of St. Omobone, Rome (Tagliacozzo 1989). In this area the bones of puppies less than two months old were found, in contexts dating to the 6th century BC. It must be pointed out that the Gauls also worshipped goddesses related to the same cult, such as Sirona, Nehalennia, Aveta or Epona, who are often depicted as having a puppy on their lap or curled up at their feet (Gourevitch 1968).

Another example of dogs offered to goddesses linked to the principle of procreation is that of Genita Mana, an Italic divinity presiding over the menstrual cycle and matters connected with fertility. Both Pliny the Elder (*Nat. Hist.*, XXIX, 58) and Plutarch (*Quaest. Rom.*, 52, 277) describe the ritual sacrifice of a puppy to this goddess, whom Plutarch also identifies with Hecate. Over time, the cult of Hecate in ancient Greece incorporated a number of entities, so much so that by the 5th century BC Artemis was also identified with Hecate (Mainoldi 1981; 1984).

In the area of the Kolonos Agoraios in Athens, in a well deposit dated to the 2nd century BC, the bones of 450 infants, nearly all newborn or fully developed foetuses and 150 dogs were found (Shear 1939; Angel 1945; The association of the dogs and babies in this well has been interpreted as evidence of rites of purification associated with childbirth (Little 1999; Rotroff 1999; Snyder 1999). Following the description of the Agora offered by Pausanias (I, 14, 7), Osanna (1993) links the well with the temple of Aphrodite who was worshipped there as Ourania and was the goddess of the dead and protectress of burial and buried (Shear Jr. 1984: 24). Nevertheless archaeological excavations beginning in the 1980s and continuing today have proved that this sanctuary is actually far separated from the area of the well, by two major thoroughfares, the Sacred Way and the Panathenaic Way (Shear 1997: 497). Dog offerings were also performed in the sanctuary of Aphrodite Kolias, on Cape Kolias in Attica as described by Pausanias (I, 5) where the goddess was worshipped together with the nymphs Genetillidae, protectresses of marriage and birth. Osanna (1993) notes additional instances of dog sacrifice in areas sacred to Aphrodite, such as the sanctuary of Locri Epizefiri (Torelli 1977) where dog bones were found in as many as 56 bothroi (Lissi *et al.* 1958–61). The infants found at the Kolonos Agoraios at Athens (Greece) and the Xanthian purification rite inevitably come to mind. Also the newborns and/or foetuses found in the Agora well may have been victims of famine or an epidemic (Osanna 1993: 90). Moreover, the dismembering of dogs is similar to that practised during the Xanthian purification sacrifice. In fact, the previously mentioned case of the dog where the right jaw was buried with the forequarters and the left jaw with the hindquarters closely resembles the rite decribed by Ancient historians.

Dog remains have been found in wells and bothroi associated with sanctuaries dedicated to a number of deities, including the sanctuary at Pyrgi. In this instance the sacrifice is interpreted as a real and proper piaculum, a compensatory sacrifice offered during the closure of the well (Colonna 1988–1989). In the sanctuary at Torre di Satriano in Lucania, Italy, an articulated dog skeleton was found in a great pit containing votive items (Tagliente *et al.* 1991). The skeleton was positioned in the centre of a burnt area, suggesting that a ritual act directly related to the closure of the sacred pit may have been performed just before the sanctuary was abandoned (Osanna and Giammatteo 2001). Dog remains were also recovered from a bothros consecrated to Eolo on the acropolis of Lipari (Villari 1991). Bones from at least five dogs and an ox were found in a heap in the Lavello sanctuary in Basilicata, Italy (Sublimi Saponetti 1991). Here, as at Lucania, the dogs seem to have been sacrificed and buried as the sanctuary was abandoned. A most interesting deposit was found in one of two bothroi associated with a temple of the late 4th century BC at the mouth of the Sele River in Italy. This bothroi had been filled by a 1.5m deep deposit of ceramics, bones and charcoal, upon which lay the skeleton of a dog (Zancani Montuoro 1937). In nearly all these cases, the stratigraphy of the deposits containing the dogs suggests a ritual act directly connected with the closure of a sacred pit. This is particularly evident in the bothroi connected with the Heraion at the mouth of the Sele and at Torre di Satriano. However, the significance of these rituals is unclear. Were they associated with rites of purification and passage, or with sacrifices to the gods for propiation or protection?

In another instance, a necropolis of infants and child burials at Lugnano in Teverina, Italy also contained the skeletons of a number of dogs. In this cemetery, dating to the middle of the 5th century AD, pagan rites should have long since disappeared and given way to Christian practices. In this instance, however, among the burials of 47 infants, the skeletons of at least 12 puppies less than six months old at death, and a one year old animal were found (Soren *et al.* 1995). Although four of the dog skeletons were apparently intact, a number had apparently been broken apart or dismembered. In one instance, only a puppy skull was found, four of the puppies were found without mandibles, while three had mandibles but no skulls. One had apparently been split in half at the pelvis, with a single mandible buried with each half of the carcass. Finally, the older dog had no skull. The dog burials appeared to accompany the premature or newborn infants only, and all the burials apparently occurred within a short time interval.The excavators suggest that the deaths may have had a common cause such as malaria, and the dogs may have been associated with magic or therapeutic rites related to the deaths of the infants.

Dogs as healing agents

In the ancient world, dogs were sometimes believed to have special healing powers. The dog was sacred to the cult of Aesculapius. We must remember that the primary role of this god was cthonic and oracular and only later did he become part of therapeutic cult (Gourevitch 1968). Pliny the Elder (*Nat. Hist.*, XXIX, 58, 98–101, 111, 114, 117, 133; XXX, 21–22, 27–8, 35, 46, 51, 53, 69–70, 72–4, 76, 81–2, 93, 98, 105, 109, 111, 114, 119, 121, 123, 133) notes the many therapeutic roles of dogs (see also Reinach 1884; Burriss 1935). It was also believed, as reported by Aelianus (*De Nat. anim.*, IV, 40), that dogs were affected by only three diseases: rabies, distemper and gout.

As scapegoats in curing disease, puppies were rubbed over the diseased portion of the patients' body so that they might absorb the ailment. Then, according to Pliny (*Nat. Hist.*, XXX, 42, 64), the animals were killed and buried in a sacred space. The use of puppies to cure illnesses by mere contact with the diseased was also apparently practiced by the Gauls. A stele found near the source of the Seine River in France shows worshippers of the healing divinity Sequana holding puppies in both hands and rubbing them against their bodies (Toynbee 1973).

Dogs in funerary contexts

Funerary practices of combining dog and human burials or burying dogs in pits separate from their masters are documented in several Roman and Greek cemeteries (Day 1984), such as in the two Roman necropolae located at Fidenae and at the cross-road between the Nomentana and Palombarese near Rome (De Grossi Mazzorin and Minniti 2000; 2001). It is possible that these animals were intended to act as companions or guardians in the journey to the Underworld, although they may have been buried there because their masters were very fond of their pets.

Agricultural rituals

Rituals associated with agriculture sometimes involved the sacrifice of dogs. An Etruscan text, the *Eugubinae Tabulae* (IIIa:15ff) which dates to the 2nd century BC describes such a sacrificial rite, in honor of Hondia (Devoto 1948: 94–97). In this ritual, a portion of the limbs and viscera were burned, while the unburned portion of the animal was buried at the foot of the altar.

Another agricultural ritual very similar in nature is the Robigalia (Ovid, *Fasti*, IV, 905–942; Columella, *Res Rustica*, X, 337–347), a festival to protect the harvest held in honour of the god Robigus/Robigo (Smith 1996). In the Robigalia, a procession to the sacred wood was followed by the sacrifice of a sheep and a female dog and the "Flamen's prayer", an archaic text which links the Robigalia rites to Etruscan practices (Santini 1991), which kept the corn rust away (Gianferrari 1995).

Other agricultural rites included the offering of a puppy before planting, and the "Augurium canarium", in which red dogs were sacrificed at the end of April (Columella, *Res Rustica*, II, 21, 4). Another agricultural rite consisted of the burnt offering of a puppy near one of the gates of Ancient Rome, in consequence of which the gate was called the "Porta Catularia" (*Festus*, 39, 50).

Foundation offerings and protection

Dogs were also sometimes offered as sacrifice for the protection of a building, the walls of a city, or defensive installations. At Fidenae, Italy, the skeleton of a dog appears to have been intentionally interred under a tuff and clay wall (Carandini and Carafa 2000: 278). A structure interpreted as a bastion of the Porta Mugonia was uncovered on the slopes of the Palatine hill in Rome. This structure contained the remains of three dogs with evident signs of butchering in a layer rich in ashes, intact vessels and animal bones (Ricci *et al.* 2000). A similar deposit was recently uncovered in the Meta Sudans, where a pit dated to 506 BC and probably related to the rebuilding of the Curiae Veteres sanctuary, was found. According to historical texts this sanctuary was located in the northeastern corner of the Romulean Pomerium. In addition to ceramic sherds, the pit produced an assemblage of burned and partially burned animal bones which included a number dog bones, one of which was an innominate fragment which bore clear signs of butchering (De Grossi Mazzorin nd). In Ariminum, Italy, a number of skeletal elements of a small dog were found in the earth shoring up the foundations of one of the colonial Roman defence walls (Ortalli 1990; 1995). These bones were scattered and had perhaps been disturbed by damage to the area during pillaging in the Middle Ages. Giusberti (1990), however, does not rule out the possibility that the dog remains may have been deposited as part of a ritual which including the dismemberment of the animal and internment of the body segments at various points along the wall.

At Paestum, Italy, a pit containing the skeleton of a dog was found during excavation of the northern bastion of the Porta Marina (Roberts 1993). Although the "porta" itself was built when the city was reduced to a colony in 273 BC, the pit containing the dog was dated by the ceramics it contained to the late 6th through 5th centuries BC. Dogs buried in the foundations of the city walls were also discovered in the Roman town of Chester-le-Street and at Caerwent in England (Merrifield 1987).

While the ancient texts do not speak directly about special foundation rites, the rites performed during the Roman festival of Lupercalia may in some manner explain their significance. During these rites a goat and a dog were offered to the god Faunus. This festival also involved a procession of "luperci" in which youths dressed only in goat skins ran through the streets scourging the women they met with leather straps in order to insure their fertility (Plutarchus, *Quaest. Rom.*, 68, 280b–c; 111, 290a–c; *Romulus*, 21, 10). In addition, Liou-Gille (1980: 180–194) suggests that the Lupercalia is based on the legend of the foundation of Rome. In Liou-Gille's interpretation, the luperci were the primitive inhabitants of Rome before the city was founded; the race round the Palatine recalls the furrow of the sulcus primigenius drawn by Romulus; the sacrifice or Lupercale recalls Romolus's childhood when he was raised by the Lupa; and the goat dismemberment recalls Romulus' dismemberment.

Comments and conclusions

In this context, the attributes of the god Faunus, to whom a goat and dog were offered as part of the Lupercalia, are also pertinent (Roberts 1993). Indeed, Faunus is the entity who watches over the rural world or countryside. Thus, this particular dog sacrifice appears to complete the ritual cycle. In brief, with this sacrifice, passage from the primitive to the urban world is officially marked and the city walls become the boundary between the inner city and the wild, external world. The entities known as the Lares praestites may also play a part in this concept of city protection or security. These beings, who watched over the security of the city and especially over its defensive walls, were often depicted dressed in dogs skins and with a dog at their feet. Ovid (*Fasti*, V, 133–142) explains the nature of the Lares praestites and their dogs thusly: they "both guard the house, both protect the master". Moreover, the Lari in the quality of earth gods are integrated with the Parentes or the Mani that as part of the cult of Genita Mana or Hecate, the goddess that watches over crossroads, frontiers and more generally the border between the world of the living and the world of the dead.

So the circle is completed. Dog sacrifice is linked to a number of divinities directly connected to the idea of passage from one stage to another, be they divinities of the earthly world related to the principle of procreation and development, or divinities that watch over a line that distinguishes two diverse and contrasting worlds of wild and urban, life and death.

References

Angel J. L. 1945. Skeletal material from Attica. *Hesperia* **14**, 311.

Barthell E. E. Jr. 1973. *Gods and Goddesses of Ancient Greece.* Miami: University of Miami Press.

Bodson L. 1980. Place et fonction du chien dans le monde antique. *Ethnozootechnie* **25**, 13–21.

Burriss E. E. 1935. The Place of the Dog in Superstition as Revealed in Latin Literature. *Classical Philology* **XXX**, 32–42.

Caloi L. and Palombo M. R. 1980. Il cane domestico di Pyrgi. *Studi Etruschi* XLVIII, 293–328.

Carandini A. and Carafa P. 2000. Palatium e Sacra Via I, pp. 31–33, in Carandini A. and Carafa P. (eds), *Bollettino di Archeologia.* Roma 1995.

Colonna G. 1988–1989. I due pozzi antistanti il tempio A, in Pyrgi. Scavi del Santuario Etrusco. *Notizie degli Scavi*, XLII–XLIII, Suppl II, 11–138.

Day L. P. 1984. Dog burials in the Greek world. *American Journal of Archaeology* **88(1)**, 21–32.

De Grossi Mazzorin J. and Minniti C. 2000. Le sepolture di cani della necropoli di età imperiale di Fidene – Via Radicofani (Roma): alcune considerazioni sul loro seppellimento nell' antichità, pp. 387–398, in Abaco, R. (ed.), *Atti del 2° Convegno Nazionale di Archeozoologia.* Asti 1997.

De Grossi Mazzorin J. and Minniti C. 2001. Caratterizzazione archeozoologica: le sepolture di cani, in pp. 81–93, *Ad deverticulum. Scavi archeologici lungo la bretella Nomentana-GRA.*

Delort R. 1987. *L'uomo e gli animali dall'età della pietra a oggi.* Bari, Laterza.

Devoto G. 1948. *Le tavole di Gubbio.* Firenze: Sansoni.

Gianferrari A. 1995. Robigalia: un appuntamento per la salvezza del raccolto, in pp. 127–140, Quilici, S. and Quilici G. (eds) *Agricoltura e commerci nell'Italia antica.* Roma.

Gimbutas M. 1989. *The Language of the Goddess.* San Francisco: Harper and Row.

Giusberti G. 1990. I resti ossei sacrificali delle mura di Ariminum. *Etudes Celtique* XXVII, 119–130.

Gourevitch. D. 1968. Le chien, de la therapeutique populaire aux cultes sanitaires. *Mélanges d'Archéologie et d 'Histoire* LXXX(1), 247–281.

Jenkins F. 1957. The role of dog in Romano Gaulish religion. *Latomus*, XVI, 60–78.

Liou-Gille B. 1980. Les cultes "heroiques" romains. Les fondateurs, I, *Les Belles Lettres*: Paris.

Lissi E., Blanc A. C., Cardini L. and Cassoli P. 1958–1961. Determinazione delle faune dei Bothroi di Locri. *Quaternaria* V, 298–299.

Little, L. M. 1999. Babies in Well G5:3: preliminary results and future analysis. *American Journal of Archaeology* **103**, 284.

Mainoldi C. 1981. Cani mitici e rituali tra il regno dei morti e il mondo dei viventi. *Quaderni Urbinati di Cultura Classica*, n.s. **8.37**, 7–41.

Mainoldi C. 1984. *L'image du Loup et du chien dans la Grèce Ancienne d'Homère à Platon.* Paris.

Majupuria T. C. 1991. *Sacred Animals of Nepal & India.* Bangkok: Craftsmen Press.

Markussen E. P. 1993. *Painted Tombs in Etruria. A Catalogue.* Roma.

Menache S. 1997. Dogs: God's worst enemies? *Society & Animals* **5(1)**, 23–44.

Merrifield R. 1987. *The Archaeology of Ritual and Magic.* New York: New Amsterdam Books.

Ortalli J. 1990. Le mura coloniali di Ariminum e il deposito di fondazione con "semuncia" a testa di gallo. *Etudes Celtiques* XXVII, 24–30.

Ortalli J. 1995. Nuove fonti archeologiche per Ariminum: monumenti, opere pubbliche e assetto urbanistico tra la fondazione coloniale e il principato augusteo, in Calbi A. and Susini G. (eds), *Atti del Convegno Internazionale: "Rimini antica. Una respublica tra terra e mare*": 469–529. Rimini, ottobre 1993.

Osanna M. 1993. Il problema topografico del santuario di Afrodite Urania ad Atene. *Annuario della Scuola Archeologica di Atene* LXVI–LXVII: 73–95.

Osanna M. and Giammatteo T. 2001. VI. Azioni rituali e offerte votive, pp. 107–122, in Nava, M. L. and Osanna, M. (eds), *Rituali per una Dea Lucana. Il santuario di Torre di Satriano.* Cavano, Editrice Cerbone.

Reinach S. 1884. Les chiens dans le culte d'Esculape. *Revue archéologique* IV: 129–135.

Ricci G., Brocato P. and Terrenato N. 2000. L'età delle mura. La fase 2. Le prime mura, pp. 31–33, in Carandini, I. A. and Carafa, P. (eds), *Palatium e Sacra Via. Roma, Bolletino di Archeologia.*

Roberts R. 1993. Rites de protection et de défense. A propos des ossement d'un chien découverts au pied du rempart de Paestum. *AION* XV, 120–142.

Rotroff S. I. 1999. The artefacts from Well F 5:3 and some conclusions concerning the deposit. *American Journal of Archaeology* **103**, 284–285.

Rudhart J. 1958. *Notions fondamentales de la pensée religieuse dans la Grèce classique.* Genève.

Santini C. 1991. Fast. 4, 905–942: ruggine del grano e ruggine del ferro, pp. 169–182, in Gallo, I and Nicastri, L. (eds), *Cultura, poesia, ideologia, nell 'opera di Ovidio.* Napoli.

Shear T. L. 1939. The Athenian Agora: The campaign of 1938. *Hesperia* **8**, 238–239.

Shear T. L. Jr. 1984. The Athenian Agora: Excavations of 1980–1982. *Hesperia* **53**, 1–57.

Shear T. L. Jr. 1997. The Athenian Agora: Excavations of 1989–1993. *Hesperia* **66**, 495–234.

Smith C. 1996. Dead dogs and rattles: time, space and ritual sacrifice in Iron Age Latium, pp. 73–89, in Wilkins, J. B. (ed), Approaches to the Study of Ritual: *Italy and the Ancient Mediterranean, Vol. 2, Accordia Specialist studies on the Mediterranean.* London.

Snyder, L. M. 1999. The animal bones from Well G 5:3: domestic debris, industrial debris, and possible evidence for the sacrifice of domestic dogs in Late Hellenistic Athens. *AJA* **103**, 284.

Soren D., Fenton D. and Birkby W. 1995. The Late Roman Infant Cemetery near Lugnano in Teverina, Italy: some implications. *Journal of Paleopathology* **7(1)**, 13–42.

Sublimi Saponetti S. 1991. I resti animali di Gravetta (Lavello PZ), pp. 105–108, in Mertens, J. and Lambrechts, R. (eds), *Comunità indigene e problemi della romanizzazione nell'Italia centro-meridionale (IV-III sec. av.C.).* Bruxelless – Rome.

Tagliacozzo A. 1989. Analisi dei resti faunistici dell'Area Sacra di S. Omobono, pp. 65–69, in *Il viver quotidiano in Roma Arcaica.* Roma: Edizioni Procom.

Tagliente M., Fresa M. P., Bottini A. 1991. Relazione sull'area daunio-lucana e sul santuario di Lavello, pp. 93–104, in Mertens, J. and Lambrechts, R. (eds*), Comunità indigene e problemi della romanizzazione nell'Italia centro-meridionale (IV–III sec. av.C.).* Bruxelless – Rome.

Torelli M. 1977. I culti di Locri, pp. 148–148, in Locri epizefiri, in *Atti del sedicesimo Convegno di Studi sulla Magna Grecia.* Napoli.

Toynbee J. M. C. 1973. *Animals in Roman Life and Art.* Ithaca: Cornell University Press.

Villari P. 1991. The faunal remains in the Bothros at Eolo (Lipari). *ArchaeoZoologia* **4(2)**, 109–126.

Zaganiaris M. J. 1975. Sacrifices de chiens dans l'Antiquité classique. *Platon* **27**, 322–329.

Zancani Montuoro P. 1937. Heraion alla foce del Sele. *Notizie degli Scavi* **13**, 299–331.

Università degli Studi di Lecce – Dip. Beni Culturali

jacopo.degrossi@ateneo.unile.it

c_minniti@:hotmail.com

9th ICAZ Conference, Durham 2002
Dogs and People in Social, Working, Economic or Symbolic Interaction
(eds Lynn M. Snyder and Elizabeth A. Moore) pp. 67–76

9. Bronze Age Dogs from Graves in Borger (Netherlands) and Dimini (Greece)

Wietske Prummel

Bronze Age dog skeletons or parts of skeletons are rarely found in human graves in Central and Western Europe. Only two sites with dog cremations are known so far. Both sites are fields of burial mounds. Dogs are rather common in the contemporaneous Mycenaean tholos and chamber tombs in Greece. New finds of dogs in Bronze Age graves are presented here. The possible meanings of these dogs in human graves are discussed.

Introduction

Dog bones in human graves are rare in the Bronze Age of Central and Western Europe (Andralojc 1993). Only two sites with dog cremations are known so far. These are Borger in the Netherlands (this paper) and Tornow in Germany (Teichert and Teichert 1976). Inhumations are completely unknown in Central and Western Europe for this period. On the other hand, dog inhumation or the deposition of dogs and parts of dogs in human graves is a well-known phenomenon in the Mycenaean world of Greece (Fig. 1). These dog burials are only found in tholos and chamber tombs (Day 1984; Hamilakis 1996).

Two new burial sites with dog remains are presented in this paper. These are the Borger dogs (c. 1430–1210 cal. BC) and the dogs from the Lamióspito tholos tomb in Dimini (Thessaly, Greece) (Late Helladic III A 2, which is in the second half of the 14th century BC, c. 1340–1320 BC). The paper ends with a discussion of the possible meanings of dog cremation and dog inhumation in Europe in the Middle and Late Bronze Age. Hamilakis' thesis that the deposition of dogs in Mycenaean tholos and chamber graves was associated with the concept of hunting (Hamilakis 1996) is made up a stand against. Alternative meanings of dog burials and depositions in Bronze Age graves are presented, which also take the dog's functions in daily life into account.

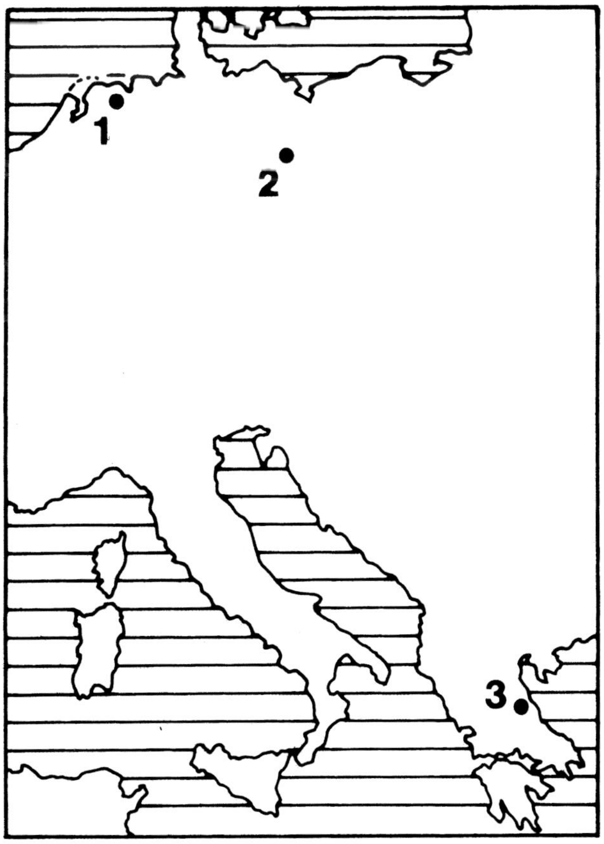

Fig. 1. Map of Europe with the situation of the Bronze Age burial sites of 1) Borger (Netherlands), 2) Tornow (Germany) and 3) Lamióspito in Dimini (Greece)

Fig. 2. Borger, burial mound XI, urn 1. Distal part of left metacarpus II of the cremated dog. Scale bar = 1 cm.

Fig. 3. Borger, burial mound XI, urn 1. Phalanges 1 of the cremated dog. Scale bar = 1 cm.

Fig. 4. Borger, burial mound XI, urn 1. Phalanges 2 of the cremated dog. Scale bar = 1 cm

Fig. 5. Borger, burial mound XI, urn 1. Phalanges 3 of the cremated dog. Scale bar = 1 cm

Borger, Netherlands

The base of the levelled Middle Bronze Age burial mound XI, one in a row of burial mounds along the Drouwenerstraat between the villages of Borger and Drouwen in the province of Drenthe (Netherlands), was excavated in 1987. The mound was 27 m long and 11 m wide and was surrounded by a 1.4–2 m wide and 0.9–1.2 m deep ditch. The mound was NNE-SSW oriented and dates from the first half of the Middle Bronze Age (Lanting *et al.* 2001b: 80).

Two urns were found at the southern end of the burial mound. Urn 1 was located within the ditch. It had been dug half into the soil below the ditch. This urn had been hit by ploughing. Urn 2, which was undamaged, was found 0.5 m outside of the burial mound and its ditch. Urn 1 and 2 were 6 m apart. The urns date from the end of the Middle Bronze Age or the beginning of the Late Bronze Age typologically (Lanting *et al.* 2001b: 80). The contents of the urns were taken into study in 2001.

Urn 1 contained 76.5 g of cremated bone. A total of 22.1 g could be identified as parts of the skull and the fore feet of a dog (Figs 2–5, Table 1). No human cremated bone was found in this urn. The measurements of the

Table 1. Borger, burial mound XI, urn 1. Numbers and weights of the identified cremated bones, and weight of the residue. MNI: minimum number of individuals; frg.: fragment(s); cf. dog: identification as dog not 100 % certain

Cremated dog bones, 22.1 g: MNI = 1

8 cranial frg. (cf. dog),	0.4 g
1 left os carpale quartum,	0.8 g
2 frg. of carpus/tarsus bones (cf. dog),	0.1 g
1 frg. of metacarpus I,	0.1 g
1 frg. of left metacarpus II,	0.6 g
1 frg. of left metacarpus III,	2.6 g
1 frg. of left metacarpus V,	0.5 g
1 frg. of right metacarpus V,	1.1 g
7 frg. of metacarpi,	1.0 g
18 frg. of metacarpi/metatarsi,	7.3 g
1 complete phalanx 1 of toe III or IV,	1.9 g
1 almost complete phalanx 1 of toe II or V,	0.9 g
5 frg. of phalanges 1	1.9 g
1 complete phalanx 2 of left toe I,	0.3 g
2 almost complete phalanges 2	1.7 g
2 frg. of phalanx 2,	0.2 g
3 frg. of phalanges 3,	0.5 g
2 frg. of sesamoids,	0.2 g
Residue (bone):	*54.4 g*

Table 2. Measurements of cremated dog bones from urn 1 of Borger burial mound XI. N.B. the bones have been shrunk by the burning; therefore measurements are minima

	Maximum length (GL)	***Proximal width (Bp)***	***Minimum width of diaphysis (SD)***	***Distal width (Bd)***
Phalanx 1 of toe III or IV	33.5	10.8	7.0	9.2
Phalanx 1	-	-	-	8.4
Phalanx 2	20.1	9.6	6.5	-
Phalanx 2	21.1	9.4	6.5	9.2
Phalanx 2 of toe I	14.1	6.7	4.6	-

Table 3. Borger, burial mound XI, urn 2. Numbers and weights of the identified cremated bones, and weight of the residue. MNI: minimum number of individuals; frg.: fragment(s) ; cf. dog/human: identification as dog/human not 100 % certain

Cremated dog bones, 6.6 g: MNI = 1	
8 cranial frg. (cf. dog),	2.9 g
1 frg. of upper first molar,	0.1 g
2 tooth frg.,	0.1 g
1 frg. of humerus (cf. dog),	2.1 g
1 frg. of radius (cf. dog),	0.4 g
Human bones: 2.6 g, MNI = 1, child	
7 cranial frg. (5 of them cf. human),	1,7 g
1 frg of cervical vertebra,	0.4 g
2 frg. of long bones,	0.5 g
Residue (bone mixed with sand):	*174.5 g*

phalanges 1 and 2 (Table 2) suggest that the dog was of considerable size, e.g. a sheepdog. The phalanges 1 and 2 had fused proximal epiphyses, which means that the dog was at least 4–5 months old (all the age criteria are after Habermehl 1975).

Urn 2 contained 183.7 g of a mixture of cremated bone and sand. A total of 6.6 g of cremated bone was identified as dog bones. The identification of some dog bones was made with some reservation (Tables 1 and 3). The size and age of the dog are unknown. Saddha Cuijpers, a specialist in human cremated bone, identified 2.6 g of cremated bone as from a young child (Lanting *et al.* 2001b) (Table 3).

Various body parts have been recognized among the dog remains from urn 1 and 2 (Tables 1 and 3). This means that the dog bones in urn 1 and urn 2 most probably represent complete dogs and not partial skeletons such as legs, feet or a skull.

The urns also contained grave goods. Urn 1 contained unburnt fragments of a bronze bracelet and the eye-side end of an unburnt sewing needle. These objects had been put into urn 1 together with the cremated bone after the cremation. A burnt decorated bone toggle made out of a sheep radius was found in urn 2. The toggle was presumably attached to the clothes of the child during the cremation (Fig. 7).

Samples of cremated bone from the two urns were dated with the AMS-radiocarbon dating method for cremated bone, which uses calcium carbonate instead of collagen (Lanting *et al.* 2001a). These samples dated the contents of the urns as from the periods 1430–1210 cal. BC and 1410–1210 cal. BC, respectively (Table 4). Both dates are at the very end of the Middle Bronze Age.

Dog cremations are very rare in the Bronze Age in Northwest and Central Europe. Andralojc (1993: Fig. 4) gives no instances of cremated dogs for the Early and Middle Bronze Age in Central Europe (Germany, Denmark, Poland, Czech Republic, Slovakia, Hungary, Bulgaria and Romania) and they are neither known for Western Europe. The cremation of dogs in a funerary context seems to start at the very end of the Middle Bronze Age and becomes rather common in the Iron Age (Andralojc 1993: Fig. 5). The two Borger urns are early examples of this funerary custom.

Nine cremated dogs were found in the Late Bronze Age burial mounds field of Tornow, municipality of Calau (southeast Brandenburg, Germany) (Teichert and Teichert 1976; Breddin 1965). Eight of them were found in burial mounds, the ninth in a plain grave. The Tornow dogs were cremated together with horses, cattle, sheep/goats and pigs and a red deer (Teichert and Teichert 1976: Tabelle 2). The ashes of the Tornow cremated dogs and other animals were found in pits, not in urns like in Borger.

The Borger and Tornow cremated dogs may have been grave gifts to deceased human beings. That no human remains have been identified among the ashes in urn 1 of the Borger burial mound (Table 1) may be accidental. Perhaps no ash from the cremated human being, perhaps a child like in urn 2, was collected from the pyre and put into the urn. The unburnt bracelet and sewing needle fragments suggest that urn 1 was also connected with a human cremation.

That most of the cremated dogs were found in burial mounds (i.e., the two Borger dogs and eight of nine Tornow dogs (Teichert and Teichert 1976: Tabelle 2)), suggests that the cremated dogs were grave gifts to elite persons.

Fig. 6. Borger, burial mound XI, urn 2. Tooth fragments of the cremated dog. Scale bar = 1 cm

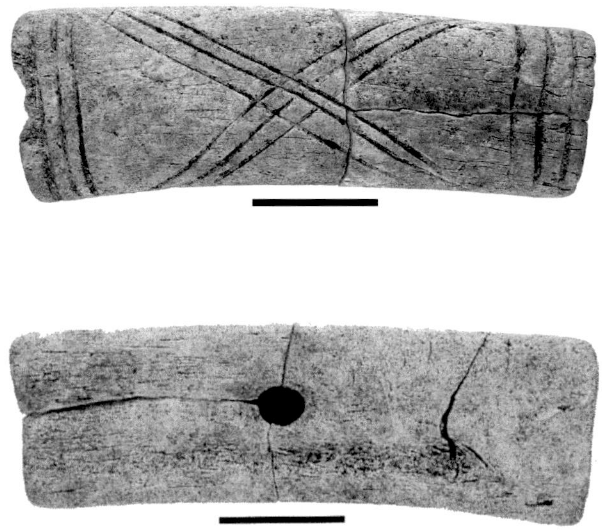

Fig. 7. Borger, burial mound XI, urn 2. Burnt bone toggle made out of a sheep radius, which was presumably attached to the clothes of the cremated child. Top: anterior side with a decoration, bottom: posterior side with a hole. Scale bar = 1 cm

Dimini: the Lamióspito tholos tomb, Greece

The Lamióspito tholos (vaulted) tomb is situated 300 m northwest of the Neolithic and Bronze Age (Mycenaean) site of Dimini (Adrími-Sismáni 1990; 1991; Adrími-Sismáni *et al.* 1990). The archaeological site of Dimini is situated on a small hill 5 km west of the town of Volos, the capital of the district of Magnisia, on the way from Dimini to Sesklo. A tholos tomb consists of an entrance passage, the *dromos*, a narrowing in the dromos, the doorway or *stomion*, and the circular, vaulted, subterranean tomb itself, the *thalamos*. Tholos tombs are generally considered as the burial places of the local elite (Taylour 1983: 79–83).

H. G. Lolling and P. Wolters discovered the Lamióspito tholos tomb at the end of the 19th century and made excavations in the *thalamos* and the *dromos* (Lolling 1884: 99–103; Lolling and Wolters 1886; 1887). The Lamióspito *thalamos* has a diameter of 8.5 m and a height of 9 m; the *stomion* is 3.6 m high. Although the tomb had been plundered the excavation yielded rich finds, such as gold jewellery, beads and necklaces of glass-paste, ivory items and bronze weapons. A double human burial was also found.

The pottery found in the *dromos* dates the Lamióspito tholos tomb as from the Late Helladic III A 2 period, which is placed in the second half of the 14th century BC (c. 1340–1320 BC) (Adrími-Sismáni *et al.* 1990: 33; Adrími-Sismáni 1991). Lolling and Wolters (1886: 437) found some bones and ashes together with pottery and golden sheets at either side of the *dromos* 2 m in front of the door. They recognised some of the bones as not human, but gave no species identifications.

A second Mycenaean tholos tomb is located in the hill of Dimini itself. This tholos tomb dates from the Late Helladic III B period (c. 1320–1200 BC). Elite inhabitants of the site of Dimini in the Mycenaean period may have been buried within the two tholos tombs (Adrími-Sismáni 1991).

The 13th Ephorate of Prehistoric and Classical Antiquities of the Greek State in Volos excavated a 5.5 m

Table 4. AMS-^{14}C-dates of samples of burnt (calcined) dog (and/or human) bone from the urns 1 and 2 from Borger burial mound XI (calibration carried out with OxCal)

	Uncalibrated ^{14}C date	*Calibrated date and probability*
Urn 1 (GrA-17601)	3065±40 BP	1430–1210 cal. BC (95.4 %)
Urn 2 (GrA-17602)	3045±40 BP	1410–1210 cal. BC (90.6 %)

Table 5. Animal and human bones found in pit 1 and pit 2 in the Mycenaean tholos tomb Lamióspito in Dimini (Greece), excavated in 1989. Period: LH III A 2 (second half of 14th century BC). L: left-hand side, R: right-hand side, L/R: left- and right-hand side (cranium and vertebrae) or left-hand or right-hand side, MNI: minimum number of individuals for each element (columns) and for the pits (row), vert.: vertebrae, cart.: cartilage

	Pit 1				***Pit 2***			
	L	**R**	**L/R**	**MNI**	**L**	**R**	**L/R**	**MNI**
Dog bones								
cranium			2	2			1	1
mandible	1	3		3	1	1		1
atlas							2	2
epistropheus			1	1			1	1
vert. cervicales			7	2			5	1
vert. thoracales			8	1			13	1
vert. lumbales			7	2			9	2
sacrum			2	2				
costae			33	2			38	2
sternum							4	1
cart. costo-sternum							3	1
scapula	1	1		2	2	2		2
humerus	2	1		2	2	1		2
radius	1	1		1	1	1		1
ulna		1		1	1	1		1
metacarpus II			2	2	1	1		1
metacarpus III					1	1		1
metacarpus IV	1	1		1	1	1		1
metacarpus V						1		1
pelvis	2			2	3	3		3
femur	3	3		3	1	2		2
tibia	2	1		3	2	1		2
fibula	2	2		2	1	1		1
calcaneus					1	1		1
metatarsus II	1	1		1		1		1
metatarsus III			3	2	1	1		1
metatarsus IV			3	2	1	1		1
metatarsus V			3	2	1	1		1
baculum							1	1
phalanx 1							6	
phalanx 2							3	
number of dog bones	16	15	71		21	22	83	
MNI of dogs				5				3
Human bones								
cf. radius			1	1				
ulna			1	1				
femur			1	1				
Foetal pig bone								
ulna							1	1
cf. Sheep/goat								
cf. femur							2	1
Testudo sp.								
carapace fragment							1	1

long, 0.5 m wide feature in the *thalamos* of the Lamióspito tholos tomb in 1989. The feature was just right of the entrance to the *thalamos* and followed the curvature of the wall. It had been dug into the natural rock. Two concentrations of unburnt animal bones were found in it.

Mrs. V. Adrími-Sismáni, the director of the 13th Ephorate of Prehistoric and Classical Antiquities, asked me in 1999 to study the bones from these two pits, which are called pit 1 and pit 2. At that moment I was working on the animal remains from the Hellenistic town of New Halos (Prummel 2003). I took the opportunity to study the Lamióspito bones.

The bones from the two pits are in excellent preservation condition. Most of the bones are complete. No cut marks are visible. The bones are mainly dog bones. The numbers of dog bones in pit 1 and pit 2 amount to 102 and 126, respectively (Table 5). The distribution of the bones over the skeleton (Table 5) and the pairs of left and right bones of equal size (Table 6) suggest that the dog bones in each pit originate from a limited number of complete or partial dog skeletons. The minimum numbers of individuals are five for pit 1 and three for pit 2 (Table 5). I labelled the dogs from pit 1 A through E and those from pit 2 a through c.

Pit 1, dog A. The completely fused pairs of left and right humeri and left and right radii are attributed to dog A. The estimates of the height at the withers for these bones are between 50.3 and 51.5 cm (Table 6). The skull with fused sutures, a pair of left and right mandibles with the permanent dentition and a fragment of a right ulna may originate from this dog because of the similar size and age. Dog A was older than 9 months.

Pit 1, dog B. A pair of left and right femora with almost fused proximal and distal epiphyses are labelled as dog B. The fusion lines are still visible. A left tibia with fused distal end and a still visible proximal fusion line may also belong to this dog. This dog was about 6–11 months old on account of its almost fused epiphyses. Dog B had a height at the withers of about 53.8 cm (Table 6).

Pit 1, dog C. A pair of left and right femora with completely fused epiphyses and a left tibia are attributed to dog C. This dog measured 55.8–55.9 cm at the withers and was older than 9 months.

Pit 1, dog D. A right tibia and a pair of fibulae are attributed to dog D, which measured about 57 cm at the withers (Table 6). The fibulae have completely fused epiphyses at both ends, whereas the fusion line of the proximal end of the tibia is still visible. This dog was about 6–11 months old.

Pit 1, dog E. A proximal half of a humerus with open epiphysis and the proximal halves of a left and a right femur both with open proximal epiphysis are attributed to dog E. Dog E died younger than 6–9 months old.

The dog bones found in pit 1 that are not attributed to a specific dog probably originate from the dogs A–E. A cranium fragment consisting of the left and right frontals of a larger skull than that attributed to dog A, but with unfused sutures, may belong to dog B or to dog D. Two right mandibles of adult dogs may belong to dogs B, C and/or D.

The vertebrae from pit 1 originate from at least three dogs, a smaller adult one (perhaps dog A), a larger adult dog (perhaps dog C) and a dog with unfused vertebrae epiphyses (perhaps dog B). The scapulae come from a smaller dog (perhaps dog A or dog B) and a larger dog (perhaps dog C or dog D). The two left pelvis halves have fused acetabula. One pelvis half has fused ilium and ischium epiphyses, whereas those of the others are unfused. These epiphyses fuse at 20–24 months. The two left pelvis halves may belong to dog A and dog C. All the metacarpi and metatarsi have fused epiphyses. They represent at least two dogs, which are presumably among the dogs A–D (Table 5).

Pit 1 did not contain any dog phalanges, sesamoids or caudal vertebrae. That the carpus and tarsus bones are also lacking suggests that the small bones were overlooked during excavation or were never buried into the pit. There is no indication that the dogs had been skinned (cf. Hamilakis 1996: 160).

Pit 1 also contained three human bones (Table 5). Their presence suggests that the human bones and the dog bones had been re-buried into the pit. The incompleteness of the five dog skeletons confirms this hypothesis.

Pit 2 contained the remains of three dogs (Tables 5 and 6). The largest dog bones in pit 2 are attributed to dog a. It had a height at the withers of 58.5–60.8 cm, and is thus the largest dog in the Lamióspito (Table 6). The skeleton of this dog is almost completely present. An atlas, the epistropheus and most of the other vertebrae (Table 5) may belong to dog a. The sacrum, caudal vertebrae, the carpus bones and the smaller tarsus bones and most of the phalanges are lacking. The tooth wear of dog a suggests an age of about 2 years.

A series of smaller dog bones from pit 2 (an atlas, some of the lumbar vertebrae, the scapulae, humeri, pelvis halves, femora and tibiae) are attributed to dog b, which had a height at the withers between 48.8 and 51,5 cm and was more than 9 months old. The third pair of left and right pelvis halves of a dog smaller than dog a and dog b, was attributed to dog c. The pelvis bones were not as far developed as those from dog a and dog b. This suggests that dog c was a young dog.

A single baculum was found in pit 2, which means that at least one of the dogs in pit 2 was a male dog. The baculum may originate from dog a because of its large size (Table 6). All the dog pelvis bones from pit 2 have sharp pubis rims. Although the shape of the pubis is not as reliable a sex criterion as the baculum, it might suggest that all three dogs in pit 2 were males.

The foetal pig radius found in pit 2 (Table 5) may originate from the last meal of one of the dogs. That dogs do eat pig foetuses has been demonstrated archaeozoologically before. Large parts of a foetal pig were in the belly of a dog in the early medieval cemetery of Oosterbeintum in the Netherlands (Knol *et al.* 1995/96, 324–325). Two fragments of perhaps a sheep/goat femur and a tortoise carapace fragment in pit 2 (Table 5) are perhaps accidental finds. Pit 2 represents either the original place of burial of dog a to which the remains of

Table 6. Measurements of dog bones from pit 1 and pit 2 of the tholos tomb Lamióspito in Dimini. The bone measurements are in mm, the heights at the withers in cm (calculated after Harcourt 1974: 154 and Clark 1995: 22). The measurements were taken after Von den Driesch (1976). The numbers between brackets for the cranium and mandible measurements refer to the Von den Driesch system. L: left-hand bone, R: right-hand bone. The characters A-D and a-b refer to individual dogs in pit 1 and pit 2 (only given if the bone was attributed to an individual dog – see main text).

Cranium	**pit 1**	**pit 2**
	cf. A	a
Basal length, basion-prosthion (3)	-	174.0
Length basion-synsphenion (4)	45.4	51.5
Basifacial axis (5)	119.6	126.7
Upper neurocranium length (7)	98.8	105.3
Facial length (9)	110.2	116.5
Length M2–P1 (15)	61.5	67.0
Length M1–M2 (16)	18.3	18.5
Length P1–P4 (17)	47.9	50.9
Length of P4	19.3	20.3
Width of P4	9.6	11.2
Length of M1	13.8	14.3
Width of M1	15.4	15.7
Width otion – otion (23)	66.4	71.1
Width at occipital condyles (25)	38.0	40.3
Max. width paraoccipit. processes (26)	50.2	52.9
Width of foramen magnum (27)	18.8	20.8
Height of foramen magnum (28)	14.6	17.3
Max. neurocranium width (29)	56.0	60.1
Zygomatic width (30)	108.2	111.0
Frontal width (32)	55.2	56.6
Least width between orbits (33)	35.9	41.9
Least palatal width (35)	33.2	36.7
Width at the canine alveoli (36)	36.6	38.7
Height akrokranion – basion (40)	45.7	48.6

Mandible	**pit 1**	**pit 2**
	cf. A	a
Total length (1)	136.9	146.4
Length angular proc. ramus – infradentale (2)	137.8	147.2
Length indentation ramus – infradentale (3)	132.0	141.5
Length M_3–C (7)	76.8	80.7
Length M_3–P_1 (8)	71.4	76.7
Length M_3–P_2 (9)	66.5	71.6
Length of M_1 (13)	22.0	22.6
Width of M_1 (13)	8.5	9.2
Height of the vertical ramus (18)	59.5	62.2

Scapula	**pit 1**	**pit 1**	**pit 2**	**pit 2**	**pit 2**	**pit 2**
dog/side	L	R	a: L	a: R	b: L	b: R
HS	137.9	128.0	148.5	148.0	-	-
SLC	24.4	24.3	27.3	27.1	25.1	24.9
GLP	29.6	32.5	35.1	35.6	31.2	31.7
LG	25.5	27.3	28.4	28.8	25.5	26.1
BG	17.2	17.5	19.0	19.0	18.0	17.9

Humerus	**pit 1**	**pit 1**	**pit 2**	**pit 2**	**pit 2**
dog/side	A: L	A: R	a: L	a: R	b: L
GL	156.7	154.5	180.7	182.1	150.0
GLC	152.6	151.0	174.5	175.9	145.1
Bp	28.4	27.9	29.7	30.5	31.7
Dp	38.4	38.1	41.0	42.9	41.0
SD	13.8	13.9	14.7	14.5	12.7
Bd	32.4	32.6	36.9	36.2	32.7
H. at the withers	51.1	50.3	59.1	59.8	48.8

Radius	**pit 1**	**pit 1**	**pit 2**	**pit 2**
dog/side	A: L	A: R	a: L	a: R
GL	154.8	155.7	177.7	178.6
Bp	18.3	18.8	19.2	19.5
SD	13.8	14.3	14.0	14.0
Bd	25.3	24.4	26.0	25.7
H at the withers	51.2	51.5	58.5	58.7

Table 6. cont.

Ulna	**pit 1**	**pit 2**	**pit 2**
dog/side	cf. A: R	a: L	a: R
GL	-	209.0	211.2
DPA	24.1	26.5	26.1
SDO	20.0	22.9	23.0
BPC	17.4	20.4	19.4
H. at the withers	-	58.7	59.3

Metacarpus II	**pit 1**	**pit 1**	**pit 2**
dog			a
GL	59.4	60.5	61.0
H at the withers	54.3	55.3	55.8

Metacarpus III	**pit 2**
dog	a
GL	69.6
H at the withers	55.7

Metacarpus IV	**pit 1**	**pit 1**	**pit 2**
dog	L	R	a
GL	69.2	69.2	69.3
H at the withers	55.5	55.5	55.6

Metacarpus V	**pit 2**
dog	a
GL	59.8
H at the withers	57.0

Pelvis	**pit 1**	**pit 2**	**pit 2**
dog/side	L	L/R	L/R
GL	147.0	161.0	143.0

Femur	**pit 1**	**pit 1**	**pit 1**	**pit 1**	**pit 2**	**pit 2**	**pit 2**
dog/side	C: L	C: R	B: L	B: R	a: L	a: R	b: R
GL/GLC	-	182.3	175.5	175.0	197.9	197.8	168.2
Bp	39.0	39.4	39.0	39.4	39.6	40.7	37.3
DC	18.9	19.1	18.4	19.1	20.1	20.2	19.4
SD	15.1	15.0	13.8	13.7	14.7	14.7	13.0
Bd	-	32.2	32.1	31.8	34.6	33.9	31.8
H at the withers	-	55.9	53.8	53.7	60.8	60.8	51.5

Baculum	**pit 2**
dog	cf. a
Length	106.1
Maximum width	8.7

Tibia	**pit 1**	**pit 1**	**pit 1**	**pit 2**	**pit 2**	**pit 2**
dog/side	D: R	C: L	B: L	a: L	a: R	b: L
GL	192.4	188.0	181.0	197.7	198.1	169.5
Bp	35.1	34.3	34.4	36.4	36.4	-
SD	14.3	14.8	13.1	14.4	14.2	13.6
Bd	23.1	22.3	23.8	24.4	24.4	23.4
H at the withers	57.1	55.8	53.8	58.7	58.8	50.4

Fibula	**pit 1**	**pit 1**	**pit 2**	**pit 2**
dog/side	cf. D: L	cf. D: R	a	a
GL	170.4	168.8	186.2	188.0

Calcaneus	**pit 2**	**pit 2**
dog/side	L	R
GL	45.6	45.5
GB	19.7	20.0

Metatarsus II	**pit 2**
dog	a
GL	69.3
H at the withers	57.6

Metatarsus III	**pit 1**	**pit 1**	**pit 2**
dog			a
GL	75.6	67.2	77.4
H at the withers	56.0	49.5	57.3

Metatarsus IV	**pit 1**	**pit 1**	**pit 2**
dog			a
GL	66.6	59.0	79.0
H at the withers	47.3	41.6	56.6

Metatarsus V	**pit 1**	**pit 1**	**pit 2**
dog			a
GL	66.8	59.2	71.1
H at the withers	53.7	47.4	57.3

dog b and dog c had been added or the re-burial place of (parts of) the dog skeletons a, b and c. The second possibility seems to be the more probable of the two, also considering the partial dog skeletons and the few human bones in pit 1.

The Lamióspito tholos tomb of Dimini is the fourteenth Greek burial site from the Mycenaean period where dog skeletons or dog bones were found in human graves (the possible dog burial in a human tomb at Vapheio (Day 1984: nr. 20) is not included in this count). Day (1984) and Hamilakis (1996: 162) gave overviews of the Mycenaean dog burials. The other thirteen dog burials in human graves are from Crete (Knossos, Mavrospelia), Archanes (Phourni, and Gournes), mainland Greece (Mycenae, two graves in the Kalkani Cemetery), Dendra, Asine, Kokla, Kallithea, Galatas, Thebes (Kolonaki Cemetery, Perati) and Euboia (Oxylinthos). Lamióspito is the most northern grave with dog remains. The nearest neighbours are Oxylinthos and Thebes. The Peleponnese shows a concentration of dogs in human graves.

Five of the Mycenaean graves with dogs are tholos tombs (Archanes, Dendra, Kallithea, Oxylinthos and Lamióspito (Dimini). The other nine graves with dogs are chamber graves (Knossos, Gournes, both graves in Mycenae, Asine, Thebes, Kokla, Galatas and Perati). The dog bones that were found in these graves are skeletons, partial skeletons or isolated bones. The dog skeletons or dog bones were hardly ever found in articulation, but were mostly scattered (Day 1984; Hamilakis 1996: 162). Tholos and chamber graves were presumably the graves of the local elites (Taylour 1983).

The tholos and chamber graves with dog bones or dog skeletons mainly date from between 1390 and 1200 BC (Day 1984; Hamilakis 1996: 162). The Perati chamber tomb, which contained a cremated dog, is a little later, between 1200 and 1100 BC. All the other dogs were unburnt like the Lamióspito dogs.

Information on size, age and sex of the dogs from the other thirteen graves is rare. Galatas dog number 1 measured between 36.2 and 39.1 cm at the withers (Hamilakis 1996: 159) and was thus much smaller than the dogs from the Lamióspito tomb in Dimini (height at the withers between 49 and 61 cm, n = 6). Some mandible measurements of the Kokla dog (Boessneck and von den Driesch 1984: 333) suggest that this dog was of comparable size as the Lamióspito dogs (as far as tooth size correlates with the height at the withers).

The use of dogs in a funerary context in the Middle and Late Bronze Age

Hamilakis (1996: 163–165) associated the dogs in Mycenaean tholos and chamber graves with hunting. He mainly based his theory on the Mycenaean iconography, which suggests that hunting was associated with high status (Morris 1990; Marinatos 1990). Slightly higher game proportions in the archaeozoological records from the Mycenaean period seem to support Hamilakis' thesis (Hamilakis 1996; Halstead 2003: 260).

Because most Mycenaean elite sites are rather poor in bones of wild fauna Hamilakis (1996) portrayed the hunting by the Mycenaean elite not as real hunting, i.e. going out with a dog and trying to find and capture wild animals, but as the concept of going out for a hunt. He saw the link between the Mycenaean elite and hunting as mainly imaginary. The elite adhered to the concept of being hunters, even though real hunting was not very important in daily life. Hamilakis (1996) saw the dogs in the tholos and chamber graves as graves goods that confirmed the status of the elite as hunters.

Halstead (2003: 257) put forward that Mycenaean textual references to wild mammals are limited. Only deer are mentioned at two instances. Halstead suggests that the importance of hunting for food was more important than the texts suggest (Halstead 2003: 257). There are many passages in these Mycenaean texts that deal with animals, but they are mainly livestock records that reflect the importance of livestock and herding for the palatial society (Halstead 2003:258) (even allowed for the restrictions in the interpretation of these records discussed by Halstead (2003)).

Halstead (2003: 257) also noted that dogs are virtually absent in the Mycenaean texts and that the importance of dogs in the elite funerary customs is not reflected in these texts. This comment can be expanded with the observation that the functions of living dogs in daily life got neither much attention in these texts. Shepherd dogs that defended the flocks against predators and kept them together were certainly important in the Mycenaean world.

My suggestion is to expand Hamilakis' association of the dogs from tholos tombs and chamber graves with the concept of hunting by considering the possible functions of living Mycenaean dogs. Who never goes hunting, will not keep hunting dogs and cannot kill a hunting dog when there is a funeral. The function of the dogs buried in the tholos and chamber graves might have been hunting dog, shepherd dog, watchdog, pet, fighting dog, status symbol and perhaps a combination of these and other functions.

A dog that is killed during or because of a funeral and is buried into a grave gets a new meaning or new meanings. I disagree with Hamilakis that the only possible association of the dogs in tholos and chamber graves should be that of hunting. The dogs could have symbolised one or more values like hunting, animal husbandry, housekeeping and the maintenance of the family, love, combat, warfare and perhaps others. The dogs cremated in Borger and Tornow may have had comparable meanings.

Acknowledgements

The 13th Ephorate of Prehistoric and Classical Antiquities of the Greek state in Volos is thanked for the kind permission to publish the data of the Lamióspito animal pits. I thank R. J. Kosters and T. P. Jacobs, collaborators of the Groningen Institute of Archaeology for the first sorting out of the cremated bone from the Borger urns.

References

Adrími-Sismáni, V. 1990. The prehistoric settlement of Dimini. *Archaiologia* **34**, 25–30 (in Greek language with English summary).

Adrími-Sismáni, V. 1991. Le site préhistorique de Dimini. *Dossiers d'archéologie* **159**, 18–19.

Adrími-Sismáni, V., Z. Malakasióti and A. Bátiziou-Evstathíou 1990. The Mycenaean Magnesia. *Archaiologia* **34**, 31–39 (in Greek language with English summary).

Andralojc, M. 1993. *The Phenomenon of Dog Burials in the Prehistoric Times on the Area of Middle Europe*. Bruxelles, Ollodagos. Mémoires de la Société Belge d'Études Celtiques/ Belgisch Genootschap voor Keltische studies.

Boessneck, J. and A. von den Driesch 1984. Die zoologische Dokumentation der Reste von vier Pferden und einem Hund aus einem mykenischen Schachtgrab in Kokla bei Argos (Peloponnesos). *Spixiana* **7**, 327–333.

Breddin, R. 1965. Untersuchungen eines Lausitzer Hügelgräberfeldes. *Ausgrabungen und Funde* **10**, 127–131.

Clark, K. M. 1995. The later prehistoric dog: the emergence of canine diversity. *ArchaeoZoologia* **7(2)**, 9–32.

Day, L. P. 1984. Dog burials in the Greek world. *American Journal of Archaeology* **88**, 21–32.

Driesch, A. von den 1976. *A Guide to the Measurement of Animal Bones from Archaeological Sites*. Peabody Museum Bulletin 1. Harvard: Harvard University.

Halstead, P. 2003. Text and bones: Contrasting Linear B and archaeozoological evidence for animal exploitation in Mycenaean southern Greece, pp. 257–261, in Kotjabopoulou, K., Y. Hamilakis, P. Halstead, C. Gamble and P. Elefanti (eds), *Zooarchaeology in Greece, Recent Advances* (British School at Athens Studies 9). London: British School at Athens.

Hamilakis, Y. 1996. A footnote on the archaeology of power: animal bones from a Mycenaean chamber tomb at Galatas, NE Peloponnese. *The Annual of the British School at Athens* **91**, 153–166.

Harcourt, R. A. 1974. The dog in prehistoric and early historic Britain. *Journal of Archaeological Science* **1**, 151–175.

Knol, E., W. Prummel, H. T. Uytterschaut, M. L. P. Hoogland, W. A. Casparie, G. J. de Langen, E. Kramer and J. Schelvis 1995/ 96. The early medieval cemetery of Oosterbeintum (Friesland). *Palaeohistoria* **37/38**, 245–416.

Lanting, J. N., A. Aerts-Bijma and H. van der Plicht 2001a. Dating of cremated bone. *Radiocarbon* **43**, 249–254.

Lanting, J. N. W. Prummel and A. G. F. M. Cuijpers 2001b. Eindelijk de hond in de pot gevonden. *Paleo-aktueel* **12**, 80–84.

Lolling, H. G. 1884. Mittheilungen aus Thessalien. *Mittheilungen des Kaiserlich Deutschen Archaeologischen Instituts, Athenische Abtheilung* **9**, 97–116.

Lolling, H. G. and P. Wolters, 1886. Das Kuppelgrab bei Dimini. *Mittheilungen des Kaiserlich Deutschen Archaeologischen Instituts, Athenische Abtheilung* **11**, 435–443.

Lolling, H. G. and P. Wolters, 1887. Das Kuppelgrab bei Dimini II. *Mittheilungen des Kaiserlich Deutschen Archaeologischen Instituts, Athenische Abtheilung* **12**, 136–138.

Marinatos, N. 1990. Celebrations of death and symbolism of the lion hunt, pp. 143–148, in R. Hägg and G. C. Nordquist (eds), *Celebrations of death and divinity in the Bronze Age Argolid.* Stockholm: Åström.

Morris, C. 1990. In pursuit of the white tusked boar: aspects of hunting in Mycenaean society, pp. 149–156, in R. Hägg and G. C. Nordquist (eds), *Celebrations of Death and Divinity in the Bronze Age Argolid.* Stockholm: Åström,.

Prummel, W. 2003. Animal husbandry and mollusc gathering in Hellenistic Halos (Thessaly), pp. 175–223, in H. R. Reinders and W. Prummel (eds), *Housing in Hellenistic Halos, a Hellenistic town in Thessaly, Greece*. Balkema Publishers: Lisse/ Abingdon/Exton (PA)/Tokyo.

Taylour, W. 1983. *The Mycenaeans*. London, Thames & Hudson.

Teichert, M. and L. Teichert, 1976. Osteoarchäozoologische Untersuchung der Tierleichenbrandreste von einem Lausitzer Hügelgräberfeld bei Tornow, Kr. Calau. *Veröffentlichungen des Museums für Ur- und Frühgeschichte Potsdam* **10**, 101–106.

University of Groningen
Groningen Institute of Archaeology
Poststraat 6
NL-9712 ER Groningen
Netherlands

w.prummel@rug.nl

9th ICAZ Conference, Durham 2002
Dogs and People in Social, Working, Economic or Symbolic Interaction
(eds Lynn M Snyder and Elizabeth A. Moore) pp. 77–84

10. An Ethnoarcheological Study of Chase Hunting with Gundogs by the Aboriginal Peoples of Taiwan

Atsushi Nobayashi

*This paper presents the results of an ethnoarchaeological analysis of hunting activity by the Tsou people, one of Taiwan's aboriginal groups. They hunt wild boar (*Sus scrofa taivanus*) for their own use. The age structure of animals captured by Tsou while hunting with dogs is then compared to animals taken during snare hunting by the Paiwan, a second aboriginal group (Nobayashi 1999). Mortality patterns, based on age at death estimations have often been used in zooarchaeological analysis to reconstruct seasonality in prehistoric hunting activity. A seasonal pattern in prey taken is then interpreted as changing subsistence choices, or site mobility. In this paper, two different hunting techniques (gundog and snare) are described in their ecological and cultural contexts, providing a model for interpretation of archaeofaunal hunting assemblages.*

Introduction

The research area and the Tsou

This paper examines the hunting activities of the Tsou people of S village in Chayi prefecture, in the middle of the island of Taiwan (Fig. 1). The field research of this study was done in August 1999 and from July to August 2000. The research utilized two types of surveys, one was interviews conducted among the Tsou people, the other was analysis of the bones of the animals which were hunted by Tsou hunters. S village lies in a mountainous area above 600m elevation. Nearly all inhabitants of the village are Tsou. The village lies in an area of broad leaf forest, which provides good habitat for wild boar, deer, muntjak, mountain goat and monkey, all of which have been favored game for the aboriginal peoples of Taiwan.

The Tsou people

Today, aboriginal or indigenous people make up just 1.4% of Taiwan's population. Their traditional languages fall in the Austronesian group, although today they primarily speak Mandarin. The Tsou people are a relatively small group, numbering about 7000 individuals. They live in the mountainous areas around Ari Mountain and Yu Mountain. Anthropologists have divided the Tsou into

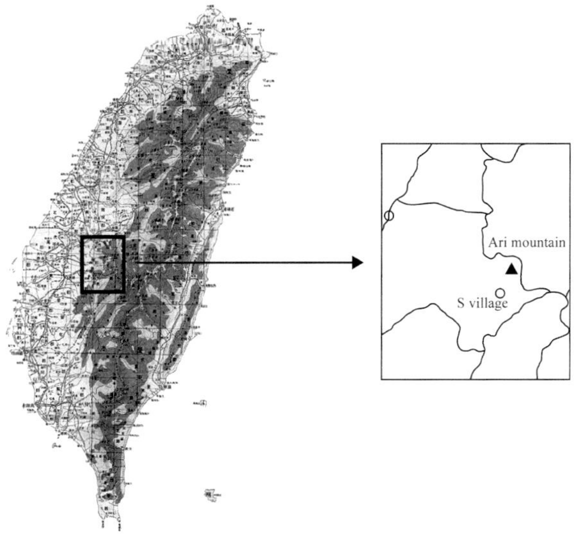

Fig. 1. The research area

Fig. 2. Tsou dogs

two groups, based on differences in language, customs and social structure (Miyaoka 1998). One group is called the "Arisan Tsou". The second, the "Southern group", is located in northern Kaoshun prefecture. "Tsou" mean "people" in the language of the Arisan Tsou, and this research was carried out among these northern Tsou people.

Subsistence and agriculture

As traditional agriculturalists, the Tsou cultivated gardens cleared by the slash-and-burn method. In these gardens they cultivated millet, rice and adlay, sweet potato, taro and some beans including peanut and adzuki bean. All of these garden products were traditionally raised for their own consumption. During Taiwan's colonial period, the Japanese colonial government encouraged the Tsou to abandon their traditional gardens and cultivate rice in irrigated fields (Miyaoka ibid.). As the Taiwanese economy developed, the Tsou tended to work away from their villages and many immigrated to the cities, where they have come to depend on cash incomes.

Traditional hunting

Hunting was also an important part of Tsou subsistence. Hunting was considered men's work. Women did not engage in hunting activities according to a report on Taiwan natives produced during the Japanese colonial period. This report further states,

> "What they most enjoy is hunting. When they go hunting, they track game, forgetting to eat or sleep. They may track game for several days. They have a number of hunting methods. A single man may go hunting with his gun and dogs. Five to ten people sometimes go hunting together. At times, all the villagers will join in the hunt, burning off a field and driving the game. Each villager has his own hunting field, and each village has its own hunting territory. However, when a pursued animal runs into another hunter 's field, the original hunter can chase and hunt it. If he is successful, he must give some of the meat from the kill to the owner of the hunting field. In general, meat is shared equally when taken in the common hunting fields. When game is taken by a hunter in a field not his own, the owner of the field receives some of the meat, even though he has not taken part in the hunt himself. Further, if the owner of the field requests the skin of the animal killed, the original hunter must give it to him. When field owners join in hunting groups, they share the skin and tail of the game taken"
> (Sayama 1915:63; translated by the author).

From the above description, it is clear that hunting was not only important in traditional subsistence, but also an exciting activity for the Taiwanese peoples. These feelings were also expressed by aged Tsou people interviewed during the course of this fieldwork.

The Tsou's traditional hunting practices were very similar to those of other Taiwanese native groups. On the other hand, they have their own system for sharing the game from hunting. I came to understand that the way in which meat of game animals was shared depended on where the animals were hunted. The Tsou owned two types of land, one was for farming and the other was for hunting. The farming land was worked by each family while the hunting area was for use by the members of each clan. The hunting area was larger than the farming area and the former included the latter. The members of a clan usually hunted in their hunting area. When they obtained game in another villagers farming area, they had to give the meat of that game to the land owner. In the course of my survey among the groups in this study, I found that each group hunted. Yet only the Tsou have tended to maintain this unique hunting tradition, using dogs. During these interviews, Tsou hunters insisted that chase hunts with dogs were the most exiting and their favorite type of hunting activity.

An ethnographic description of Tsou hunting

Tsou dogs

Tsou hunters normally use dogs when chase hunting (Fig. 2). Some hunting dogs are called *dougou* in Mandarin, which means simply "native dog". The general morphological features of these animals include short brown or black hair, a pointed nose, short and standing ears, and a slim body form. Their body length is about 1m and height at the shoulder is about 45cm. They are very aggressive and have a temperament suited to chasing game, especially wild boar. In the Tsou language, *avuo* means dog and the Tsou people do not make a linguistic distinction between their native dogs and other modern dog species.

In general, Tsou hunters who do chase hunting keep

4 to 5 dogs. However one of my informants, Pasuya, who was known as a very good hunter, kept 17, more than any other hunter in the village. Pasuya was in his middle forties. He lived together with his wife, his children and his father in S village. Pasuya and his wife were farmers and they also earned cash income by part time work in the Ecotourism Park near the village. He was not a professional hunter, nor did he sell the meat from his hunts to a restaurant. He, however, sold the meat to other people when he was asked personally to do so. When Pasuya went hunting, he usually asked his brothers or neighbors to accompany him, and the group often took along 14 to 15 dogs. Although the basic owner of these dogs was Pasuya, who bred them in his house, other members of the hunting party also shared ownership of some of the animals. Others hunters could also use some of Pasuya's dogs, even when hunting without him. As a practical matter, a single individual, Pasuya, owned, bred, and housed the dogs to prevent fights and injury among the animals during hunts. If dogs were kept and fed separately, they invariably fought when brought together for a group hunt. The Tsou hunters therefore believed that it worked best if Pasuya kept all the dogs, which they then used in hunts.

Pasuya did not necessarily consider all his dogs equal. Among his dogs, he distinguished a number of special characteristics and hunt roles which can be summarized as: Type A dogs, which had a keen nose and were excellent for finding game. Type B dogs, which could run fast and catch up with game more quickly than other dogs. These dogs then barked and threatened the game. Type C dogs, which were especially fierce and brave. These dogs would actively bite at and attempt to injure the game. Type D dogs, which only barked while around the hunters, and did not participate in chasing or cornering game.

At the time of this study, Pasuya had three Type A dogs, five Type B, five Type C and four Type D. Types B and C were morphologically basic native dogs. Although interbreeding was not observed during the course of this study, it is possible that some of the Type A dogs were interbred with modern beagles. Pasuya recognized the usefulness of beagles in scent tracking and finding game, and might have selected native/beagle mixes when breeding his own Type A dogs. Type D dogs included aged native dogs which had formerly hunted but could no longer participate, and other village mongrels. Type A, B and C dogs were usually kept in cages or on chains. All dogs except Type D were released only when fed or taken hunting. Dogs were usually given food once a day. Their food normally consisted of leftovers from their owners' meals, or sweet potato. They were also given food after hunting and they were treated to meat and bones if the hunt had been successful.

Pasuya and the other hunters gave special consideration to the Type C dogs. They were always kept away from other types. This was in part because they were quick to fight with the other dogs, on occasion even killing them, and Pasuya and the other hunters sometimes had to yell or hit them to stop their fighting. In addition, the hunters thought Type C dogs were the most important because wild boars might fight back against the dogs and hunters if their Type C dogs were not sufficiently trained and aggressive. In the other words, the success of chase hunting depended partly on Type C dogs' ability and condition. Therefore, Tsou hunters thought they should always keep several adults of Type C if they hoped to hunt. These dogs worked best between the ages of 2 and 4 to 5 years because their role was very hard during the hunt. They were sometimes injured or exhausted by attacking the game. Even if a hunter could successfully train a few Type C dogs, they usually retired at the age of about 5 years. He therefore had to breed the good dogs continuously.

Most Tsou hunters recognized these basic qualities in Type C hunting dogs, and thought that all dogs which actually participated in hunts must have some of these qualities. One man however, who hunted by himself and kept only four or five dogs, considered that animals with the qualities described as Types A and B above were the most important.

Nearly all Tsou hunters also recognized that body size and sex had nothing to do with a dogs hunting ability. They also did not breed dogs for specific characteristics or "Types", but selected them for their particular roles in the hunt based on observing them as they grew. In fact, in the Tsou language, there are no specific terms for the "types" or roles noted above. The Tsou bred their own hunting dogs, and sold puppies among themselves for low prices, or sometimes gave them away. They would not, however, sell their hunting dogs to the Han Chinese, even though the Han desired to purchase such animals.

Dogs did not begin hunting until they were more than one year old. Since the Tsou believed that puppies would learn desired behaviors from other dogs, they attempted to keep young puppies with already trained adult animals. In selecting a puppy as suitable for hunting, they would grasp it beneath the front legs, and hold it up. A puppy which acted pleased and wagged its tail was likely to be a good hunting dog.

The Tsou did not have a special method of dog training. A chosen puppy was taken along on the hunt and released after game had been captured, so that it might run around the downed game with the other dogs. The hunters gradually increased the time the puppy spent on the hunt and encouraged it to watch and understand hunting activity. They then decided the role of a puppy by observing its behaviour during the hunt.

Wild boar hunting was dangerous to both people and dogs, and in cornering game, dogs were sometimes injured. When a dog was injured, the hunters had to treat it. When one of Pasuya's dogs was injured, for example, he injected the animal with an antibiotic. When a dog was injured or killed during a boar hunt, the hunters took it back to their village. If the dog died, the hunter who owned it buried it somewhere near the village, usually in an area separate from the village cemetery. Pasuya stated that he had buried his dogs on his own premises. Other villagers did not bury hunting dogs in a single area. These hunters decided where they would bury the dogs on an individual basis. It was sometimes around the house and sometimes away from the villages. The hunters sometimes forgot the site of the grave and they did not have a special ceremony or build a monument for memory of their dogs. On the other hand, Pasuya sometimes buried dogs with part of a deer skin. During the course of this study, an old person died and no dogs were sacrificed.

The Tsou hunting party

Men might go hunting in a group or individually. When hunting in a party, the owner of the dogs was the hunt leader, and might ask his brothers, neighbors and good friends to accompany him. The membership of a hunting party was not fixed and there were no formal hunting groups or organizations. Hunting parties, however, often had at least some regular members who knew each other and their individual hunt roles well, and thus could hunt efficiently. These hunt parties usually maintained good relationships.

When hunting in a group, individuals often had different roles. A few men actively pursued and captured the game with the dogs. This was considered the main hunt group, and always included the owner of the dogs. Others took the role of pursuing game which had evaded the main party; this group included several people but no dogs. A third group moved more widely around the hunt area, watching for game movement. These men did not carry guns, but rode their motorcycles around the hunt area.

On the hunt, each hunter usually carried a gun, a bushknife, items for smoking, a transceiver, and a handful of rice or a small container of rice wine. The rice or rice wine was for use in a ceremony when game was caught. Food was not taken for consumption by men or dogs, because hunts with dogs were not considered as long hunts. With dogs, if it took more than about three hours to locate game, the hunt was considered a failure. For example, Pasuya stated that he usually took 5 or 6 hours at most on a hunt. He thought that he was able to judge whether there was game in a hunting area with about 3 hours of surveying. He partitioned off the hunting area into a few sections according to the geographical conditions and the hunt party surveyed each section for an hour. Wild boars cannot travel over so large a territory as deer or muntjak during a given period of time. Therefore, if no traces of boar were found within 3 hours, there were none within the hunting district.

The time length of a hunt also depended on the physical abilities of the hunters and their dogs. Hunts were usually started in the early morning and finished soon after noon, as air temperatures rose and both hunters and dogs became tired and could not hunt as effectively. A longer hunt would also necessitate food and supplies for both people and dogs, all of which had to be carried throughout the tracking and the chase. If a hunt could be started early and ended before noon, such inconvenience could be avoided. Occasionally however, a hunt lasted longer because of the distance traveled, or because the dogs were following a scent. Even then, the hunters did not stay in the mountains or construct special hunting stands, but returned to their villages.

Tsou hunting: A case study

The amount of time spent on a single hunt depended on the distance from the village to the hunting area, the topography of the hunt area, and the number of hunters and dogs participating in the hunt. What follows is an example of a group hunt with dogs near the village. The hunt took place at the end of August, on a cloudy but not rainy day.

The leader of the hunting party, Pasuya, decided that they should start at 5:00 AM. This hunt was initiated when a resident in the area heard the roar of a wild boar and reported it to Pasuya. The hunting areas were usually made up several rolling hills. These hills were separated by a ridge, gully, or stream. Each of the hills was usually considered a unit area for hunting. Hunters surveyed across one hill and then moved to another.

Pasuya was accompanied on this hunt by his two little brothers and neighbors who usually hunted with him. He put his Type C dogs, and others, in his small truck and drove them to the edge of the hunting areas. The other hunters traveled separately to the area by motorcycle and car.

When Pasuya arrived at the hunting area, he took all the dogs down from the truck. Although the dogs were very excited, they did not run ahead, but circled around him. They then followed Pasuya onto one of the hills in the hunting area, where, at his command, they ran off ahead of him. The main hunt party, consisting of Pasuya and one other man, proceeded along the ridge of the hill, sometimes advancing a short way into the ridge or the gully. The rest of the group separated into two support parties who traveled forward on both sides of the main party. After passing over the hill, these parties exited the area, to wait for game coming toward them at the edge of the hill. They did this in order to detect the location of the dogs in the mountainous terrain.

The scent dogs (Type A) were first to run. When they came back after a few minutes it meant that they had detected no scent in that direction, and they ran off in another direction. If the Type A dogs continued to return at short intervals, the hunters recognized that there was no game nearby, and they moved to another hunting hill. While the main party moved across a hill, the support teams ranged throughout the same area also hunting for evidence of the boar. If they detected that a boar was on another hill, they let the main party know this by radio

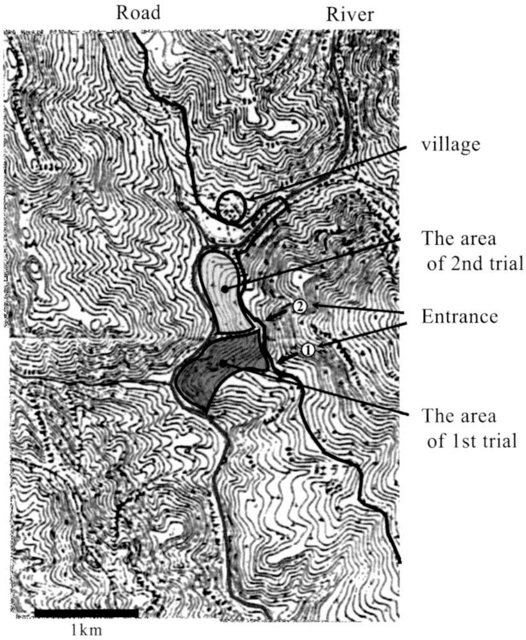

Fig. 3. The hunting area

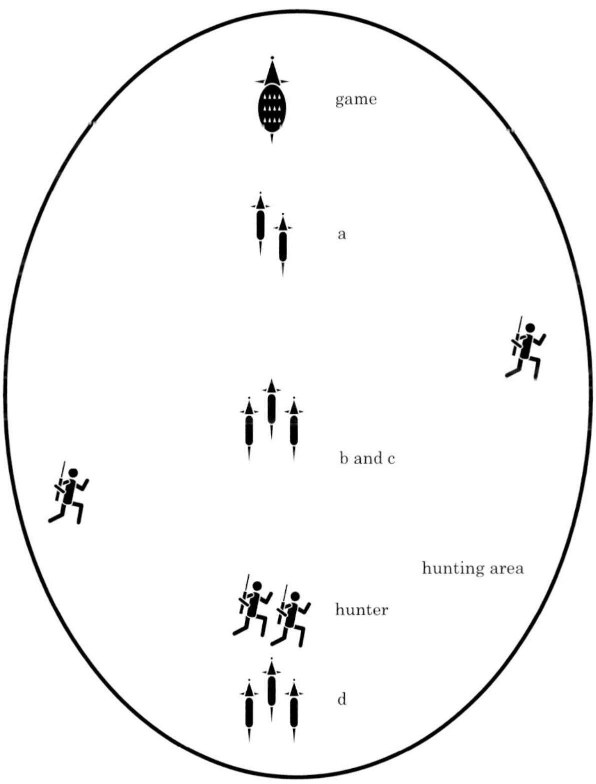

Fig. 4. The formation of the hunter and dogs

transmission. The main party then gave up the hill it was investigating, and prepared to move to another hill, based on information from the support teams. The hunters in the main party returned to the truck with the dogs and drove to the edge of the next hunting unit. Figure 3 shows the location of the hunting area which was continuously surveyed in the first and second trials.

When the Type A dogs got a scent, the other dogs also soon located it and joined in the hunt. The hunters followed the dogs. The role of the dogs was to corner the game but not to make a kill. Some dogs, especially the Type C dogs, however, tried to pounce upon or worry the game (Fig. 4). The hunters thought this too dangerous for the dogs, and tried to shoot the game as soon as possible. While a small animal might be successfully be taken by dogs, a large male boar, weighing over 50kgs and equipped with long sharp canines, could easily injure the dogs.

Traditionally, when a hunter put an end to a boar's life, he used a spear, sword or gun. The "right way" to do it, approved among the Tsou, was to hold the boar with the hands, while a sword was thrust into its side. Today however, they most often use a gun. A single-shot gun is preferred because a scatter shot load does not have enough power to kill a wild boar, and the scattered shot might also injure the dogs swarming around the prey. In order to most effectively shoot the boar, a hunter tries to approach within 20m of the animal, and aim for the side in the area of the heart. This is the most dangerous moment in the hunt, as if the hunter fails to deliver a deadly shot, the stricken animal will surely try to attack the hunter and dogs.

During this hunt, Pasuya was able to shoot an adult boar, about 90 kg. He got it in the second trial. The animal was transported to the village and then divided by Pasuya and the other hunters.

Age pattern analysis of captured prey

The sample

The samples used in analysis consist of the mandibles of wild boar which were hunted by the Tsou people, and another aboriginal group, the Paiwan. It is the custom of the Taiwanese aboriginal peoples to keep the mandibles and, in some cases, crania of their prey in their homes, as hunting trophies. Thus, it was possible to locate a number of collections with good documentation and context. Two samples (TS1, TS2) were taken by Tsou hunters by chase hunting with dogs. Two additional samples (PA1, PA2) were taken by the Paiwan hunters by snare hunting (Nobayashi 1999)

The TS1 sample was taken by a Tsou hunter using several dogs. It represents 45 animals, hunted over a period of several years. The hunter hunted alone, using dogs. From interviewing him, we knew that his hunting activity was not seasonal. Rather, he had hunted throughout the year. Sample TS2 was taken by Pasuya over approximately 8 months time (February through August), and represents 38 animals. He kept all mandibles of the game which he hunted both while alone and with others hunters. He did not divide them into those taken while hunting alone, or with other people. All the mandibles of the hunted animals were hung in Pasuya's house. Pasuya's hunting activity was also not seasonal.

The snare hunt samples, PA1 and PA2, were taken throughout the year, e.g, the hunters set snares at all times of year. Interviews with these hunters indicate that the PA1 sample represented about 30 years of hunting. The PA2 population was captured over about 15 years. Sample PA1 represents 158 animals, and PA2 100 animals. With the exception of the TS2 hunter, Pasuya, all hunts were basically made on foot and alone; therefore Pasuya may have had a slight hunting advantage.

Methods

The age at death of the animals represented by the four collections (TS1, TS2, PA1, PA1) was estimated using tooth eruption data (Genov *et al.* 1991: 400). According to these data, canines and 3rd incisors are erupted by 12 months, and the 2nd incisors erupt at about 22 months. Therefore, in this analysis, an erupted 3rd incisor was taken as indicative of an animal older than one year, while an erupted 2nd incisor represented an individual more than two years old at death.

Figure 5 presents the mortality profile for wild boar in Kampinos National Park (KNP) in Poland. KNP was established in 1959 and covers about 40,700 ha, 70% of which is covered by forests. Jezierski presents a natural die off pattern or mortality profile under no hunting pressure in the park (Jezierski 1977: 337–348). The KNP sample shows a relatively high mortality rate in the first and second year of life. KNP is at a higher latitude than Taiwan and we cannot know how this mortality profile might compare to Taiwans' wild populations. Unfortunately, there is no data on natural mortality profiles of Taiwan's wild boar. High mortality of wild boar at younger ages is also suggested in Japan and Italy,

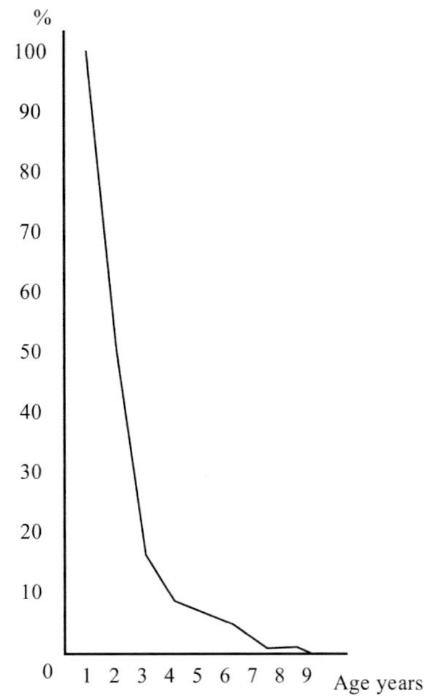

Fig. 5. The mortality of wild boar

and in temperate zones or mountainous area in northern Australia (Massei *et al.* 1997; Nakaya 2001; Saunders 1993). I therefore hypothesized that the natural mortality profile of the Taiwan wild boar was relatively high for the younger ages, and then compared the hunt data from Taiwan to the natural mortality profile of KNP.

Results

Figure 6 presents the results of the analysis of eruption patterns in each of the four sample populations, and Figure 7 is a triangular diagram based on the ratio of

Stage	Eruption pattern	PA-s	PA-l	TS-m	TS-p
I	i1/i2/i3/c/m2/m3/m4	5	4	0	0
II	i1/i2/i3/c/m2/m3/m4/M1	12	9	0	2
III	i1/i2/i3/c/P1/m2/m3/m4/M1	37	22	3	2
IV①	i1/i2/i3/C/P1/m2/m3/m4/M1	3	4	0	0
IV②	i1/i2/I3/c/P1/m2/m3/m4/M1	7	3	0	0
IV③	i1/i2/I3/C/P1/m2/m3/m4/M1	2	3	0	3
V	i1/i2/I3/C/P1/m2/m3/m4/M1/M2	15	3	1	0
VI①	I1/i2/I3/C/P1/m2/m3/m4/M1/M2	10	10	2	1
VI②	I1/i2/I3/C/P1/m2/m3/P4/M1/M2	7	3	2	0
VI③	I1/i2/I3/C/P1/m2/P3/m4/M1/M2	1	1	0	0
VI④	I1/i2/I3/C/P1/m2/P3/P4/M1/M2	2	2	1	2
VII	I1/i2/I3/C/P1/P2/P3/P4/M1/M2	6	5	3	2
VIII	I1/I2/I3/C/P1/P2/P3/P4/M1/M2	7	6	4	2
IX	I1/I2/I3/C/P1/P2/P3/P4/M1/M2/M3	6	8	4	7
X	I1/I2/I3/C/P1/P2/P3/P4/M1/M2/M3	37	17	25	17
	Total	157	100	45	38

Figure 6. The number of the samples according to the eruption patterns

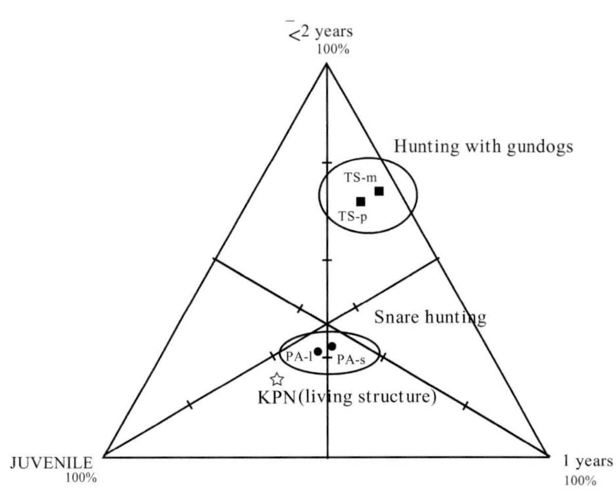

Fig. 7. A triangular diagram of the captured populations

individuals which were one year, two years and more than two years old at death. The data for the KNP is also plotted on this diagram. Although samples TS1 and TS2 represent different hunting seasons, these two samples of animals taken by chase hunting with dogs were very similar in composition. TS2 had been captured over 7 months, from February to August, while TS1 represents animals taken throughout the year. The hunter who maintained the TS1 sample stated his hunting activity did not vary seasonally, and that he used to go hunting a few times each month.

PA1 and PA2, the samples taken by snare hunting, also lie close to each other in Figure 7. The KNP population sample also lies close to PA1 and PA2, indicating that the age distribution of animals taken by snare hunting closely resembles a natural death profile in composition. In contrast, the two samples taken by chase hunting (TS1 and TS2) stand apart, due to the greater number of older individuals they contain.

Discussion

Variations in prey taken, by hunting method

The age composition of wild boar taken by chase hunting with dogs varies from that taken by snare hunting, and from the die off patterns of the KNP sample. This difference might be caused by the age distribution of the populations being hunted, e.g. a base population bias, or the variation may be a result of deliberate selection on the part of the chase hunters. When a natural population has long been under severe hunting pressure, the age profile of prey trends toward younger animals (Kanzaki 1993). Since the age structure of samples TS1 and TS2 is weighted toward older rather than younger animals, this age distribution cannot be attributed to a bias in the base game populations caused by hunting pressure.

Rather than a bias in the base population of prey animals, the age structure of animals taken by chase hunting is more likely due to deliberate prey selection, and the methods used by the Tsou chase hunters. When they go hunting, the Tsou usually spend no more time than necessary because of the physical difficulties encountered when hunting in such difficult terrain. In addition, they often begin a hunt only when informed by others about the location of adult wild boars, or when they come across animal tracks or evidence that animals have been feeding in an area. In addition, because adult boars are active over a wider geographic area than younger animals, the hunters and dogs might be more likely to come across their scent or trail.

Conversely, there are additional aspects of wild boar ecology which may explain why snare hunters tend to capture more juvenile individuals. On Taiwan, wild boar usually come into heat from September through October, and breed between October and December. The young are born the following March and April (Chao and Fang 1988: 14–18). If it is assumed that the juvenile animals (aged 6 to 9 months) in the PA1 and PA2 samples were born in March or April, then they were probably captured in August through January. These months correspond to the seasons in which wild boars come into heat and mate. At this time the female boar would probably already be away from her young of the previous year, because female wild pigs come into heat within one year of birth, at which time they are on their own and have left their litters of the previous year (Nakaya ibid.; Chao 1988). Thus, the juveniles of the previous season would probably already be on their own and more vulnerable to capture by snaring.

The relationship between social system and hunting activity

To Tsou hunters, the taking of adult wild boar has special meaning, and they recognize that chase hunting with dogs allows them to preferentially hunt these large and dangerous animals. In Tsou society, aged people have control over adults in political and ritual matters. However, skilled hunters are also admired and appreciated. Those hunters who have been injured by wild boar while hunting are especially recognized as brave, and their position in society is elevated. Only these brave hunters are allowed to wear a symbolic arm ring made from two of the long canines of the adult male boar, thus marking them to all as good and brave hunters.

The methodology and symbolic importance of Paiwan hunting contrasts sharply with that of the Tsou (Nobayashi 2001). Paiwan hunters capture prey by snare hunting, and do not preferentially pursue adult game. Paiwan society has traditionally had a strict hierarchy with only two ritual classes, chiefly and common. Membership in each class is dictated by succession, with both males and females assuming roles in these ritual classes. For the Paiwan, the primary purpose of hunting is reduced to the capturing of animals for food, and therefore hunters are not necessarily focused on acquiring the more prestigious adult or large individuals. Still, the Paiwan do value objects made from wild boar canines. These objects, however, are associated only with people belonging to the chiefly class, and thus confer no great honor on the hunters of boar themselves.

Conclusion: Archaeological Implications

Through chase hunting with dogs, the Tsou are able to preferentially take large adult male wild boars, because of the prestige associated with the hunting and killing of such a dangerous animal. A predominance of adult individuals in a hunted zooarchaeological population thus might be taken to indicate preferential hunting by methods such as those practiced by the Tsou. Additionally, it was shown that hunting during either limited periods or throughout the year led to similar composition in the captured population age profile. This means that a difference in archaeofaunal mortality patterns might not necessarily reflect differences in hunting seasons.

Conversely, a zooarchaeological population with a younger age profile, might reflect a more general hunting method such as practiced by the Paiwan snare hunters, in which the hunters earn no further status or honor by preferentially taking large and dangerous animals. Thus cultural or social values may be indirectly reflected in these very different hunted population age profiles.

References

Chao, J. and Fang, K. 1988. *The Ecological and Behavioral Study of Formosan Wild Boar* (Sus scrofa taivanus) (I). Taipei: The Council of Agriculture, The Exective Yuan.

Genov, P. V., Massei, G., Barbalova, Z. and Kostova, V. 1991. Aging wild boar (*Sus scrofa* L.) by teeth. *Proceedings of Ongules/Ungulates* **91**, 399–402.

Jezierski W. 1977. Longevity and mortality rate in a population of wild boar. *Acta Theriologica* **22(24)**, 337–348.

Kanzaki, N. 1993. Study on Population Dynamics, Hunting and Commercialization of Japanese Wild Boar (*Sus scrofa leucomystax*). PhD. thesis, Tokyo: Tokyo University of Agriculture and Industry.

Massei, G., Genov, P. V., Staines, B. W. and Gorman, M. L. 1997. Mortality of wild boar in a Mediterranean area in relation to sex and age. *Journal of Zoology* **242**, 394–400. London.

Miyaoka, M. 1998. Tsou, pp. 87–92 in Japanese Research Group on Indigenious Peoples of Taiwan (eds) *The Invitation of Taiwan Aboriginal Studies*. Tokyo, Fukyosya Press.

Nakaya, A. 2001. The unknown ecology and social of wild boar, pp. 87–92, 200–220 in Takahasi, S. (ed.), *People and Wild Boar*. Tokyo: Kokon-Shoin Press.

Nobayashi, A. 1999. An Ethnoarchaeological Analysis of Paiwan (Taiwan) Snare Hunting: A Methodological Discussion of the Interpretation of Faunal Remains. *Bulletin of the National Museum of Ethnology* Vol. **25**, No. 2.

Nobayashi, A. 2001. Taiwan native Tsou people and wild boar, pp. 79–100 in Takahasi, S. (ed), *People and Wild Boar*. Tokyo: Kokon-Shoin Press.

Saunders, G. 1993. The demography of feral pigs (*Sus scrofa*) in Kosciusko National Park, New South Wales. *Wildlife Research* **20**, 559–569.

Sayama, Y. 1915. *The Report on the Taiwan Natives, Tsou*. The committee of research on the old customs in Taiwan, The Japanese colonial government: Taihoku.

Atsushi Nobayashi
National Museum of Ethnology, Osaka
Senri Expo. Park
Suita, Osaka
Japan 568511

nova@idc.minpaku.ac.jp

9th ICAZ Conference, Durham 2002
Dogs and People in Social, Working, Economic or Symbolic Interaction
(eds Lynn M. Snyder and Elizabeth A. Moore) pp. 85–95

11. Variability in Medieval Dogs from Hungary

Márta Daróczi-Szabó

While there is a rich iconographic record of medieval dogs in Western Europe, this type of documentation was largely destroyed during past wars in Hungary. Only a few masterpieces survived, mostly beyond the former borders of the Ottoman Empire. Archaeological excavations in modern-day Hungary (i.e., the central part of the Carpathian Basin), however, offer osteological information complementary to this scanty art historical record. Skulls of over a dozen medieval dogs were first metrically analysed, and the results interpreted by comparing them with 57 modern dog and 13 wolf skulls. Morphometric variability in the medieval dog skulls from Hungary corresponds to that found in medieval art across Central and Western Europe. Textual evidence, while also rare, provides a link to medieval attitudes toward these animals.

Introduction

In this paper a comparison will be briefly made between the archaeological remains of medieval dogs in Hungary and coeval iconographic evidence of these animals. Why is such a comparison important? It is a truism that dogs are the oldest of human companions, and even today are the most popular of all pets. In spite of this, medieval Hungarian textual sources regarding dogs are relatively scarce. These texts usually pertain to extreme circumstances, in relation to punishment (Vörös 1991) or in legal documents, such as a ban on the selling of dog meat by the Buda butchers' guild (Bevilaqua Borsodi 1931). Medieval, largely negative, attitudes to dogs also seem to survive in the ethnolinguistic record (Bartosiewicz 1998). Proverbs such as "you cannot make bacon from a dog", "considered less than a dog" or "a dog's world" are typical examples. While there is a rich iconographic record of dogs from Medieval Europe, this type of documentation was largely destroyed during the 16th century Ottoman Turkish occupation and subsequent warfare in Hungary. Nonetheless, a few paintings did survive, mostly from beyond the former borders of the Ottoman Empire, often in peripheral regions of the Carpathian Basin which are part of Slovakia and Romania today. This, as well as the normal, peacetime "attrition" of artwork through time, has created a historical/geopolitical bias in the coeval pictorial record.

Archaeological excavations in present-day Hungary, however, offer osteological information complementary to this scanty art historical record. Compared to the art historical and textual sources, archaeological evidence concerning dogs is more plentiful. Indirect evidence of the presence of dogs is provided by the common occurence of gnaw marks on animal bones in the food refuse of medieval settlements. Direct evidence of medieval dogs is provided by their skeletal remains, most often found as articulated skeletons in wells, isolated burials, etc. These finds represent both casual and deliberate disposal of animals after death, since the meat of dogs was usually not eaten in Hungary. This assumption is based on both the absence of butchered dog bone from archaeological sites and textual evidence. The aforementioned prohibition of the sale of dog meat by the butchers' guild in Buda (Bevilaqua Borsodi 1931) also indirectly points to this food taboo. Single dog burials occur more commonly in early medieval contexts. A very special case, an apparently "non-Christian" burial, was unearthed in medieval Visegrád. Six dogs were interred at this 11th century settlement together with a woman who had been cut into four pieces (Vörös 1991). Quartering represented an unusually harsh punishment in Medieval Hungary, a sentence typically handed down for treason. In this case, the reason is unknown.

Material and methods

Based on archaeological faunal materials, the size and general morphology of dogs can sometimes be reconstructed, depending on the completeness and preservation of skeletal remains. Even with the best possible preservation, however, modern breeds can be traced back archaeologically at most as far as the Middle Ages, since domestic animals are far too variable and adaptable to remain unchanged over 500 to 600 years. This is especially the case with prolific, multipara dogs, since large litters make selection possible at an even higher rate (Bartosiewicz 2002). In some instances, the sex of the animal may be identified on the basis of size and skeletal robusticity. The only unambiguous indicator of sex, however, is the bacculum (penis bone) of male dogs which may easily be lost or overlooked during excavation. Age can be determined on the basis of dental eruption and wear patterns as well as the degree of epiphyseal fusion (Habermehl 1961, Schmid 1972).

Osteological analyses in this paper were limited to the evaluation of the cranial measurements summarized in Table 1. Calvaria were selected for this study, since they display greater variability than other bones of the skeleton. While long bones show the size of animals, they lack more subtle, qualitative traits such as the head's profile line or the shape of dentition. Seven measurements were selected from a total of 31 measurements taken on 61 modern dog skulls as well as 14 wolves (Appendix 1). The archaeological specimens included 43 medieval and 15 Roman Period crania. Many of them originate from more-or-less complete skeletons, however, these were not identified as special ritual deposits. In terms of the broader context, the calvaria under discussion here are listed in Appendix 2. Because of differential preservation, not all measurements could be taken on all archaeological individuals. The sample was large enough, however, to identify several trends which set medieval dogs apart from their modern brethren. In this analysis, pairs of cranial measurements (taken with callipers to a precision of 0.1 mm) were plotted against each other, in order to outline trends in modern breeds. Linear regression equations provided by the Excel program were used in quantifying these trends. The great variety of modern dog calvaria, many of which could be identified to breed, provided regression equations, showing how 1 mm increases in the measurement chosen as the independent variable (x) is, on average, followed by an increase in another variable (dependent variable, y). Coefficients of determination (R^2) were calculated to show the degree to which measurements in a pair were related to each other. The importance of trendlines characterized by regression equations in this study is that by studying the relation of known breeds to these trends, one may draw inferences concerning comparable medieval dogs, although direct analogies should be avoided.

In dogs, as in all animals, there are many characteristics of body shape and appearance which are not reflected in skeletal remains. In an archaeological context, these characteristics are commonly observable only in mummified specimens. These traits include the length, colour and texture of the coat as well as the positions of the ears and tail. Mummified dog remains, however, are practically unknown in Hungary owing to the prevailing climatic conditions and cultural traditions. It is these characteristics, however, that can be relatively easily recognised even in simple drawings. This type of iconographic evidence can thus add to reconstructions based on archaeological remains.

Iconographic representations of dogs occur in a variety of forms in Hungary. Medieval paintings and drawings were surveyed for the purposes of this study. Although many of these were lost or destroyed during Hungary's tumultuous medieval history, this group of iconographic sources remains the richest. While not included in the present analysis, dogs are also sporadically depicted on

Table 1. Cranial measurements used in the study of medieval and modern dog skulls.

Measurement	*Abbreviation*	*Definition in* von den Driesch 1976
Total length	**A-P**	Fig. 14a: **1**
Basal length	**B-P**	Fig. 14c: **3**
Greatest frontal width	**Ect-Ect**	Fig. 14a: **32**
Median palatal length	**St-P**	Fig. 14c: **13**
Palatal width	**Mol-Mol**	Fig. 14c: **34**
Greatest mastoid breadth	**Ot-Ot**	Fig. 14d: **23**
Length of the upper carnassial (P4)		Fig. 15a: **L**

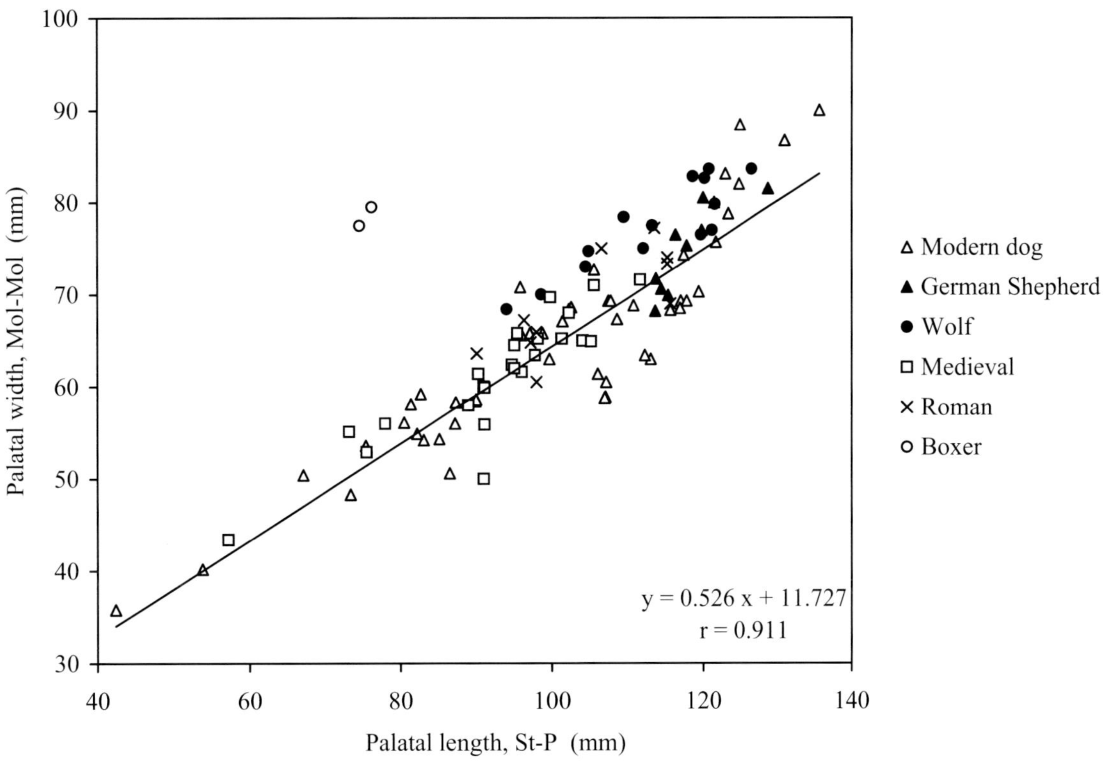

Fig. 1. The relationship between palatal measurements

sarcophagi and tombstones as well as on architectural stone carvings, especially after the medieval period. Images of dogs were also used to decorate utilitarian objects (pottery, belt mounts, bone carvings, oven tiles etc.). The sources of these images vary. Owing to the detail shown (shape, color etc.) paintings were considered the richest source of zoological information. This study is based on a survey of coeval paintings from Hungary, 23 of which showed dogs. There may be another dozen such pieces of art in existence, but not many more than that.

Results

In this analysis, aspects of the physical characteristics of medieval dogs were reconstructed based on the previously described analysis of measurements of archaeological specimens. Patterns were then established for the modern breeds, based on the same suite of measurements, and the characteristics of the medieval dogs were evaluated against the modern data. All measurements of archaeological and modern specimens were taken by the author. These data were then compared to the iconographic evidence.

Cranometric studies

Characteristic measurements from 43 medieval dog skulls were compared to those of modern and Roman Period dogs as well as wolves. Of the modern breeds, German Shepherds were treated separately owing to the presumed morphological similarity of their skulls to wolves. Boxers are also shown separately in diagrams due to their special skull morphology. In the majority of cases, the sex of animals was not recorded. Sexual dimorphism seems to be manifested mostly in size variability within breeds. Since in some cases the sex of the specimens could not be documented, differences within breeds may be hypothetically influenced by sexual dimorphism.

Palatal dimensions: The width to length proportion of the palate was successfully used by Peters (1997: 515) in characterizing the degree to which the snout, in fact the entire head, was elongated in various dogs. Wolves are commonly considered to be not simply larger but also more robust than domestic dogs. When palatal width (Mol-Mol) is plotted against palatal length (St-P) this difference becomes very clear between wolves and German Shepherds (Fig. 1). The skulls of only a few large breeds (Great Dane, St. Bernard) are larger than those of wolves as reflected in palatal proportions. Naturally, larger bodies are correlated with larger skulls and hence palatal dimensions. However, while palatal

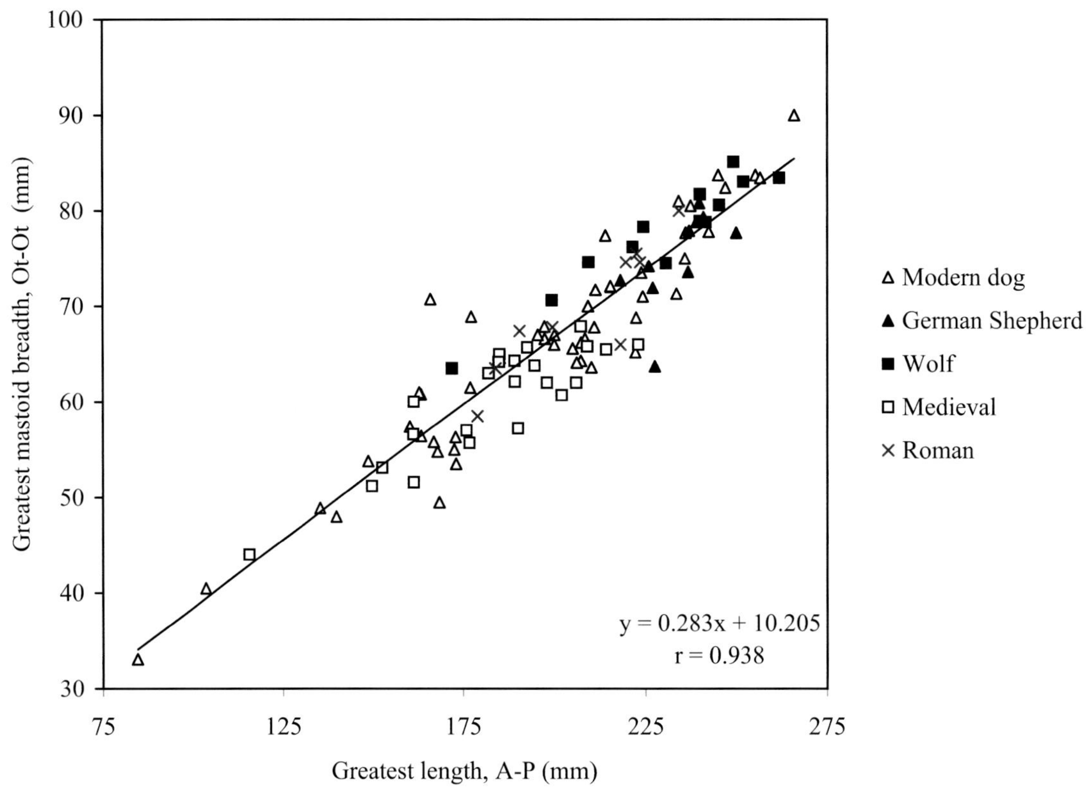

Fig. 2. The relationship between overall skull measurements

length follows the size of total skull length, relative palatal width may be more variable (e.g. in boxers). Small modern breeds, represented by the skulls of the Rattler and a Spitz, fall onto the trend line in spite of their small sizes. Boxers, on the other hand, stand out with their unusually short snouts. Medieval dog skulls are spread along the trend set by modern dogs, but none are particularly large. Only one specimen, brought to light during excavations at the 15th-16th century Pauline monastery of Márianosztra-Toronyalja, was as large as a modern German Shepherd. Palatal widths vary among [the] medium size medieval dogs, while the small specimens are comparable with modern skulls. The smallest individual, from an urban deposit in the Buda Royal Castle, compares closely to a modern Spitz in terms of palatal proportions. (The Castle Hill in Buda was fortified and settled as late as the 13th century. It became a royal centre by the last third of the 14th century; Bartosiewicz 2001: 37). In terms of palatal width, Roman Period dog skulls from Hungary seem to be larger and more robust than those from the Middle Ages. The set of Roman dog skulls does not include small and small-medium size individuals.

Greatest length and greatest mastoid breadth: These two dimensions largely characterize skull size. Greatest length includes the aboral end-point of the saggittal crest (A-P). Greatest mastoid breadth (Ot-Ot) was chosen as a relatively well preserved measurement near the dense and thus damage resistant auditory region. Among the modern sample, the skulls of wolves and large breeds are somewhat broader at the mastoid. Most of the medium size and small medieval skulls, on the other hand, are narrower than would be expected on the basis of the same trend (Fig. 2). This difference seems to result from the allometric relationship between the two measurements. The data suggest that longitudinal skull growth may slow down in larger dogs, while a slight broadening continues. Most of the medieval dog skulls fall within a medium size range, where mastoid width is still relatively small.

Greatest length and greatest frontal breadth: As opposed to mastoid breadth, in terms of greatest frontal breadth (Ect-Ect) wolf skulls seem to be relatively narrow. Among modern dogs, boxers have relatively broad foreheads (comparable to those of wolves), emphasizing the extreme shortening of the skull. Archaeological specimens (both Roman and medieval) display a trend similar to those of the previously studied measurements, although the small medieval dog from the Buda Castle stands out with its unusually broad forehead, displaying proportions similar to those of boxers (Fig. 3). In the case of this specimen, neoteny, the retention of youthful morphological

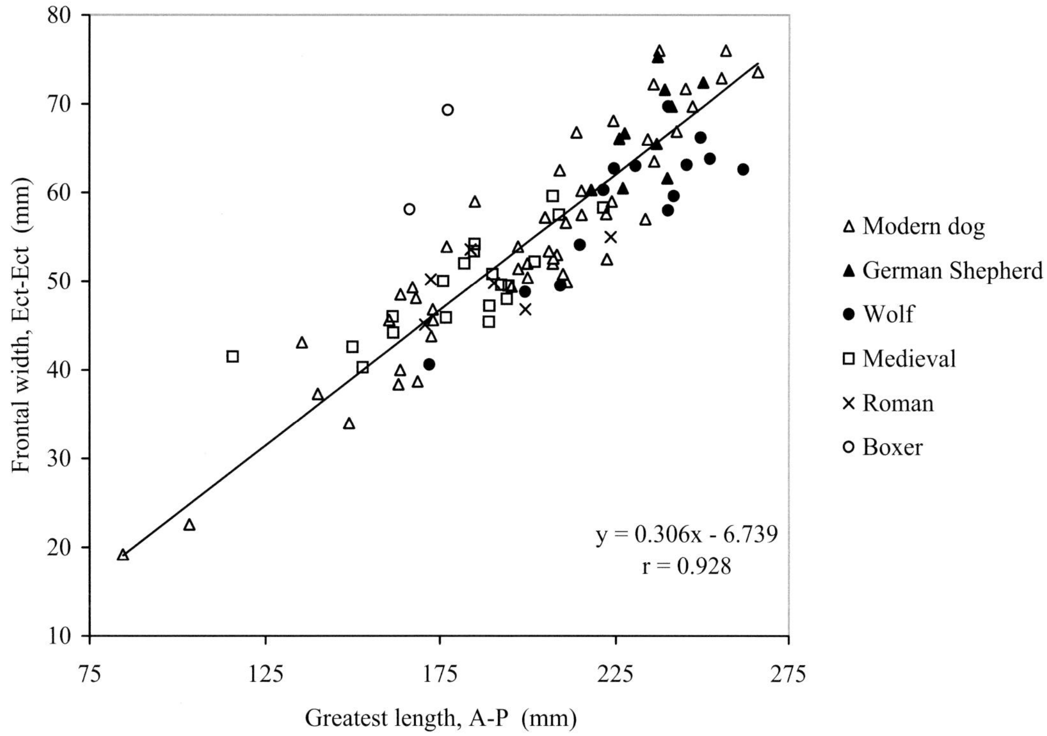

Fig. 3. The relationship between greatest skull length and frontal breadth

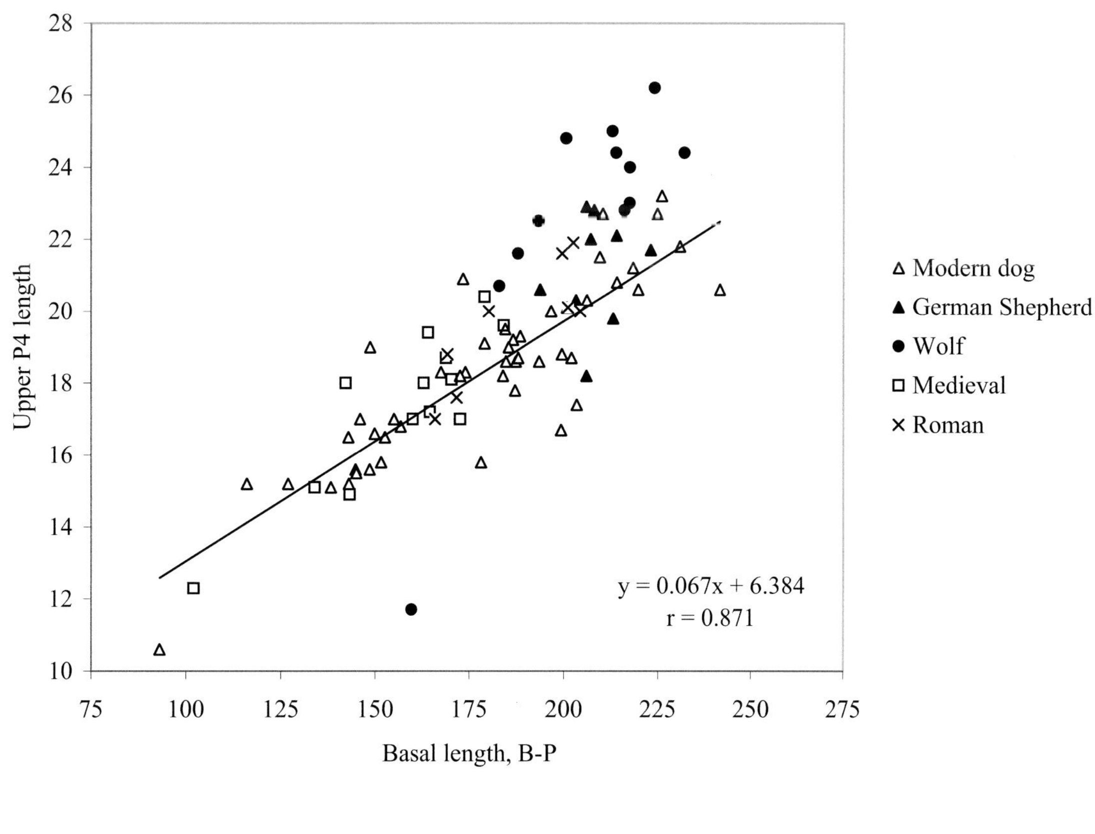

Fig. 4. The relationship between basal length and upper P^4 [carnassial] tooth length

characteristics in adulthood, comes to mind. This phenomenon is often exploited in pets, bred for a "puppy-look" (Lawrence 1989: 57).

Basal length and upper P^4 carnassial tooth length: The length of the upper carnassial tooth was studied in relation to the skulls' basal length (B-P). The superior strength of the carnassial tooth in the wild ancestor is evident in this graph. Domestication generally results in a decrease in body size, although this tendency is supposed to be slower in tooth measurements (Bökönyi 1975) and seems to be concentrated in the functionally less important premolar region. In addition, dental reduction and oligodontia (the inherited lack of one or several teeth) also seem to be more concentrated in the functionally less important premolar region. Carnassials of appropriate size are of vital importance to the individual in maintaining the ability to properly capture prey, chew and, defend itself. It is logical, therefore, that the length of the upper P4 is greater in wolves than in modern dogs of comparable size. It is of special interest that some of the medieval and Roman dogs had upper P4 teeth of proportions similar to that of wolves: these animals may be seen above the trend line of modern dogs in Figure 4. This may be due to a lesser degree to deliberate breed control, allowing the retention of "wolf-like" traits, of functional importance. Interestingly, five medium-size dogs with large upper carnassials originate from 9th–13th century deposits (Fancsika, Jánosszállás, Keszthely, Visegrád, Zalavár). The largest medieval dogs with strong carnassials, possibly bred as guard dogs, date to the late medieval 15th–17th centuries (Sümeg and Vác).

A review of iconographic evidence

In addition to osteological evidence, attention in this study was paid to pictorial representations, paintings and drawings, since paintings contain the most detailed and reliable information on the physical traits of dogs. Possibly owing to their aforementioned negative image, dogs are rarely depicted in medieval coats of arms. A unique example from Hungary is the dog's head in the coat of arms of the founder of the Hont-Pázmány family. The surname Hont is often identified with the words or names *Hunt* or *Hund*. In general, however, wild beasts (lion, wolf) or mythical monsters (griffins, dragons) were the preferred animals used as symbols in Hungarian heraldry, which makes this "hound" with its hanging ears even more interesting (Fig. 5). In this case, based on the family name, the dog portrayed would appear to represent a hunting dog, similar to that shown "in action" in the late 14th century "Illustrated Chronicle" (Szántó ed. 1987). This book, describing the history of Hungarians until 1330, was made for King Lajos I of Hungary and his daughter around 1370. It was illustrated by colourful miniatures. Its text, however, was compiled from earlier documents and is dated to 1358. The illustrator is unknown, but may be Miklós Meggyesi one of the King's artists. In medieval Hungary, dogs are first depicted in major numbers only in the 15th and 16th centuries.

Fig. 5. Head of a "hound" depicted on a shield in the late 14th century "Illustrated Chronicle"

Previously, only sporadic representations may be found. This may be explained by the stricter rules of early medieval religious iconography: with the emergence of Renaissance art, the increasing number of mundane topics seems to correlate with the depiction of dogs. However, the possibility of sampling bias owing to the small number of Hungarian paintings surviving after the Ottoman Turkish occupation (1526–1699) must also be considered.

Dogs found in paintings and drawings will be discussed here by iconographic contexts: a rigid categorisation by "breeds" or even by tight functional categories could lead to the over-interpretation of a mere two dozen images. Even attempts to classify morphological features such as the position of ears and tail or colour by the following broad contexts remained largely unsuccessful.

Fig. 6. Hound shown in a falconry scene in the late 14th century "Illustrated Chronicle"

Hunting scenes: Hunting scenes in which dogs are depicted are among the earliest images from the Middle Ages. Their presence in this context requires little explanation. There is abundant evidence that the use of hunting dogs far predates the Middle Ages and, in fact, may have been one of the oldest forms of exploiting animals for work. A hound is depicted, among others, in a falconry scene in the "Illustrated Chronicle" (Fig. 6), and greyhound-like, gracile dogs can also often be seen in other images from this work. Hunting dogs, both hounds and greyhounds, look most consistent in their appearance. They are short-haired, with droopy ears, long tails, light brownish in colour and lack markings.

Images from the life of Jesus: Sheepdogs appear with shepherds in early nativity scenes, and such scenes are relatively common in both Hungarian and non-Hungarian examples. Many such images are known from areas outside the present-day borders of Hungary, especially Slovakia, where churches were not destroyed by Turkish

Fig. 7. Various dogs on a 13th century sketch from the Buda court of King Sigismund

occupation. Dogs also sometimes appear as companion animals to the Three Wise Men who came to visit Jesus. Paralleling the great stylistic variability of these pictures, and the lesser emphasis on dogs within the composition, these animals tend to be modest in appearance (i.e. show no extreme variability of shapes or colours), but look more diverse than the aforementioned hunting dogs. A number of other scenes from the life of Jesus contain dogs in explicit symbolic roles, reflecting the dualistic perceptions of this animal (Bartosiewicz 1998). One example is an 1480 painting from the parish church of Bárfa (present-day Bardejov, Slovakia) showing Jesus appearing before Pilate. In this instance one dog, a simple-looking animal, is standing by Jesus, opposing Pilate. The other, an ugly little animal with a devilish look, lies near the feet of Pilate on the steps of the throne of his master. The contrast between these two dogs speaks for itself. Scenes of the crucifixion of Jesus also sometimes contain dogs. The symbolic meanings behind the depictions of these animals, however, are less clear. In the Middle Ages, dogs could represent fidelity, envy or even the evil that temporarily overtook Jesus until resurrection.

Royal courts and aristocratic households: Such pictures, very common in Europe, are also found in Hungary. One Hungarian 15th century example is a miniature showing King Matthias and Queen Beatrix in which a small dog rests in the background. In these royal and artistocratic contexts, the dogs were no ordinary beasts or pariah dogs, but animals of privilege. As such, they cannot be mistaken for generic, scavenging rural canines. Rather, these pictures show dogs of great variability, both in terms of size and other traits such as coat quality, color and ear position (Fig. 7, Bartosiewicz 1995: 61). It seems that these artists attempted to provide naturalistic images of the great variability of dogs bred for the upper classes. The positive attitude toward high status dogs is clearly illustrated by the instructions of King Lajos II given before he left for the disasterous battle of Mohács against the Turks in 1526: "Take good care of the dogs! Bathe them twice a week..." (Ortvay 1914: 413). The first portrait of

Fig. 8. "Pariah" type dog following pilgrims depicted on the 15th century main altar from the cathedral of Kassa (Košice, Slovakia)

a nobleman with his dog in Hungary comes only from the mid-17th century. In comparison to Western Europe, this example from Hungary is relatively late. The contemporaneous paintings from Hungary, showing a dog resting at his master's feet are stylistically rather similar.

Everyday scenes from secular art: This genre is relatively rare in Hungary, but is well represented elsewhere in Europe. By the 16th century, a wide variety of dogs appear in any number of scenes from the mundane world. In these images, dogs of every description are shown beneath the dinner table, in the company of courtesans, and indeed in nearly every venue of daily life. Such depictions confirm the common presence and great adaptability of this "first domestic animal".

Discussion

The cranial characteristics of medieval dogs identified by the metric analysis of archaeologically recovered remains suggest that they were mostly medium size animals with rather non-descript looks. Comparisons were then made between the craniometric traits of these dogs and those of modern breeds. The traits of these medieval animals can then be compared to coeval images in medieval paintings.

While lap dogs occur relatively infrequently in the few paintings from Hungary, such little creatures often accompany girls and ladies in these images. Possession of these small puppies or toy-like dogs was therefore apparently regarded as a primarily feminine attribute. Such pets are commonly depicted by the 15th–16th century in paintings from elsewhere in Europe. Since miniature dogs are found only in pictures from later than the 15th-16th centuries in Hungary, the osteological evidence for such dogs from the Buda Royal Castle is of special importance. Aside from these small animals, the aforementioned greater variability of size, shape and color seems to have been characteristic of dogs in royal or aristocratic households.

Because relatively few high status medieval sites have been excavated, the available sample of archaeological specimens comes primarily from low status contexts. In general, these animals seem to have been of medium size and completely average appearance. Although jackals have long been excluded as the ancestors of the dog whose monophyletic origins unambiguously point to wolf, the head shape of many feral dogs breeding freely, appears more similar to jackals, rather than wolves. They are gracile, of medium size and often brownish or agouti in colour, sometimes with white markings. It is only their ears that often stand or fall in unmatched positions. The "jackal-look" of pariah dogs probably represents an optimum that results from "natural" selection in a human environment. On some pictures, these characteristics can be clearly recognized, even in the case of less elaborate representations. The size and shape of many medieval dog long bones point to this form as well: extremely small or large forms had to be maintained by consistent breeding work. The non-distinct and relatively homogeneous, "pariah" look of dog remains is suggestive of the absence of such efforts in many periods (e.g. prehistoric sites: Bartosiewicz 2002).

Fig. 9. Shepherd's dog in a nativity scene painted by Master M. S. in 1506

Hunting scenes and pictures of aristocratic/royal courts often show unique and special looking dogs. Mundane scenes are seldom depicted, therefore fewer images of common dogs are known from medieval paintings. One nice example, however, is shown on a 15th century altar from Kassa (present-day Košice, Slovakia) where a pariah-like dog is shown following a group of pilgrims (Fig. 8). Another appears as a shepherd's companion in the painting of "The Nativity" by Master M.S. (Fig. 9; Bökönyi 1974: 199).

Fig. 10. A dog being castrated instead of Prince Béla II in the late 14th century "Illustrated Chronicle"

Animal symbolism played a complex role in medieval thinking. With a few exceptions (such as the lamb as a symbol of Jesus in Christianity), a single species might embody both positive and negative concepts. "Faith" was probably the only positive attribute associated with dogs in the Middle Ages, and even this concept may have been a relatively late development. For example, the fuzzy little dog which appears in the 1434 portrait of "Giovanni Arnolfini and his wife" by Jan Van Eyck is interpreted as another symbol of faith (Végh 1977: Taf. 17). More commonly, dogs represented envy in religious Christian iconography. On a number of altar pieces from Hungary depicting the seven cardinal sins, dogs are often used as a symbol of envy. One example is the late 14th century altarpiece from Lőcse (present-day Levoča, Slovakia).

A special interface with humans was created by the use of dogs as real time or actual substitutes for humans in various situations, usually with negative connotations. A late medieval painting from Poland produced in 1504 and depicting the legend of the 11th century St. Stanislaw, shows unfaithful wives being punished by having to suckle puppy dogs while their own babies were placed under bitches for the same purpose. An example of a more complex aspect of the dog/human relationship is shown in the aforementioned "Illustrated Chronicle" from the late 14th century. In this instance, it appears that an unfortunate dog was substituted for a human. When in his childhood the future King Béla II was supposed to have been castrated on the order of a rival king (Fig. 10), the executioner entrusted with the job castrated a puppy instead (as portrayed to the right in Figure 10), taking its testicles to the king (as shown on the left).

Conclusions

The medieval dog crania available for study originated mostly from medium size dogs. Very few small animals were represented and larger individuals, reaching the size of at least the modern German Shepherd, were rare. The socio-economic status of the inhabitants of the excavated sites surely influenced the types of dogs kept. Unfortunately, dogs from former high status centers are less well represented archaeologically since most such settlements developed into continuously occupied and built-up urban areas. Iconographic evidence, however, suggests that different types of dogs were indeed common to high status vs rural settlements. The smallest medieval dog, whose skull was recovered from a 15th century deposit in the Buda Royal Castle, may well have been the lap dog of an aristocrat or a rich burger. In contrast, the skull of a large 15th century dog was recovered from the isolated, hilltop monastery of Márianosztra-Toronyalja. Since a greyhound-like skull also came from this site, it is possible that these dogs were used in hunting, although the food remains from this site contained only a few bones from wild animals (Bartosiewicz 1997).

It is of special interest that early medieval (10th–13th century) dog skulls from rural or early urban sites are of medium size but have relatively large carnassials, attributes that are somewhat similar to those of wolves. Stronger dentition, related to prey capture and intra-specific competition, may be seen as a result of stronger natural selection in primitive forms, prior to the development of conscious medieval dog breeding. These average looking, "pariah"-like dogs, most frequently encountered in archaeological assemblages, are also known from paintings. In the paintings they are often shown as gracile, medium-size animals with brownish coats and non-distinct ears. In contrast to their dominance in the archaeological record, however, these animals are far less frequently depicted in Hungarian art than their aristocratic, high status counterparts.

Hundreds of dog breeds have been created and consolidated by conscious breeding work during the last 100–150 years. The dogs portrayed in early medieval painted images, in contrast, can only be divided into broad or general breed or type classifications. Moreover, it should be kept in mind that these pictures were not painted for the sake of the dogs themselves. Instead, in these images, they often play only a symbolic, decorative or representative role and may appear only in a sketchy form. In this study the reconstructed physical features of dogs from archaeological contexts were linked with the morphological features and human attitudes towards these animals as depicted in paintings from medieval Hungary. By combining the information provided by medieval paintings and texts with morphometric data from archaeologically recovered dog crania, a more coherent picture of dogs in their medieval social environments emerges.

Acknowledgements

Modern reference specimens were measured by the author in the Osteological Collections of the Hungarian

Agricultural Museum: assistance by Andrea Körösi is gratefully acknowledged here.

Dóra Nyékhelyi and László Daróczi-Szabó of the Budapest History Museum gave permission to use their unpublished data. Data on the dogs from both Vác and Márianosztra were put at my disposal by László Bartosiewicz, whose help and support is acknowledged here. I would also like to thank Alice Choyke and László Bartosiewicz for their scholarly and linguistic help with the preparation of this manuscript and its presentation at the 9th Conference of ICAZ in Durham, Great Britain.

References

Bartosiewicz, L. 1995. *Animals in the urban landscape in the wake of the Middle Ages*. Oxford: BAR International Series 609.

Bartosiewicz, L. 1997. Márianosztra – Toronyalja állatcsontleleteinek elemzése (The analysis of animal remains from Márianosztra – Toronyalja). *Váci Könyvek* **8**, 159–182.

Bartosiewicz, L. 1998. Attitudes to pets in the ethnolinguistic record, pp. 65–78, in P. Anreiter, L. Bartosiewicz, E. Jerem – W. Meid (eds) *Man and the Animal World. Studies in memoriam Sándor Bökönyi*. Budapest: Archaeolingua Kiadó.

Bartosiewicz, L. 2001. Buda, pp. 36–38, in P. J. Crabtree (ed.) *Medieval Archaeology: an Encyclopedia*. New York–London, Garland Publishing Inc.

Bartosiewicz, L. 2002. Dogs from the Ig pile dwellings in the National Museum of Slovenia. *Arheološki Vestnik* **53**, 77–89.

Bevilaqua Borsody, B. 1931. A budai és pesti mészároscéhek ládáinak okiratai 1270–1872 [Documents from the chest of the Buda and Pest butchers' guilds 1270–1872] I. Budapest: Athenaeum.

Bökönyi, S. 1974. *History of Domestic Mammals in Central and Eastern Europe*. Budapest: Akadémiai Kiadó.

Bökönyi, S. 1975. Vlasac: an early site of dog domestication, pp. 167–178, in A. T. Clason (ed.) *Archaeozoological Studies*. Amsterdam–New York: North Holland and American Elsevier.

Driesch, A. von den 1976. *Das Vermessen von Tierknochen aus vor- und frühgeschichtliche Siedlungen. Diss.* München: Institut für Paläoanatomie, Domestikationsforschung und Geschichte der Tiermedizin der Universität München.

Habermehl, K.-H. 1961. *Altersbestimmung bei Haustieren, Pelztieren und beim jagdbaren Wildtieren*. Hamburg und Berlin: Paul Parey.

Lawrence, E. A. 1989. Neoteny in American perception of animals, pp. 57–76 in, R. J. Hoage (ed.) *Perceptions of animals in American culture*. Washington DC–London: Smithsonian Institution Press.

Ortvay, T. 1914. *Mária, II. Lajos magyar király neje* (Mária, the wife of King Lajos the Second). Budapest: Historia.

Peters J. 1997. Der Hund in der Antike aus archäozoologischer Sicht. *Anthropozoologica* **25–26**, 511–523.

Schmid, E. 1972. *Atlas of animal bones*. Amsterdam – London – New York: Elsevier Publishing Company.

Szántó, T. (ed.) 1987. *Képes krónika* [The Illustrated Chronicle]. Budapest: Helikon Kiadó.

Végh, J. 1977. *Fifteenth century Nederlandish painting*. Budapest: Corvina.

Vörös, I. 1991. Kutyaáldozatok és kutyatemetkezések a középkori Magyarországon [Dog sacrifices and dog burials in Medieval Hungary] II. *Folia Archaeologica* XLII, 179–196.

Institute of Archaeological Sciences
Loránd Eötvös University
H-1088 Budapest, Múzeum körút 4/B

hadarcska@yahoo.co.uk

Appendix 1 The composition of cranial assemblage by breed and sex. Reference specimens and wolves: Osteological Collections of the Hungarian Agricultural Museum

	Male	*Female*	*?*	*Total*
German Shepherd	8	2		10
Afgan Greyhound	1	1		2
Airedale Terrier	1	1		2
Basset Hound		1		1
Black Puli	1			1
Boxer	1	1		2
Collie	1			1
Dwarf poodle	1			1
English Greyhound	1			1
English Hound		1		1
English Setter		1		1
Fox Terrier		2		2
German Pointer		1		1
Gordon Setter	1			1
Great Dane	2	2		4
Hungarian Greyhound	1	1		2
Hungarian Pointer	1	1		2
Irish Setter	1			1
Komondor	2	2		4
Rattler		1		1
Skye Terrier		1		1
Snautzer		1		1
Spitz		1		1
St. Bernard	1			1
White Puli	1	1		2
Breed unknown	6	1	9	16
Wolf		2	12	14
Medieval dogs	3	1	39	43
Roman dogs			15	15
Total	**34**	**26**	**75**	**135**

Appendix 2 The origins of medieval archaeological specimens

Site type	*Period*	*Number of individuals*
Urban settlement:		
Buda	15th c.	3
Vác	15h c.	2
Vác	16–17th c.	2
Rural settlement:		
Doboz-Hajdúirtás	10–12th c.	1
Visegrád-Várkert	11th c.	6
Jánosszállás-Katonapart	11–13th c.	1
Tiszaeszlár-Bashalom	11–13th c.	1
Bóly	12th c.	1
Kardoskút-Hatablak	12th c.	1
Fancsika	12–13th c.	3
Visegrád-Sibrikdomb (Árpád Period)	10–13th c.	6
Túrkeve-Móricz	15–16th c.	1
Sümeg-Sarvaly	15th c.	1
Central settlement:		
Monastery		
Márianosztra-Toronyalja	15–16th c.	13
Bayliff's seat		
Szabolcs	10–12th c.	1
Non-specified:		
Keszthely (Conquest Period)	10th c.	1
Kunhegyes-Jajhalom	10–13th c.	1
Cemetery:		
Magyarhomorog	10th c.	1
Zalavár	10th c.	1
Eperjes	11th c.	1
Zalavár (Árpád Period)	10–13th c.	1

9th ICAZ Conference, Durham 2002
Dogs and People in Social, Working, Economic or Symbolic Interaction
(eds Lynn M. Snyder and Elizabeth A. Moore) pp. 96–119

12. Companions from the Oldest Times: Dogs in Ancient Greek Literature, Iconography and Osteological Testimony

Katerina Trantalidou

In Attica the first known image of a dog comes from a vase of the third millennium BC. In Classical and Hellenistic Greece there are many representations of dogs in sculpture and iconography (Beazley's archives along record 237), showing literally and metaphorically the relationship between humans and the "most vigorous of domestic animals" as Pausanias tells us. Among those representations, one of the most tender is a Hellenistic sculpture of a small boy covering a dog with his arms (National Archaeological Museum at Athens). Dogs have provided for the practical, ideological and sentimental needs of man. They were complementary food animals in prehistory, and in later times in northern Greece, symbols of power for the emerging nobles, who eclipsed even the king himself. They have served as religious attributes; funeral guards; companions in games and at home. From varying points of view, we will attempt to learn more about our common history with dogs through time.

Introduction

In virtual reality and in real life, as it has been perceived by the Greeks, dogs (ὁ and ἡ: dog, bitch, κύων το ὑλακτοῦν ςῷον: Hesychius, *Lexicon),* gifted with special qualities (Pollux, *Onomasticon,* V 51–60) such as excellent smell and hearing, accompanied gods, heroes and men during hunting activities ('κύνε εἰδότε θήρης', 'κυσί θηρευτῆσι': Homer, *Iliad*, 10, 360; 11, 325). Dogs were also the guards of men's houses and sheepfolds day and night, thus protecting their masters from potential dangers such as enemies, thieves, and environmental factors such as sun or moon eclipses and earthquakes. Dogs also took part in festivities. For instance, they are often seen under the tables of the banquet, representing the social life in contrast with wild animals. Unwonted they walked around the streets, the crossroads and even the cemeteries looking for food, in the form of other animal or even unburied human carcasses ('κυνοσπάρακτον σῶμα Πολυνείκους' Sophocles, *Antigone* 1198).

Through time, the status of the dog gradually changed; and from an edible mammal (κυνοφαγέω: eat dog's flesh) in prehistoric and early historic times in southern Greece and Crete (Trantalidou 1996: 100; Snyder and Klippel 2003), Tables 1 and 2, it became an element in the ritual of the god's cult. Still, it is occasionally mentioned in the list of animals eaten in later times (cf. Parker 1983: 357–8), in Hellenistic Kassope (Boessneck 1986), in Imperial Corinth (Reese 1987), and in Hellenistic Pella (Yielding in Trantalidou 2001: 268), where it was most often used for curative purposes.

It is essential, however, to note that in Greek religion animals did not represent gods. They were dedicated to them; and they could be a god's attribute. The sacred status of the dog was in many cases controversial. Dogs were used for curative purposes and purification rites. Very early in the development of Greek religious ideology, dogs became connected with hunting and birth as well as death (Mainoldi 1984: 37–59) and sorcery, they were also attributes of the deities of the night and the crossroads (Fig. 1.1). Yet dogs were denied entry to the Athenian acropolis, to Delos and other sacred islands (Plutarch, *Moralia* 111b; *Aetia Romana* 68, 280c; Parker 1983: 357).

Table 1. Relative frequencies of Canis familiaris bones from different domestic faunal assemblages (wild taxa included) during the Neolithic sequence. To unify the data and to examine as many samples as possible the quantification of the species was done on the basis of the Number of Identified Specimens (NISP). Usually the evaluation of species abundance on the basis of Minimum Number of Individuals does not change dramatically the proportions among the species

AceramicSites	*%*	*References*
Argissa, East Thessaly	0.18	Boessneck 1960, ib 1962, 50
Dendra, East Peloponnese	0.32	Kotjabopoulou 1992, 114
Knossos, Central Crete	0.22	Jarman & Jarman 1968, 243

Early Neolithic Sites	*%*	*References*
N.Nikomedia, West Macedonia	0.22	Higgs 1962, 271–72
Achilleion I, East Thessaly	0.94	Bökönyi 1989, 316
Achilleion II, East Thessaly	1.14	Bökönyi 1989, 316
Sesklo, East Thessaly	0.41	Schwartz 1982, 136
Lerna, East Peloponnese	0.60	Gejvall 1969, 10
Knossos Ia, Central Crete	0.93	Jarman & Jarman 1968, 243
Knossos Ib, Central Crete	1.92	Jarman & Jarman 1968, 243

Middle Neolithic Sites	*%*	*References*
Dimitra Ia, East Macedonia	17.87	Yannouli 1997, 105
Dimitra Ib, East Macedonia	6.41	Yannouli 1997, 105
Sitagroi, East Macedonia	1.57	Bökönyi 1986, 68
Vassilika I, Central Macedonia	1.01	Yannouli 1994, 346
Achilleion IIIa, East Thesssaly	1.27	Bökönyi 1989, 316
Achilleion IIIb/IVa, East Thesssaly	1.59	Bökönyi 1989, 317
Achilleion IV, East Thesssaly	0.29	Bökönyi 1989, 317
Magoula Zarkou, West Thessaly	1.94	Becker 1991, 618
Lerna, East Peloponnese	1.01	Gejvall 1969, 10

Late, Final, Neolithic and Chalcolithic Sites	*%*	*References*
Makri II, Aegean Thrace	0.40	Curci & Tagliacozzo 1997, 47
Paradeisos, Aegean Thrace	1.37	Larje 1986, 107
Kryoneri, East Macedonia	2.09	Mylona 1999
Dimitra II, East Macedonia	6.83	Yannouli 1997, 106
Dimitra III, East Macedonia	5.23	Yannouli 1997, 106
Sitagroi II, East Macedonia	1.88	Bökönyi 1986, 68
Sitagroi III, East Macedonia	2.04	Bokönyi 1986, 68
Thermi B, Central Macedonia	3.80	Yannouli 1990, 225–27
Thermi B, Central Macedonia	6.78	Yannouli 1990, 225–27
Vassilika, Central Macedonia	0.39	Koufos in Grammenos 1984, 158
Vassilika II, Central Macedonia	0.96	Yannouli 1994, 346
Vassilika III, Central Macedonia	1.12	Yannouli 1994, 346
Vassilika IV, Central Macedonia	0.17	Yannouli 1994, 346
Stavroupoli, Central Macedonia	3.99	Yannouli 2002, 741
Ay. Sofia, East Thessaly	1.93	von den Driesch & Enderle 1966, 33
Arapi, East Thessaly	1.87	Boessneck 1956, 61
Dimini, East Thessaly	3.96	Halstead 1992, 34
Pefkakia, LN, East Thessaly	0.93	Jordan 1975, 710
Pefkakia, FN, East Thessaly	2.19	von den Driesch 1987, 5
Magoula Zarkou, West Thessaly	1.47	Becker 1991, 18
Ay. Dimitrios, LNIIa, West Peloponnese	6.32	Rusche & Halstead 1987
Kastria, Cave of Lakes, LN Ib/IIa, North Peloponnese	1.13	Trantalidou 1997, 439
Tharrounia Ia, Skoteini Cave, Euboea	1.09	Kotjabopoulou & Trantalidou 1993, 402
Tharrounia Ib, Skoteini Cave, Euboea	1.74	Kotjabopoulou & Trantalidou 1993, 402
Tharrounia IIa, Skoteini Cave, Euboea	0.96	Kotjabopoulou & Trantalidou 1993, 402
Kalythies I, Rhodes, Dodecannese	0.80	Halstead & Jones 1987, 140
Saliagos, Cyclades	0.90	Higgs & allii 1968, 114–17

Table 2. Relative frequencies of Canis familiaris bones from different domestic faunal assemblages (wild taxa included) during the Early Bronze Age sequence. To unify the data and to examine as many samples as possible the quantification of the species was done on the basis of the Number of Identified Specimens (NISP). Usually the evaluation of species abundance on the basis of Minimum Number of Individuals does not change dramatically the proportions among the species

Early Bronze Age Sites	*%*	***References***
Skala Sotiros I, Thasos, North Aegean	1.05	Yannouli 1994, 406
Skala Sotiros II, Thasos, North Aegean	0.90	Yannouli 1994, 406
Skala Sotiros I, II, Thasos, North Aegean	0.88	Yannouli 1994, 406
Poliochni, Limnos, North Aegean	1.16	Sorrentino 1997, 158
Sitagroi IV, East Macedonia	1.80	Bökönyi 1986, 68
Sitagroi V, East Macedonia	1.85	Bökönyi 1986, 68
Aggitis Cave FN/EB, East Macedonia	3.82	Trantalidou, personnal observation
Pentapolis I, East Macedonia	0.49	Yannouli 1994, 396
Pentapolis II, East Macedonia	1.64	Yannouli 1994, 396
Aggitis Cave FN/EB, East Macedonia	1.65	Yannouli 1994, 406
Mesimeriani Toumba, Central Macedonia	1.39	Yannouli 2002b, 352
Kastanas, Central Macedonia	0.58	Becker 1986, 333
Magoula Zarkou, West Thessaly	1.15	Sorrentino 1991, 18
Pefkakia, East Thessaly	1.33	Jordan 1975, 7-10
Pefkakia, East Thessaly	1.96	Amberger 1979, 16-7
Tiryns, EH II, East Peloponnese	0.91	von den Driesch & Boessneck 1990, 81
Tiryns, EH III, East Peloponnese	1.12	von den Driesch & Boessneck 1990, 81
Lerna, EH II, East Peloponnese	1.30	Gejvall 1969, 10
Lerna, EH III, East Peloponnese	3.38	Gejvall 1969, 10
Ayios Dimitrios, FN/EB, West Peloponnese	0.80	Rusche & Halstead 1987
Ayios Dimitrios, EH II, West Peloponnese	1.30	Rusche & Halstead 1987
Nichoria, South Peloponnese	8.60	Sloan & Duncan 1978, 69
Markiani III, Amorgos, Cyclades	0.10	Trantalidou, personnal observation
Markiani IV, Amorgos, Cyclades	0.10	Trantalidou, personnal observation

In the following few paragraphs, I will try to outline some of the instances in which dogs were related to individuals (Tables 3–5) and gods as well as the properties of the dogs themselves, using examples from archaeology, literature and iconographical testimonies, mindful that the attributes and the qualities of the deities in the popular and national religion are sometimes extremely complicated. A single cult might differ from place to place, assimilation and association of gods was plausible, and the scholarly commentaries are not always in accordance with one another, since the sources are often unclear and the archaeological data are incomplete. All interpretations depend upon the origin of the deity, the different versions of myths, the chronological period in which the adoration took place, and the economic, political and military influences of each city-state by which the cult was spread. In addition, we must take into consideration variation in ideology and cultural level between city and countryside, social classes and sexes, as well as the small close communities involved in special celebrations such as the Bacchic or Eleusinian 'mysteries'.

With all these parameters in mind, we will try to understand (without using any stylistic, typological, grammatical, or aesthetical reading of the data) how dogs were associated with birth and healing, as well as the rites of passage in youth and the rites of purification in death.

The hounds

When society was transformed from the Paleolithic period to stable settlements and wild animals were no longer an important component of subsistence, the role of hunting was minimized throughout the Greek peninsula and adjacent areas. From the Neolithic onwards, food provisioning relied on domestic livestock for meat. Little by little hunting become a social marker (territorial control, training for war) and these activities became very important among young men. The Gods commonly reflected current ideology, and heroes such as Tithon (see for instance the red-figure pelike at Louvre G 230 in Paris: Scheffer 2001: fig. 4) were often represented as hunters. A young person after his death could also gain the statue of a hero, as in the 4th century BC heroic votive relief representing a young horseman with two dogs in the Piraeus Archaeological Museum (Stainhauer: pl. 344).

In Arrian's *Cynegeticus* the following special usages/ epithets also occur after the 5/4th centuries BC: 'ἀγαθαὶ

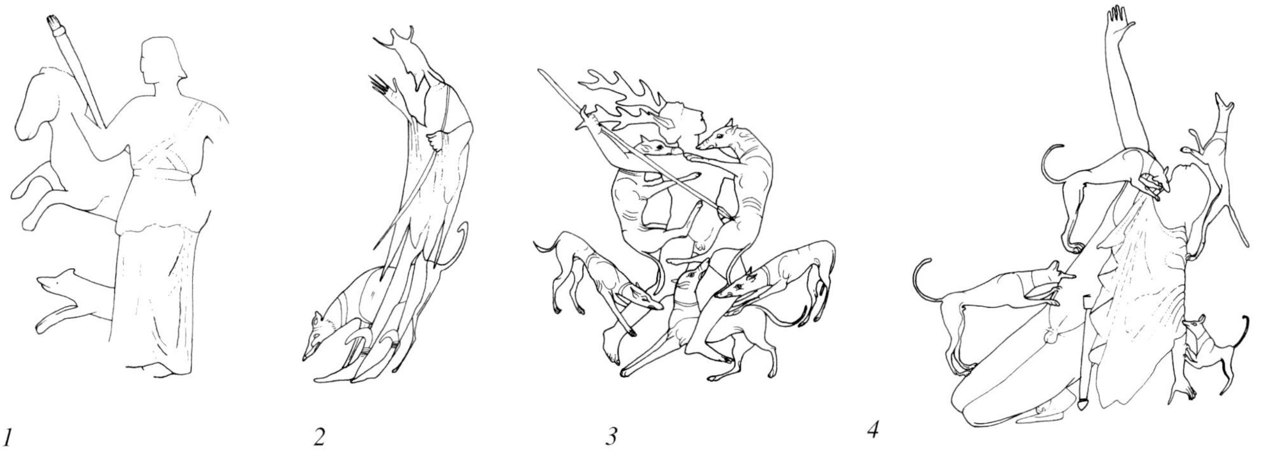

1 2 3 4

Fig. 1. Gods and Heroes
1. Goddess Enodia, escorted by a horse and a dog, her sacred animals, on a marble votive relief dedication found at Exochi Eordaias, Ptolemaïs basin, in West Macedonia, (sk. after Chrissostomou 1998, fig. 14b). Enodia is holding two torches
2. Hermes and his dog on a black-Figured amphora showing Dionysos, Athena and Hermes. New York Metropolitan Museum of Art 06.1021.68a, Rogers Fund, 1906 (sk. after Scheffer 2001: fig. 1)
3. Greek and Roman artists had often portrayed the punishment of Actaion by Artemis. This sketch is from a Poseidonian skyphos of 400–350 BC, Carlsrouhe, Baadishes Landesmuseumm 76/106 (sk. after Kakridis 1986, Elliniki Mythologia: fig. 41)
4. Aktaion being killed by his dogs. Bell, red-figured krater from Cuma. Pan painter, 530–470 BC, Boston, Museum of Fine Arts 10.185 (sk. after Boardmann 1975: fig. 335.2)

κύνες' (good greyhounds, one of the most ancient of the foundation breeds) and 'ὠκεῖαι κύνες' (fast gazehounds: Hull 1964, 204; synonymous with 'κυσίν ταχείαις': Eurypides, *Hippolytus* 17–18; 'κυνῶν 'ὠκυπόδων': ibid. 1127–30 etc.). We are also informed of the existence of the following breeds: the sheepherders (Eur. *Ajax* 297), κυνόλυκος, resembling a wolf (wolfhound?); 'Ινδικοὶ (Aristotle); Μολοττικαὶ κύνες, which appear to be guardian dogs (Eur. Thesm. 416–7; Athenaeus); Laconian (Λακαίνης: Sophocles, Ajax, 7–8), a type of hunting dog also illustrated on ceramics (Ashmolean Museum, Oxford 1966.447; Mainoldi 1984: 181); and χονδρόσκυλο, a dog specializing in hunting big animals illustrated in mosaics all around the Mediterranean basin during the early Byzantine era (Loberdou-Tsigarida 2000: 82–3); λαγοκυνήγιο, a hound specializing in hunting small game, represented on a bone slab (ibid. fig. 9).

Skeletal variation in dog stature

Based on metrical anlysis of archaeological canid materials (Table 6), the ancient dog populations in the south Balkan Peninsula (Koudelka 1885) appear to have consisted of small to medium sized animals, and researchers have concluded that in the earlier strata, they were quite similar to modern variations of the Schnauzer or terrier like dogs. Such animals are reported from Anza, the first phases of Lepenski Vir, Sitagroi, Stavroupoli, Otzaki, Arapi Magoula, and Lerna I (Gejvall 1969: 14; Bökönyi 1976: 332–3; Yannouli 2002, 691). Other animals have been compared to the modern beagle (Larje 1987: 96). From Early Helladic III however, researchers have identified three different sizes of dogs and "at least one (possibly two) new races of dogs which will, of course, show combinations with the types known earlier" (Gejvall: 16–8; von den Driesch 1987: 16; von den Driesch and Boessneck 1990: 145).

Similar developments and changes in size are seen in other European populations. In Britain, in contrast (Harcourt 1974: 151–75), dogs are larger during the Mesolithic (60 cm in shoulders height) and Neolithic (43–62 cm). A reduction in height appears to occur during the Iron Age (23–72 cm) in which two, and possibly three populations have been identified. In Switzerland, individuals of medium height have been observed in the Gallo-Roman period from the end of the 1st century BC through the middle of the 3rd century AD (Chaix 1980: 172). In Italy, again as shown by stature estimations based on limb bones measurements, during the Neolithic withers height varies from 35.3–55.6 cm. There is an increase in stature from the Bronze (36.0–52.1 cms) through the Iron Age (73.4–60.8 cm). During the Roman period, the presence of both small and large dogs (29.4–69.7 cm) is noted (Mazzorin and Tagliacozzo 2000: 141–161), including small lap-dogs with slightly brachymelic limbs.

Table 3. Dog remains in human burials in Peloponnese during the Mycenean period. Other animals recovered in burials where dogs were not found have not been recorded. Relative chronology defined mainly on the basis of changes in pottery style (after Simpson 1981)

Conventional Dating	***Site***	***Type of Tombs***	***Burial Group***	***Animal Offerings***	***Grave Goods***	***References***
LHII 1450–1405 BC	Vapheio, Laconia	Tholos tomb	No skeleton was found	Teeth of several dogs	Whole arsenal of weapons, gold and silver cup, stone lamps, alabaster vases, amber beads, jewelery, mirror, pottery, etc.	Tsountas 1889 Tsountas & Manatt 1897, 152 Andronikos 1968, 87 Day 1894, 24 Kilian-Dirlmeier 1987, 197–212
LHI–LHIIB 1550–1405 BC	Kallithea, Patras, Achaia	Tholos tomb		Remains of dogs, cows, sheep/goats, horse (skull)		Papadopoulos 1987, 69–72 Hamilakis 1996, 162 Papadopoulos 1998, 267 Papadopoulos & Kontorli-Papadopoulou 2001, 134
LHIIB–LHIIIC 1320–1100 BC	Apatheia, Galatas, Troizinia	Chamber tomb	31 inhumations, primary burials and re-use	2 dogs (82 frgs) – probably skinned – frgs of sheep/goat, hare, roe deer and bird bones	Pottery, vessels, sprindle whorls, glass beads	Hamilakis 1996, 153–166
LHIIIA1 1405–1375 BC	Dendra, Argolid	Royal "Tholos sacrificial", Pit 2 (1,30×0,50) in the chamber	Inhumations	A well-preserved skull of a dog, animal bones (according to Persson the remains of a servant and a dog, according to Mylonas remains of previous burials)	Glass, paste, faience beads, stirrup vase, bronze nails, gold-foil	Persson 1931, 18, 39, 68–70 Mylonas 1966, 128–29 Andronikos 1968, 87 Furumark 1972, 53 Day 1984, 24 Hamilakis 1996, 162
		Main chamber (Ø 7,00m)	Inhumations of 3 MNI (at least 3 individuals)	3 dog teeth on the floor of the tomb	9 gold objects, 4 semi-precious stone objects, 3 gl, 8 faience, 1 ivory, 4 bronze, 2 steatite potery	
LHIIIA2 1375-1320 BC	Asine, Argolid	Chamber tomb 1		Dog skull in the middle of the chamber, offering to the latest inhumation		Frödin & Persson 1938, 358 Furumark 1972, 62 Andronikos 1968, 87 Day 1984, 24 Hamilakis 1996, 87
LH$_{IIIA2}$ 1375–1320 BC	Mycenae, Argolid, Kalkani cemetery	Chamber tomb 505	2 inhumations in the dromos deposits	Animal remains including the skulls of a dog, a pig and a horse	Sherds	Wace 1932, 116, n. 1 Andronikos 1968, 87 Furumark 1972, 62 Day 1984, 24 Hamilakis 1996, 162
LHIIIA-B 1405–1200 BC	Mycenae, Argolid, Kalkani cemetery	Chamber tomb 533		1 dog scattered near the door		Wace 1932, 116 Andronikos 1968, 87 Day 1984, 24 Hamilakis 1996, 162
LH$_{IIIA2}$ 1375–1320 BC	Kokla, Argolid	Chamber tomb II		1 medium size dog and 4 horses were found inside the tomb		Demakopoulou 1989, 83–5 Boessneck & von den Driech 1984, 327–33

From natural to cultural: hounds in art

Animals as decorative elements in rows or bands

Dog are among the animals often depicted in bands of repeated images on Archaic pottery (Fig. 2). In Chian pottery dogs appear either running in a row as on the Al Mina and Emporio oenochoe, or chasing animals such as a boar (shown on the inside wall of the Aphrodite bowl) or goats (Lemos 1991: 29–30, pl. 352, 310, 311, 252, 388–9, 453, 455, 887). On Corinthian pottery dogs (Fig. 2.1–4) are most often depicted chasing hares as seen on the Aryballos decorated by the Huntsmen painter (British Museum A2 1883, London); fragments of pottery decorated by the painter of the Corinth Hare-hunter (Corinth Archaeological Museum C-32–139); an aryballos executed by the Head-in–air painter (Trustees of the British Museum 1860: 4–4.16); an olpe, from c. 630 BC (Munich, Antikensammlungen 8764); an aryballos by the Shambling Bull Painter (Bonn 25A); an aryballos of the Kerameikos group (Vienna IV.51); and an olpe from the Campana Painter (Louvre, Paris 10477) (Amyx 1988: pl. 5/2d, 13, 16/1, 17/2,3, 31; Ohly 1986: 24, pl. 6). Other decorative motifs found on Corinthian pottery are: dog and boar, as shown on an olpe in Syracuse (13580: Amyx 1988: pl. 15), dogs chasing stags on an olpe, executed by the painter of the Frankfurt olpe, in the Museum für Vor und Frühgeschichte (Amyx 1988: pl. 16/2b), and a row of dogs on a painted aryballos in the collections of the Copenhagen Museum (4713: Amyx 1988: 17/1).

In Athenian ceramics, the decorative syntax based on bands of dogs is seen on middle Protoattic bowls (Brann 1962: pl. 512), on attic and atticizing amphorae of the protogeometric and geometric periods (CVA by Kourou 2002: pl. 60–5), and on an attic black-figure skyphos

Table 4. Dog remains in human burials in Crete. Other animals recovered in burials where dogs were not found have not been recorded (chronological table after Simpson 1981

Conventional Dating	***Site***	***Type of Tombs***	***Burial Group***	***Animal Offerings***	***Grave Goods***	***References***
EM 3400–2100 BC (Evans) 2000–1800 BC (Levi) 2740–2000 BC (Hood)	Krasi, Pepiados near Malia	Tholos		Fragments of 2 hares (*Lepus creticus*, Barrett-Hamilton), teeth from 2 sheep/goat, teeth from 1 cattle, 1 pig tooth (usual deposit), 1 hedgehog (*Erinaceus nesiotes* Bate), the mandible and loose teeth of a dog of medium size	One amulet made on a shark (*Lamna cornubica*) vertebra	Marinatos 1932, 102–141
LMIII 1405-1100 BC	Mavrospelio, Knossos	Chamber Tomb IX, Chamber A	Inhumation in a larnax	Skull and leg bones of a dog in a grave below the larnax		Forsdyke 1926–27, 248–64 Day 1984, 24
LMIIIA *c*.1405–1375 BC	Phourni, Archanes	Tholos B	Re-use	At the dromos were found skeletons of dogs some complete, some without their heads. Isolated dog bones, pigs and hare, were disovered under the blocks sealing the entrance		Sakellarakis 1966, 178 Sakellarakis & Sakellarakis1991, 91 Day 1984, 23 Hamilakis 1966, 162
LMIIB *c*.1320–1200 BC	Gournes, Herakleion	Chamber Tomb I	Inhumation in a larnax in a pit in the dromos	One metre above the pit, in the till, among burned material, a small dog and sheep bones were deposited	Sealstones in the larnax	Hazzidakis 1918, 64 Kanta 1980, 47 Day 1984, 23–4 Hamilakis 1996, 162
LMIIIC *c*.1200–1100 BC	Praisos		Human teeth	Bones of a dog and an ox		Bonsanquet 1901–1902, 242 Kanta 1980, 179 Pini 1968, 104 Day 1984, 25
SUBMINOAN PERIOD *c*.1100–1200 BC	Karphi, Lasithi	Joint M 16–17	4 individuals	Bones of dogs, sheep and goat		Pendlebury and Money-Coutts 1937–38, 107 Andronikos 1968, 88 Day 1984, 24
PROTO GEOMETRIC PERIOD 1050–900 BC	Siderospilia, Prinias, Herakleion	Tholoi, Tomb BU	Inhumations	2 horses, stretched out on their left sides. A dog was laid between them		Rizza 1978, 42–3, fig. 37 Rizza 1979, 295 Rizza 1985, 160–61 Day 1984, 25 Reese 1995, 295
		Grave BV		A horse and a dog skeleton		Rizza 1979, 295 Reese 1995
		Tomb BO		Bones of dogs and a horse skeleton		Rizza 1979, 295 Reese 1995
		Tomb BE		Bones of dogs and horses		Rizza 1979 Reese 1995
	Tekke cemetery Knossos	Tomb F		A nearly complete skeleton of a donkey, dog and cow bones		Catling 1976–77, 16 Day 1984, 25
GEOMETRIC-EARLY ORIENTALIZING PERIOD 10th–end of 9thc. BC	North cemetary, Knossos	Tomb 79	Secondary burial in a pit containing two ash urns	Two dogs, one fairly complete, above two horse skeletons	Number of small pots	Catling 1976–77, 50 Day 1984, 25 Cavanagh 1996, 674 Wall-Crowther 1996, 704–9
EARLY IRON AGE	Bronda, Kavousi, East Crete	Tholos, tomb X		Numerous puppies, a fox in a pit beneath the burial chamber. Some equid bones also		Gessell, Day & Coulson 1983, reported in Day 1984

from the Athenian Agora (P2710a) of the early 5th century BC (Moore and Philippides 1986: pl.105/1607). Hounds in pursuit of other animals are seen on three askos vases of the late 5th century in which they chase a fox (Munich 2541), a hare (Athenian Agora P5330) and a deer (Athenian Agora: P100541) (Moore 1997: 289–90, pl. 109–11). Two races of local hounds are present in these Athenian representations, having either large straight ears or short ones and long or short muzzels.

The same decorative vocabulary (e.g. a dog chasing a hare) is used in the Boeotia workshops as illustrated by a quadruped kothon in the collections of the National Archaeological Museum in Athens (12687, Kilinski 1990: pl.13/2).

Table 5a. Dog remains in human burials in Attica and the adjacent areas

Conventional Dating	*Site*	*Type of Tombs*	*Burial Group*	*Animal Offerings*	*Grave Goods*	*References*
LHIIIA2 1300–1200 BC	Oxylithos, Euboea	Tholos tomb	8 burials	Cow, sheep, goat, pig and dog bones	Lottery vases, bronze tools, sprindle whols	Papavasileiiou 1910, 26 Andronikos 1968, 87
MYCENAEAN PERIOD 1200–1100 BC	Ayioi Theodoroi (Metafio), Magnesia, East Thessaly	Tholos tomb	6 individuals	Frg. of Bovidae, Equidae, tooth of dog		PAE 1951, 150–4 Feuer 1983, 208
LHIIIC1 1070–1050 BC	Perati, East Attica	Chamber tomb 1, Lakkos 2	Three human skeletons (one of them cremation)	Burned bones of a dog	Numerous offerings	Iakovides 1969, I 159, II 32, 42, 54
LH 1550–1050 BC	Thiva, Kolonaki	Chamber tomb 6 in the dromos		A dog skeleton		Keramopoulos 1917, 137 Andronikos 1968, 87 Hamilakis 1996, 87
PROTO GEOMETRIC PERIOD 11th–9th BC	Lefkandi, PG bulding at Toumba, Euboea	Central room under the floor, revelled rock holes containing small burned bones	Discoloration of the rock was due to the great heat of the "pyre" in which the warrior was cremated. South shaft contained the human burials	1bone belonged to a dog. The North shaft contained horse burials	Boxes, coffin weapons, amphora, remains of a cloth	Lemos 2002, 143–6
MIDDLE GEOMETRIC PERIOD I 850–800 BC	Athens, Areopagus	Grave I in the filling earth over the grave	1 cremation	Dog bones		Day 1974,24
LATE GEOMETRIC PERIOD II 735–700 BC	Athens, Kerameikos	Grave	1 individual	2 dogs		Day 1974, 24
GEOMETRIC PERIOD 900–700 BC	Argos, Rembelos plot, Peloponnese	Tumulus	1 individual	1adult dog burial		Barakari (exc), unpub.; Trantalidou,.pers. obs.
6th *c*. BC	Volos (Palia), East Thassaly	Cist grave	1 individual	1 dog		
1th *c*. BC	Athens, Agora	Pit	175 human infants	Bones of 85 dogs, sheep, goats, pigs and horses		Angel 1945 Day 1984,24
IMPERIAL PERIOD	Athens, Syntagma cemetery	"pit" under a group burial of late Roman times		Dog, hind limbs and caudal vertebra are missing, 1 dog mandibula of a larger animal		Trantalidou, pers. obs.
		A separate dog burial				
1st–2nd *c*. AD	Athens, Syntagma cemetery	Grave 82, a separate dog burial in a cist grave built with bricks			2 glass vases, nails from the dogs collar	Zachariadou 2000, 157; Trantalidou, pers. obs.
			Human humerus and phalanx	Bones of a dog, an equid, tarsals and metatarsals of Bos, Sus, Murex sp.and Pecten sp.		

Table 5b. Dog remains in human burials in Macedonia and Thrace

Conventional Dating	*Site*	*Type of Tombs*	*Burial Group*	*Animal Offerings*	*Grave Goods*	*References*
7th *c*. BC	Drama, industrial area	Tumulus B		1 adult dog burial		Koukouli-Chryssanthaki, Arch.Delt.34 (1979), 333–4
CLASSICAL PERIOD 5th–4th *c*. BC	Acanthos, Central Macedonia			6 horses, 4 dogs skeletons		Trakasopoulou- Salakidlou 1996
MIDDLE OF THE 4th*c*. BC	Rigio, Didymoticho, Thrace	Tumulus B	Cremation	2 horses, 1 dog		Triantafyllos-Terzopoulou, Arch.Delt.50 (1995), 662–4
LATE HELLENISTIC PERIOD	Mithimna, Lesvos			Solitary burial of a dog	2 vases	"Eleutherotypia" 06/05/98
2nd *c*. AD	Mikri Doxipara, Aegean Thrace	Tumulus	Cremations	15 horses, 1 adult dog	Numerous objects	Triantafyllos & Terzopoulou 2005

Table 6. The stature of animals according to withers height

Site	*Period*	*Element*	*Greatest Length in mm.*	*Withers Height in cm.*	*Comments on Size*	*References*
Paradeisos on Nestos river, Aegean Thrace	LN, Chalcolithic Period (about 1000yrs)	Radius	112.9	~40	Two breeds a smaller and a bigger, 'a modern beagle'	Larje 1987, 96, 116
Dikili Tash, plain of Drama-Philippoi, Macedonia	LN, Chalcolithic Period				"Taille moyenne"	Julien 1992, 151
Sitagroi by the river Angitis, Drama plain, Macedonia	II. 5200–4600 BC	Humerus	115.2	38.92		Bökönyi 1986, 121–2
	III. 4600–3500 BC	Humerus	135.5	44.65		
		Radius	143.5	46.20		
		Radius	131.0	42.18		
		Tibia	136.0	39.71		
		Tibia	143.5	41.90		
	IV. 3500–3100 BC	Humerus	131.0	46.84		
		Humerus	152.0	51.22		
		Radius	132.0	42.50		
	V. 3100–2200 BC	Radius	158.0	50.87		
		Calcaneum	40.0	48.80		
Piges Angiti, Drama, East Macedonia	Chalcolithic Period	Radius	154.0	49.58		Trantalidou, personnal observation
		Calcaneum	49.7	54.53		
Stavroupoli I–II, plain of Thesssaloniki, Macedonia	LN	Humerus	133.0	~36/37 to 53.11	Small or medium size animals	Yannouli 2002, 691
		Radius	142.3			
		Tibia (3)	159.0–181.9 $\bar{x}$: 172.9			
		Calcaneum (4)	29.9 – 35.2 $\bar{x}$: 32.2			
Kastanas, Axios valley, Macedonia	~2400–~2000 BC	Calcaneum (7)	39.2 – 52.8 $\bar{x}$: 44.8	54.65	"Zwischen Kleinpudel / Woltsspiz-Airdale / Boxer"	Becker 1986, 93–6, 358
Anza, Bregalnica valley, F.Y.R.O.M	Anza III c. 100–5000 BC	Radius	129.0	41.54	"small to medium size" in the lowest portion of the size of a small Schnauzer variation	Bökönyi 1976, 332–3
	Anza IV				"*palustris type* " either of Spitz group (Torfspitz) or terrier like dog	
Argissa Magoula, by Pinios river, Thessaly	Aceramic-MBA				Larger than those of Anza Aceramic " Typ des Kleinen schlankwüchsigen Torfhundes'	Boessneck 1962, 48–9 Bökönyi 1976, 333 von den Driesch 1987, 16
Ayia Sofia, near Larissa, Thessaly					*Canis familiaris* intermedius Woldrich 1878	von den Driesch & Enderle 1962, 27–8
Pefkakia, Volos bay, Thessaly	Rachmani, 3 mill. BC	Calcaneum	43.0	52.46	"vom Kleinen Spitz bis zum Schäferhund reicht"	Jordan 1975, 110
	Early Bronze Age 2600–2000 BC	Calcaneum	41.0	50.02		Jordan 1975, 110
		Calcaneum	39.0	47.58		Hinz 1979, 110
	Mycenaean Period 1500–1200 BC	Calcaneum	46.0	56.12		Jordan 1975, 110
Achilleion, Thessaly	Achilleion I. 6500–6200 BC	Radius		37.5	1. "small dogs with often crowded upper and lower premolars". "a very small dog the size of a modern Welsh terrier, Stratfordshire terrier, or a Hungarian pulis". "The small dog would represent a second level of domestication" 2. a medium size specimen	Bökönyi 1989, 321

Table 6. cont.

Site	*Period*	*Element*	*Greatest Length in mm.*	*Withers Height in cm.*	*Comments on Size*	*References*
Dhimini, East Thessaly	Late Neolithic Period				"small stature, more akin to those seen today in and around Greek villlages"	Halstead 1992, 46
Galatas, NE Peloponnese	Mycenaean Period (LHB_LHIIIC Early)	Radius	118.73		1."36.2cm based on ulna". " a drachumel dog, variety which in Eastern Mediterranean is documented as early as 1900 BC in Egypt"	Hamilakis 1996, 160
		Radius	118.18	39.1	2."even smaller than the first one"	
Lerna, Argolid plain, Peloponnese	EH II	Humerus	139.5	47.01	EN. "slightly larger than a 'turf dog' (*Canis palustris*) or a modern Schnauzer" MN. "size of a dingo" larger individuals EH II. "more heavily bult individuals, oligodonty", Another comes next to a cross between a wolf and a greyhound EHIII. "three different sizes of dogs, one smaller, one medium, one larger"	Gejvall 1969, 14-8, 67-9
	EH II	Radius	154.0	49.58		
	MH	Calcaneum	39.5	42.09		
	Classical Period	Tibia	188.0	54.89		
	Classical Period	Calcaneum	42.8	52.21		
		Calcaneum	41.5	50.63		
Kokla, Argos, Peloponnese					medium size 'ein Kleiner Schäferhund'	Boessneck & von den Driesch 1984, 333
Tiryns	EHIII			73–78		von den Driesch & Boessneck 1990, 145
Nichoria, South Peloponnese	MHI – Byzantine Period			*c*.55.0	"10% larger than a recent population sample of *Canis aureus* "	Sloan & Duncan 1978, 69
Argos, tumulus, Rebelos plot	Geometric Period	Radius	172.25	68.55		Trantalidou, personal study
Eretria, Euboea	Geometric Period, 2nd half of the 8th c. BC	Humerus	139.2	47.0	Two breeds: 1.looks like "Epagneul breton 46–51cm / courant suisse 45–50cm" 2.a large breed	Chenal-Velarde 2001, 124
Ayio Galas, Chios island	LN/ EBA				"size of present day terrier"	Clutton-Brock 1982, 681
Knossos, Crete	Aceramic Period				Small canid	Jarman 1968, 243
Dictaean cave, Crete	Bronze Age				Small dog	Boyd-Dawkins 1902, 165
Knossos, Crete, Tomb 79	Geometric- Early Orientalizing Period	Sk I. Tibia	187.0	54.6	"modern greyhound or whippet"	Wall-Crowther 1996, 708
		Calcaneum	47.3	57.70		
		Sk II. Humerus	172.0	57.96		
		Tibia	188.0	54.69		
		Calcaneum	45.2	55.14 $\bar{x}$: 56.78		
Knossos, Crete, Wine press	Late Hellenistic Period	Humerus		56.3		Wall 1994, 376

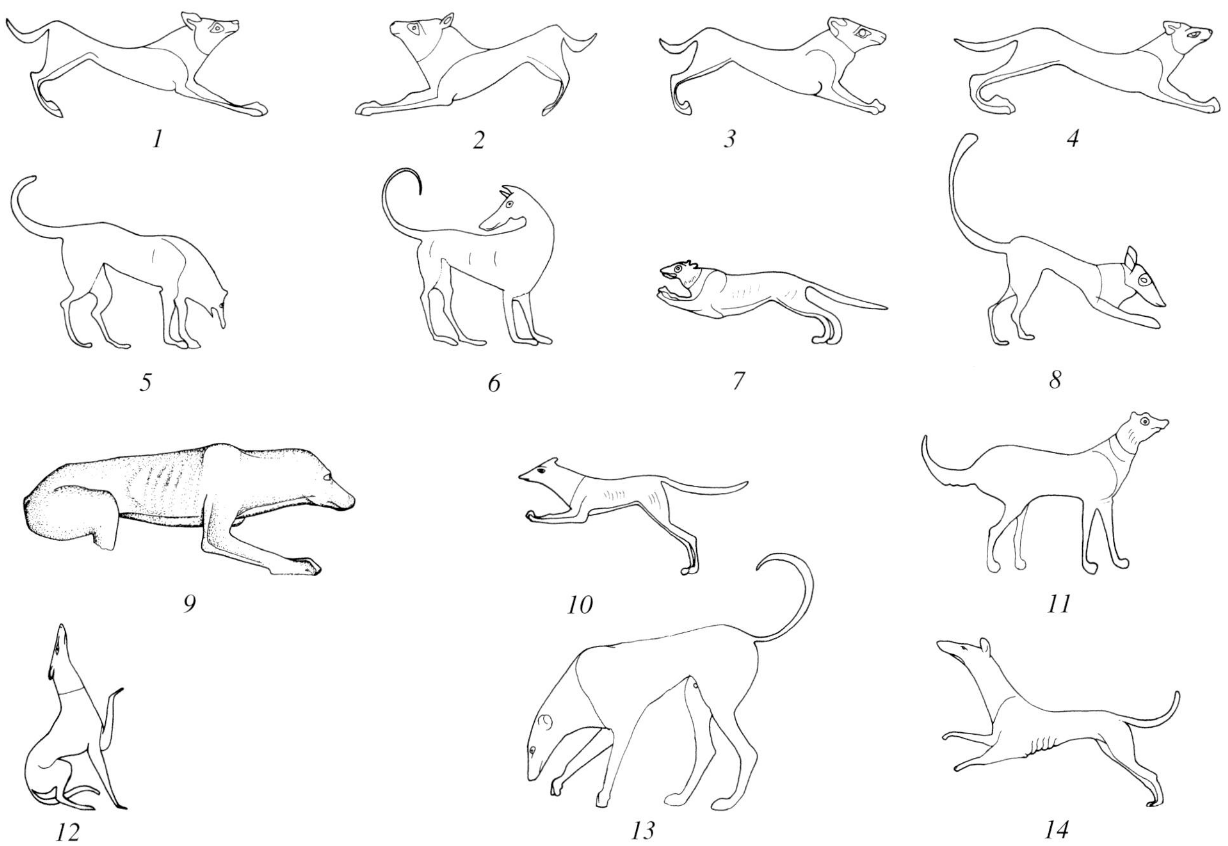

Fig. 2. Hounds

1,4. Dogs on a Late Proto-Corinthian Olpe decorated with three animal friezes where among other animals two dogs are confronted, the painter of the Frankfurt Olpe (650–630 BC), Frankfurt MFV 335, (sk. after Amyx 1988: pl. 16, 2a–b)

2,3. Dog on a Late Proto- Corinthian Olpe decorated with three animal friezes, in one of the earliest narrative contexts showing hounds chasing hares, the painter of the Frankfurt Olpe (650–630 BC), Munich 8764, (sk. after Amyx 1988, pl. 16, 1). The Corinthian vase-painters depicted dogs with admiration and respect

5. Dog on a black-figured skyphos showing Pan and Mainades at Thebes, Archaeological Museum, 25542, (sk. after Sabetai 2001, Corpus Vasorum Antiquorum: pl. 45)

6. Dog on a black-figured skyphos from Ritsona at Thebes, Archaeological Museum, 17078, (sk. after Sabetai 2001: Corpus Vasorum Antiquorum: pl. 46)

7. Dog on a black-figured kantharos showing a frieze decorated with men on horseback (sk. after a pl).

8. Dog on a black-figured lekythos showing Actaion bitten by his dogs, National Archaeological Museum in Athens A 488 (sk. after Waern-Sperber 2001: fig. 4)

9. Marble votive statue of a dog found at the sanctuary of Artemis in Brauron, c. 530 BC, Akropolis Museum (sk. after M. Brouscari, 1978, Acropole d'Athènes et son Musée).

10. Dog on a black-figured attic belly amphora by the Amasis Painter, 550/540 BC, Munich Antikensammlungen 8763 (sk. after Ohly 1986: 15)

11. Dog on a black-figured lekythos representing a man mounted on a chariot accompanied by a dog, from the Athenian Agora, made by the Gela painter, c. 500 BC, P 24105 (sk. after Moore and Philippides, The Athenian Agora 1986, vol. 22, 870: pl. 79)

12. Dog on a red-figured wine jar, a stamnos by the Eucharides painter, showing a young man visiting hetaerae, from Athens, c. 460 BC, National Museum, Copenhagen 3239 (sk. after Lund and Bundgaard Rasmussen 1995: pl. 78)

13. Dog on red-figured attic amphora by the Kleophrades Painter representing the soldier's farewell, 500–490 BC, (sk. Munich Antikensammlungen 2305 WAF (sk. after Ohly 1986: 32).

14. Dog on a red-figured pelike representing Eos and Tiphon with his dog. Paris, Louvre Museum G. 230 (sk. after Scheffer 2001: fig. 4)

Hunting (θήρα) scenes with dogs

The Greek language is accurate. There could be no hunt or chase (κυνηγία/κυναγία, κυνήγιον, κυνηγεσία, κυνηλασία, κυναγετική τέχνη, κυνοδρομία) without a dog leader. Verbs and nouns reflecting the imagery of the act include κυνηλατέω: follow the hounds; κυνοδρομέω, κυνηγέω/κυναγέω, κυνηγέσσω/ κυνηγέττω, κυνηγετέω: run or chase with dogs; κυναγός, κυναγωγός, κυνηγέτις/κυναγέτις (epithet of Artemis), κυναγέτας, κυνηγητήρ: hound leader, huntsman; Κ(ο)υναγίδας: title of Heracles (Macedonia 2nd century BC); κυναγετικοί τόποι: hunting places; and κυνηγέσιον/κυναγέσιον: hunting establishment. According to the principles of Homeric society, war, athletic games and hunting were important aspects of a superior man's fame. In classical Greece these activities were very closely connected, and in iconography can be distinguished in the following groupings.

Hunting scenes.

Among the many scenes representing hunting ('*κυσίν θηροκτόνοις*': Eur. *Helena*, 153–4) we can cite a Mycenaean wall painting (Boulotis 1988; 35), a Bronze Age complex of figurines depicting a hunter (a hero?) with his hound attacking a lion from the end of 8th century BC in the Archaeological Museum of Samos (Boardman 1980; fig.17), and a marble sarcophagus decorated with relief scenes depicting a hunting scene with horsemen, hounds and one lion. This object, found at the cemetery of Sidon and dated to the end of the 4th cent. BC is in the collections of the Istanbul Archaeological Museum (Boardman 1980: pl. 205). A mosaic executed by Gnosis in Pella, Macedonia c. 300 BC (Fig. 3) depicts two hunters and a stag which is being attacked by a dog (Boardman 1980: pl. 229). Dogs are shown on the architrave frieze, dating to c. 400–380BC, from the Nereid's monument at Xanthus depicting bear hunting (London 889: Boardman 1999: pl. 218.10), and on the base of a statue of the 3rd century BC from Messene (Peloponnese) which is decorated with scenes of lion hunting (Paris 858: Boardman 1999: pl. 154).

Hunters

Scenes depicting hunters were widely appreciated. As examples we can cite a stone seal of the LM period which depicts a hunter (Muenzer 2000: 126). On an oenochoe from Rhodes, by the Amasis painter (British Museum B 52) the hunter, returning from the hunt is accompanied by his dog. He wears a leather cap and carries a hare and a fox hanging from his stick (Karouzou 1956: 10). A panel-amphora decorated by the painter of the Andromeda group shows a horseman and his dog (Berlin Staatliches Museum F 1632: Amyx 1988: pl.123/2). A panel amphora (550–540 BC) by the Amasis Painter (Fig. 2.14) shows a procession of riders (Antikensammlungen 8763: Ohly 1986: 28, pl. 15) and a black-figured kantharos depicting horsemen and a running dog was found in Boeotia. (Cambridge, Fogg Museum 1960.390: Kalinski 1990: pl. 21/1). A red-figured lekythos (c. 470 BC) was decorated by the Pan Painter with a scene of a hunter and his dog, (Museum of Fine Arts, Boston: Boardman 1980; pl. 162). On a marble funerary relief from c. 460 BC a hunter holding a hare returns home with his dog, (Berlin Staatliche Museum: Boardman 1980; pl. 111). Hunters are also portrayed on a 5th century BC limestone funerary block of Denomachos, from Akraiphnion, Boetia (Thebes Museum 44: Dimakopoulou and Konsola 1981: 42, fig. 8) and a marble funeral relief from Ilissos (c. 330 BC). which depicts the dead hero as a hunter accompanied by his dog, his elderly father and his young servant (Athens, National Archaeological Museum 869), a scene which portrays not only of the dead peron but also the dog's loyalty as stressed by the presence of the servant. A funeral stele from Thespies of the 4th century BC portrays a hunter and his two dogs (Thebes Museum 33: Dimakopoulou and Konsola 1981: 73, fig. 25).

Athletes

Scenes in which dogs accompany athletes can be illustrated by the following examples. A marble relief base for a funeral statue, found near the Kerameikos cemetery in Athens, shows four athletes in relaxed poses watching two other individuals, the owners (?) of a dog and a cat, which are fighting (c. 510 BC. Athens, National Archaeological Museum 3476: Karouzou 1967: 31; Tzachou-Alexandri 1989: 167). On a marble funerary relief stele (Fig. 4.2) of the athlete Stephanos found at Tanagra in Boeotia a dog accompanies his master on his way to the palestra or wrestling ring (early 4th cent. BC, Athens, National Archaeological Museum 2578: Tzachou-Alexandri 1989; 70). On a funeral stele of Agathocles, son of Phrynichos found at Chassani, Attica, a human figure (the athlete, Fig. 4.1) and a dog have been sculpted (c. 440/420 BC, Athens, National Archaeological Museum 742: Karouzou 1967: 39; Tzachou-Alexandri 1989: 225).

Other human figures with dogs

Dogs began to appear on stelai in the last quarter of the 6th century BC, continuing until the half of the 4th century BC. On stelai, animals as well as humans were represented as servants and in some instances animal companions, including dogs, also accompanied the deceased in burials (Perrson 1931: 69; Mylonas 1966: 128–9; Day 1984: 26). Gravestones depicting human figures with their dogs become very popular in the first half of the fifth century, some examples of which are: fragments from the shafts of two stele found at the Athenian Agora (c. 535–530 BC. Agora Museum S1276a, S1276b: Richter 1961: 34–5/49); a marble funerary stele from Orchomenos in Boeotia sculpted by Alxinor from Naxos c. 480 BC (Athens, National Archaeological Museum 39); and a marble stele relief fragment found on

*Fig. 3. A dog and a fallow deer (*Dama dama*) on a mosaic floor of an andron at a house, depicting a hunting scene Pella, Central Macedonia, hellenisic period (sk. after M. Lilimpaaki-Akamati and I. M. Akamatis 2003, Pella and its environs, Thessaloniki: fig. 17)*

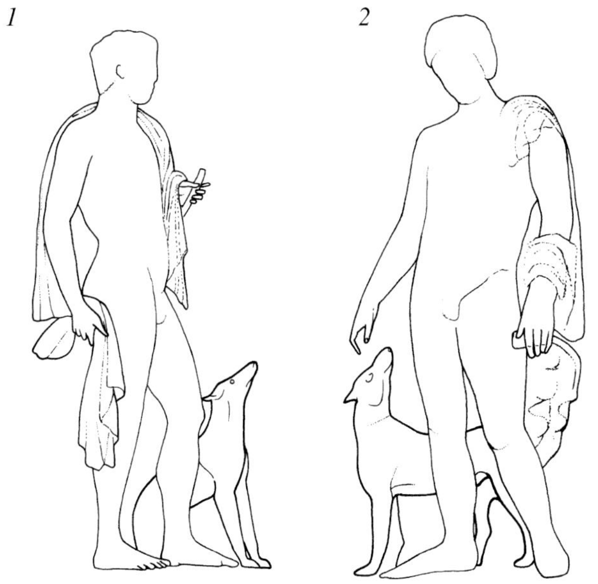

Fig. 4. Athletes
1. Dog and young man on the funeral relief of athlete Agathokles , c. 440 BC, National Archaeological Museum in Athens 742 (sk. after Tzachou-Alexandri 1989: fig. 224)
2. Dog and his master on the marble funeral relief of the athlete Stephanos from Tanagra, Boeotia, beginning of the 4th century BC, National Archaeological Museum in Athens 2578 (sk. after Tzachou-Alexandri 1989: fig. 70)

Anaphe in the Cyclades. (c. 460–450 BC. Athens, National Archaeological Museum 3205: Karouzou 1967). A marble funeral stele depicting a young and an older man with a dog between them, was found near the Kerameikos cemetery (c. 410 BC, Athens, National Archaeological Museum 2894: Karouzou 1967: 78). On a marble stele found at Piraeus a lone woman is depicted seated with a dog at her feet (c. 4th century BC, Athens, National Archaeological Museum 882: Karouzou 1967).

Warriors/ Chariot scenes

In Greek κυνομαχέω mean to fight with dogs. In iconography, dogs are often present in the procession of riders and at the warrior's farewell, as in the following examples: a black-figured lekythos from the Athenian Agora on which a chariot pulled by four horses,and carrying two men is accompanied by a dog (P24105 in the Agora Museum, Moore and Philippides 1986: pl.79/ 870); an attic black-figure neck-amphora from c. 550 BC with a chariot race scene on side A, attributed to the Castellani Painter (San Antonio Museum of Art, Texas, 86.134.169: Shapiro *et al.* 1995: 78, pl. 35); an attic black-figure neck-amphora, attributed to the Nikoxenos painter, on which two mounted Amazons on horseback are accompanied by yapping dogs (c. 500 BC, San Antonio Museum of Art, Texas, 86.134.43a, b: Shapiro *et al.* 1995: 112, pl. 55); an the attic amphora (Fig. 2.13) by Kleophrades Painter (500–490 BC, Munich Antiken-sammlungen 2305 WAF: Ohly 1986: 47, pl 32).

Pet animals

Small sized dogs were also kept as household pets. The commonest of these seems to be an animal resembling the Maltese (Μελιταία κυνάρια), an animal with small upright ears and long hair (Figs. 5 6). Representations of such dogs include: twenty terracotta figurines (Fig. 6) depicting Maltese dogs from Hellenistic and Roman towns including Tanis, Zaouiet el Maietin, Antinoe, from Egypt, and from the Italian peninsula, all housed in the Louvre Museum (E 15033, E 26851, E 29799, AF 8329, AF 1048 B, E 12446, E 20845, AF 1307, AF 1306, E 20846 [dog holding a hen], AF 8484, AF 8486, AF 9127, AF 1305, AF 8952, E 12445, D/E 4540, D/E 4541, D3785, D 3786; Dunand 1990: 288–93, numb. 862–880; Besques 1986: pl. 78f /79,b, pl.80,d, f), and four examples of the 3rd century BC in the Tübigen and Dresden museums (1120–25: Fischer 1994: 419–20, pl.119–20). Roman terracotta figurines in the shape of Maltese type animals are found throughout the Roman provinces (Gonzenbach 1995: 228–37). Funeral reliefs depict children of all ages accompanied by small pet dogs and a funeral lekythos showing two twin brothers with their parents and their pet, comes from Attica/ Peristeri (3rd quarter of the 4th century BC, Archaeological Museum of Piraeus: Stainhauer 2001: pl. 440). A naiskos on limestone from Alexandria now at the Louvre also shows such a breed

(Ma 4203 Hamiaux 1992: 163). In all these scenes the dogs are rarely seated. One exception is a funeral relief dated to the 3rd or the 2nd century BC in the Rhodos Archaeological Museum (IV.16: Konstantinopoulos 1996, 44). In another instance a pet dog is jumping to catch a bird (Fig. 5.2). Kneeling girls have pets in their raised arms. Sometimes other common domestic species (a pigeon, a calf, etc) are also present. Perhaps the depiction of young or small animals was thought to be an appropriate attribute for the representation of childhood, as larger types of dogs such as the Laconian hound were rarely depicted in such settings. It is also rare that an adult is represented with a pet dog. One example of such a scene is found on a funeral stele from Halicarnasse, Asia Minor (Louvre Ma 2927; Ma 945: Hamiaux 1992: 163, 7, pl. 180, 5). On choes (Fig. 5.3) pet dogs often engage in play with little children. In one such instance, a red-figured chose from c. 430–426 BC, the animal is standing on its hind legs (A 15272; Parlama-Stambolidis 2000, 355). On a red-figured aryballos from 490–480 AD, found at the Kerameikos cemetery (A15535) a malteze dog is scratching itself (Parlama-Stambolidis 2000: 309–10). A small boy holding a maltese dog was sculpted in marble during the 1st century BC (Fig. 5.5). The statue was discovered at Gerontiko in Asia Minor (Athens National Archaeological Museum 3485: Karouzou 1967: 182, pl. 67).

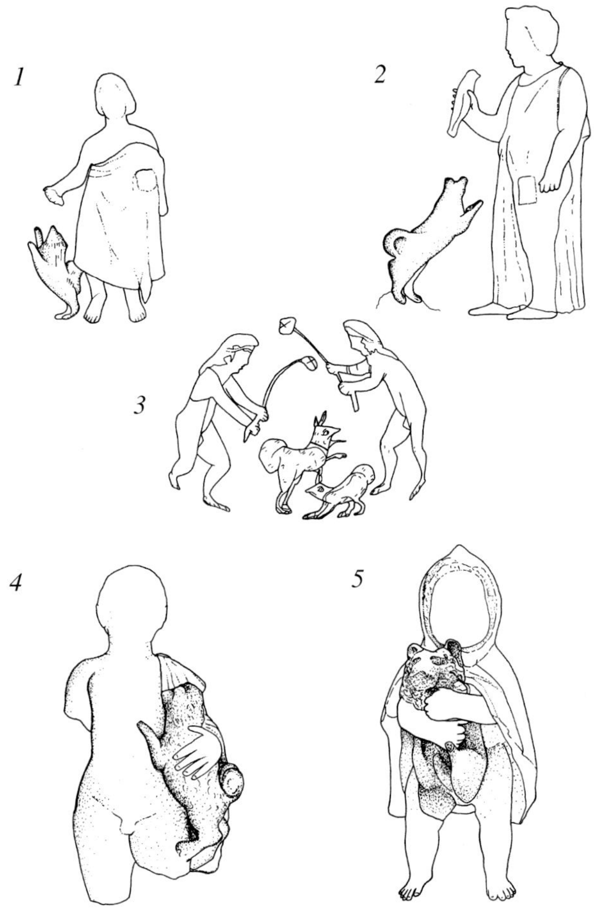

Fig. 5. Children and pets dogs of Maltese breed
1. Complex of a boy, Theocles, and his dog, shown jumping up, on a grave relief of the beginning of the 4th century BC found in Attica, National Museum in Athens, 3661 (Karouzou 1967: 37; sk. after a photo). The theme is connected to the death of a child
2. Funeral marble stele representing a child holding a dove on his right hand, while a pet-dog jumps to catch the bird, Attica, National Museum in Athens, 748. Pigeons and long-haired maltese dogs are the attributes of children in Classical grave-reliefs
3. Children playing with balls and maltese dogs participating in the game on red-figured choe from Kerameikos cemetery in Athens, 430–426 BC, A 15272, (sk, after Stampolidis and Parlama 2000: fig. 389)
4.Marble statue of a boy holding a dog on his left hand at the National Museum in Athens
5. Marble statue of an infant bearing a cape, known as the little refugee, holding a pet-dog, found at Gerontiko Nissis, Asia Minor, 1st century AD recreating an earlier model, National Museum in Athens, 3485 (sk. after Karouzou 1967: fig. 67)

Familiar dogs participating in domestic life and in social events.

Dogs as watchdogs and guardians escorting people on their trip the Underworld.

Among the many representations of dogs in domestic scenes is a Laconian rhyton representing a hound's head executed by the Brygos Painter (500–490BC) in the collections of the Museo Nazionale di Villa Giulia, Rome: Hull 1964: 223). It just reminds us of our close relationships and familiarity with this animal. On an Attike pelike showing a market scene, two dogs are shown fighting each other (Scheibler 1992: pl. 7). On a black-figured pelike in Dunedin (Otago Museum E 48.226) where rhapsodes are performing, a dog accompanies listeners who are waiting their turn to perform (Shapiro 1989: 46, pl. 22b–c). Scenes with musicians and a dog are also shown on Boeotian skyphoi (Sabetai, CVA, Thebes, pl. 45–6).

Dogs are important elements in illustrations of symposia, when young men visit hetaerae. They appear also in banquet scenes, under the couches and the tables. They are seen near the beds in the rooms of gods, such as on a lekythos of the Leagros group showing Dionysos, Ariadne and their son banqueting (Bochum 496: Shapiro 1989: 94, pl. 42d–e). They are shown with heroes such as Hercules, Iphitus, Iolas on a Corithian crater of c. 600–590 BC; and Tydeas and Ismene on a Corinthian

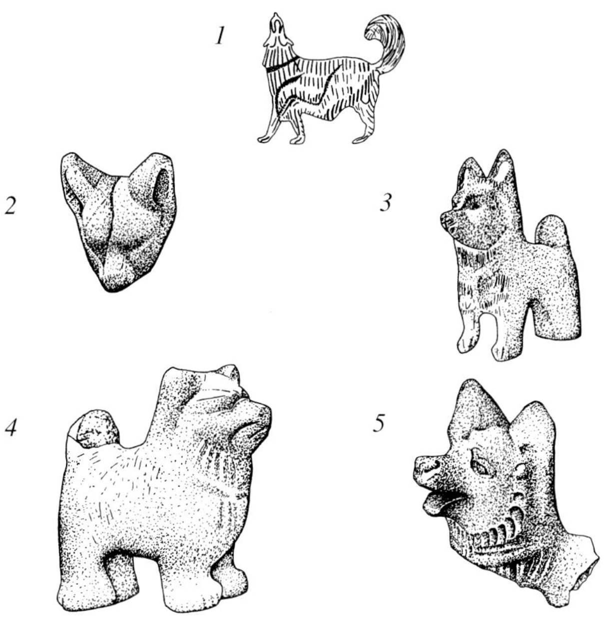

Fig. 6. Maltese dogs
1. A maltese dog rising his head painted on a red-figured aryballos from Kerameikos cemetery in Athens, 490–480 BC, A 15535, (sk, after Stampolidis and Parlama 2000: fig. 311)
2. Terracotta dog head bearing traces of painting (H: 6,8 cm), from Antinoe, 2nd–3rd century BC, Paris, Louvre Museum, E 12446 (sk. after Dunand 1990: fig. 880)
3. Terracotta dog Fig. with white painting (H. 17,3 cm) roman period, Paris, Louvre Museum, E 29805 (sk. after Dunand 1990: fig. 866)
4. Terracotta dog Fig. with white painting (H. 10,5 cm) from Antinoe, 2nd–3rd century BC, Paris, Louvre Museum, E 12445 (sk. after Dunand 1990: fig. 864)
5. Terracotta dog head (H. 13,8cm) roman period, Paris, Louvre Museum, AF 9127 (sk. after Dunand 1990: fig. 874)

amphora of c. 560 BC in the Musée du Louvre, Paris (E635 and E640: Elliniki Mythologia IV, pl. 73 and 145). On a black-figure neck-amphora from Vulci, dating to c. 530–520 BC, Dionysos appears on a banqueting couch, while a dog is shown feasting on a bone (Fitzwilliam Museum, GR 27.1864: Vassilikou 1998, 30–31). From the Mycenean era come two miniature representations of tables and cakes at which small dogs are feeding (Piraeus Archaeological Museum: Stainhauer: pl. 41–2), these dogs are described as τραπεςῆες.

In the funeral rites of Patroclos, the dogs were cut (*Iliad* 23, 171–77; Day 1984: 26). Dogs are also present on funeral reliefs depicting funeral meals, where they lurk under the beds and the tables eating anything that has fallen from above (see for instance a marble relief in Athens, National Museum 1501, c. end of the 5th century BC). On a grave-stele of Aristeas (middle of the 3rd century AD) the deceased is shown with his pet dog (Fitzwilliam Museum GR 21.1865: Budde and Nicholis 1967, 135). On a wine jar, a stamnos, by the Eucharides Painter, a young man (Fig. 2.12) visiting hetaerae (Athens, c. 460 BC, in Copenhagen National Museum) is depicted with his dog (Lund and Bundgaard Rasmussen 1995, 78). Dogs are also present (drawn by the smells?) on scenes where men are courting youths such as an attic black-figured amphora, attributed to the Berlin Painter of Berlin (1686, c. 540BC, San Antonio Museum, Texas, 86.134.44: Shapiro *et al.* 1995: 92–3, pl. 43).

Dogs were essential to the comfort and dignity of the dead in the under world (Tables 3–5). At the cemetery adjoining with the Gymnasium in Messene (Peloponnese) infant burials of the 2nd/1st century BC were accompanied by young dog burials (Themelis 2000, 124). Funeral monuments were used to perpetuate the memory of the dead. At times, figures of lions or dogs might take the place of the funeral vases that decorated the enclosure where each family buried its members. As such, they represent the guardians which never sleep. A hound smelling the earth was found on a funeral monument from Salamis Island (Attica, c. 350 BC, Munich 497:Boardman 1999: pl. 113). Another found in Attica is housed at the Athens National Archaeological Museum (4763: Karouzou 1967: 117). A funeral monument at the Gymnasium in Messene, Peloponnese has a marble frieze decorated with running dogs, stags and other animals (Themelis 2000: pl. 102).

Gods and eponymous heroes

Hunting dogs

The domination of the gods over animals was expressed by hunting scenes in which gods and heroes triumphed over wild animals. During these hunts, dogs were their indispensable attendants, and their dogs often preceded them. In these scenes the dogs were at the god's service and they proved their competence (Fig. 1).

Artemis

Goddess of the hunt (κυναγέτις: huntress), Artemis led human hunters through the steep mountains of the Peloponnese, from Taygetos to Eurymanthos, followed by nymphs (*Homeric hymn* II, 2/ XXVII. 1; Plutarch, *Moralia*, 379 D; Decharme 1959: 152; Prieur 1988: 133–5). Callimachus observed that she received her dogs from Pan. Pan himself can be seen on an Athenian relief of the 4th. century BC from Pnyka with a Nymph and a dog (Metrorama 30/05/02). Artemis presented Cyrene, a nymph, with two hounds and she taught Atalante how to manipulate those animals. The Cretan goddess *Dictynna*, identified with Artemis, also kept hounds and her temple was guarded by dogs (Callimachus, *Hymn to Artemis*, 90–100, 206–7, 215–17; *Dionysiaka* XVI, 187). According to Xenophon of Ephesos (*Habrocomes and Antheia* I, 2.6–7), the sacred procession to the

Artemision started with a girl dressed like the goddess and followed by dogs (Bevan 1986: 115). Artemis and Hekate were known as *Skylakitis*, protectors of dogs (*Orphic Hymns*, I, 5; XXXVI, 12) and *Skylakotrophos*, nurse of puppies (*Dionysiaka*, XLVIII, 15; XLIV, 195). A votive inscription to Kynagia, found in Thessaly could be dedicated either to Hekate/Enodia or to Artemis (Bevan 1986: 118).

Representations of dogs (Artemis and her dog, hunting motifs, single representations of dogs) were found in the sanctuaries of Artemis Orthia at Sparta. At the Artemision of Ephesos, a Greek gem of the Imperial Period was found which shows the many-breasted Ephesian Artemis flanked by two bitches. Dogs (Fig. 2.9) are also found in association with the Artemision of Delos, the Delion of Paros, the Artemis Hemerasia at Lousoi, the Artemis Laphria at Kalydon, the Brauron sanctuary, the Artemis Knakeatis at Tegea, the altar of Artemis at Olympia, the Artemis Limnatis at Kombothreka, the Artemis in the Asklepieion of Epidaurus, the Artemis Orthia in Sparta, the Diktynnaion of Crete, the Artemision at Scala Greca in Sicily, and the Artemis Tauropolos at Aricia beside Lake Nemi in Italy and at Pherai, all dating from the Mycenean era through the 3rd century AD (Bevan 1986). Two marble dogs, found on the Athenian Akropolis (Museum 143) and dated to 520–510 BC suggest the presence of Artemis (Shapiro 1989: 65, pl. 31c).

Animal groups, often showing dogs and hares, were very popular in Cypriot coroplastic art of the 6th century BC and later in stone sculpture. Such groupings were usually votive offerings given by successful hunters in the sanctuary of Amathus, and were sometimes dedicated to Apollo or Aphrodite (74.51.2741; 74.51.2666; 74.51.2623 in the Metropolitan Museum of Art: Karageorghis *et al.* 2000: 260. 224–5, National Museum at Athens: Karageorghis 2003: V3247; 11611 at the Kunsthistorisches Museum in Vienna).

Kephalos and Prokris

Kephalos (Cephalus) from Phokis lived in Athens and was married to Prokris. She is sometimes represented with lance and a dog. In myth and imagery a dog named "Lailaps" (Storm, a dog catching everything it hunts), is a gift to Kephalos from Zeus or Artemis or even Eos (the dawn in Hymettos mountain, Attica), and accompanies him as he hunts on mount Hymettus. On a red-figured crater (c. 440–430 BC) in the British Museum (E 477), the death of Prokris, caused by a mistake by Kephalos, is portrayed (Elliniki Mythologia III, pl. 14). Kyanippos and Leukonoe, are the heroes of the Thessalian version of the story. Kichyros and Anthippe also appear in a similar myth with the same nucleus and naturalistic symbolism (Elliniki Mythologia III, 33–6).

Actaion

Actaion (Actaeon) was a famous hunter with 50 hounds who ranged over Kithairon Mountain, in Boeotia. Among his greyhound were: *Charon* (death), *Arpyia* (harpy), *Pamphagos* (omnivorous), *Tigris* (tiger), *Nevrophonos* (killer of young deer, deerhound), and *Corax* (crow, rapacious). Having seen, by mistake, Artemis in the nude, he was transformed into a deer and subsequently attacked and killed by his own dogs. In this narration dogs represented the emissaries of Artemis' will (Dionysaiques V, 300–70; Bevan 1986: 115; Prieur 1988: 140). These scenes of metamorphosis (Fig. 1.3–4) are represented on a black-figured lekythos (Athens NM A488: Waern-Sperber 2001: fig. 4), a red-figured fragment (Athens NM 760: ibidem, fig.5), and a Poseidonian skyphos (c. 400–395 BC) in the Karlsruhe, Basishes Landesmuseum 76/106 (Elliniki Mythologia III, pl. 41; Waern-Sperber 2001: fig.3). A red-figured crater (c. 480 BC) from Cuma in the Museum of Fine Arts (Boston 10.185: Elliniki Mythologia II, pl. 69; Boardman 1975: pl. 335.2; Hill 1964: 215) depicts hounds which Waern-Sperber (2001: fig. 8) recognizes as Laconian. A Roman statue of the 2nd century AD also represents Actaeon being attacked by his dogs (Woodford 2003: 169, pl. 129).

Peleas

Peleas was a hunter from Aigina who took part in the hunt for the Caledonian boar (Central Greece), as well as hunts on mount Pelion, before becoming king of Iolkos in Thessaly. On a black figure hydria he is represented accompanied by his dog (c. 520 BC, Staatliche Museum F 1890: Elliniki Mythologia III, 74).

Meleagrus

Meleagurs (Meleager) was a famous hunter from Aetolia, in Central Greece who killed the boar sent by Artemis against the area of Calydon (Iliad IX, 529–45: Pausanias, I, 27), His dog's names were *Korax, Marpsas* (catches violently), *Egertis* (rising above others), *Methepon* (follows closely), *Charon* (death), *Podagros*, *Phero*, *Podis*, etc. This myth has many versions. In early versions, only a few hunters are involved while in the poems of Appolodoros and Ovidios they reach as many as 35 in number (Elliniki Mythologia III, 158–9). In these latter poems, Atalante, the only woman among these many male heroes, took part. On a black-figure crater known as the François vase the hunting scene as narrated by Homer is represented (Florence, Archaeological Museum 4209: Elliniki Mythologia III, pl. 83; Tiverios 1976, pl. 86a, 93b). The same scene is depicted on a cylix created c. 540 BC (Munich, Staatliche Antikensamlungen 2243: Elliniki Mythologia III, pl. 86). The myth is probably also depicted by a scene on a black figured hydria created c. 575–525 BC (Rome, Musei Capitolini 65: LIMC, III, pl. 535: Beazley Archives 100) in which horsemen attack a boar. On an Apulian amphora, executed about 330 BC, Meleagrus is shown giving the hide of the boar to Atalante (Bari, National Museum, 872: Elliniki Mythologia III, pl. 84). On a Roman sarcophagus the leading hero, who has organized the hunt, is shown hunting with his dogs while

Atalante shoots an arrow (180–200 AD Palazzo Doria, Rome: Woodford 2003: 186, 148a, b).

Castor and Pollux.

The Dioscouroi (Kastor and Polydeukes), were Elena's (Helen's) brothers and hunters from the Peloponnese. As shown on a black-figured amphora of c. 503 BC, they were always connected with cavalry, a sign of their aristocratic origin (Rome, Musei Vaticani: 16757: Elliniki Mythologia III, pl. 109). At the end of their life they become heroes. A black-figured amphora (c. 550–540BC) depicts the two brothers arriving at the palace of Zeus. In this scene, Poseidon, Ares and a dog attend them (Copenhagen, National Museum, 14347: Elliniki Mythologia III, pl. 84; Shapiro 1989: 114, pl. 48a). A similar scene has been identified on an hydria acquired by the University of Bochum 1165 (Shapiro 1989: 152, pl. 67b). The animals of these Spartan heroes symbolized their relation with the light and the dark, the light of Heaven and the darkness of Earth. On a lekythos by Amasis painter, found in Athens, Helen is shown with her brothers (Karouzou 1956: 11).

Egests

Egests is a Trojan hero who founded the town of Segesta in Sicily. On coins he is depicted wearing a cap, holding two lances and accompanied by two dogs.

Hippolyte

On the south slope of Acropolis in Athens there is a sanctuary dedicated to this hero. Hippolyte is represented as a hunter having a dog (pers. comm. I. Leventis, Associate Professor at Volos University). On a Roman sarcophagus Hippolyte attacks a boar on horseback accompanied by his dogs (180–190 AD, Campo Santo, Pisa, Woodford 2003: 188, 150a, b)

Adonis

On two roman sarcophagi the departure of Adonis for the hunt is depicted. The resultant confrontation of Venus' beloved did not have a happy outcome (2nd century AD, Palazzo Giustiniani, Rome; c. 220 AD, Musei Vaticani, Vatican City, Woodford 2003:187–9, pl. 149a, b, 1512b).

Orion

This hunter of the sky ('Ωρίων) is followed by the hound Sirius. Each year, on the island of Keos in the Cyclades, priests made a sacrifice before the rising of his constellation. Coins from Keos also bore the head of a hound surrounded by rays of light (Decharme 1959: 250–1).

Pastoral dogs

Pares

While acting as a shepherd, the Trojan prince Pares was called upon to judge which goddess was the most beautiful. On an Etruscan black-figured amphora (c. 530 BC, Munich Antikensammlungen) a dog, three cows and a bird accompany Pares, establishing a purely bucolic scene (Woodford 2003: 90, pl. 61). On an attic red-figure hydria, the Pares Painter (c. 400 BC), depicts the Trojan hero and his dog sitting in front of Hermes. The three goddesses to be judged, and Zeus, are also shown awaiting Paris' decision (Badisches Landesmuseum, Carlsruhe B36, 259; Boardman 1980: pl. 175; Elliniki Mythologia V, pl. 9; Woodford 2003: 92, pl. 63).

Dogs in domestic life

Odysseus

Odysseus was associated with the Caledonian hunt, which involved dogs. It is also well known that on his journey home from Troy Circe transformed a number of his companions in animals, primarily pigs. This episode is depicted in an image on a red-figured crater (c. 450–430 BC) in the collections of the Metropolitan Museum, New York (No. 4183, Elliniki Mythologia V, pl. 186) in which pigs, horses and a dog are represented. Meanwhile, Argos, his beloved dog was faithful to his master while Odysseus was gone from Ithaca, suffering all types of humiliations during his absence, as Odysseus himself was persecuted during his journey home. When this faithful animal died, Odysseus gave his canine tooth to the king of Ithaca.

Dogs as guards of Hades and as symbols of death

En(n)odia

Ennodia, the goddess of roads and crossroads, and the goddess of death, evolved slowly into the national goddess of Thessaly. Her cult was autonomous until the late Roman period. She was worshiped in such places as Krannon, Phalanna, Gonnoi, and Phythion. At Thebes of Phthiotis or Pagassai, En(n)odia Patroa, was worshipped as the national goddess. At the city of Larissa, she was worshipped as Enodia Astike. As Enodia Stathmia, she was worshiped at the city gates as was Hekate. As Enodia Mykaike she is associated with the underworld and related to Poseidon and earthquakes; as Enodia Alexeatis she is an apotropaic character. At Pherai, the second most important city of Thessaly and the center of the cult, four sanctuaries of Enodia Pheraia have been located, three of them near the cemeteries of the city. Here, she was worshipped from early Geometric times (Chryssostomou 1998: 25–69; 104–12, with a detailed bibliography). She was also worshipped in Macedonia. At Pella as Beroea-Hosia, she was the goddess who supervised purification rites and burial customs, Eordaia, Derriopos, Elimeia, and Mygdonia (ibid. 70–103). In the cities of southern Greece, on the islands of Euboea and Thera, and in Athens, she acted as the goddess of the funeral rites (Sophocles, *Antigone,* 1199), and as the goddess of cemeteries and ghosts (Euripides, *Ion* 1048–52, and *Helena,* 569–70). Enodia was also associated with the deities *Artemis*, as Artemis Pheraia in the Peloponnese and Sicily, and *Hekate*, both of whom controlled daemons and ghosts. Because she was associated with burial rites, she was also related to *Pluton* (*Antigone* 1196–1200, before 442 BC).

The horse (Chryssostomou 1998: 131, 145–50) and the dog ('κύων μελαίνα', κυνώ σκυλοκάγεια') were animals sacred to Enodia, and are often shown with her (Fig. 1.1). On a coin from Pherai, Thessaly, the head of Enodia on the body of a dog is seated below the Hypereia spring. This coin was circulated during the administration of Jason tyrannous, which began in the 4th century BC (ibid. 141). The goddess and a dog are shown on a marble votive relief from Larissa, Thessaly, also dated to the 4th century BC (ibid. 154, pl. 15γ). On a marble votive relief from Krannon, Thessaly (360–350 BC), a torch bearing Ennodia is accompanied by both a horse and a dog (ibid. 152–3, cover sheet). From Perseis, modern Debreste, F.Y.R.O.M., two terracotta busts of Enodia dated after 183 BC show her with a horse, and a dog jumping over her shoulder (ibid. 154–5, 269). On a marble inscribed relief votive (2nd century BC) from the area of Exochi village, Eordaia the goddess is escorted by her sacred animals, a dog and a horse (Museum of Kozani, Macedonia, 895, ibid. 74–6, 151–2, pl. 14β). Also from Exochi is an inscribed marble altar with a hunting scene involving hare and dog, also dated to the 2nd century BC (ibid. 76–7). A seated dog is shown with the goddess on a marble statue dated to classical times from Pella, Macedonia (Archaeological Museum of Pella ΒΠ 1986/11, ibid. 70, pl. 17). Enodia and a dog are shown in relief on a marble altar of the Hellenistic period from Mygdonia, Macedonia (Archaeological Museum of Thessalonica 12333, ibid. 84, 163–5, pl.18β). From Elimeia, the village of Ayia Paraskevi, in Macedonia comes a marble votive relief showing the goddess astride a horse, with a dog walking in front of them (Museum of Kozani 848 (ibid. 149–51, 14a). Finally, on a statue which is probably from Attica, and dated to c. 300 BC, two dogs are seated with two women who are facing each other; one of whom is likely Enodia (Louvres Museum, ibid. 160–3).

Apollo Pythios

Apollo Pythios (Phoebus, Xanthus) was the god of purification rites and, as with the goddess Hekate, dogs were used in these ceremonies (Chryssostomou 1998: 104–33). At Temnos in Asia Minor, Apollo was worshipped as Kynneios (Polybius, XXXII, 37.12). Representations of dogs were discovered in the sanctuaries of Delphi, and of Apollo at Amyclaion, at Thermon, and on Delos. The shrine of Apollo Maleatas at Epidaurus contained terracotta figurines, a bronze dog, part of a mirror and a possible marble relief. The hill where he was worshipped at Epidaurus, called Kynortion, was a Mycenaean cult-place to a female god or a chthonian deity (possibly Artemis or Artemis-Hekate), located between the temples of Asklepios and Artemis, according to two inscriptions. Archaeological evidence for this cult has been found in contexts dating from the Geometric period to the 5th century BC (Bevan 1986). An amphora by the Amasis painter (Berlin 1688) depicts two archers, Apollo and Idas, who fought for Marpessa, with their dogs (Berlin 1688, Karouzou 1956: 5).

Zeus

In Thessaly Zeus was worshiped with Hekate as Zeus Thaulios, the god who punishes murder and crime, the god of the Underworld and death; or as Zeus Meilichios, the god who purified murderers from the miasma. Representations of dogs were found at the sanctuaries of Zeus at Olympia and Dodone (Beaven 1986).

Hercules

The attic painters of the 6th century presented Hercules (Herakles) capturing and taming the beast Cerberus, a monster with 50 heads, 3 of which were dogs (Sophocles *Trach.* 1097–9). This beast guarded the entrance to the underworld, preventing the living from entering and the dead from leaving. In early iconography Cerberus was often giving snaky extremities; in later representations it might have only one head (Fig. 7). A terracotta figurine from Roman Egypt represents the dog Cerberus with three heads and long hair (Louvre Muséum, E 20912 bis: Durand 1990: 293, pl. 881). The myth of the dog as guard of the gates of Hades was an ancient one (*Iliad* VIII, 368; *Odyssey* XI, 623; Hesiod, *Theogony*, 311; Pausanias, III, 25.6). The journey to Hades was the march of Hercules towards death. His taming of Cerberus represents the domination of the hero over death, and achievement of immortality.

These motifs are illustrated by a Caeretan black-figured clay vase from Cervetri, (c. 530–520 BC.), on which Herakles introduces Cerberus to Eurystheus (Paris, Louvre Museum, E 701: Elliniki Mythologia IV, 39; Boardman 1980: pl.73; Woodford 2003: 177, pl. 138). On an Athenian red-figured amphora, by the Andokides Painter (c. 520 BC.) Heracles captures Cerberus (Paris, Louvre Muséum, F 204: Elliniki Mythologia IV, pl. 65; Woodford 2003: 177, pl. 136), and similar images appear on an attic red-figured plate by Paseas (c. 520–510 BC, Museum of Fine Arts, Boston: Woodford 2003, 177, pl. 137), and on a Roman sarcophagus of AD 160–170 in the Musei Vaticani, Vatican City (Woodford 2003: 180, pl. 141). The myth of Cerberus is still remembered today in popular songs from the island of Zakynthos, west Greece.

Hercules on Olympos is the subject of a number of vases attributed to the Amasis painter (amphora Berlin 1688, Berlin 1689) where he is drawn with a dog at his feet (Karouzou 1956: 5–6). Conquering Cerberus is represented in another version in the myth of Geryones (Geryon). In this myth Hercules carries off Geryones' bovids from an island connected with the underworld, in which the dog keeper is Órthos (before the daybreak).

1

2

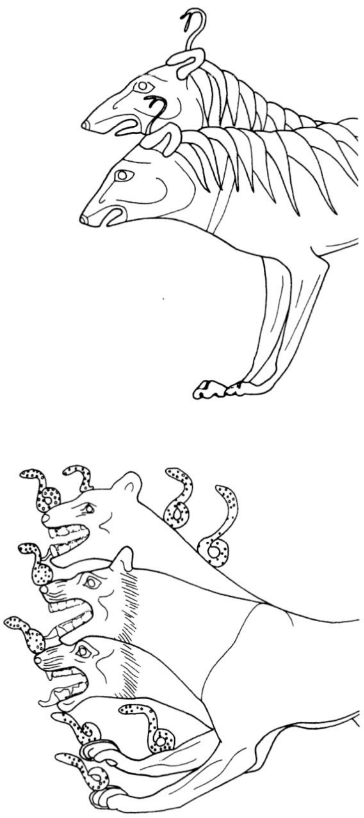

Fig. 7. Cerberus
1. The Attic painters of the end of the 6th century BC showed a vivid interest for the myth of Heracles and Cerberus Detail of a two headed Cerberus on a red-figured amphora, around 520 BC, Paris, Louvre Museum, F 204
2. The three heads and body of Cerberus on a Caeretanean hydria, 520 BC, Paris, Louvre Museum, E 701. (both sketches based on the photos after Kakridis 1986, Elliniki Mythologia, vol. IV, on Heracles, fig. 38, 39)

Figural scenes in which Hercules is killing both the giant and his dog were composed on an Attic black-figured amphora (mid 6th century BC), where the two-head Orthros (Prieur 1988: 62) is seen trying to escape Herakles (Prieur 1988: 62; Musei Vaticani, Vatican city, Woodford 2003: 179, pl. 140). On a Chalcidician amphora (c. 530 BC) Orthros lies dead as Herakles fights with Geryon (Paris, National Library 202: Elliniki Mythologia IV, pl. 32–3), and on a red-figured cylix (c. 510 BC), the dog Orthos is represented with two heads and a snake tail (Munich, Staatliche Antikensammlungen 2620: Elliniki Mythologia IV, pl. 35; Woodford 2003: 179, pl. 139). In each case, the capture of the oxen or the giant was not of supreme importance; the central point of the myth was the defeat of death.

The third infant of Typhon and Echidna, after Cerberus and Orthos, was *Hydra*, an entity also sometimes represented as a dog, as on a skyphos from Athens (Archaeological Museum 1306), a skyphos at Copenhagen, and an oenochoe at Boston painted during the first quarter of the 5th century (Euripides, Heracles, 419–20: «πολύφονον κύνα»; Tiverios 1980: 111, fig 1; pl 39). Hydra was established at Lerna where there was an entrance to the underworld. In this guise, the role of Hydra was equal to that of Cerberus, a myth also recorded by Virgilius (Aenias VI 287–8).

Skylla

Skylla was a female daemon with several animal features including a bark like a newborn puppy, the bust of a woman, two fish fins, three dog's heads and a serpent's tail (*Odyssey* XIII, 85–100). Several depictions are known. Perhaps the most famous is the work of the 4th century painter Nikomachus from Thebes (Plinius, *Nat. Hist.*, 35, 109). Others included a black-figured lekythos, an Etruscan funeral relief, and a red figure crater from Olynthus (n. 272) which could be depicting earlier motifs. Skylla is also depicted on a bronze mirror from the Euboean city Eretria (Berlin Antiquarium 8391, now in Athens), the image of Skylla and a shipwreck survivor on the altar from Pergamos, a bronze mirror found in a grave on the peninsula of Taman (Hermitage 643D), bronze coins from Acragas, a bronze sheet from Dodoni (Athens, National Archaeological Museum 82), a bronze sheet from Eretria (Athens, National Archaeological Museum 12742), a mosaic from Eretria, three bronze Etruscan patera (one at the British Museum 882), funeral bas-reliefs from Taras, a sarcophagus from North Africa, mosaics from Paphos on Cyprus and a villa near the gate of Marancio at P. San Sebastian. In addition, images of Skylla appear on a number of utensils or sculptures, like those at Sperlonga and Instanbul, inspired by the Odyssey and spanning a time period from the 6th /5th century BC to the 5th century AD (Themelis 1979: 118–53).

Brimo

The daughter of Perseus, Brimo is represented in three forms. The priestess Cassandra predicted to her mother that she would be transformed into a female dog, to become the companion of Brimo, barking at night and feared by all those mortals who disregarded the deity (Lycophron, *Alexandra,* 1174–1180, Schol. on *Alexandra* 698 and 1176 by Tzetzes, 12th century AD; Schol. 35/36a on *Pharmaceutries* by Theocritus). A correlation of this entity with Hekate and En(n)odia Pheraia is indicated by Apollonius Rhodius, (*the Argonautica*, 1211; Chryssostomou 1998, 125–7; Propertius, *Elegies,* II, 11–2; Arnobius, *Adversus Nationes,* V, 20).

Athena, Hera, Demeter, Poseidon

Representations of dogs were found at the sanctuaries of Athena on the Acropolis of Athens, Athena Alea at Tegea, Athena Chalkioikos in Sparta, and Athena Soteira at Asea; at sanctuaries of Hera (Hera Chtonia) at Hera Akraia/ Limenia at Perachora, at Samos, at the Argive

Heraion; at sanctuaries of Demeter at Souvala in Phokis and Souvala, and of Poseidon at Penteskoufia in Corinth (Bevan 1986). These deities, however are not always attributed with a chthonic significance. On a black-figured hydria (Munich Antikensammlungen 1727) the figure of Athena Promachos is shown with a dog (Shapiro 1989: 29, pl. 8d). On an amphora (Geneva MF 154) on which Athena emerges from of Zeus as a miniature Promachos, a dog is seen under the throne of Zeus (ibid. 40, pl. 14c–d).

Hermes

As a chthonic deity leading the souls of the dead, or as Hodios protecting travelers, Hermes was probably related to Enodia (Chryssostomou 1998). On a black-figured amphora (c. 550–480 BC) in the New York Metropolitan Museum of Art (06.1021.68a) Dionysus, Athena and Hermes (Fig 1.2) are seen enjoying each other's company, and in this scene Hermes is accompanied by a dog (Scheffer 2001: 129, fig. 1).

Dogs as healers of the wounded

Aesculapius

The famous doctor son of Apollo, Aesculapius (Asklepios) could heal all wounds, healing even the dead. For this reason, Zeus killed struck him dead with a thunderbolt (Elliniki Mythologia II, 213–7). One of the attributes of Aesculapius was the dog, as symbol of treatment, and an assistant in healing (Farnell 1921: 260; Bodson 1988: 86). It was thought dogs could heal the sick by sucking or licking the infected area. Dogs were also thought to cure blindness or mysterious diseases (Day 1984: 28). When Aesculapius was born, he was abandoned on mount Thittion, near Epidaurus, where two female dogs fed him (Pausanias II, 26, 5: thus the dog was also associated with childbirth (Bodson 1988: 86; Prieur 1988: 24).

At the sanctuary at Epidaurus, the sculptor Thrasymedes placed a dog next to Aesculapius (Pausanias II, 27, 2). The family of Aesculapius is escorted by dogs (Athens, National Archaeological Museum 142: LIMC sv Asclepios, 204/ 4th century BC). On the founding stele of the Asklepieion at Athens (5th century BC), a dog is seated under the chair of Hygeia, and Telemachos, the founder, is shown leading a hound. At the Asklepieion at Piraeus (district of Zea), those faithful to the Epidaurian Aesculapius, who was intimately associated to Apollo Maleatas, offered cakes (popana) to the dog guarding the sancturay (Farnell 1921: 261; IG II 2, 4962, 9–10; Guarducci, Epigrafia Creca IV, 1978).

Amphiaraus.

The hero Amphiaraus was a healer who traveled by chariot, alive, to the underworld. Upon his return he used the water of Lethaios (forgetfulness) to treat the sick. On a lost Corinthian crater decorated c. 560 BC the departure of the hero from Thebes is depicted (Berlin, Staatliche Museen F 1655: Elliniki Mythologia III, 202, pl. 134).

Dogs associated with childbirth

In the sanctuary of Artemis at Brauron (Attica) and at Lindos (Rhodes) where she was worshiped as a fertility goddess, in the sanctuary of Artemis at Brauron (Attica) and at Lindos, Rhodes, where she was adorated as a fertility goddess, marble representations of a boy and a dog were dedicated, possibly as thank-offerings a successful childbirth (Bevan 1986: 124–5). Dog representations offered at the Argive Eileithia, and those likely offered to Eileithia at Olympia, as well as to the deities at Kalydon, Ephesos, Artemis Orthia, Aricia, Argive Heraion, Perachora, Samos and Souvala, referred to as Kourotrophoi, could also be associated with childbirth. At Smyrna, the images of dogs are included in a bronze hoard. This deposit is likely connected with the eastern worship of the mother goodness, Cybele, a fertility deity (Cesme, near Smyrna, 6th century BC in Fitzwilliam Museum GR 12.1904: Vassilikou 1988: 24–5). Dogs also possessed a special place in the fertility cult of Astarte-Aphrodite in Cyprus.

Dogs as sacrificial animals

In the context of sacrifice, the dog was employed primarily for rites of purification (Parker 1983: 357). This practice was widespread in both Greece, including Boeotia and Lacedaimon, and in Rome (Plutarch, *Moralia, Aetia Romana,* 111). The primary festival in which dogs were sacrificed, was called κυνοφόντις (Athenaeus 3. 99e).

Patroclus (Patroklos)

In the funeral pyre of the hero Patroclus (*Iliad* 23, 171–77) sheep, oxes, horses, nine domesticated dogs and twelve young Trojans lay around his body (Poplin 1995: 253–265). The inclusion of dogs in funeral rites seems most common during the Bronze and Iron ages (Tables 3–5a). Yet, it continued in some areas of the Greek world into later periods (Table 5b) At Mycenaean Argos people were buried together with animal bones after some natural disaster (Cavanagh and Mee 1998: 114). The "burials" of neonatal dogs in a domestic area at Late Neolithic Dhimini hint at the close connection between dogs and people, although there may be other explanations for this deposit (Halstead 1992: 34–6). It is interesting to emphasize, however that human burials with canids have been documented at archaeological sites such as Ein Mallaha and Hayonim as early as the Natufian period (Clutton-Brock 1995: 11–2).

Hekate

Hekate (κυνοκέφαλος: Suidas, *Lexicon*) was a chthonic deity, also known as Philoskylakos (dog-lover) (*Dionysiaka,* XLIV, 195). In early periods, the goddess was worshipped in the Northern areas of Greece and

Thrace. At first she gained Thrace. Hecuba (motherhood), metamorphosed in a dog and roamed with Hekate through the Thracian forests. The statue of Hekate Lampadephorus at Byzantium was erected to commemorate the alarm given by the dogs when Philip II of Macedon attacked the city by night (Farnell 1896: 508). Through time, the sacred aspects of the dog became widespread in the religion of Boeotia and Attica.

The animal that was by priority dedicated to Hekate ('τεκμαιρομένηἐκ τῶνὠρυγμῶν τῶν κυνῶν' Schol. 35/36a *Pharmaceutries* by Theocritus; 'ἱπποκύων'; Orphica, *Αργοναυτικά*, 983, cum notis) and sacrificed to her was the dog (κυνοσφαγής: Lycophron, *Alexandra*, 77; Farnell 1896: 508; Decharme 1959: 154–5; Parker 1983). Hymns and literary sources for this witch-goddess document that in Samothrace, Athens, and Syracuse or Colophon in Asia Minor superstitious people scarificed dogs. Slaughtering dogs for this goddess related to sorcery was a rather common rite, as evidenced from the following passages; from the Late Hellenistic: 'χαίρουσα σκυλὰκων ὑλακῇ καὶ αἵματι φοινῷ' (Hippolitus, *Ελεγχος* IV, 35), in *Mimos* of Sophron (5th century BC), in the *Pharmaceutries* of Theocritus (Gow, II, *Idyll* II, 33–34), in Pausanias III, 14.9, and in Plutarch, *Moralia*, 277B, 280C (Bevan 1986: 116–7). Still, as the birth-goddess Artemis Hekate (Aeschylus, *Suppliant Women*, 674; Bevan, op. cit) the dogs sacrificed to her could also be associated with birth.

The attributes of Hekate were also close to the moon character of Artemis, who sent her brightness from very far in the dark sky. Like Artemis at Lykosoura and Eleusis (Pausanias, VIII, 37, 1–6; I, 38,6), Hekate was a protector of gates such as those at the entrance of the Acropolis of Athens (ibid. II, 30, 2). The image of the goddess running with a dog was found on a plaque in a Laconian tomb and as a terracotta at Brauron, a sanctuary associated with women who had died in childbirth. In these cases, the goddess was identified as Artemis-Hekate.

In known imagery, the goddess is seen with her dog, or a dog stands alone, as a representation of the goddess. In some cases, the representation are of a figure having the body of a woman and a dog's head ('Εκάτης ἄγαλμα: Hesychius, *Λεξικόν*: Arist. fr. inc. LXXXII; Tragicorum Graecorum Fragmenta: Euripides fr. 968; Euripides, *Hecuba*, 1265; the fragments of Attic Comedy: Aristophanes, fr. 204/ 594; Apollodorus, Epitome, V, 24; Dio Chrysostom, 35.39). Hekate is seen with a dog in votive reliefs from Attica, and in the form of Kore in a votive relief from Cyzique in Asia Minor, both dated to the 3rd century BC (Louvre MA 2849, MA 2723; Hamiaux 1992: 170, 82, pl. 189, 202). She is also seen with a torch, identified as Iphigeneia or Artemis (Bevan 1986: 124). In tripartite form, she is often represented with dogs, including in a Hellenistic figure (406) from Macedonia in the Archaeological Museum of Beroea in Macedonia (Chryssostomou 1998: 174); and two figures from Thessaloniki (Archaeological Museum of Thessaloniki, 228 (ibid. 176–7). In each of these figures, one or more of the three images has a dog at her side. In the *Alexandra*, the poet correlates Hekate Zerynthia, the goddess of the Strymon area in Macedonia, with Brimo and En(n)odia Pheraia, presumably having the same qualities and iconographic typology (Chryssostomou 1998: 125–33).

Aesculapius

Dogs were sacrificed to the Epidaurian Aesculapius, who was intimately associated with Apollo Maleatas. In these cases the victim was not eaten (Porphyrius, *De Abstinentia*, I, 14), as also attested by an inscription of the 4th century BC (S.I.G.[3], 1040, 9–100; Farnell 1921: 261; Bodson 1988: 121; Parker 1983: 358), and narrated by Plutarchus as a rite in Lacedaimon area (*Moralia, Aetia Romana*, 111). Hygieia (Health), one of Aesculapius' daughters, was also related to dogs.

Ares (Enyalius)

The dog, considered as the most vigorous of domestic animals 'το ἀλκιμώτατον ζῷον', was sacrificed to Ares, the sturdiest god 'ϑεῶν τῷ ἀλκιμωτάτῳ' (Pausanias III,14,9; 'σκύλακας ἐντέμνουσι' (Plutarchus, *Aetia Romana*, 111; Graf 1985: 422; Bodson 1988: 126; Parker 1983: 358). At Sparta the dog sacrifices seem to have had a pacificing significance (Day 1984: 27). On an amphoriskos in the Louvre Ares is represented as a hunter (Fig. 25 from Vulci; Karouzou 1956: 12). He holds a splendid dog on a leash.

Linos

The heroic persona of Linos, son of Apollo and Psamathe, was deeply rooted in the native legends and public ritual of the Argive region. His mother, fearing the anger of her own father, exposed the him as an infant. The infant Linos was then found by a shepherd and was protected until one day by accident dogs attacked him and he was torn to pieces. The sacred infant torn to pieces recalls the Dionysian infant dismembered by his worshippers. There could also be affinities between Linos and Adonis since both of them belonged to the category of vegetation-deities (Farnell 1921: 26–28). According to literary sources, once a year the the Argives collected all the dogs they met and massacred them. This may have been undertaken during the month in which the festival of Linos was observed, since, in Argos, these rites included the sacrifice of dogs (κυνοφόντις). Another possible explanation for the timing of this event might be that the animals were killed at the time of the dog-stars greatest heat, to minimize its effects (ibidem).

Other entities

Other entities associated with dog sacrifice include Eiletheia or Eilonia, (Parker 1983: 358). At Argos dogs and cocks were sacrificed to ease a woman in childbirth (Plutarch, *Moralia*, 277B; Athenaeus, 99 E; Day 1994: 28, citing Scholz; Bevan 1986: 117) Selene, Genetyllida,

Aphrodite Erykine, Hephaistos and Adranos were also associated with dogs, probably in the form of sacrifices (Chryssostomou 1988: 179). A possible ritual deposit indicated by the skeleton of a dog was identified in a bothros at the Hera Argiva in Selenunta, Sicily. At Sardis (Lydia, Asia Minor) puppies were killed and dismembered but not eaten. In this instance, at least 26 puppies under 3 months in age were buried in cooking pots, and may have been offered to Hermes Kandaulas (Day 1984: 28; Harvey 1995: 282–5). There is also evidence of keeping and sacrificing temple hounds at the sanctuary of Astarte-Aphrodite in Cyprus (Bernhard *et al.* 1999: 203).

Conclusions

The performance of work by dogs when human subsistence still depended on hunting and gathering, including such tasks as guarding and herding livestock as well as providing us company; the effects of owner personality and attitudes on dog behaviour; the loyalty and devotion of dogs in human – dog interactions; the value placed on dogs by peoples worldwide; the positive socialization effects of dogs for people; the physical and psychological benefits of canine companionship; and the welfare of dogs in human care have been investigated and discussed at length (e.g. Bodson 1980: 13–21; Mainoldi 1984; Hart 1995: 162–78; Hubrecht 1995: 180–98; Linseele 2004). In addition, while recognizing all these complex interactions between dogs and people, a nearly universal ambivalence towards the domestic dog has also been noted, as evidenced by the prevalence through time and in many parts of the world of the use of dogs for sacrifice and as food.

Cynophagy was common during the whole of prehistory, but zooarchaeological analyses of the age distribution of the animals eaten indicates their secondary role as meat animals, since very few bones come from immature (juvenile and sub adult) specimens. Primarily, they seem to have been used in hunting, or were left to lie around the villages where they might be useful as watchdogs, warning villagers when strangers approached. The shepherds' dogs, if we can distinguish such a breed, must have had value in watching and guarding the flocks as well as in herding and control of caprovine populations (Gejvall 1969: 14–8; Coy 1973; Bökönyi 1976: 332–3; Becker 1986: 88–97; Nordquist 1987: 36; Larje 1987, 95; Yannouli 1994: 208; Ib. 2002, 691).

Later in time, dogs became a status animal. The evidence of the funeral data (Tables 3–5b) reconstructs the social and political organization of the Aegean. The warrior graves display symbols of power and wealth. Despite the apparent contradiction in the symbolic role of the dog as a human ally, which was lost when the dog was regarded as a true animal, Greek mythology and historical events known through iconography, archival sources and archaeological evidence point to an important evolution in the role of dogs in Greek thought.

Acknowledgments

L. Boloti has given expression to my ideas in her drawings of animal figures. E. Belegrinou typed some of the tables and L. Snyder had the courage to invite me to participate in the ICAZ session on Dogs and People and the resulting publication, and to face my text. Many thanks to them all.

References

Amberger, K. P. 1979. Neue Tierknochenfunde aus der Magula Pevkakia in Thessalien. II. Die Wiederkäuer. PhD thesis, Munich: University of Munich.

Amyx, D. A. 1988. *Corinthian Vase-Painting of the Archaic Period.* III vol. Berkeley: University of California Press.

Andronikos, M. 1968. *Totenkult. Archaeologia Homerica.* Göttingen: Vandenhoeck & Ruprecht.

Becker, C. 1986. *Kastanas. Die Tierknochenfunde.* Berlin: Wissenschaftsverlag Volker Spiess.

Becker, C. 1991. Die Tierknochenfunde von der Platia Magoula Zarkou, neue Untersuchungen zu Haustierhaftung, Jagd und Rohstoffverwendung im neolithisch- bronzezeitlichen Thessalien, *Praehistorische Zeitschrift* **66**, 14–66.

Besques, S. 1986. *Catalogue raisonné des figurines et reliefs en terre cuite grecs étrusques et romains.* Paris: Réunion des Musées Nationaux, IV–I, II.

Bevan, E. 1986. *Representations of Animals in Sanctuaries of Artemis and other Olympian Deities.* Oxford: BAR International Series 315.

Bingham Hull, D. 1964. *Hounds and Hunting in ancient Greece.* Chicago: The University of Chicago Press.

Boardman, J. 1975. *Αθηναϊκά Ερυθρόμορφα αγγεία. Αρχαϊκή περίοδος.* Athens: Kardamitsas.

Boardman, J. 1980. *Αρχαία Ελληνική Τέχνη.* Athens: Ypodomi.

Boardman, J. 1999. *Ελληνική Πλαστική. 'Υστερη Κλασική Περίοδος.* Athens: Kardamitsas.

Bodson, L. 1980. Place et fonction du chien dans le monde antique. *Le chien, évolution des races, de l'élevage et d'utilisation du chien. Ethnozootechnie* **25**, 13–21.

Bodson, L. 1978. *'Ιερὰ Ζῴια. Contribution à l'étude de la place de l'animal dans la religion grecque ancienne.* Mémoires de la Classe des Lettres. Bruxelles: Palais des Académies.

Boessneck, J. 1962. Die Tierreste aus der Argissa-Magula vom Präkeramischen Neolithicum bis zur Mittleren Bronzezeit, pp. 27–99, in Vl. Milojčić, J. Boessneck und M. Hopf, *Die Deutschen Ausgrabungen auf der Argissa-Magula in Thessalien.* Bonn: Rudolf Habelt Verlag.

Boessneck, J. 1986. Zooarchäologische Ergebnisse an den Tierknochen – und Molluskenfunden, pp. 136–40, in W. Hoepfner und E. L. Schwander (ed.), *Haus und Stadt im Klassischen Grechenland.* Munich: Deutscher Kunstverlag.

Boessneck, J. and von den Driesch, A. 1984. Die zoologische Dokumentation der Reste von vier Pferden und einem Hund aus einem mykenischen Schachtgrab in Kokla bei Argos (Peloponnes), *Spixiana* **7(3)**, 327–33.

Bökönyi, S. 1976. The Vertebrate Fauna from Anza, pp. 313–63, in M. Gimbutas (ed.), *Neolithic Macedonia as reflected by Excavations at Anza, Southern Yugoslavia.* Los Angeles: Monumenta Archaeologica.

Bökönyi, S. 1986. Faunal Remains, pp. 63–132, in C. Renfrew, M. Gimbutas and E. S. Elster (eds), *Excavations at Sitagroi. A prehistoric Village in Northeast Greece*, 1.

Bökönyi, S. 1989. Fauna, pp. 315–39, in M. Gimbutas, Sh. Winn, D. Shimabuku (eds), *Achilleion. A Neolithic Settlement in Thessaly, Greece, 6400–5600 BC.* Los Angeles: Monumenta Archaeologica.

Boulotis, C. 1988. Mycenaean wall painting, in K. Demakopoulou (ed.). *The Mycenaean World. Five Centuries of Early Greek Culture 1600–1100 BC.* Athens: Ministry of Culture-I.C.O.M.: 35–7.

Brann, E. T. H. 1962. *The Athenian Agora. Late Geometric and Protoattic Pottery. Mid 8th to late 7th c. BC.* Princeton, The American School of Classical Studies at Athens. Vol. VIII.

Budle, L. and Nicholis, R. 1967. *A catalogue of the Greek and Roman Sculpture in the* Fitzwilliam *museum.* Cambridge: University Press.

Cavanagh, W. G. 1996. The burial customs, pp. 651–75, in J. N. Coldstream and H.W. Catling (eds), *Knossos North Cemetery. Early Greek Tombs. BSA,* Suppl. Vol. **28** (II).

Cavanagh, W. G. and Chr. Mee 1998. *A private place: Death in Prehistoric Greece.* Studies in Mediterranean Archaeology. Jonsered: P. Åströms Förlag.

Chaix, L. 1980. La faune du vicus gallo-romain de Lousonna-Vidy (Vaud, Suisse, fin du 1er s. av. J.-C.- milieu du IIe s. ap. J.C.), in G. Kaenel, M. Klausener and S. Fehlmann, *Nouvelles Recherches sur le vicus gallo-romaine Lousonna.* Lausanne: Cahiers d'Archéologie Romande **18**, **2**, 168–75.

Chenal-Velarde, I. 2001. Etude archéozoologique, pp. 121–6, in Reber, K., Chenal-Velarde, I, Metzer, I. R. E., Ein hellenistischer Brunnen im Bezirk B von Haus IV in Eretria, in R. Frei-Stolba and K. Gex, *Recherches recentes sur le monde hellenistique.* Actes du colloque international organise à l'occasion du 60e anniversaire de P. Ducrey (Lausanne, 20–21 novembre 1998). Bern: P. Lang.

Chenal-Velarde, I. 2001b. Des festins à l'entrée du temple ? Sacrifices et consommation des animaux à l'époque géometrique dans le sanctuaire d'Apollon à Erétrie, Grèce. *Archaeofauna* **10**, 25–35.

Coldstream, J. N. and Catling, H. W. 1996. *Knossos North Cemetery. Early Greek Tombs. ABSA,* suppl. vol. **28** (I, II).

Catling, H. W. 1978. Knossos, 1978, *AR* 1978–1979, 43–58.

Clutton-Brock, J. 1982. The Animal Bones, in S. Hood (ed.), *Excavations in Chios 1938–1955. Prehistoric Emporio and Ayio Gala. ABSA,* suppl. Vol. **16**, 678–97.

Clutton-Brock, J. 1995. Origins of the dog: Domestication and early history, pp. 8–20, in Serpell, J. (ed.) *The domestic dog, its evolution, behaviour and interactions with people.* Cambridge: Cambridge University Press.

Chryssostomou, P. 1998. *Η Θεσσαλική θεά Εν(ν)οδία ή Φεραία θεά.* ADeltion 64. Athens: Ministry of Culture.

Coy, J. P. 1973. Bronze Age Domestic animals from Keos, Greece, pp.239–43, in Matolsci, J. (ed.), *Domestikationsforschung und Geschichte der Haustiere.* Budapest: Akadémiai Kiadó.

Curci, A. and Tagliacozzo, A. 1997. Preliminary Analysis of the Fauna of Makri, pp. 11–62, in Efstratiou, N. *et al.*, Excavations at the Neolithic settlement of Makri, Thrace, Greece (1988–1996) A preliminary report. *SAGVNTVM (PLAV),* **31**.

Day, P. L. 1984. Dog Burials in the Greek World. *AJA* **88**, 21–32.

Decharme, P. 1959. *Ελληνική Μυθολογία.* (Translated by I. Oikonomidis). Athens: Χρήσιμα Βιβλία.

Demakopoulou, K. and Konsola, D. 1981. *Musée Archéologique de Thèbes. Guide.* Athènes, Direction Générale des Antiquités et de la Restauration.

Demakopoulou, K. 1989. Κόκλα, μυκηναική νεκρόπολη. *ArchDeltion* **37** (1982, chron.) 83–5.

Driesch (von den), A., and Enderle, K. 1966. Die Tierreste aus der Agia Sofia Magula in hessalien, pp. 15–54, in Milojçiç, V. L., von den Driesch, A., Enderle, K. Milojčić-v. V., Zumbusch and Kilian, K. (eds) *Magulen um Larisa in Thessalien 1966.* Bonn: Rudolf Habelt Verlag.

Driesch (von den), A. 1987. Haus-und Jagdtiere im vorgeschichtlichen Thessalien. *Praehistorische Zeitschrift* **62**, 1–21.

Driesch (von den), A. and Boessneck, J. 1990. Die Tierreste von der Mykenischen Burg Tiryns bei Nauplion/ Peloponnes, in Weishaar H.-J., I.W. Hiden, A. von den Driesch, J. Boessneck, A. Rieger and W. Böser (eds), *Tiryns* Band XI: 87–129. Deutsches Archealogisches Institut Athen.

Dunand, F. 1990. *Catalogue des terres cuites gréco-romaines d'Egypte.* Musée du Louvre, département des antiquités égyptiennes. Paris: Réunion des musées nationaux.

Farnell, L. R. 1896. *The cults of the Greek states.* Vol II. Oxford: Clarendon Press.

Farnell, L. R. 1921. *Greek hero cults and ideas of immortality.* Oxford: Clarendon Press.

Fischer, J. 1994. *Griechisch-Römische Terrakotten aus Ägypten.* Berlin: Ernst Wasmuth Verlag Tübingen.

Frödin, O. and Persson, A. 1938. *Asine: Results of the Swedish Excavations, 1922–1930.* Stockholm: A. Westholm.

Furumark, A. 1972 (1941). *The Mycenaean Pottery: Analysis and Classification.* Stockholm: Svenska Institutet i Athen.

Gejvall, N-G. 1969. *Lerna. A preclassical site in the Argolid. The fauna.* Princeton: American School of Classical Studies at Athens.

Gonzenbach, V. (von), 1995. *Die Römischen Terrakotten in der Schweiz.* Tübingen: Francke Verlag Tübingen und Basel.

Graf, F. 1985. Nordionische Kulte. Religionsgeschichtchen und Epigraphische Untersuchungen zu den Kulten von Chios, Erythrai, Klazomenai und Phokaia. *Schweizerisches Institut in Rom,* 1–490.

Guarducci, M. 1978. *Epigraphia Greca. Epigrafi Sacre Pagane e Christiane.* Istituto Poligrafico dello Stato. Roma: Libreria dello stato.

Hamiaux, M. 1992 *Les sculptures grecques. La période hellénistique (IIIer-Ier siècles av. J.-C.).* Paris: Reunion des Musées nationaux.

Halstead, P. and Jones, G. 1987. Bioarchaeological Remains from Kalythies Cave, Rhodes, pp 135–52, in Αδ. Σάμψων (ed.), *Η Νεολιθική περίδος στα Δωδεκάνησα.* Athens: Arch. Deltion **35**.

Halstead, P. 1992. Dimini and the "DMP": Faunal Remains and Animal Exploitation in Late Neolithic Thessaly. *ABSA*, 29–59.

Hamilakis, Y. 1996. A Footnote on the Archaeology of Power: Animal Bones from a Mycenaean Chamber Tomb at Galatas, NE Peloponnese. *ABSA* **91**, 153–66.

Harcourt, R. A. 1974. The dog in prehistoric and Early Historic Britain, *JAS* **1**, 151–75.

Hart, L. A. 1995. Dogs as human companions: a review of the relationship, pp. 161–78, in Serpell, J. (ed.) *The domestic dog, its evolution, behavour and interactions with people.* Cambridge: University Press.

Harvey, D. 1995. Lydian Specialities, Croesu's golden Baking-Woman, and dog's dinners, pp. 273–85, in Wilkins, J., Harvey, D. and Dobson, M. (eds) *Food in Antiquity.* Exeter: University of Exeter Press.

Hatzidakis, J. 1912. *Τύλισος Μινωική.* Archaiologiki Ephemeris, 231.

Higgs, L. S., Clegg, I. M. and Kinnes, I. A. 1968. Saliagos Animal Bones in Evans, J. D. and Renfrew, C. (eds), *Excavations at Saliagos near Antiparos. ABSA,* suppl. vol. **5**, 114–7.

Hinz, G. 1979. *Neue Tierknochenfunde aus der Magula Pevkakia in Thessalien.* I. *Die Nichtwiederkäuer.* PhD thesis, Munich.

Hubrecht, R. 1995. The welfare of dogs in human care, pp. 179–98, in Serpell, J. (ed.) *The domestic dog, its evolution, behaviour and interactions with people.*

Jarman, M. R., and Jarman, H. N., 1968. The fauna and the economy of Early Neolithic Knossos, in J. D. Evans. Knossos Neolithic. Part II. *ABSA*, **63**, 241–64.

Jones, G. 1978. Appendix: bone report, in Callaghan P. J. (ed.) Excavations at a Shrine of Glaukos, Knossos, *ABSA* **73**, 29–30.

Jordan, B. 1975. *Tierknochenfunde aus der Magula Pevkakia in Thessalien.* PhD thesis, Munich.

Julien, R. 1992. Les faunes domestique et sauvage, pp. 147–53, in R. Treuil (ed), *Dikili Tash, Village Préhistorique de Macédoine Orientale*. Paris: CNRS – Université de Paris I.

Iakovides, S. 1969. *Περατή. Το νεκροταφειον*. Athens: Archaiologiki Etaireia **67**, 3 vols.

Kakridis, I. T. 1986. *Elliniki Mythologia*. Athens. Ekdotiki Athinon, vol. III–V.

Karageorghis, V., Mertens, J. R. and Rose, M. E. 2000. *Ancient Art from Cyprus. The Cesnola Collection in the Metropolitan Museum of Art*. New York: Metropolitan Museum of Art.

Karageorghis, V. 2003. *'Αρχαία Κυπριακή Τέχνη στο 'Εθνικό 'Αρχαιολογικό Μουσεῖο Αθηνών*. Athens: Idryma Leventi, National Archaeological Museum.

Karouzou, S. 1956. *The Amasis Painter*. Oxford: Clarendon Press.

Karouzou, S. 1967. *'Εθνικόν 'Αρχαιολογικόν Μουσειον. Συλλογή Γλυπτῶν*. Athens: Geniki Dieythynsis Archaiotiton kai Anastiloseos.

Keramopoulos, A. 1917. *Θηβαϊκά*. Athens: Arch. Deltion.

Kilian-Dirlmeier, I. 1987. Das Kuppelgrab von Vapheio: Die Beigabenausstattung in der Steinkiste. Untersuchungen zur Sozialstruktur in Spathelladisher Zeit, *RGZM* **34**: 197–212.

Kilinski, K. 1990. *Boeotian Black figure Vase Painting of the Archaic Period*. Mainz am Rhein: Verlag PH. von Zabern.

Klippel, W. E. and Snyder, L. M. 1991. Dark-Age Fauna from Kavousi, Crete. The Vertebrates from the 1987 and 1988 excavations. *Hesperia* **60**, 179 –86.

Konstantinopoulos, G. 1996. *Το Αρχαιολογικό Μουσείο της Ρόδου*. Athens: Adam.

Kotjabopoulou, E.A. 1992. The Faunal Remains from Dendra. A Preliminary Analysis, pp. 113–7, in E. Δεϊλάκη, Παρατηρήσεις στην Προκεραμεική. *Διεθνές Συνέδριο για την Αρχαία Θεσσαλία*. Athens: Arch. Deltion **48**.

Kotjabopoulou, E. and Trantalidou, K. 1993. Faunal analysis at the Skoteini cave, pp. 392–434, in Ad. Sampson, *Skoteini at Tharrounia. The Cave, the settlement and the cemetery*. Athens.

Koudelka, F. 1885. Das Verhältnis der Ossa longa zur Skeletthöhe bei den Säugetieren. *Verhandl. Naturf. Ver Brünn*, **24**, 127–53.

Koufos, G. 1997. Το παλαιοςωολογικό υλικό της Δήμητρας (ανασκαφικές περίοδοι 1979, 1980), pp. 97–100, in Δ. Γραμμένος, *Νεολιθική Μακεδονία*. Athens, Arch. Deltion **56**.

Kourou, N. 2002. *Corpus Vasorum Antiquorum. Greece. Athens, National Museum. Attic and Atticizing Amphorae of the Protogeometric and Geometric Periods*. Athens: Academy of Athens. Fasc. 8.

Larje, R. 1987. Animal Bones, pp. 89–118, in Hellstöm, P. (ed.), *Paradeisos, A Late Neolithic Settlement in Aegean Thrace*, Stockholm: Medelhavsmuseet **7**.

Lilja, S. 1976. *Dogs in Ancient Greek Poetry*. Helsinki Societas Scientiarum Fennica **56**.

Linseele, V. 2004. Cultural identity and the consumption of dogs in western Africa, pp. 318–26, in O'Day, S. J., van Neer, W. and Ervynck, A. *Behaviour Behind Bones*, 9th ICAZ Conference, Durham 2002. Oxford: Oxbow Books.

Lemos, A. 1991. *Archaic Pottery of Chios. The Decorated Styles*. Oxford University Committee for Archaeology. Monograph No. 30.

Lemos, I. S. 2002. *The Protogeometric Aegean. The Archaeology of the Late Eleventh and Tenth Centuries BC*. Oxford: Oxford University Press.

Loberdou- Tsigarida, A. 2000. *Οστέινα Πλακίδια. Διακόσμηση ξύλινων κιβωτιδίων από τη Χριστιανική Αίγυπτο*. Athens. Arch. Deltion **73**.

Lund, J. and Bundgaard Rasmussen, B. 1995. *Guides to the National Museum. Near Eastern and Classical Antiquities Greeks, Etruscans, Romans*. Copenhagen: The National Museum.

Mainoldi, C. 1984. *L'image du loup et du chien dans la Grèce ancienne (d'Homère à Platon)*. Paris: Ophrys.

Masson, O. 1950. A propos d'un rituel hittite pour la lustration d'une armée: purification par le passage entre deux parties d'une victime. *Revue de l'histoire des religions* **137**, 5–25.

Mazarakis-Ainian, A. 2000. *'Ομηρος και αρχαιολογία*. Athens: Institouto tou bibliou.

Mazzorin, J. de Grossi and Tagliacozzo, A. 2000. Morphological and Osteological Changes in the dog from the Neolithic to the Roman Period in Italy, pp. 141–61, in Crockford, S. J. *Dogs Through Time: An Archaeological Perspective*. Proceedings of the 1st ICAZ Symposium on the History of the Domestic Dog. Oxford: BAR International Series 889.

Moore, M. B. and Pease Philippides, M. Z. 1986. *The Athenian Agora. Attic Black-figured pottery*. Princeton: The American School of Classical Studies at Athens. Vol. XXIII.

Moore, M. B. 1997. *The Athenian Agora. Attic Red-figured pottery*. Princeton: The American School of Classical Studies at Athens. Vol. XXX.

Morin, J. 1991. *Le dessin des animaux en Grèce d'après les vases peints*. Paris: Librairie Renouard.

Muenzer, P. J. 2000. What the Throne-and-Sceptre Sign of Linear B really means. *AAA* 1996–1998, 125–6.

Mylona, D. 1999. Οστά δώων από τα ΥΝ στρώματα του Κρυονερίου Σερρών. Προκαταρκτική παρουσίαση, pp. 523–38, in Δ. Μαλαμίδου, Ανασκαφή στον προϊστορικό οικισμό του Κρυονεριου, Νέα Κερδύλια. *Archaiologiko ergo sti Makedonia ke Thraki (AEMTHR)* **11** (1997).

Mylonas, G. 1966. *Mycenae and the Mycenaean Age*. Princeton: University Press.

Nordquist, G. C. 1987. *A Middle Helladic Village. Asine in the Argolid*. Upsala: Acta Universitatis Upsaliensis Boreas.

Ohly, D. 1986. *Guide to the Munich Antikensammlungen*. Bayern: Stiftland-Verlang Waldsassen.

Papadopoulos, T. 1987. Ανασκαφή Καλλιθέας Πατρών. PAE, 69–72.

Papadopoulos, T. and Kontorli-Papadopoulou, L. 2001. Death, Power and Troubles in Late Mycenaean Peloponnese. The Evidence of Warrior-graves, in P. M. Fischer (ed.) *Contributions to the Archaeology and History of the Bronze and Iron Ages in the Eastern Mediterranean*. Studies in Honour of P. Åström. Österreichisches Archäologisches Institut, Sonderschriften Band **39**.

Papavasileiou, G. A. 1910. *Περὶ τῶν ἐν Εὐβοίᾳ 'Αρχαίων Τάφων*. Athens: Archaiologiki Etaireia, 1–107.

Parlama, L. and Stambolidis N. 2000. *Η πόλη κάτω την πόλη. Ευρήματα από τις ανασκαφές του Μητροπολιτικού Σιδηροδρόμου των Αθηνών*. Athens, Goulandris foundation: Museum of Cycladic Art.

Parker, R. 1983. *Miasma. Pollution and Purification in Early Greek Religion*. Oxford: Clarendon Press.

Persson, A. W. 1931. *The Royal Tombs at Dendra near Midea*. Lund: Gleerup.

Pini, I. 1968. *Beiträge zur minoischen Gräberkunde*. Wiesbaden: Fr. Steiner.

Popham, M. R. and Lemos, I. S. 1996. *Lefkandi III. The Toumba Cemetery. The Excavations of 1981, 1984, 1986 and 1992–4. ABSA* Suppl. vol 25.

Poplin, F. 1995. L'homme et l'animal dans le Bûcher de Patrocle (Iliade, XXIII). *Anthropozoologica* **21**, 253–65.

Prieur, J. 1988. *Les animaux sacrés dans l'antiquité. Art et religion du monde méditerranéen*. Rennes, Ouest France.

Reese, D. S. 1987. A Bone Assemblage at Corinth of the Second Corinth of the Second Century after Christ. *Hesperia* **56**, 255–74.

Reese, D. S. 1995. Equid Sacrifices/ Burials in Greece and Cyprus: An Addendum. *JPR* **9**, 35–42.

Richter, G. M. A. 1961. *The archaic Gravestones of Attica*. London: The Phaidon Press.

Rizza, G. 1973. Tombes de chevaux, communication, in Karageorghis, V. (ed.), Acts of the International Archaeological Symposium *The Relations Between Cyprus and Crete, ca 2000–500 BC*, 294–7. Nicosia.

Rizza, G. 1985. Prinias – The horse burials, *Ancient Crete. A hundred Years of Italian Archaeology (1884–1984)*. Rome: Italian Archaeological School of Athens, Ministry of Cultural and Environmental Heritage, De Luca ed.

Rushe, C. and Halstead, P. 1987. The animal Bones from Ayios Dimitrios, in C.L. Zachos, *Ayios Dimitrios, a prehistoric Settlement in the Southwestern Peloponnesos: the Neolithic and Early Helladic Period.* PhD thesis, Boston University.

Sabetai, V. 2001. *Corpus Vasorum Antiquorum. Greece, Thebes, Archaeological Museum.* Athens: Union Academique Internationale.

Sakellarakis, J. and Sakellaraki, E. 1991. *Crete. Archanes.* Athens: Ekdotiki Athinon.

Scheffer, C. 2001. Gods on Athenian vases: their function in the Archaic and Classical periods, communication in Scheffer, C. (ed.) *Ceramics in context.* Proceedings of the Internordic Colloquium on Ancient Pottery held at Stockholm, 13–15/06/97, 128–38. Stockholm: Acta Universitatis Stocholmiensis, Almqvist & Wiksell International.

Scheibler, I. 1992. *Ελληνική κεραμική, Παραγωγή, εμπόριο και χρήσμ των αρχαίων ελληνικών αγγείων.* Athens: Kardamitsas.

Serpell, J. 1995. From paragon to pariah: some reflections on human attitudes to dogs, communication in J. Serpell (ed.) *The domestic dog, its evolution, behaviour and interactions with people, 245–56.* Cambridge: Cambridge University Press.

Shapiro, H. A. 1989. *Art and Cult under the Tyrants in Athens.* Mainz am Rhein: Verlag Ph. von Zabern.

Shapiro, H. A., Picon, C. A. and Scott, C. D. 1995. *Greek vases in the San Antonio Museum of Art.* San Antonio, Texas: San Antonio Museum of Art.

Simpson, R. H. 1981. *Mycenaean Greece.* New Jersey: Noyes Press.

Smithson-Lord, E. 1974. A Geometric Cemetery on the Aeropagus: 1897, 1932, 1947. *Hesperia XLIII* **3**, 325–90.

Sloan, R. E. and Duncan, M. A. 1978. Zooarchaeology of Nichoria, pp. 60–77, in Rapp, G. and Aschenbrenner, S. E. *Excavations at Nichoria in Southwest Greece.* I, Minneapolis: Minnesota University Press.

Snyder, L. M. 1991. Barking Mutton. Ethnohistoric, ethnographic, archaeological and nutritional evidence pertaining to the dog as a Native American food resource on the plains. *Illinois State Museum Scientific Papers* **23**, 359–78.

Snyder, L. M. and Klippel, W. E. 1999. Dark Age Subsistence at the Kastro site, East Crete. Exploring Subsistence Change and Continuity During the Late Bronze Age – Early Iron Age Transition, pp. 65–83, in S. J. Vaughn and W. D. E. Coulson (eds), *Palaeodiet in the Aegean.* Oxford: Oxbow Books.

Snyder, L. M. and Klippel, W. E. 2003. From Lerna to Kastro: Further thoughts on dogs as food in Ancient Greece; Perceptions, prejudices and reinvestigations, pp. 221–232, in Kotjabopoulou, E., Hamilakis, Y., Halstead, P., and Gamble, C. (eds), *Zooarchaeologyin Greece: Recent Advances.* Oxford: David Brown Book Company (British School at Athens).

Sorrentino, C. 1997. Poliochni: Il materiale faunistico, pp. 157–67.,in Doumas, C. R. and La Rosa, V. (eds), *Poliocnhi e l'Antica età del Bronzo nell'Egeo Settentrionale.* Athens, Scuola Archeologia Italiana di Atene: University of Athens.

Stainhauer, G. 2001. *Το αρχαιολογικό Μουσείο Πειραιώς.* Athens: Eurobank.

Schwartz, C. A. 1982. The fauna from Early Neolithic Sesklo, in W. H. J. M. N. Wijnen, *The Early Neolithic I settlement at Sesklo: An early Farming Community In Thessaly, Greece. Analecta Praehistorica Leidensia* XIV, 135.

Tiverios, M. 1976. *Ο Λυδός και το έργο του. Συμβολή στην έρευνα της Αττικής Μελανόμορφης αγγειογραφίας.* Athens: Arch. Deltion **23**.

Tiverios, M. 1980. Μια νέα παράσταση του άθλου του Ηρακλή με Λερναία 'Υδρα (;) *Archaiologiki Ephimeris 1978.*

Themelis, P. G. 1979. Σκύλλα Ερετρική. *Archaiologiki Ephimeris.*

Themelis, P. G. 2000. *'Ηρωες και Ηρώα στη Μεσσήνη.* Athens: Archaiologiki Etaireia, 210.

Trakasopoulou-Salakidou, E. 1987. Αρχαία 'Ακανθος. Πόλη και νεκροταφείο. To *Archaiologiko Ergo sti Makedonia ke Thraki (AEMTHR)* **1**, 295–9.

Trakasopoulou-Salakidou, E. 1996. Αρχαία 'Ακανθος 1986–1996. To *Archaiologiko Ergo sti Makedonia ke Thraki (AEMTHR)* **10**, 297–307.

Tzachou-Alexandri, O. 1989. *Το πνεύμα και το σώμα. Οι αθλητικοί αγώνες στην Αρχαία Ελλάδα.* Athens: Ministry of Culture-I.C.O.M.

Trantalidou, K. 1996. Agriculture, Animal Husbandry, Hunting, Fishing, pp. 95–101, in Papathanassopoulos, G. A. *Neolithic Culture in Greece.* Athens: Museum of Cycladic Art.

Trantalidou, K. 1997. Θηράματα και οικόσιτα ζώα από το σπήλαιο των Λιμνών, pp. 415–55, in Sampson, A. *The Cave of Lakes at Kastria of Kalavryta.* Athens: Etaireia Peloponnisiakon Spoudon **7**.

Trantalidou, K. 2001. Producing and Recording leather and other animal products, in pp. 267–317, Michailidou, A. (ed.), *Manufacture and Measurement.* Athens: Research Centre for Greek and Roman Antiquity.

Triantafyllos, D. and Terzopoulou, D. 1995. Ανασκαφή ταφικών τύμβων στο Ρήγιο Διδυμοτείχου. To *Archaiologiko Ergo sti Makedonia ke Thraki* **9**, 473–85.

Triantafyllos, D. and Terzopoulou, D. 2005. 'Αμαξες και καύσεις νεκρών οτον Τύμβο της Μικρής Δοςιηὰρας – Ζώνης του Δήμου Κυηρινου, in *Archaiologiko Ergo sti Makedonia ke Thraki 17, 2003*, 1–12.

Tsountas, C. and Manatt, J. I. 1897. *The Mycenaean Age. A study of the Monuments and Culture of Pre-Homeric Greece.* Chicago, Argonaut Publishers. Reprinted 1969.

Vassilikou, E. 1998. *Greek and Roman Art.* Fitzwilliam Museum. Cambridge: Cambridge University Press.

Waern-Sperner, A. 2001. Ancient Perception of Time in Metamorphosis scenes on Greek Vases, pp. 156–51, in Scheffer, C. (ed.) *Ceramics in context.* Proceedings of the Internordic Colloquium on Ancient Pottery held at Stockholm, 13–15/06/97. Stockholm: Acta Universitatis Stocholmiensis, Almqvist & Wiksell International.

Walcher, B., Dembski, A., Gschwantler, K., and Karageorghis, V. 1999. The Collection of Cypriote Antiquities in the Kunsthistorisches Museum. Wien; Foundation A.G. Leventis.

Wall, S. 1994. The Animal Bones, in J. Carrington Smith, A Late Hellenistic Wine Press at Knossos. *ABSA* **89**, 375–6.

Wall-Crowther, S. 1996. The animal bones, pp. 703–10, in J. N. Coldstream and H.W. Catling (eds), Knossos *North Cemetery. Early Greek Tombs. ABSA,* Suppl. Vol. **28**(II).

Woodford, S. 2003. *Images of myths in Classical Antiquity.* Cambridge: University Press.

Yannouli, E. 1990. Η προϊστορική πανίδα της Θέρμης Β, pp. 262–78, in Δ. Β. Γραμμένος, Ανασκαφή Νελοιθικού οικισμού Θέρμης Ανασκαφική περίδος 1987. *Makedonika* **27**.

Yannouli, E. 1994. *Aspects of Animal Use in Prehistoric Macedonia, Northern Greece. Examples from the Neolithic and Early Bronze Age.* PhD thesis, Cambridge.

Yannouli, E. 1997. Dhimitra, a Neolithic and Late Bronze Age Village in Northern Greece: the faunal remains, pp. 101–27, in Δ. Γραμμένος, *Νεολιθικο Μακεδονία.* Athens: Arch. Deltion **56**.

Yannouli, E. 2002. 'Ημερη και άγρια πανίδα από το Νεολιθικό οικισμό στη Σταυρούπολη Θεσσαλονίκης, pp. 683–742, in Δ.

Γραμμένος and Σ. Κώτσος (eds), *Σωστικές Ανασκαφές στο Νεολιθικό οικισμό Σταυρούπολης Θεσσαλονίκης*: 683–742. Thessaloniki: Archaiologikon Institouto Boreiou Elladas 2.

Yannouli, E. 2002b. Μεσημεριανή Τούμπα. Τα ζωικά κατάλοιπα, pp. 321–58, in Δ. Β. Γραμμένος and Σ. Κώτσος, *Ανασκαφή στον προϊστορικό οικισμό «Μεσημεριανή Τούμπα» Τριλόφου, Ν. Θεσσαλονίκης*. Thessaloniki: Archaiologiko Institouto Thessalonikis.

Zachariadou, O. 2000. Σταθμός Σύνταγμα, in Λ. Παρλαμά. and N. Χρ. Σταμπολίδης (eds), *Η πόλη κάτω από την πόλη*. Athens, Goulandris Foundation: Museum of Cycladic Art.

Katerina Trantalidou
Ephorate for Paleoanthropology-Speleology
Ministry of Culture
11636 Athens
Greece

Department of History, Archaeology and Social Anthropology
University of Volos, Argonauton and Phililinon
38221 Volos
Thessaly

ktrantalidou@yahoo.gr

9th ICAZ Conference, Durham 2002
Dogs and People in Social, Working, Economic or Symbolic Interaction
(eds Lynn M. Snyder and Elizabeth A. Moore) pp. 121 –131

13. Dog-wolf Hybrid Biotype Reconstruction from the Archaeological City of Teotihuacan in Prehispanic Central Mexico

Raúl Valadez, Bernardo Rodríguez, Linda Manzanilla and Samuel Tejeda

*Between 1992 and 1996 the archaeological project "The Study of Tunnels and Caves at Teotihuacan", of the National University of Mexico, under the direction of Linda Manzanilla, was undertaken in the prehispanic city of Teotihuacan, located to the northeast of modern Mexico City. Initial analysis of the assemblage of identified canids (455 individuals), resulted in 20 being considered possible wolves. Although their cranial and dental characteristics were similar to the Mexican wolf (*Canis lupus baileyi*), their dimensions were smaller. In 1999 additional analysis indicates that these individuals were really hybrids of wolves (*Canis lupus*) and dogs (*Canis familiaris*).*

While the best example (of this proposed hybrid) was the complete skeleton of a young animal, there were many other individuals represented by just the inferior mandible and teeth. Their reconstructed shape is of a bigger dog with a wolf-like look, with a shoulder height of up to 20 inches, and length up to 30 inches. The data from the young individuals indicate a strong asincrony in their development. Quantification of bone strontium and zinc indicates that their diet was primarily herbivorous, with minimal access to meat. This condition could only be explained by owners who took care of them and gave them food.

Most of the samples recovered were dated between the 8th and 12th centuries AD, and were discovered inside the tunnels, where they were left in locations oriented to the west. The association of caves, west and wolves in Prehispanic Indian symbolism indicates that these animals were used in rituals associated with the passage of the Sun and its entrance to the underworld, the night space associated with the god Xolotl, an Indian god with a dog shape, who was considered the sun's night companion.

Teotihuacan tunnels

The archaeological project "The Study of Tunnels and Caves at Teotihuacan" was directed, between 1992 and 1996, by Dr. Linda Manzanilla of the National Autonomous University of Mexico. Four Prehispanic volcanic scoria quarry tunnels were extensively excavated under the prehispanic city of Teotihuacan, located to the northeast of modern Mexico City (Manzanilla *et al.* 1996). The main goal was to determine the importance of these tunnels for the Epiclassic and Postclassic groups that occupied this site: the tunnels as extraction sites, dwelling sectors, storage areas, working sites, and ritual places.

Through an interdisiciplinary methodology involving the participation of archaeologists, osteologists, archaeobotanists, archaeozoologists, geophysicists, geochemists, and geneticists, a series of activity areas and occupational levels were established for Coyotlatelco, Mazapa, Aztec and modern people (c. AD 600–present times) (Fig. 1).

The faunal remains studied belong to different periods of the human occupation, from the 7th century to the beginning of the 20th century AD. During this time the tunnels were used as a place where the people lived, worked, where ritual and domestic activities were frequently held. From the 7th until the 12th centuries, the occupants implemented diverse subsistence strategies

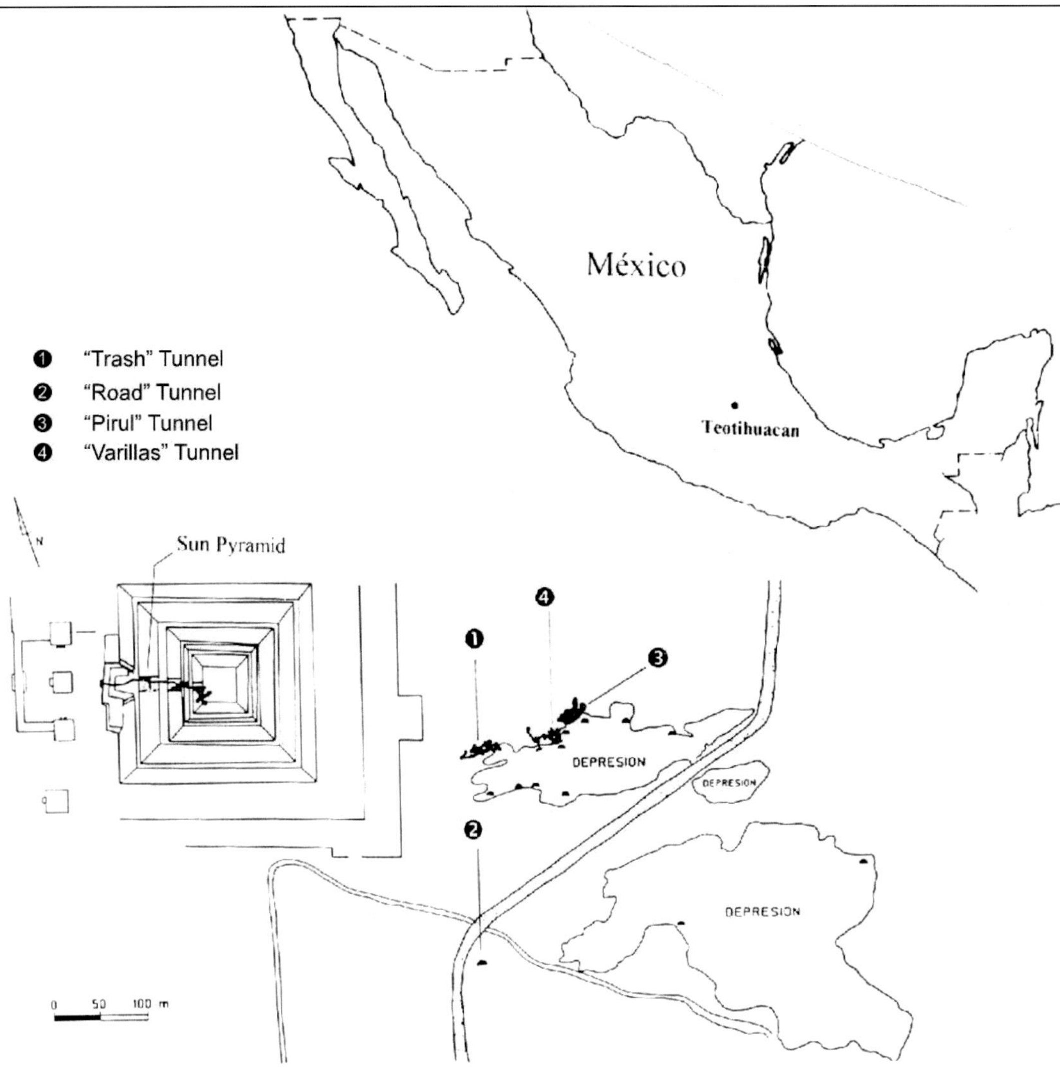

Cultural phases	*Period (centuries AD)*	*Life style*
Coyotlatelco	VII–X	Smalls villages with simple life style
Mazapa	X–XII	
Aztec	XIII–XVI	Agriculture and turkey breeding
Colonial	XVI–XIX	Ranchs
Recent	XIX–XX	

Fig. 1. The location of the tunnels studied in the project "The Study of Tunnels and Caves at Teotihuacan" and general characteristics of the discovered contexts

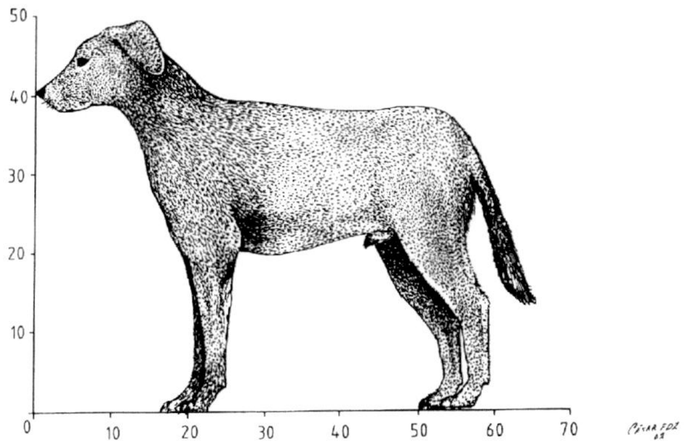

Fig. 2. Mesoamerican common dog, discovered in a burial (16998 registered number) in the Pirul Tunnel

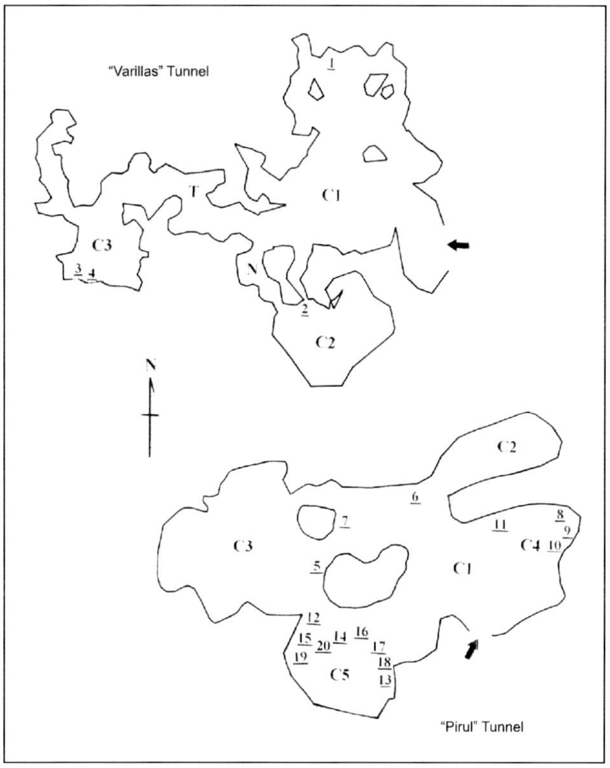

Fig. 3. "Las Varillas" and "Pirul" tunnels. The numbers indicate the hybrid number (see Table 2) and the place where each individual was found

when compared to Classic Teotihuacan, where a more mobile element was present. It is possible that this more diverse strategy had its origin in the Bajío area, in northcentral Mexico.

Archaeofauna registered

From this project, an archaeofaunal collection was obtained that included a MNI total of 2,845 vertebrates and 294 mollusks, and 16% (455 animals) of the vertebrates were canids (Fig. 2 and Table 1).

Recent research of prehispanic dogs of Mexico (Blanco *et al.* 1999; Valadez and Mestre 1999; Valadez *et al.* 1999) indicates the existence of four types of authoctonous dogs; the most abundant type was named the "Mesoamerican common dog". These were medium-sized animals, 14–18 in (36–46 cm) high, and 23–28 in (60–70 cm) in length. This was the common type from which other types of dogs were derived; was the most abundant type in prehispanic Mexico, and was uniform in characteristics.

In the collection there were 20 distinct individuals that were identified as Mexican wolves (Rodríguez 2000). Based on bone morphology and teeth size, these individuals were more similar with the *Canis lupus baileii* than with *Canis familiaris*. In 1999 the comparison with the archaeozoological remains of the wolves discovered in the Teotihuacan valley and confirmation that the contexts in which they appear indicated clear evidence of human activity, led us to the conclusion that these individuals were wolf-dog hybrids.

Diagnostic elements of the hybrids skeleton

The hybrids appear in two tunnels: the Varillas tunnel and the Pirul tunnel (Fig. 3), but the majority were discovered in the area known as the "Chamber 5" (C5) in the Pirul tunnel. The chronology of these individuals goes from 500 to 1,350 years BP, although the majority are dated in the Coyotlatelco and Mazapa phases (c. AD 600–950). With the exception of one complete young individual (Fig. 4), individuals are only represented by a few bones. Many of them had cut marks, and several bones were cooked (Table 2).

The bones (of the proposed hybrid specimens) are similar or larger than the dog bones, but none of them are as large as the Mexican wolves. The mandibles have dimensions similar or superior to the dogs (Table 3 and Fig. 5), but, more significantly, they have a close resemblance to the morphology of the Mexican wolf mandible (Fig. 6).

Table 1. Canid collection discovered in the tunnels

	Types of canids					
	Dogs					
	Mesoamerican Common	*Mexican hairless*	*Europeans*	*Unidentified*	***Wolf-like canids***	***Coyotes (Canis latrans)***
No ind	43	3	3	384	20	2
%	9.4	0.7	0.7	84.4	4.4	0.4

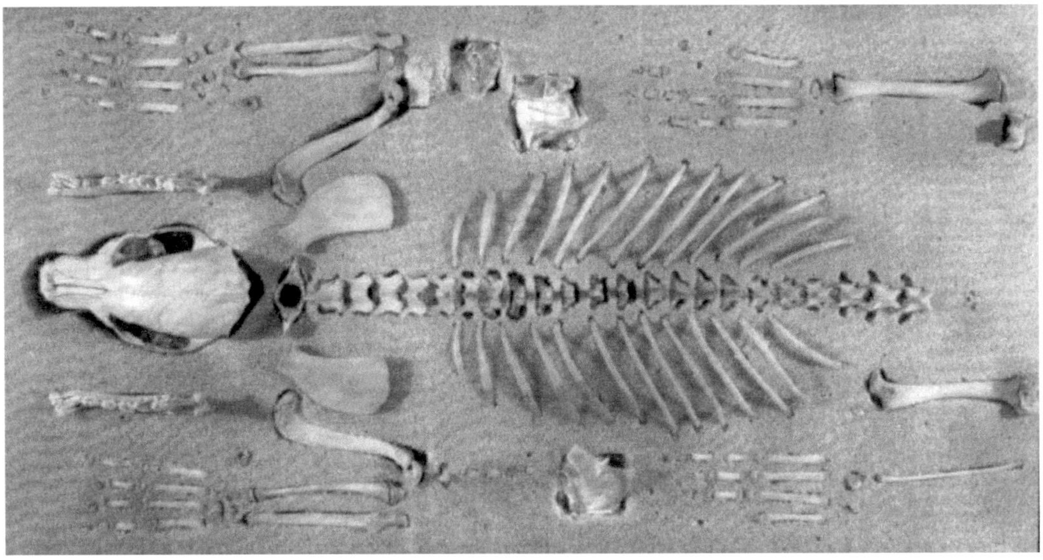

Fig. 4. Juvenile hybrid

Table 2. Wolf-dog hybrids discovered in the Teotihuacan tunnels

Hybrid number	Archaeological information			Bone remains registered		
	Bag number	***Tunnel/ camera***	***Cultural phase***	***Cranium***	***Dental pieces***	***Poscraneal bones***
1	6507	Varillas/C1	Coyotlatelco	Right mandible	Pm/3–4, M/1–2	
2	14973	Varillas/C2		Mandibles right and left	Cd,i, Pm/2–4d,i, M/1–2d,I	Calcáneo left
3	14824	Varillas/C3	Mazapa	Left mandible	Pm/3–4, M/1–2	Atlas, 5th dorsal vertebrae, first-2nd lumbar vertebrae; rib; right scapula; 3rd right metacarpus; proximal epiphysis to right femur
4	14152				I3 (pd)	Right Isquion
5	25223	Pirul/C1	Late Coyotlatelco		M/2d	5th left metatarsus
6	17352	Pirul/C1	Mazapa	Left mandible	Ml/2–3	
7	16058	Pirul/C1	Azteca			Right and left femur; ulna, rib
8	21154	Pirul/C4	Coyotlatelco	Neurocranium and left mandible (&)	M/1	Right ulna; right radium; left calcaneum; two caudal vertebrae
9	23402					Right humerus; pelvis acetabulum (&)
10	20923	Pirul/C4	Late Coyotlatelco			Left ulna
11		Pirul/C4	Mazapa	Skeleton		
12	24136	Pirul/C5	Late Coyotlatelco	Right maxilla	C, Pm3–4, M1–2	
13	24206			Right mandible	I/1, C, Pm/2–4, M/1–3	
14	24671	Pirul/C5	Late Coyotlatelco - Mazapa	Left mandible	Pm/4, M/1–2	Atlas–5th cervical vertebrae and caudal vertebrae. Right pelvis(&)
15	24020			Right mandible (&)	M/2i	
16	24032	Pirul/C5	Coyotlatelco-Mazapa transition	Left mandible, right premaxilla	I1–2, Pm/2,4	
17	24192			Left mandible	I/1, C (pd) I/2, C, Pm/3–4, M/1–2	
18	24029					Fibula diaphysys
19	23426	Pirul/C5	Mazapa	Left maxilla	Pm3–4, M1–2	
20	22795	Pirul/C5	Azteca	Left maxilla	Pm4	

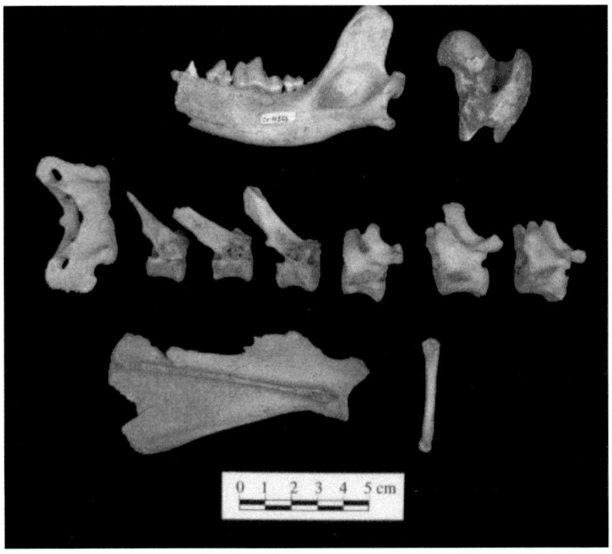

Fig. 5. Individual 14824, discovered in the Varillas Tunnel. The teeth possess a morphology of the "wolf type", although the individual dimensions are only higher than a dog

Only one neurocranium was discovered (Fig. 7), and it was possible to take three measurements (Table 3): one of them is similar to the dogs, the second to the wolves and the last one have a intermediate value. The form of the mastoid region (Fig. 8) indicated a hybrid condition (Yates 2000). One hybrid burial was discovered, with a five months old animal that belongs to the Mazapa phase (AD 900). While the individual presents a large head, the diagnostic teeth elements also show permanent and deciduous incisors and canines together, an unusual condition in the dogs that indicates an irregular dental development, a reasonable condition derived from its hybridism.

Dentition

The dental measurements of the molars and fourth superior premolar help to distinguishes the hybrid condition of the individuals. These measurements frequently range between Mesoamerican dogs and Mexican wolves (Fig. 9). Although all of them show a "like-dog" morphology, in general it is clear that these animals possess a dentition larger than that of the dogs (Fig. 10).

Table 3. Mean measurements of the skull, teeth and some large bones in the Mexican wolf and Mesoamerican common dog and comparison with the measurements obtained in the discovered hybrids

Measurements	**Promedium length (mm)**		
	Canis lupus baileyi	***Mesoamerican common dog***	***Hybrids***
Total cranium length	235	164	163–182 (4 ind)
Greatest neurocranium breadth	62	52	49.1 (1 ind)
Greatest mastoid breadth	76	57	64.3 (1 ind)
Least skull breadth	40	33	37.4 (1 ind)
Greatest breadth across tooth rows at P or M	76	56	52.7 53.4 (2 ind)
Length from the angular process to the infradental	175.3	119	120.1–135 (5 ind)
Height of ascending ramus	71	48	48–55.9 (6 ind)
Breadth to the horizontal ramus	41	29	27.7–36.1 (8 ind)
Greatest height from M1 to base of jaw	29	20	20.8–26 (8 ind)
Ulna	249	140	183.5–185 (2 ind)
Radium	214	119	151.2 (1 ind)

Table 4. Dimensional comparation of diverse parts of the hybrid skeleton and of a common dog of the tunnels. The result indicates individuals of more than 500 mm of height and 714 mm of length

Measurements from a Mesoamerican common dog, buried in the Pirul tunnel (individual 16998)

Cranium length	160 mm	Radium length	115 mm	Height	390 mm
Scapula length	100 mm	Pelvis length	130 mm	Head-body length	628 mm
Ulna length	134 mm	Atlas-sacrum length	468 mm		

Dimensional reconstruction of four hybrids, derived from calculated measurements and its appearance in the 16998 dog

Hybrid number (number bag)	***Calculated cranium length***	***Height (mm)***			***Head-body length (mm)***		
		Bone	*Dimensional relationship with 16998*	*Calculated value*	*Bone*	*Dimensional relationship with 16998*	*Calculated value*
14824		Scapula (100 mm)	1:1	390	Six vertebrae (98.1 mm)	0.96 smaller	607 mm
14973	182.3	Ulna (183.5 mm)	1.36 bigger	530 mm			
21154	161.5	Radium (151.2)	1.32 bigger	499 mm			
24671	170.6	Pelvis (130 mm)	1.1	430 mm	Atlas-fifth cervical vertebrae (151 mm)	1.16 bigger	543 (spine) + 170.6 (head) = 714 mm

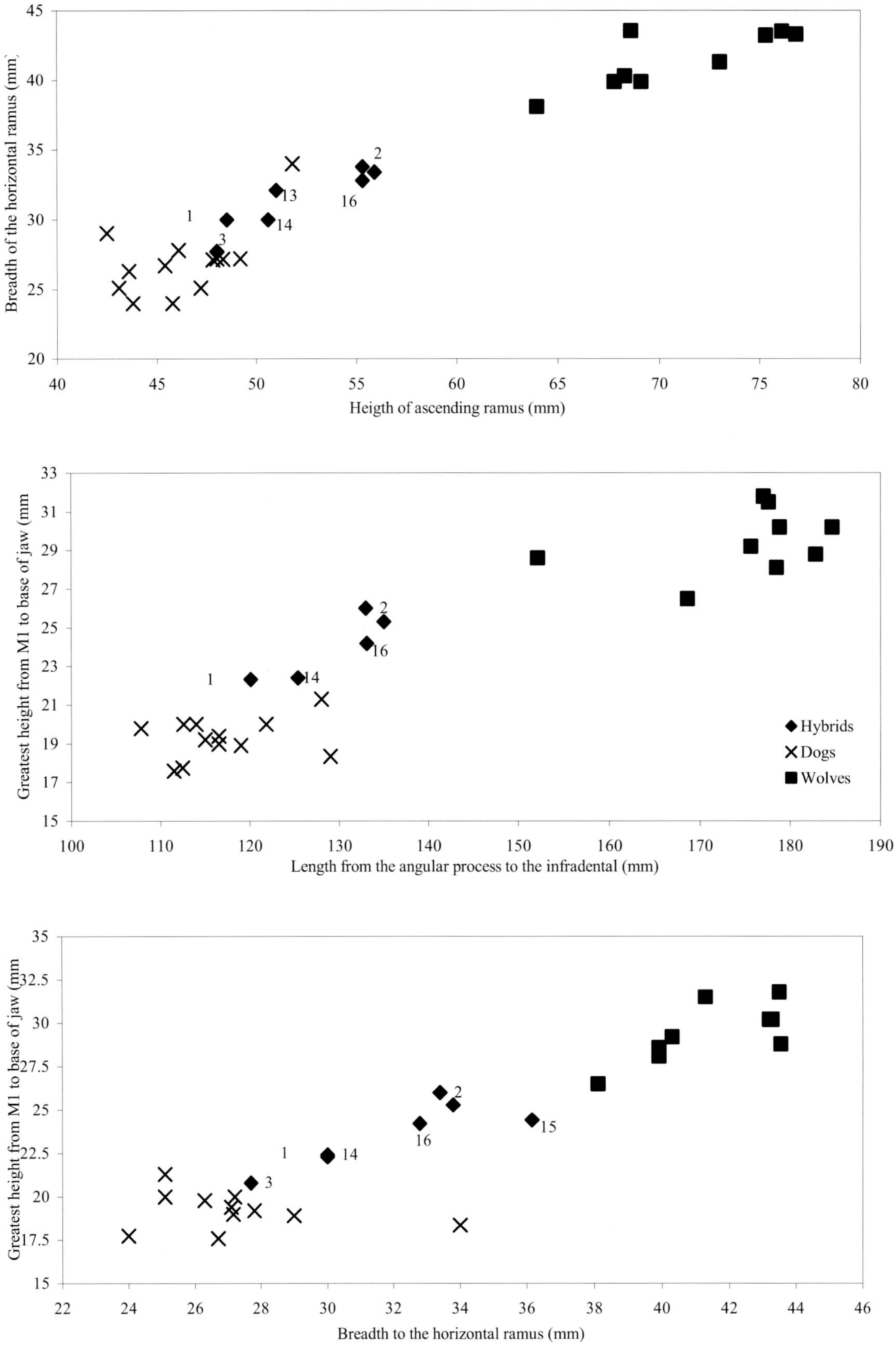

Fig. 6. Graphics in which the relationships between cranial measurements in dogs, wolves and hybrids location are shown (the number shown in the graphics is the hybrid number of Table 2)

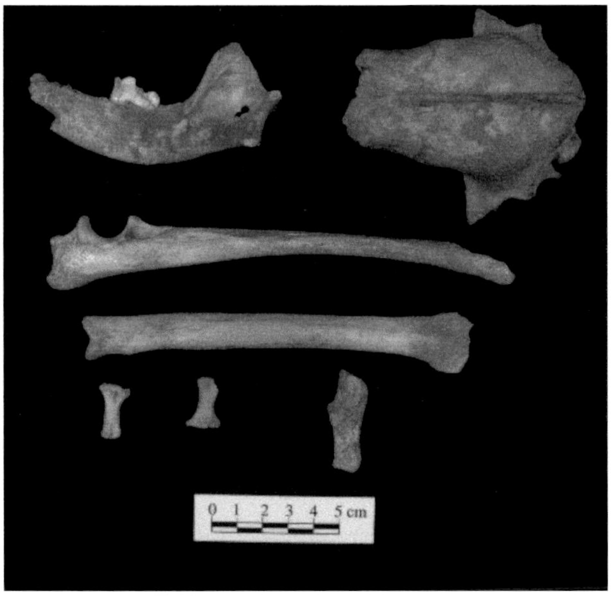

Fig. 7. Hybrid 8 (21154 bag number) The skull presents intermediate characters between dog and wolf, and the large bones are from a larger canid than a Mesoamerican dog

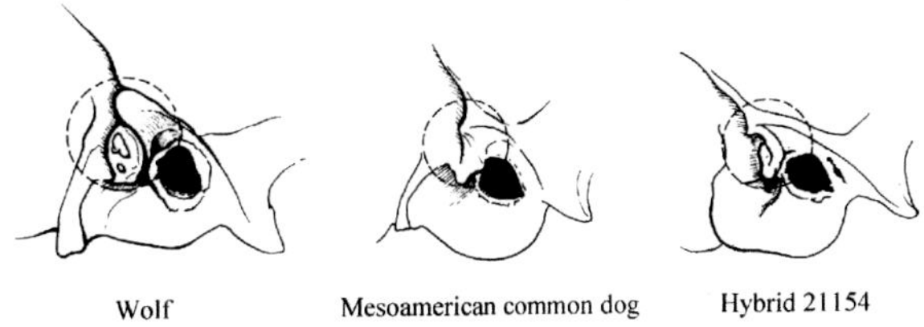

Fig. 8. Comparation between the mastoidea region to wolf, dog and hybrid with number 8 (21154 number bag). See that in this last the region possess a more complex morphology that of the dog but simpler than the wolf

Reconstruction

The cranium and mandible remains of the individuals indicate that these animals have heads that are a little larger compared to the dog's head, but are more robust. The face is larger than the dogs', but thinner, and the post-cranial bones indicate 30% larger dimensions. The comparison and the extrapolation of the hybrid measures with a dog found in the Pirul tunnel (CP16998) (Fig. 2) indicate that their withers' height goes from 390–530 mm (15 to 20.9 in), and their length, between 600 and 714 mm (23.6 to 28 in) (Table 4). Accordingly, these canids were larger and more robust than common dogs, with a wolf-like rostrum (Fig. 11).

Subsistence

One of the goals of the research that was carried out in the tunnels was the study of paleodietary indicators (Sr, Zn) in human remains, with the purpose of recognizing human subsistence trends (Burton and Price 1990; Farnum 1995; Fornaciari and Mallegni 1987; Gilbert *et al.* 1994; Manzanilla *et al.* 2000; Wing and Brown 1979). As reference points we took 36 mammal and bird bone samples, with one coyote (*Canis latrans*), eight dogs, and three hybrids among them.

The distribution of the results (Fig. 12) show that the Sr-Zn proportions in the hybrid individuals are more similar to the dogs than to the coyote. The coyote (*Canis latrans*), with a high Zn and a medium Sr concentration, points to a diverse diet with a strong protein support. The felines, in the left inferior extreme, indicate a good and a healthy meat diet. The dogs show a diverse subsistence pattern, from the ones which have a "coyote diet type", the ones that have a subsistence similar to the opossum (*Didelphis virginiana*), or the little carnivores like the skunks. This schedule is just like the typical dogs life with its masters, because domestic dogs would have been more able to look for their food in a wider variety of contexts: in the countryside, in the dumps or with its masters.

In an illogical situation, the hybrids depart from this pattern, because they feed like rabbits, skunks and opossums, revealing an herbivorous or omnivorous diet. One explication for this condition is that these animals were taken care of by people, and fed from their human food (maize, beans, insects, and occasionally bones and a little meat) with the purpose of reducing the development of their wolf-like instinct. Chronicles of the XVI century state that dogs ate the same food as the people, and at present dogs do not eat raw meat because people think that this would trigger their aggressive instincts.

Symbolism

In Mexico there has been a tradition of breeding female dogs and male coyotes, because the hybrids were considered as resistant, loyal but temperamental, and good guardians. The practice was to take the mating female dog and leave her chained in the mountain a few days, with enough food, until she was impregnated. In prehispanic Mexico, the wolf was one of the more important species in religious life (Seler 2004). It was associated with the forces that guided the world, like a symbol of war (Fig. 13) and the Sun. Wolves were sacrificed and used in high-status ceremonies. We propose that the hybrids were created by men, with the purpose of having individuals that could display the sacred attributes of the father (wolf), inside a body that could be manipulated by men. These animals could be taken care of until the sacrificial ceremony (Valadez *et al.* 2001), in

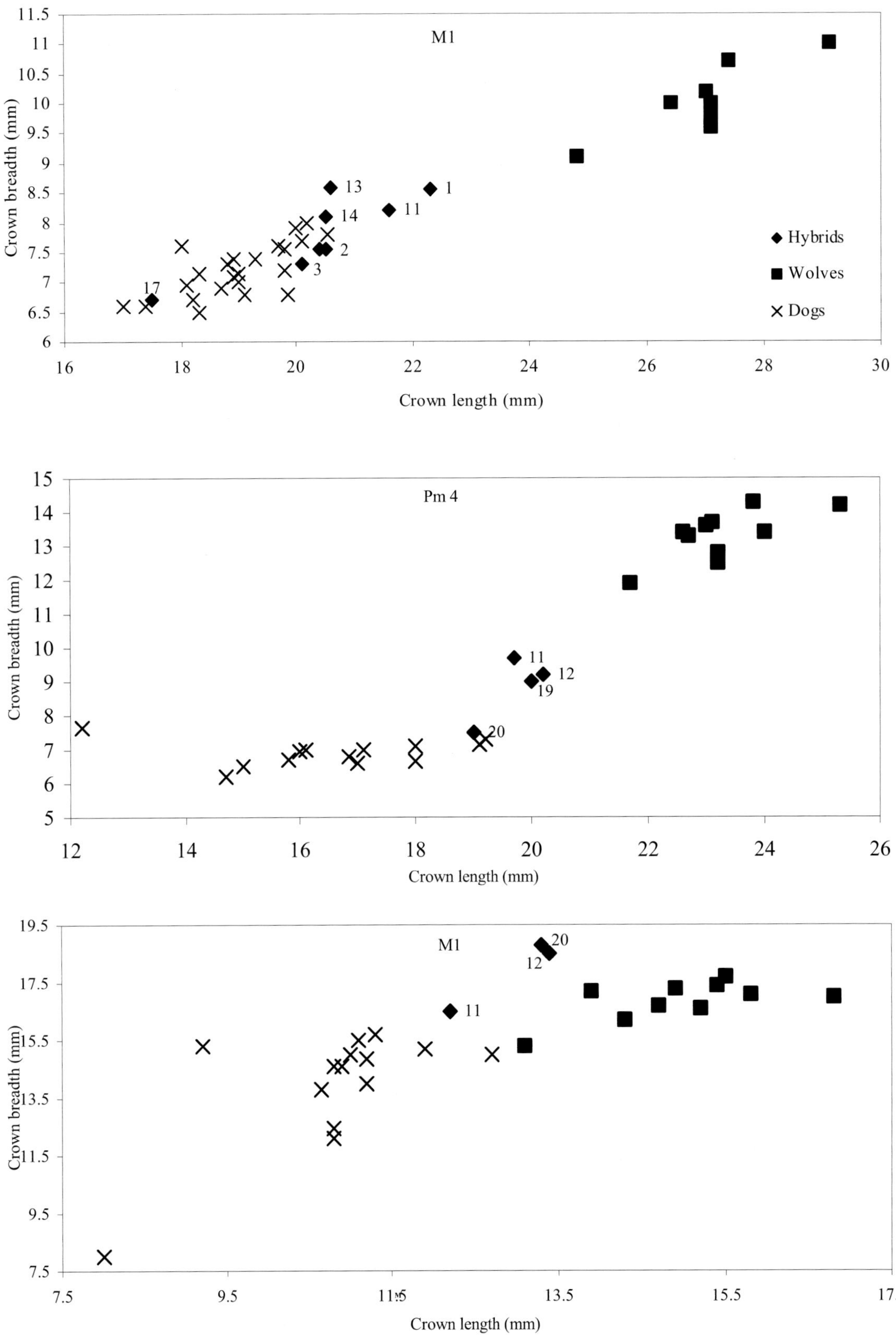

Fig. 9. Graphics that shows the relationship between many teeth measurements in dogs, wolves and hybrids. The medium condition is visible in all the hybrids (the number comes from the hybrid of Fig 7)

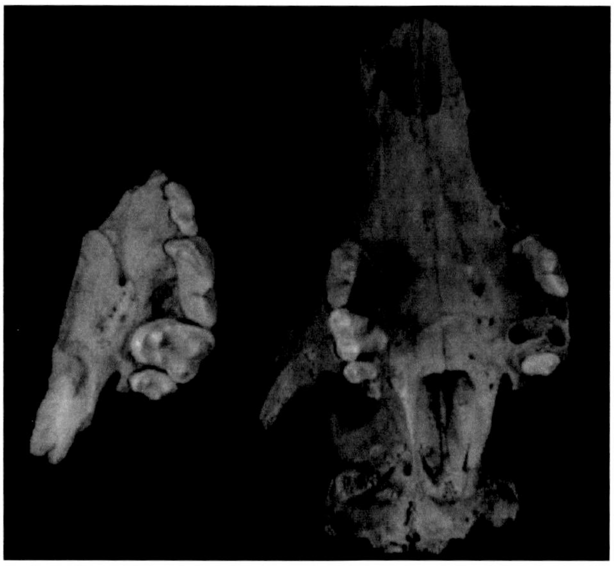

Fig. 10. Left: hybrid 19 maxilla (23426 bag number) with Pm3–4, M1–2 and a common dog (right side) from the tunnels

Fig. 11. Reconstructed image of a tunnel hybrid

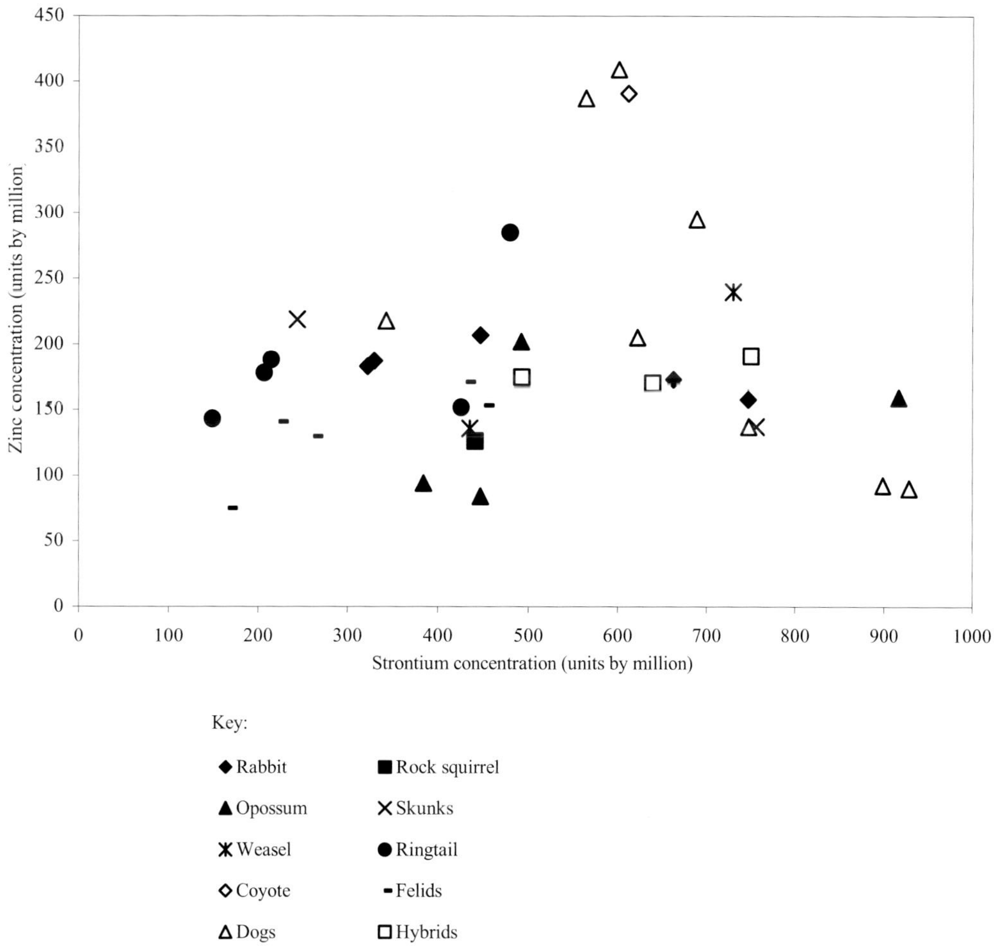

Fig 12. Relationship between strontium (Sr) content and zinc (Zn) in mammal bones discovered in the tunnels. The dogs are placed in positions that manifest diverse diets from the omnivore or herbivore "hare type" to the carnivore "coyote type". The hybrids are placed between animals like the opossums, the rabbits and the skunks, showing a type of diet in which the meat presence was very low

Fig 13. Mural representation of a wolf at Teotihuacan (Atetelco compound)

which they were cut apart and separated in pieces according to their symbolic value. The most important body parts were the heads and faces, which were used in priest and warriors attire (Valadez *et al.* 2002).

The remaining pieces, the ones that were discovered during excavation, mandibles and large bones, would be the ones with less value for these people. These individuals were deposited in places with a western orientation, the same areas that were used as funerary chambers (Manzanilla and Arrellín 1999).

For prehispanic people, the tunnels were considered as an entrance to the "underworld", as a fertility symbol, as death, and as a place where mankind had its origin (Weitlaner and Leonard 1959). The west was a place of rebirth, the region of the dead Sun (Anon 1942; Sahagún 1985), and an entrance to the "underworld", an association that we found repeatedly in the burials of the Varillas and Pirul tunnels. The association of the "cave" and western orientation leads us to consider this as a context of the nocturnal Sun (the night) inside the "underworld", a time in which this star should cross through this region in company of Xolotl, a canid god, related frequently with the dog (Seler 1963).

This research describes these hybrids as organisms that were buried with the mission of accompanying the Sun during the night, as an earthly equivalent of the Xolotl god. Since each dog was buried in the tunnels with a western orientation, we conclude that the main canid element in the rituals were the wolves. It may be that Xolotl was represented by *Canis lupus* (a wolf, not a dog), with the hybrids having the role of animals who carry on the sacred character of the wolf in the dog body that could be manipulated by men.

Acknowledgments

Drawings: César Fernández Amaro.
Photographs: Rafael Reyes Ojeda.
Graphic designer: Jonathan Valadez.

References

Anonymous. (1942) *Mitos indígenas*. México: Imprenta universitaria de la UNAM.

Blanco, A., Valadez, R and Rodríguez, B. 1999. Colección arqueozoológica de perros del sitio de Chac-Mool, Punta Pájaros, Quintana Roo. *Arqueología* **22**, 89–106.

Burton, J., and Price, T. D. 1990. The ratio of barium to strontium as a paleodietary. Indicator of consumption of marine resources. *Journal of Archaeological Science* **17**, 547–557.

Farnum, J. F., Glascock, M. D., Sanford, M. K. and Gerritsen, S. 1995. Trace elements in ancient human bone and associated soil using NAA. *Journal of Radioanalytical and Nuclear Chemistry*. **196(2)**, 267–274.

Fornaciari, G. and Mallegni, F. 1987. Paleonutritional studies on skeletal remains of ancient population from the Mediterranean area. *Antropologische Anzeige, Jg.* **45(4)**, 361–370.

Gilbert, Ch., Sealy, J. and Sillen, A. 1994. An investigation of barium, calcium and strontium as paleodietary indicators in the southwestern cape, South Africa. *Journal of Archaeological Science*. **21**, 173–184.

Manzanilla, L., López, C. and Freter, A. 1996. Dating results from excavations in quarry tunnels behind the pyramid of the sun at Teotihuacan. *Ancient Mesoamérica*. **7(2)**, 245–266.

Manzanilla, L. and Arrellín, R. 1999. Los entierros de los túneles al este de la Pirámide del Sol: proyecto UNAM 1987–1996. *In*: L. Manzanilla and C. Serrano, (eds). *Prácticas funerarias en la ciudad de los dioses. Los enterramientos humanos de la antigua Teotihuacan*. México: Instituto de Investigaciones Antropológicas-Dirección General de asuntos del Personal Académico, UNAM., 427–458.

Manzanilla, L., Tejeda, S. and Martínez, J. C. 2000. Implicaciones el análisis de calcio, estroncio y zinc en el conocimiento de la dieta y la migración en Teotihuacan, México. *Anales de Antropología*. **33**, 13–28.

Rodríguez, B. 2000. *Estudio morfológico y morfométrico, craneal y dental de perros y lobos hallados en Teotihuacan y su aplicación en la arqueozoología*. Biol. Thesis, Universidad Nacional Autónoma de México.

Sahagún, B. 1985. *Historia General de las Cosas de la Nueva España*. Libros séptimo (cap. II), undécimo (cap. I) y adiciones al libro noveno. México: colección "sepan cuántos......" No 300, Porrúa.

Seler, E. 1963. *Comentarios al Códice Borgia*. México: Fondo de Cultura Económica.

Seler, E. 2004. *Las Imágenes de los Animales en los Manuscritos Mexicanos y Mayas*. México: Casa Juan Pablos, 40–76.

Valadez, R, and Mestre, G. 1999. *Historia del Xoloitzcuintle en México*. México: Instituto de Investigaciones Antropológicas de la UNAM, Museo Dolores Olmedo Patiño, Cámara de Diputados.

Valadez, R., Paredes, B. and Rodríguez, B. (1999) Entierros de perros descubiertos en la antigua ciudad de Tula, Hidalgo. *Latin American Antiquity* **10(2)**, 80–200.

Valadez, R., Blanco, A., Rodríguez, B., Viniegra, F. and Olmos, K. 2001. Una quinta raza de perro prehispánica o, ¿una segunda especie de lobo mexicano? *AMMVEPE*. **12(5)**, 149–159.

Valadez, R., Rodríguez, B., Cabrera, B., Cowgill, G. and Sugiyama, S. (2002) Híbridos de lobos y perros (tercer acto): hallazgos en la pirámide de Quetzalcoatl de la antigua ciudad de Teotihuacan. *AMMVEPE*. **13(5–6)**, 165–176, 219–231.

Weitlaner, R. and Leonard, J. 1959. De la cueva al palacio, pp. 933–956, in C. Leonard, (coord). *El esplendor del México antiguo*. México: Centro de Investigaciones Antropológicas de México.

Yates, B. 2000. Use of the mastoid region of the crania of canids to distinguish wolves, dogs, and wolf/dog hybrids, pp. 269–270, in S. Crockford, (ed.). *Dogs through time: an archaeological perspective. Proceedings of the first ICAZ symposium on the domestic dog*. London: BAR International Series 889.

Wing, E. and Brown, E. 1979. Reconstruction of prehistoric diet, nutrients and food. *Paleonutrition* **5**, 6–44.

Instituto de Investigaciones Antropológicas
de la Universidad Nacional Autónoma de México
Circuito Exterior, s/n
Ciudad Universitaria
Delegación Coyoacán
Código Postal 04510
México D.F.
México.

raul_valadez@hotmail.com
sanber65@hotmail.com
lmanza@servidor.unam.mx

Instituto Nacional de Investigaciones Nucleares
Kilómetro 36.5 de la Carretera México-Toluca
Municipio de Ocoyoacac
Edo. de México
Código Postal 52045
México.

stv@nuclear.inin.mx

9th ICAZ Conference, Durham 2002
Dogs and People in Social, Working, Economic or Symbolic Interaction
(eds Lynn M. Snyder and Elizabeth A. Moore) pp. 132–137

14. The Sacrifice of Dogs in Ancient Italy

Barbara Wilkens

The sacrifice of dogs can be linked to a number of forms of funerary practice or ritual action. In a funerary context, the dog can be present in the grave together with the deceased or can be used in rites after the burial. This study examines the use of dogs in ritual contexts only. In Italy there is archaeological evidence for dogs used for ritual purposes from the early Neolithic through the Roman periods. There is also literary evidence, in the form of texts from later periods, indicating that by these later times dog sacrifice was seen as an aspect of ancient tradition, and that these traditions were often no longer fully understood. In the case of public cults, there is evidence in the Chalcolithic period for the sacrifice of dogs in sanctuary contexts, although dogs as a species are always a minor component of the larger animal sacrifice. In these contexts, the dogs are often butchered. In contrast to cult assemblages from large public contexts, sacrificial remains associated with private cult, practiced in the environment of daily life, are often recognizable only with difficulty. Nonetheless, we can deduce from a reading of Latin authors and pre-Roman texts that dogs were sacrificed on occasions both public and private in nature, some of which involved the consumption of meat. In other cases, the dog was buried whole.

Introduction

The association of dog sacrifice with funerary rituals, in which the animal is either directly interred within the tomb alongside the dead or in adjacent areas, has been documented in a number of contexts. For instance in Continenza cave, in the Fucino basin near Avezzano in Abruzzo (Fig. 1), the disarticulated bones of a dog, some of which showed signs of butchering, were found in a Neolithic context in an area which also contained human burials (Wilkens 1989–90). Sacrifices in non-funerary contexts, however, are sometimes more difficult to recognise. While the presence of dog remains in association with other cult materials or in association with sanctuaries may provide unambiguous evidence of ritual significance, other assemblages are far more enigmatic and difficult to interpret. This work will first deal with Roman and Italic literary sources from the 3rd century BC to the 2nd century AD. These works are

Fig. 1. map of the sites

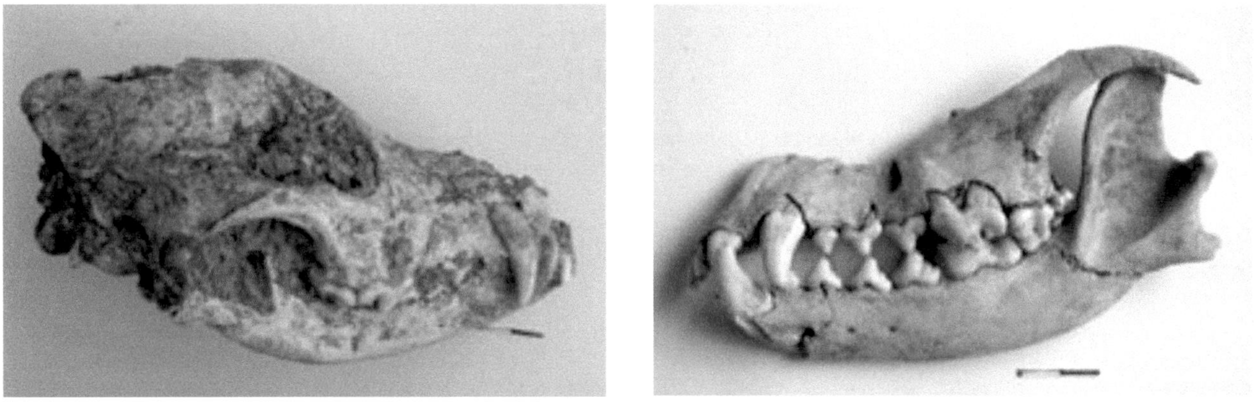

Figs 2 and 3. Canis familiaris *skulls from Porto d'Ascoli*

based on traditions dating to earlier periods, and hence may aid in interpretation of the archaeological documentation that will then be discussed.

Textual Evidence

"*In relation to the Hondia festival, the declaration of the dog is established as being at the moment of culmination of the interlunary cereal (festivals)....So as to carry out Hondia, the dog, grain, the Mefa tart, the Ficla tart, and the drink, wine are brought. Salt is ground. A table cloth is brought, as are used and unused vases, and unguent. Fire is placed upon the altar ....The sacred dog is always buried at Hondo Giovio, for the Petronia people of the Atiedii brothers.*" With this information in *Tabulae Iguvinae* (Devoto 1975), the ritual of dog sacrifice is codified. Further, this text indicates that the sacrifice must take place at the time of the full moon, after interpretation of the augury of birds to ensure the approval of the gods. The text continues: "*The sacrificial animal is laid down. The flesh of the dog is taken, as are the hind limbs. The innards are cut away with thin skewers, and thin pieces of wood are placed beneath them. The pit is observed.*" This is followed by libations and the cooked meat is brought around for the ritual meal. The participants pray in the direction of the pit. "*The flesh is laid out on the posterior part of the sacrificial altar, the parts to be shared are then taken*". After prayers and libations, the remaining parts of the dog are buried close to the altar. The *Tabulae Iguvinae* were discovered in 1444 at Gubbio, in Umbria. These are seven bronze tablets with inscriptions in the Umbrian language, written partially using the Umbrian alphabet, and partially with the Latin alphabet. They contain references to several sacrifices, and acted as a sort of guidebook for the high priests. According to G. Devoto, the tablets in the Umbrian alphabet date to between 200–120 BC and those in the Latin alphabet to between 150 and 70 BC. The codified rules are however to be considered as referring to earlier traditions. In the tablets little-known Umbrian divinities are mentioned (*Hondo Giovio*), as are *gentes* and religious organisations of the city.

In the Roman period dog sacrifice was considered by many to be an inheritance from earlier time, and represented a custom no longer fully understood or appreciated. In "*Fasti*", Ovid reacts with disgust, when he sees a bitch being sacrificed. In this collection of poetry, written in the 1st century AD, that celebrates the religious festivals of Rome, Ovid testifies that in April Quirinus' *flamen* (priest) went to the wood sacred to *Rubigo*, a divinity which represented the mould which attacked cereals (cereal rust), to enact a sacrifice to ensure the health of the crops. "*He offered incense and wine to the fire as well as the innards of a bidental ovine and we saw the repulsive innards of an obscene bitch.*" To a question which the poet poses asking for an explanation for the ancient ceremony, the *flamen* answers that the sacrifice of the dog took place in accordance with the dog constellation.

Further evidence of a more positive nature is provided in Pliny (XXIX, 14) in the 2nd century AD. He states that the "forefathers" considered suckling puppies such pure food that they could be used in sacrifices to please the gods, and notes that the dog was a sacred victim for *Genita Mana*, a goddess linked to the menstrual cycle. He also notes that dog meat was still served at banquets in honor of the gods in his times. In a more negative context, Pliny describes a ceremony which was still occurring in his time to commemorate the invasion of the Gauls in 390 BC. During this ceremony dogs were "*hung live by their shoulders on elder pitchforks between the temples Iuventatis and Summani.*" This treatment was interpreted as punishment for the dogs that, in contrast to the geese, had not been vigilant and announced the approach of the Gauls (XXIX, 14).

The Archaeological Evidence

Sacrifices associated with sanctuaries

Of the most typical sacrifices of the Roman rituals, the *suovitaurilia* is of note as it involved the sacrifice of rams, bulls and boars in equal numbers. Variations of this ritual can be found in different periods and different localities – a similar ritual is also recorded in the *Tabulae Iguvinae*.

Zooarchaeological analyses confirm that it in nearly all sanctuaries of the Roman period in which the ritual of *suovitaurilia* was enacted, dog remains, often with butchering marks, make up a small percentage of the faunal assemblages. This was the case in the 6th century BC Roman deposit of *Lapis Niger* (De Grossi Mazzorin 1990), in the sacred area of S. Omobono (Tagliacozzo 1989), at *Satricum* in Lazio (Prummel 1996, 1997) in the sanctuary which was probably dedicated to *Mater Matuta* (8th–3rd centuries BC), and at Olbia in Sardinia in the 2nd century AD sanctuary dedicated to Hercules (Wilkens 1996).

In an Italic context (c. 4th century B.C.), dogs were found among the remains of other animals in sacrificial pits in the area of the ancient temples of Eraclea in Southern Italy (Wilkens and Delussu 2002). In a number of pits which appeared to be linked to individual acts of sacrifice, dog skeletal remains bearing cut marks were found associated with two of eight deposits. It is of note that while the site of ancient Eraclea is Greek in origin, the rituals appear to be predominantly Italic, similar to *suovitaurilia*. A possibly similar, though much earlier deposit comes from the sanctuary of Monte d'Accoddi, near Sassari, in northern Sardinia. This sanctuary appears to have been of great political and social importance in the area (Wilkens 2003a). To date, only the faunal materials from the Chalcolithic (25th–18th centuries B.C.) levels of the sanctuary have been studied. In these levels dog remains, some bearing butchering marks, constitute a small percentage of the sacrificial assemblages, which also contained the bones of sheep, cattle and pigs.

Sacrifices in non-sanctuary contexts

Complete dog skeletons, apparently of sacrificed animals, have been found in deposits of a number of periods. A large pit of Final Neolithic date found in the village of Porto d'Ascoli, Marche (Wilkens 2003a) contained the articulated skeletons of two dogs (Figs 2 and 3). The sacrificial nature of this feature is uncertain, although the presence of several unusual objects in association with the dogs suggests that a ritual was involved. Other animal remains of large dimensions, belonging to bovines and ovines, and the form of the pit itself are all somewhat anomalous. A well of the Chalcolithic period in Le Cerquete-Fianello, near Rome, contained the skeletons of two puppies, plus the dismembered remains of a horse (Curci and Tagliacozzo 1995). The authors interpret this structure as being of ritual significance. Several pit deposits of a possible ritual nature were also found at the Middle Bronze Age site of Roca in Puglia (Wilkens 1995). In one a complete dog was laid close to the walls of the pit (Fig. 4). In the same deposit, a number of whole vases and the head and mandible of a bovine suggest that the deposit may have been sacrificial in nature.

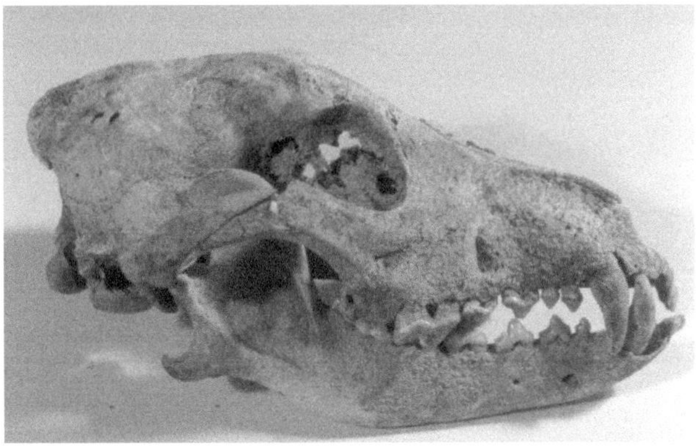

Fig. 4. Canis familiaris *skull from Roca*

At the site of Rendina 2, discovered in connection with investigations near the Rendina dam in Basilicata (Wilkens 1995), three underground structures which had been partially destroyed by modern agricultural work were uncovered. In Structure A a dog skeleton, apparently complete when deposited, was found. In this case, the dog was accompanied by the remains of a large number of wild fauna including red deer, wild boar, marten, badger and hedgehog. The association of the dog with wild taxa suggests that its role as a hunt companion was of importance in this context.

Ritual deposits in wells

The cult of sacred wells and springs appears to be limited to Sardinia. This cult did not involve merely the deposition of ritual objects in common wells or springs, as was practiced in many cultures, but rather the construction of sanctuaries with water contained within an architectonic structure in stone at the centre of the cult. These structures were of well-defined typologies and were generally monumental. The wells consisted of an underground chamber with a *tholos* roof. Access to this chamber was by way of a series of steps. In the case of springs, the architectonic structure was usually above, rather than below the ground. In general, the stratigraphic sequence in these wells starts with an initial phase in which water is being taken from the well, and only votive objects such as bronze figurines are deposited. In the second phase, when the well is no longer used for water, animal carcasses or carcass segments were thrown into the well. Sheep or goats are the most often sacrificed animals, with pigs and cattle less common. Horns cut at

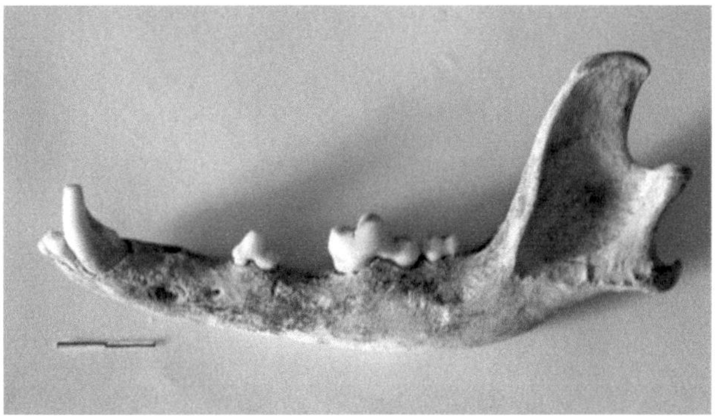

Fig. 5. Canis familiaris *mandible from Serra Niedda*

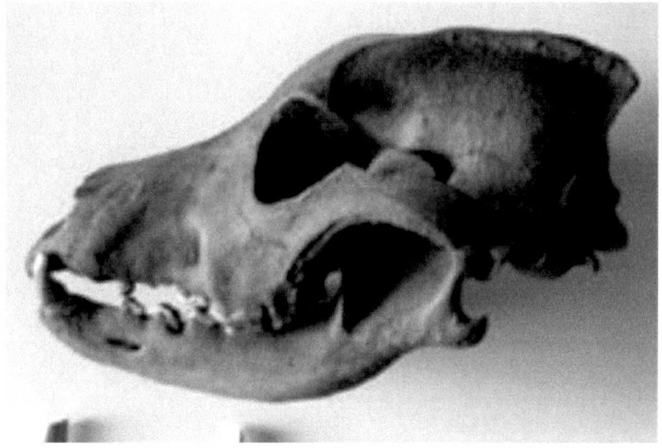

Fig. 6. Canis familiaris *skull and mandibles from Genoni*

the base were frequent. In this phase the structures of the sanctuary were outside.

The sacred well in Serra Niedda, near Sassari, in northern Sardinia (Wilkens 2000a), contained in the upper levels the skeletal remains of a dog (Fig. 5) and several goats, which appear to have been deposited whole in the well, and showed no butchering marks. Several horn cores of male goats and sheep were also found in this deposit, but postcranial elements of these animals, as well as pigs, were relatively rare. The strata in which these materials were found dates to the Nuragic period (late Bronze/early Iron Age). Besides the remains of sacrificed animals, bronze votive statues were also found in this site. At the site of Genoni-S. Antine, central Sardinia (Wilkens and Delussu, in press) a well initially dug in the Nuragic period contained a deposit of animal bones in a strata dating to the Imperial Roman period. Several goats, a sheep, a cow and newborn calf (or pregnant cow and foetus), a number of pigs, and the remains of seven dogs were found (Fig. 6). All of these animals appear to have been whole when they entered the well, with the exception of the cow, from which the horns had been cut. One of the dogs (Fig. 7) and one goat (Fig. 8) bore marks on their skulls which may have been inflicted at their death. The dog remains display fractures of the frontal, while the goat has a perforation of the occipital bone, caused by a weapon. All seven of the dogs appeared to be of adult age and approximately the same size, although the skeletons of individual animals could not be reconstructed due to the commingling of the deposit and difficult conditions during excavation. A well deposit was discovered also in Lavello, Basilicata, southern Italy, above Hypogeum 743 (Wilkens 1997). The well, which is dated to the Iron Age (c. 9th–8th century BC) Daunian culture, contained an assemblage of ceramics and bone clearly associated with ritual. As well as whole vases, the remains of seven dogs were recovered, several of which appear to have been partially butchered. The remains of a piglet, a barn owl, and a small number of isolated domestic and wild animal bones probably entered the deposit as refuse not related to ritual. Scattered and non-articulating human bone fragments found in the deposit may have been incorporated into the deposit when the digging of the well accidentally cut into one of the burials of the underlying Bronze Age hypogea. This event may have necessitated an appeasing ritual, in which dogs were sacrificed (Fig. 9).

Characteristics of the sacrificed dogs

One detail of ritual which is not provided by the Latin sources, nor by the *Tabulae Iguvinae*, is the manner in which the sacrificial victim, the dog, was to be killed. Some information can be gleaned, however, from examination of the skeletal remains themselves. The frontal bone of the dog from Fontenoce near Recanati in Abruzzo (Wilkens 2000b) shows a clear axe blow, indicating that this animal was apparently dispatched by a blow to the head (Fig. 10). This dog comes from a Chalcolithic necropolis, and hence represents a funerary sacrifice. Disarticulation of head at the atlas vertebra is possibly indicated by the position of the cranium with respect to the cervical vertebra when excavated. In fact, the skeleton was found perfectly articulated and post depositional movement due to natural causes does not seem possible given the limited room within the pit. Fractures of the frontal found in one of the dogs from the Genoni well (Fig. 7) and another from the *dromos* of the Bronze Age hypogeum in Lavello suggest that these animals were dispatched by a blow to the head with a stick or other blunt object.

In general, the dogs selected as sacrificial victims were adult in age, some even elderly. Such was the case, for example, in the well deposit at Genoni-S.Antine which contained seven dogs, all adults. However, at LeCerquete-Fianello two animals less than three months old at death were found, and newborn puppies are indicated by the

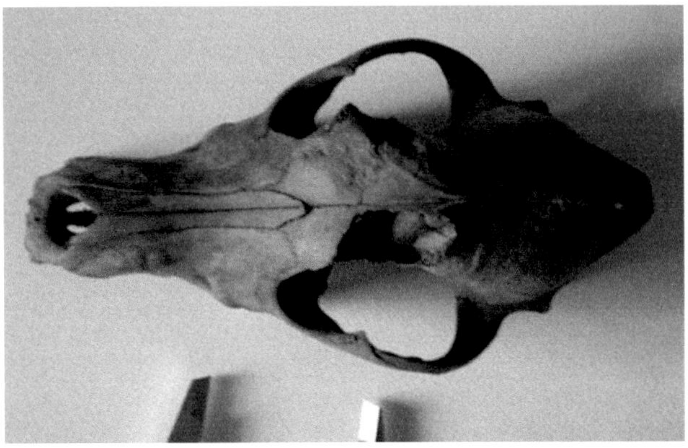

Fig. 7. Canis familiaris *skull from Genoni*

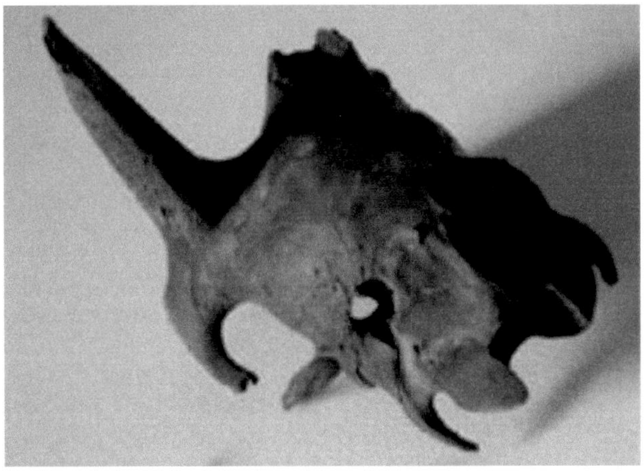

Fig. 8. Capra hircus *skull from Genoni*

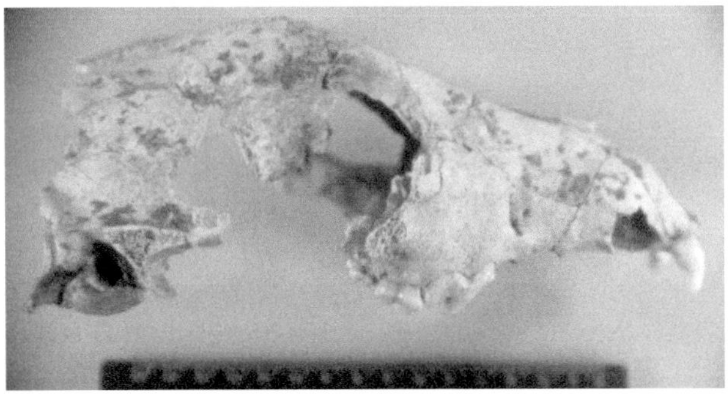

Fig. 9. Canis familiaris *skull from Lavello*

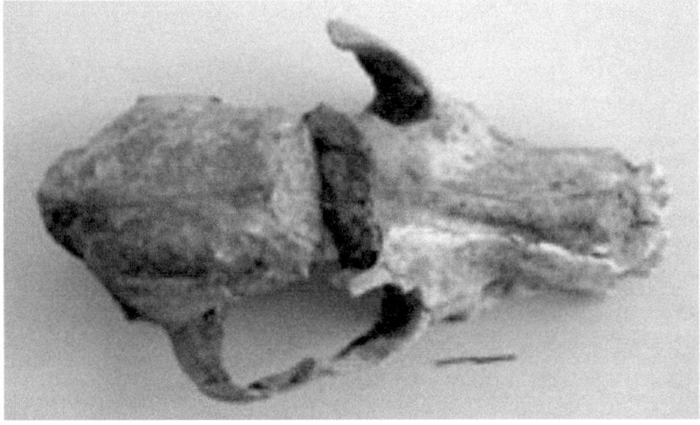

Fig. 10. Canis familiaris *skull from Fontenoce*

remains in the hypogeum at Lavello. Age at death was calculated on the basis of dentition and fusion of the epiphysis, relying on data provided by K.H.Habermehl (1961).

It is often difficult or impossible to determine the gender of the dogs which were sacrificed. While the *baculum* (penis bone) is an unequivocal indicator of a male animal, this small bone can be easily separated from disarticulated skeletons in a commingled matrix, or overlooked during excavation. In the assemblages discussed above, the presence of a *baculum* indicated that the animal from the Middle Bronze Age site of Roca was a male, as was the dog from Fontenoce. In the other deposits, the lack of *bacula* may possibly be due to the sacrifice of female animals, but certainly cannot be taken as conclusive evidence. As regards other indicators of sex, such as size difference and morphology of the skull, these are of little use given the variability of the species and the scarcity of remains from each site.

Comments and Conclusions

The identification of deposits containing dogs as sacrificial, when in association with clearly sacred spaces, is perhaps somewhat straightforward. The numerous ritual actions that may have been carried out within the home, the village or even in the fields and countryside, however, may well elude detection. Dog remains with butchering marks are common throughout Italian pre- and proto-history. In many cases, however, it is difficult to say whether these remains represent ritual actions or the consumption of dogs as a food resource. In the Middle Neolithic village of Catignano, Abruzzo, near Chieti, for instance, a pit containing a dog skull with mandibles was found within a small domestic structure. This pit was first interpreted as a posthole, but it's wide and shallow outline, and above all the presence of the dog's head, suggests a possible ritual feature in a domestic environment. (Wilkens 2003b).

It should come as no surprise that similarities exist in ritual practice through time. In some instances, this may be due to convergence phenomena rather than direct historical links. Religious rites are, however, conservative and may tend to adapt to changing political and social situations with a minimum of change. In some instances, this continuity can be demonstrated for long periods of time. In Italy, some types of cult activity have persisted throughout the whole of prehistory and into later historic periods as well. As an example one may recall the cave of Grotta di Santa Maria di Agnano close to Ostuni in Puglia (Wilkens 2003a). In this cave and the immediately adjacent area, there is evidence of cult activity from the Chalcolithic up to the present day; earlier activity is not to be excluded. The composition of the fauna does not differ greatly in the various periods; the divinity noted for the Greek phase of the sanctuary, Demetra, was transformed into the Virgin Mary with the arrival of Christianity. In terms of dog sacrifices there is less evidence, since it was not an animal commonly used as food – its use for sacrifices is consequently less common and regards only certain rituals. Another example may be that of the sacred wells in Sardinia, that, while built in the Nuragic period, were also used as places of cult in the Roman period. In some cases the cult continued up to the Medieval.

This study has investigated the use of dogs as a sacrificial animal throughout the Italian peninsula and nearby islands, an aspect of ritual which appears to have become widespread in the Iron Age. In this sense there are numerous examples. One may recall the use of dogs in Iron Age foundation sacrifices in Tell Afis, Syria (Wilkens 1998) and the important role that the dog had in Crete, where it was associated with equines, probably as a sacrificial victim at the Prinias necropolis dating to the Early Bronze Age (Wilkens 2003a). The common occurrence of dog remains in cultural and ritual contexts throughout the Mediterranean, and through time, speaks to the importance and continuing significance of this animal to human society.

References

Curci A., Tagliacozzo, A. 1994. Il pozzetto rituale con scheletro di cavallo dall'abitato neolitico di Le Cerquete-Fianello (Maccarese-RM). *Origini*, 297–350.

De Grossi Mazzorin, J. 1990. Ossa di avvoltoio, p.274 in Cristofani M. (ed.), *La grande Roma dei Tarquini*, Roma: L'Erma di Bretschneider.

Devoto, G. 1975. *Le tavole di Gubbio*, Firenze: Sansoni

Habermehl, K. H. 1961. *Die Altersbestimmung bei Haustieren, Pelztieren und beim jagdbaren Wild*, Berlin: Paul Parey Verlag.

Ovide, N. 1993. *Les Fastes*, Paris: Les Belles Lettres.

Plinio, G. S. 1982. *Storia Naturale*, Torino: Einaudi.

Prummel, W. 1996. The Sacrificial Animals in Deposit II of Borgo Le Ferriere (Satricum), in J. W. Bouma (ed.), *Religio Votiva: The Archaeology of Latial Votive Religion*, 419–479, Groningen.

Prummel, W., Bouma J. W. 1997. Animal offerings at Borgo Le Ferriere (Latium, Italy). *Anthropozoologica*, **25–26**, 531–537.

Tagliacozzo, A. 1989. Analisi dei resti faunistici dall'area sacra di S.Omobono, in *Il viver quotidiano in Roma arcaica*, 65–69, Roma.

Wilkens, B. 1989–90. La fauna dei livelli neolitici della grotta Continenza. *Rivista di Scienze Preistoriche*, XLII, **1–2**, 93–100.

Wilkens, B. 1995. Animali da contesti rituali nella preistoria dell'Italia centro-meridionale, *Padusa Quaderni*, **1**, 201–207

Wilkens, B. 1996. Un saggio di scavo sull'acropoli di Olbia: la fauna, in A. Mastino, P. Ruggeri (eds), *Da Olbìa ad Olbia. 2500 anni di storia di una città mediterranea*, 353–355, Sassari: Chiarella. Wilkens B. 1997. Restes de chiens provenant d'un puits de l'age du Fer à Lavello, Potenza, Italie, *Anthropozoologica* **25–26**, 799–801.

Wilkens, B. 1998. The faunal remains. In S.M.Cecchini, S.Mazzoni (ed.): *Tell Afis (Siria). Scavi sull'acropoli 1988–1992*, 433–450, Pisa: ETS.

Wilkens, B. 2000a. Resti rituali dal pozzo sacro di Serra Niedda (SS), *Atti del 2° Convegno Nazionale di Archeozoologia – Asti 1997*, 263–266, Forlì: Abaco edizioni.

Wilkens, B. 2000b. Il cane eneolitico di Fontenoce, *Atti del 2° Convegno Nazionale di Archeozoologia – Asti 1997*, 213–215, Forlì: Abaco edizioni.

Wilkens, B. 2003a. *Archeozoologia. Manuale per lo studio dei resti faunistici dell'area mediterranea*. CD rom, Schio.

Wilkens, B. 2003b. La fauna del villaggio neolitico di Catignano, in C.Tozzi, B.Zamagni *Gli scavi nel villaggio neolitico di Catignano (1971–1980)*, 219–238, Firenze: IIPP.

Wilkens, B., Delussu F. 2002. I resti faunistici, in G. Pianu (ed.), *L'agorà di Eraclea Lucana*, 299– 342, Roma: Carocci.

Wilkens, B., Delussu F. 2003. Wild and domestic mammals in holocenic Sardinia, in A.Legakis, S.Sfenthourakis, R.Polymeni, M.Thessalou-Legaki: *Proceedings of the XVIIIth International Congress of Zoology, Athens, 28/8–2/9 2000*, 303–308, Sophia-Mosckow: Pensoft.

Dipartimento di Storia
University of Sassari
viale Umberto I n°52
Sassari 07100
Italy

wilkens@tiscali.it

9th ICAZ Conference, Durham 2002
Dogs and People in Social, Working, Economic or Symbolic Interaction
(eds Lynn M. Snyder and Elizabeth A. Moore) pp. 138–146

15. The Evidentiary Dog: A Review Of Anthrozoological Cases And Archaeological Studies

Bonnie C. Yates and Janice Koler-Matznick

Infrequently, archaeozoologists may venture into forensic casework when they are asked to use their skills to identify incomplete clusters of bones encountered by law enforcement personnel who are searching for clues in homicide cases, remains of lost children, or identification of potential contraband. When found without skulls, remnants of pet dogs, domestic goats, and young deer can be mistaken for bones of human children to those law enforcement officers who are uninitiated in osteology. Archaeozoologists could find interest in the new field of forensic vertebrate morphology in which the skills they developed in archaeozoology can be applied to modern law enforcement cases. Cases involving wild and domestic canids serve to illustrate this new application in the broader field of anthrozoology.

Introduction

Today, all manner of animal-source objects are marketed as collectibles and trade goods. Because of laws such as CITES, the scientific name and source of each species used must be declared on items imported into countries participating in CITES, to ensure sustainable trade in species around the globe. CITES is the acronym for the Convention on International Trade in Endangered Species of Wild Fauna and Flora. It is an international agreement that has been signed by over 169 countries. The goal is to ensure that international trade in wild plants and animals does not result in extirpation.

The United States Fish and Wildlife Service's National Wildlife Forensic Laboratory [NFWFL] is a federal facility devoted to solving crimes against, or involving, wildlife. In the Mammal Unit of the Morphology Section at the Lab, our job is to identify the victim in such a crime. The evidence usually results from human/animal interactions, and then submitted to the Lab as hunting trophies, smuggled art and jewelry, clothing, medicinal parts and products, food items, and collectibles. These are sent in by international game officers and wildlife inspectors at ports of entry either because they are from improperly permitted shipments or suspected of being made from threatened/endangered species. Table 1 shows the diversity of mammalian items identified over the last 10 years of casework, tabulated by order and family. The order Carnivora accounts for 27% of all identified items, and the dog family, Canidae, is one of the few case categories numbering in triple digits. The genus *Canis* comprises one-quarter of the canid items.

Wild canids are exploited for furs and killed for sport. Canids of all kinds are sought for hides, skulls, post-cranial bones, and dried organs: anything might show up in casework (Table 1). Domestic dogs, *Canis familiaris*, sometimes serve as proxies for wild forms. For example, when remains of wolves (*Canis lupus*) are desired for craft items, but are unavailable or unattainable because of legal issues, dog parts are substituted. Conversely, while coyote and wolf pelts are traded internationally, inside the US, there are state and local laws prohibiting the use of dog pelts. Outside the US, the exploitation of

Table. 1. Diversity of mammalian items identified over the last 10 years of casework, tabulated by order and family

Order	Family	No. of Cases
Artiodactyla	Antilocapridae	*2*
Artiodactyla	Bovidae	*366*
Artiodactyla	Camelidae	*8*
Artiodactyla	Camelidae	*4*
Artiodactyla	Cervidae	*368*
Artiodactyla	Giraffidae	*7*
Artiodactyla	Hippopotamidae	*15*
Artiodactyla	Moschidae	*7*
Artiodactyla	Muntiacidae	*1*
Artiodactyla	Suidae	*48*
Artiodactyla	Tayassuidae	*3*
Artiodactyla	Tragulidae	*4*
Artiodactyla	Tyassuidae	*2*
Artiodactyla	Unsp	*8*
Carnivora	Canidae	*223*
Carnivora	Felidae	*273*
Carnivora	Herpestidae	*8*
Carnivora	Hyaenidae	*10*
Carnivora	Mustelidae	*75*
Carnivora	Odobenidae	*10*
Carnivora	Otariidae	*18*
Carnivora	Phocidae	*20*
Carnivora	Procyonidae	*24*
Carnivora	Unsp	*2*
Carnivora	Ursidae	*203*
Catacea	Mysticeti	*2*
Cetacea	Odontoceti	*5*
Cetacea	Physeteridae	*3*
Cetacea	Plantanistidae	*1*
Cetacea	Unsp	*2*
Chiroptera	Molossidae	*1*
Chiroptera	Pteropidae	*6*
Chiroptera	Vespertilionidae	*13*
Dermoptera	Cynocephalidae	*1*
Hyracoidea	Procaviidae	*3*
Insectivora	Erinaceidae	*5*
Insectivora	Soricidae	*3*
Insectivora	Talpidae	*1*
Insectivora	Tenrecidae	*2*
Lagomorpha	Leporidae	*43*
Marsupialia	Didelphidae	*9*
Marsupialia	Macropodidae	*6*
Marsupialia	Phalangeridae	*2*
Perissodactyla	Equidae	*31*
Perissodactyla	Rhinocerotidae	*21*
Perissodactyla	Tapiridae	*2*
Pholidota	Manidae	*9*
Primates	(Papionini)	*1*
Primates	Callitrichidae	*8*
Primates	Cebidae	*11*
Primates	Cercopithecidae	*58*
Primates	Pongidae	*5*
Primates	Tarsiidae	*1*
Proboscidea	Elephantidae	*58*
Proboscidea	[extinct]	*2*
Proboscidea	Mammutidae	*1*
Proboscidea	Unsp	*7*
Rodentia	Aplodontidae	*1*
Rodentia	Arvicolinae	*2*
Rodentia	Castoridae	*15*
Rodentia	Cricetidae	*1*
Rodentia	Erethizontidae	*10*
Rodentia	Geomyidae	*2*
Rodentia	Heteromyidae	*5*
Rodentia	Hystricidae	*2*
Rodentia	Muridae	*30*
Rodentia	Myocastoridae	*7*
Rodentia	Sciuridae	*29*
Rodentia	Sigmodontinae	*2*
Sirenia	Dugongidae	*1*
Sirenia	Trichechidae	*2*
Tubulidentata	Orycteropodidae	*1*
Xenarthra	Dasypodidae	*2*
Xenarthra	Megalonychidae	*1*

Carnivores = 27 % of all items identified
Canids = one quarter of those Carnivores

dogs for skins is mostly unregulated. Trade figures indicate over 160,000 dog hides were used by the fur industry in 2001. In 1997, in just one case, a shipment of 4.7 tons of dog hides was intercepted by the Hong Kong authorities for lack of permits. Italian TV recently interviewed a leather goods importer who reported annual imports of 50,000 to 100,000 dog skins, most of which are made into garments (e.g., Fig. 1b).

As a framework to explore the human /dog relationship through time, we have established six functional categories that can help reveal patterns or purposes in the material record, whether from the past or in the present (Fig. 2). Overlap is certainly possible among these categories, and, as we know from the archaeozoological record, recognition of the "purpose" of a man-made or a natural object, after the fact or even in context, can be problematic. This paper will briefly explore the present and past human use of canids (wild and domestic), drawing upon some forensic examples as modern counterparts to the past. The remainder of this paper will discuss the anthrozoological record of humans and dogs along the following framework: dogs as food, as commodities, as entertainment, as ritual objects, as controlled agents, and as scientific research subjects.

As Food

In some Western restaurants, "dog meat stew" may actually be made with goat or chicken, but the dish is listed on the menu as dog meat to cater to a strong cultural tradition in some Asian communities. Dog eating is common in many modern cultures in Asia, where an estimated 13 to 16 million dogs are consumed annually (Bartlett and Clifton 2003). The Korean dog dish "boshintang" can be translated as "a soup for health." When a group of Koreans (n = 3,097) were polled in 2000, 59% indicated "I would certainly eat dog as a health food." Yellow-colored dogs are said to be best for digestion, reports journalist Oh Byung Sang in an article in the *Jungang News* (Korea).

Evidence of dogs as food abounds in the world-wide archaeological record. Yates examined faunal remains from sites in East Texas, where prehistoric dog remains were found both in middens and as burials, with and without human interments. The indigenous people of the Americas often ate dogs (Schwartz 1997; Thurston 2000). In other time periods, many Western European cultures also had dog on their menus. Evidence of human

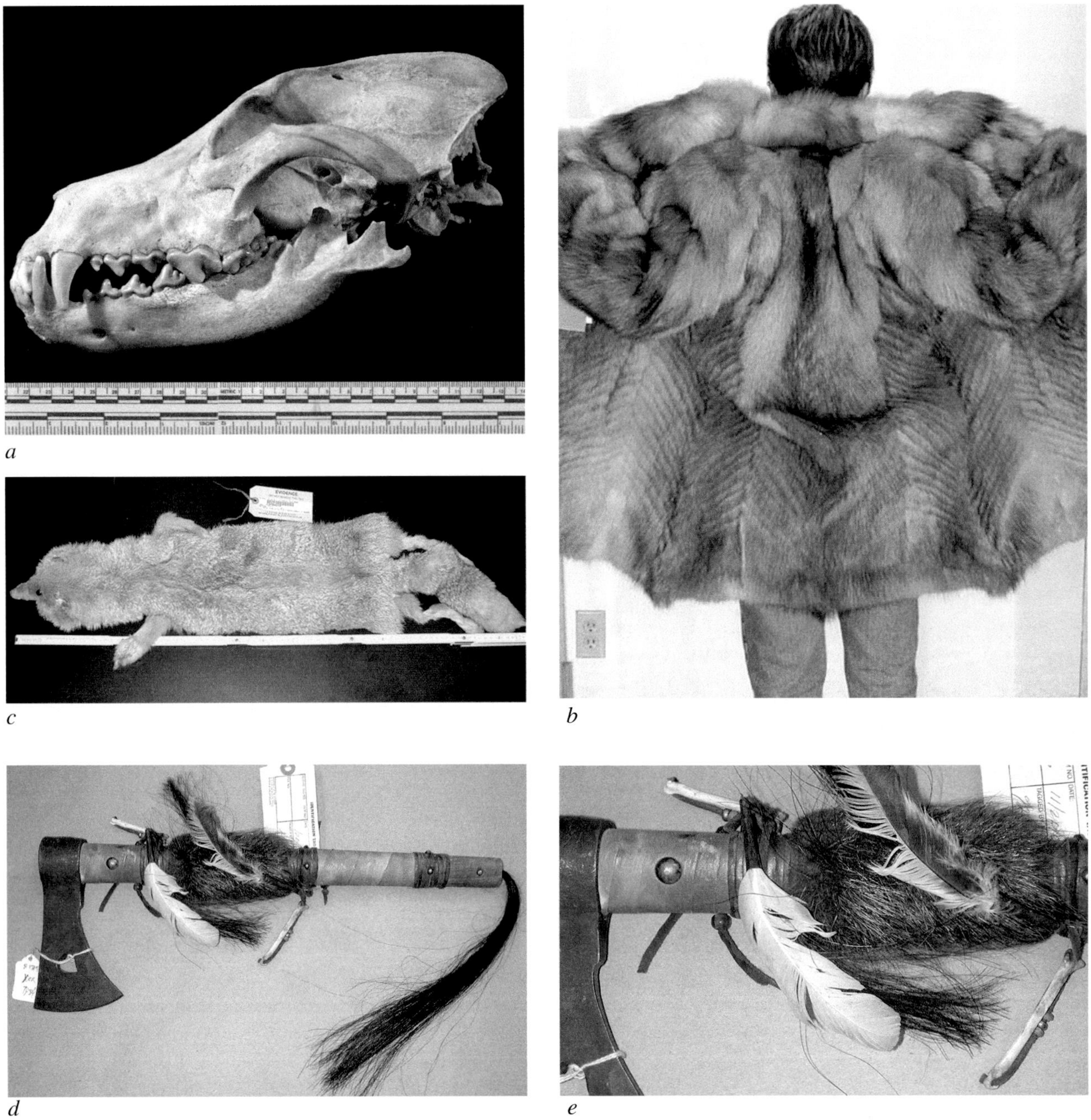

Fig. 1. Examples of canid collectibles and modern artifacts made with canid biomaterials. (a): wolf skull saved as memento of illegal wolf kill; (b): fur coat made from trimmed Asian canid hides; (c): fox stole with clip sewn into mouth; (d): hatchet adorned with metapodials of coyote; (e) close-up of coyote metapodials.

consumption of dogs has been found in many European archaeological sites, including some in France (Horard-Herbin 2000), Austria (Galik 2000) and Britain (Harcourt 1974). Since dog eating is so entrenched in certain cultures, the hot debate today in animal welfare circles is whether or not to concentrate on education and legislation concerning how the meat dogs are kept prior to their demise and how they are dispatched, rather than trying to change the cultural habit of eating dogs.

Humans interact with dogs in six ways:

1. As food

2. As non-food commodities

3. As ritualized objects

4. As controlled entities

5. In science

6. As incidental "take"

Most usually result in the death of the animal.

Fig. 2. Types of human/canid interactions used as discussion framework.

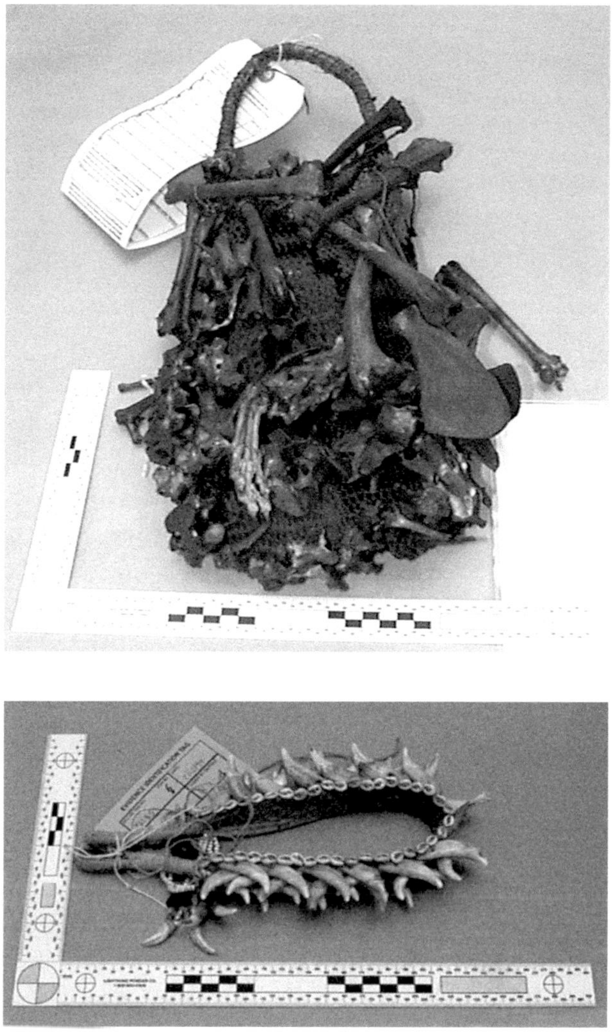

Fig. 3. Modern artifacts from New Guinea using dog bones and teeth

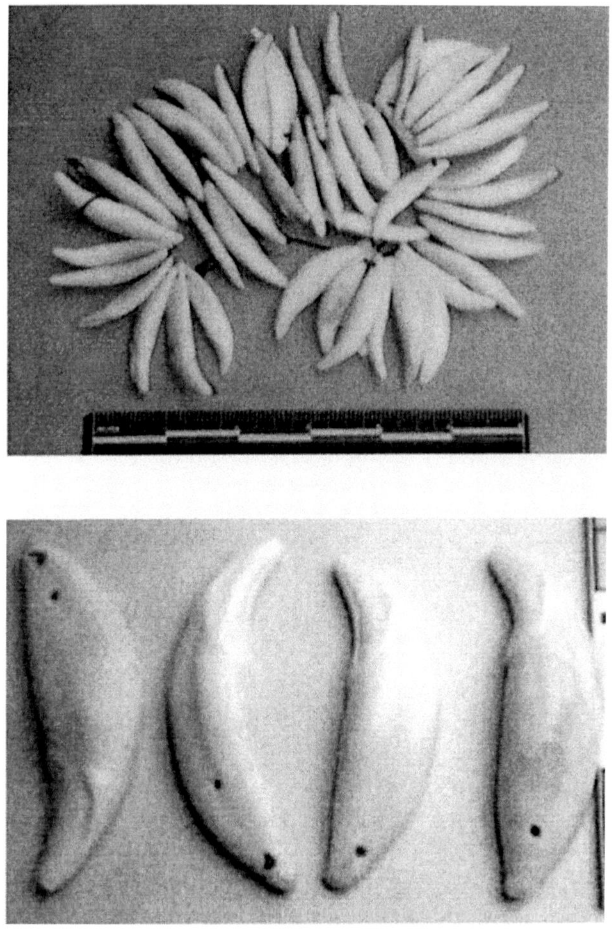

Fig. 4. Modern dog-tooth necklace (and close-up) also made in New Guinea.

As Commodities

In a post WW II plan to diversify farm income, the United States Department of Agriculture encouraged farmers to raise puppies as an alternative "crop" because booming suburban families wanted pets, and farmers needed income. As a result in the US, dogs became an agricultural commodity and were even sold at public auction. This misguided treatment of puppies as a "crop," to be produced at the lowest cost possible, resulted in a bloom of "puppy mills." The outcome has been most unfortunate for both the dogs and the consumer, because the puppies produced in this way are often psychologically and physically unfit to be pets. Some of the evidentiary items Yates has seen from this commerce include piles of pitiful puppy carcasses, leftover by-products from puppy mills.

There is a wide variety of both modern and ancient trade goods and personal items that include dog parts. Figures 3 and 4 are examples of modern artifacts crafted in New Guinea that contain dog remains; they were confiscated as tourist curios coming into the US. Drilled tooth necklaces, some with canid teeth, have origins back as far as the Aurignacian (Bednarik 1995) and are found in cultures as diverse as those of New Guinea (Titcomb 1969) and the indigenous peoples of the western coast of North America and Central America (Schwartz 1997). Their use in prehistoric times was probably the same as in historic records, that is, for ritualistic purposes and personal adornment. Prehistorically, dog teeth may have been used for trade like certain shell species and obsidian that are found far from their original sources.

As certain iconographic animals used in traditional medicines, rituals, and adornment are extirpated, artisans turn to readily available substitutes, such as the dog skin in Figure 5, which was stained with turmeric and painted with other dyes to simulate a tiger hide. In China, dog

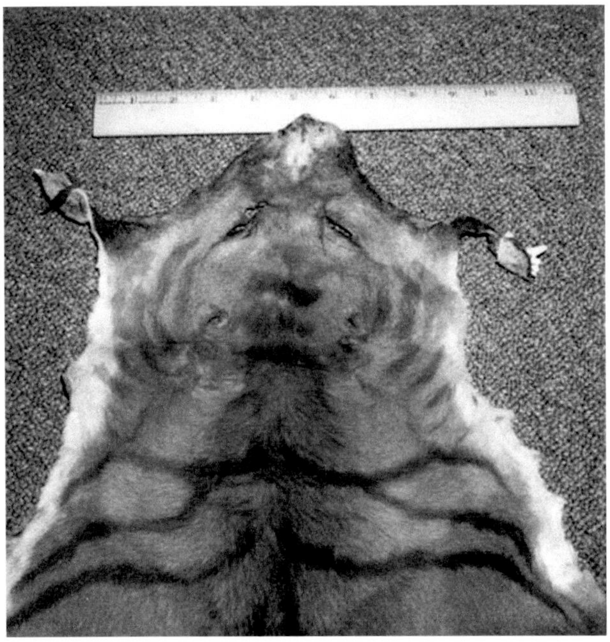

Fig. 5. Dog skin painted in India to simulate a tiger's skin.

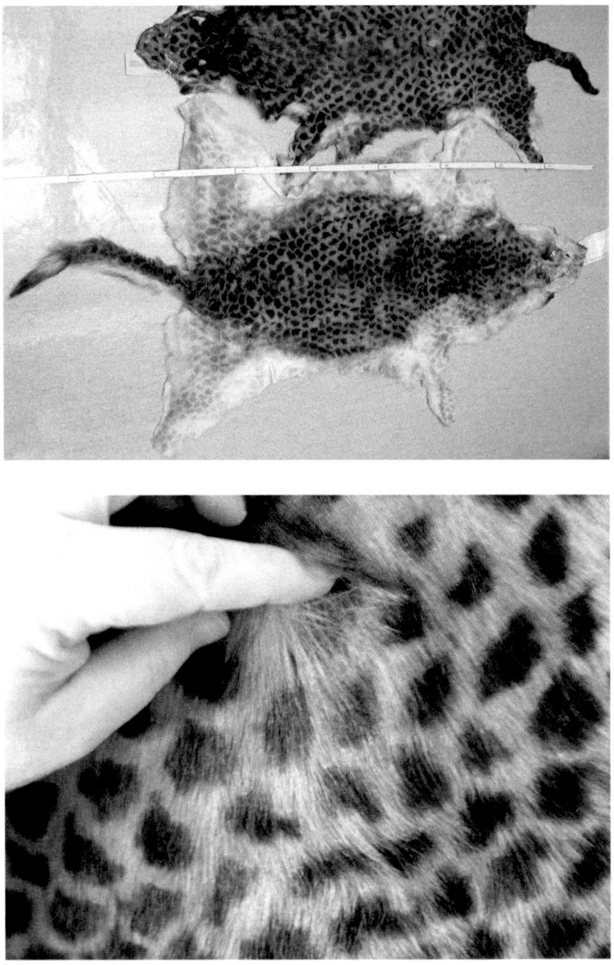

Fig. 6. Another dog skin stenciled to resemble a leopard skin; and close-up.

skins are stenciled to resemble spotted cat hides like the ones shown in Figure 6. Likewise, the fierce-looking paw in Figure 7 was constructed from two goats' feet covered in dog hide, and fixed with feline-shaped claws that were carved from cattle horn. These objects are the results of cottage industries worldwide that depend on animal remains for income.

The NFWFL was once asked by the Humane Society of the US to examine imported dog and cat figurines made of furred skins. Laws in the US prohibit the use of domestic dogs and cats in commercial products. While some of these figurines were made from hides of rabbit and squirrel (non-protected species), others were indeed dog and cat skins, sometimes parts of both. One particularly memorable forensic case was a large panda bear curio that FWS Inspectors seized because they thought perhaps genuine panda skins might have been used in the manufacture of the object. Genuine furred skins were indeed used to construct the 55–cm tall replica of the popular panda, but microscopic examination of fur from both the black and white skins indicated that they were from black dogs and white dogs, and not panda at all.

As Entertainment

The relationships between dogs and their human friends are complex and multi-faceted. For this paper, the use of dogs as companion animals (i.e., pets) seems to fit best in the general category of entertainment. Although some other species have been called "companion animals," the only species that is truly a voluntary and accepted member of human social groups is *Canis familiaris*. In the industrialized countries where most dogs serve as house pets, the sale of dogs and dog-related items such as food, toys, leashes, beds, etc., forms a significant portion of the economy.

Dogs are also raised and sold commercially for several forms of entertainment. A large and lucrative international industry has formed around dog fighting, including production of dogs physically and mentally suitable for professional matches, and the manufacture and sale of the associated equipment. Professional dog fighting is an accepted gambling "sport" in many countries, such as Japan where it has become highly ritualized. In the US, dog fighting is illegal in all 50 states, and is a felony in many states. Although a clandestine activity in almost all countries that have outlawed staged dog fights, the unusually high number

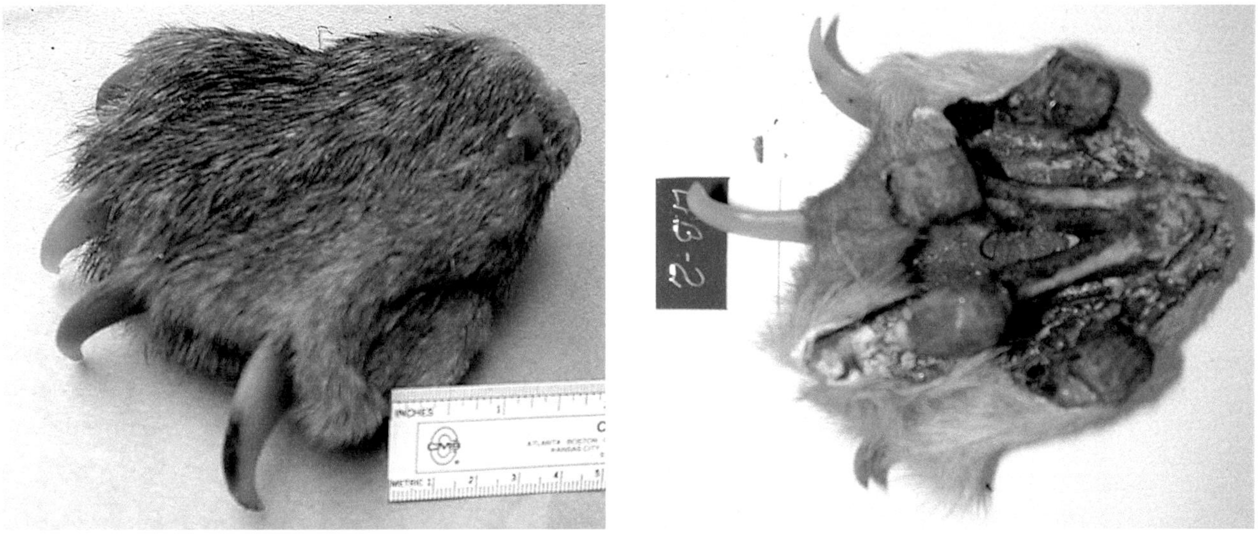

Fig. 7. Top and bottom views of goat's feet covered in dog skin and fashioned with feline-shaped claws made from cattle horn, sold to tourist as a tiger's paw

of pit bull terriers (and pit bull types) rescued from hurricane disasters in the Gulf Coast bears witness to an activity that everyone knows about but few acknowledge. Sadly, the canine losers of these encounters are sometimes found as skeletal materials discarded in country ditches or city dumpsters.

Although today in the US and elsewhere, there are groups attempting to pass laws against circuses using exotic animal acts, no one thinks twice about the dog acts so common in circuses, probably because dogs are seen as a domesticated companion animal that is adapted to traveling with humans. Throughout the history of circuses, and of variety shows on the stage, dogs have provided entertainment both in dog-only acts and combined with various exotic species or ponies. Most are treated humanely because of the investment in training and their value as objects of income-generating entertainment.

In several countries, racing greyhounds provide entertainment for millions of humans who wager on the outcome of the competitions. In the US, the United Kingdom, and South Africa, greyhound racing is a major industry. The unfortunate by-product of this industry is thousands of greyhounds discarded each year. If they do not make the grade on the track, and are not intended as part of a breeding program, the vast majority are killed. Today, there are several organizations that take in a small minority of unwanted racing greyhounds and place them in pet homes. This is possible only because the breed is by nature submissive to humans and non-offensive, so even though they have been raised in small pens or cages their entire lives, and had minimal positive interactions with humans, they adapt to pet homes.

As Ritualistic Objects

The unusual closeness of the human/dog relationship places the dog in a unique position as almost quasi-human, and as such, it often has served an important ritualized or spiritual role in many past cultures (Serpell 1995). In ancient Egypt, dogs were mummified so they could guide human spirits across into the next world. Effigies of dogs, for example, were used as funereal objects throughout MesoAmerican and North American native cultures, such as Iselin, Colima, Puebloan, and Poverty Point (Schwartz 1997).

In many cultures, dogs were given ceremonial burials or buried with humans. Dog burials occur globally, and in the last few years, dozens of dog burials have been reported: US/Alabama (Walker 1997), Greece (Williams 2000), Kazakhstan (Olsen 2000), Russia (H. Müller-Beck 1996), Ireland (O' Baoill 2000), Tenerife (Curtó Gracia 2001).

Yates (1986) investigated the Roseborough Lake dog burial (Fig. 8), dating from an eighteenth century site in eastern Texas. This burial contained fetal bones of a single pup, a retained fetus that may have caused the death of this carefully buried dog of the Caddoan people. It was found in close proximity to human burials associated with this contact-period site containing remains of French explorers. In the diary of Benard de la Harpe, dogs were noted as sacrificial subjects dedicated to La Salles's companions by the Caddoan Indians of the southcentral US, offered in rituals to impress or appease the newcomers (Gilmore 1986).

As Controlled Agents

The dog has served humans since the beginning of the relationship, certainly well before they became "pets." The first dogs to join themselves to humans over 12,000 yrs BP undoubtedly scavenged around the camp environs, thereby keeping it a bit cleaner and less attractive to more deleterious visitors such predators and insects. In this capacity as sanitary worker, dogs may even have inadvertently facilitated the establishment of the first permanent human settlements. A study of the diets of free-ranging African pariah dogs attached to a remote Zimbabwean village showed that about 23.6% of their diets consisted of human feces and 55.1% of scavenged mammal remains, mostly dog and goat carcasses left as carrion (Butler 1998). Most of the Zimbabweans stated the dogs also served as guards, not from people, but from wild animals such as baboons that tried to eat their crops. So, dogs were useful even before humans had the ability to bring them under control.

The dog's ancient use as hunting companions is well documented. However, the earliest use of dogs for hunting was probably not very "controlled." Modern accounts of the use of indigenous village dogs as hunting aids in New Guinea and Africa may describe the earliest purposeful use of dogs (Koler-Matznick 2002). One to three or four dogs are allowed to roam at will around the hunters, and they find, chase, tree, and sometimes even capture small game, which they then readily allow the humans to take (Bulmer 2001; Butler 1998). The humans do not have command control over the dogs: the dogs just follow their natural instincts and the humans follow the dogs. As dogs became domesticated, and human societies more centralized, with more concentrated populations, hunting dogs were brought under direct control. This more recent type of use is explicitly celebrated on wall art from Ur and Egypt, bronze works from China, and ceramics from ancient Greece. Royal hunts using dogs, especially of lions, were very likely propagandic depictions in examples of Hellenistic art that underscore the might of the king, such as the scenes depicted on the Krateros Monument to Alexander the Great (Pollitt 1990).

Dogs have also regularly served as beasts of burden in many times and places. The travois dogs of the North American Indians and the carting dogs of Western Europe were critically important, labor-saving agents (Schwartz 1997; Snyder 1995; Thurston 2000). This form of benign exploitation provides definite benefits to their handlers and trainers, and, therefore, deliberate mistreatment is rare. When mistreatment does occur, the penalties are civil in nature and are seldom confused with wildlife laws. Accordingly, our laboratory has had no cases emanating from this category. Usually, any violations would be investigated by the humane societies at a local or state level.

Now that studies such as Hare *et al.* (2002) and Miklósi *et al.* (2003) have shown an innate propensity of domestic dogs to follow human signals, if not a unique ability to pay attention to human speech, we know why they have made such excellent partners for the sightless, for search and rescue, and for sniffing out bombs, drugs, prohibited agricultural products, and as pet-assisted therapy animals and dogs for the deaf. Because of the apparent willingness on the part of some dogs, it may be possible to train them to even finer discrimination of scents (*e.g.*, cancerous tumor detection, see Church and Williams 2001), and thus, we may find even more ways to exploit them.

Fig. 8. Dog burials from East Texas: (a) Roseborough Lake, 41BW5; (b) Roitsch Site, 41RR16

In Science

Dogs used in laboratory work may be treated as controlled agents or as scientific subjects. It seems to depend on whether the animal is rewarded for its work. Historically, dogs used in scientific experiments lacked any access to mobility or choice about their service. As early as 1665, the first successful blood transfusion was dog to dog by Richard Lower, an Oxford physician (Starr 2000). In 1934, Dr. Robert Cornish, successfully "revivified" a series of dogs named Lazarus (*Time Magazine* 1934). One of the test subjects, Lazarus III, was resuscitated after 4 minutes of death, and Cornish recorded 3 months later that the dog was "regaining faculties."

The archive at Cold Spring Harbor Laboratory documents information about some of science's most famous dogs. For example, details of the results of behavioral response experiments conducted by Ivan Pavlov on 60 dogs are archived, along with photographs of each of his subject dogs adorned with the dog's name in what may be Pavlov's handwriting (http://www.cshl.org/PDogs/). The stories of the Sputnik dogs, Laika and Chernuska, can be found at various sites on the Internet, as well.

The stories of thousands of dogs used in medical research will probably never be known, but credit for their sacrifices has been honored by the Schweitzer Medal, named for humanitarian Dr. Albert Schweitzer by the Animal Welfare Institute (Free 2002). This award has been given 15 times since 1955 to individuals who have made efforts to improve the lives of lab animals, and specifically to the five individuals mentioned below who spoke out for the welfare of dogs in science:

1955 Dr. Robert Bay, veterinarian in charge of a colony of 500 experimental beagles, whose humane treatment of the animals exemplifies the purpose for which the Medal was struck.

1963 Ann Cottrell Free, author and journalist, whose discovery and reporting on hundreds of Food and Drug Administration test dogs, perpetually caged in a sub-basement, led to Congressional action providing comfortable kennel runways for them.

1969 Stan Wayman, Life photographer, whose "Concentration Camps for Dogs" and other picture stories brought recognition to millions of people that animals need protection.

1975 Fay Brisk, who uncovered cruelty and theft by laboratory dog dealers in the 1960s and initiated an animal port in Washington, DC to help animals transported by air. The Medal was presented by Senator Lowell Weicker.

1977 Yoko Muto, animal caretaker of Tokyo University, and representative of the Japan Animal Welfare Society, for her seven years of unstinting effort to allay the suffering of thousands of dogs used for experimental surgery, by gentle, personal nursing care given to each animal. The presentation was made by US Ambassador to Japan, Mike Mansfield. http://www.awionline.org/schweitzer/

Vast numbers of dogs aid mankind by testing vaccinations and other drugs for modern pharmaceutical companies. Yates's only forensic experience with dogs as this type of controlled agent has been in investigations of their use/abuse as laboratory subjects. Disposal of carcasses of laboratory specimens is strictly regulated, and finding bones or hairs of dogs associated with such work in the wrong disposal containers can lead to prosecution and/or fines.

At the NFWFL, we are collecting cranial and podial data on primitive dogs, wolves, and various domestic breeds in order to detect morphologically the osteological manifestations that characterized wolf/dog hybrids. Wolves are afforded federal protection in certain populations in the US, while domestic dogs and hybrids are not. To reliably enforce the protection laws, therefore, we must be able to differentiate among the various canid forms. Craniometric data have been collected on skulls from all over the US and museum specimens from the British Museum of Natural History, the Royal Museum in Leiden, the Koninklijk Museum voor Midden-Afrika in Tervuren, Belgium, the Science Museum at the University of California—Berkeley, the US National Museum of Natural History, and the University of Georgia among others. The New Guinea Singing Dogs of Koler-Matznick have been compared to the dingo and to the Arabian wolf skulls from the BM(NH) in order to discern evolutionary traits. So, even after death, these canids participate in scientific endeavors.

As Incidental Take

Humans are not always the direct cause of death to canids, wild or domestic. Environmental disasters such as wildfires and floods destroy homes of domestic dogs, as well as the habitat and denning sites of wild canids. Perhaps the symbol of incidental take most famous in archaeology is Fiorelli's cast of Primus' dog from Pompeii, preserved for conjecture as to whether the dog would have survived had its owner had time to remove its chain (Cooley 2003).

The majority of FWSL casework involving canids concerns wolves, coyotes, and foxes that are suspected to have died directly by human means. Occasionally, artifacts decorated with parts of domestic dog show up, undeclared, at border inspections. Because some artisans use "found objects," such as pieces of fur, teeth and bones, they may not themselves know the identity of the species whose remains they have chosen for their art, but they do know that tourists will buy almost anything (See Fig. 2d,e).

Conclusions

Dogs became human beings' most attentive commensal. There is evidence that brains of dogs developed special regions in part by paying closest attention to human speech and behavior. Hare's (2002) study shows that the domestic dog is extrmely talented in heeding cues from humans. They serve us, attend us, save us, and love us. We reciprocate and deprecate in kind. This symposium and others to come will continue to explore this relationship in all its complexities and undercurrents from the past, through the present, and into the future.

References

Bartlett, K. and M. Clifton 2003. How Many Dogs and Cats are Eaten in Asia? *Animal People* **12(7)**,18B–19.

Bednarik, R. G. 1995 Concept-mediated Marking in the Lower Palaeolithic, *Current Anthropology* **36(4)**,605–634.

Bulmer, S. 2001. Lapita dogs and singing dogs and the history of the dog in New Guinea, pp. 183–201, in *The Archaeology of Lapita Dispersal in Oceania: Papers from the Fourth Lapita Conference, June 2000, Canberra, Australia*, Terra Australis 17, edited by G. R. Clark, A. J. Anderson, and T. Vunidilo. Canberra, Australia: Pandanus Books.

Butler, J. R. A. 1998. The Ecology of Domestic Dogs *Canis familiaris* in the Communal Lands of Zimbabwe. PhD. dissertation: Harare, University of Zimbabwe.

Church, J. and H. Williams 2001. Another sniffer dog for the clinic? *Lancet* **358**, 930.

Cooley, A. E. 2003. *Pompeii*. London: Gerald Duckworth and Co., Ltd.

Curtó Gracia, M. 2001. The Presa Canario Dog: It's true origin. The dog in the myth and in the cult of the Guanches. http://www.irema-curto.com/iremacurto/Myth-cult.htm

Free, A. C. 1982 (2002) Animals, Nature and Albert Schweitzer. The Albert Schweitzer Fellowship, New York, The Animal Welfare Institute, Washington D.C., The Albert Schweitzer Center, Great Barrington, MA, The Humane Society of the United States, Washington D.C. http://www.awionline.org/schweitzer/

Galik, A. 2000. Dog remains from the late Hallstatt period of the Chimney Cave Durezza, near Villach (Carinthia, Austria), pp.129–137 in, *Dogs Through Time: An Archaeological Perspective,* edited by S.J. Crockford. Proceedings of the First ICAZ Symposium on the History of the Domestic Dog. BAR International Series 889. Oxford: Archaeopress.

Gilmore, K. 1986. *French-Indian Interaction at an 18th Century Frontier Post*. Contributions in Archaeology No. 3, Institute of Applied Sciences. Denton: North Texas State University.

Harcourt, R. A. 1974. The Dog in Prehistoric and Early Historic Britain. *J. of Archaeo. Sci.* **1**, 151–175.

Hare, B., M. Brown, C. Williamson, M. Tomasello 2002. The domestication of social cognition in dogs. *Science* **298**, 1634–1636.

Horard-Herbin, M-P. 2000. Dog management and use in the late Iron Age: the evidence from the Gallic site of Levroux (France), pp. 115–121, in *Dogs Through Time: An Archaeological Perspective,* edited by S. J. Crockford. BAR International Series 889. Oxford: Archaeopress.

Koler-Matznick, J. 2002. The origin of the dog revisited. *Anthrozoös* **15**, 98–118.

Miklósi, A., E. Kubinyi, J. Topái, M. Gácsi, Z. Virányi and V. Csányi 2003. A simple reason for a big difference: Wolves do not look back at humans, but dogs do. *Current Biology* **13**,763–766.

Müller-Beck , H., 1996. Palaeoecology and Archaeology of the Ekven Burial Ground and the Ekven Settlement Area near Uelen, Chukotka. INTAS-94-964. http://www.intas.be/catalog/94-0964.htm

Oh, B. S. 2000. Untitled article in *Jungang News*. http://www.admh.org/data/obs2.htm.

Olsen, S. 2000 The sacred and secular roles of dogs at Botai, Kazakhstan, pp. 71–92, in S. J. Crockford, *Dogs Through Time: An Archaeological Perspective*. BAR International Series 889. Oxford: Archaeopress.

O' Baoill, R. 2000. Dogs on the menu in medieval Northern Ireland. *British Archaeology*, Issue No. **53**.

Pollitt, J. J. 1990 *The Art of Ancient Greece: Sources and Documents*. Cambridge: Cambridge University Press.

Schwartz, M. 1997. *A History of Dogs in the Early Americas*. Yale University Press.

Serpell, J. 1995. From paragon to pariah: Some reflections on human attitudes to dogs, pp. 245–256, in J. Serpell (ed.) *The Domestic Dog; Its Evolution, Behaviour and Interactions with People*. Cambridge University Press.

Snyder, L. M. 1995. Assessing the Role of the Domestic Dog as a Native American Food Resource in the Middle Missouri Subarea A.D. 1000–1840. Unpubl. PhD. Dissertation, Department of Anthropology, University of Tennessee, Knoxville.

Starr, D. 2000. *Blood: An Epic History of Medicine and Commerce*. New York: Alfred A. Knopf.

Thurston, M. E. 2000. *The Lost History of the Canine Race*. Kansas City: Andrews and McMeel.

Time Magazine 1934. Lazarus, Dead and Alive. March 24, 1934, Vol. XXIII, No. 13.

Titcomb, M. 1969. *Dog and Man in the Ancient Pacific with Special Attention to Hawaii*. Bernice P. Bishop Museum Special Publication 59. Honolulu, Hawaii.

Walker, R. B. 1997 Late-Paleoindian faunal remains from Dust Cave, Alabama. *Current Research in the Pleistocene* **14**, 85–87.

Williams, H. 2000 Stymphalos Excavations: Project Description. http://www.csanet.org/archproj/greece/project036.html.

Yates, B. C. 1986 vertebrate faunal remains at Roseborough Lake, 41BW5, pp.107–130, in K. Gilmore, *French-Indian Interaction at an 18th Century Frontier Post*. Contributions in Archaeology No. 3. North Texas State University, Denton: Institute of Applied Sciences.

USFWS National Fish and Wildlife Forensic Laboratory
1490 East Main
Ashland
Oregon 97520
USA

bonnie_yates@fws.gov

The New Guinea Singing Dog Conservation Society
5265 Old Stage Road
Central Point
Oregon 97502
USA

jkoler@ccountry.com